What's on the CD

The CD included with the *MCSE: SQL 6.5 Administration Study Guide* contains several valuable tools to help you prepare for your exam. You can access the files on the CD through a user-friendly graphical interface by running the CLICKME.EXE file located in the root directory.

SQL Server 6.5 Administration Exam Prep Program

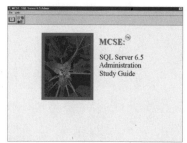

A custom exam prep program that allows you to quiz yourself on all of the review questions found at the end of each chapter in the book. Test yourself chapter by chapter or randomly to ensure that you're ready to take the real exam. Brief explanations of correct answers are provided.

NOTE: During installation, you may be prompted to allow the program to update system files. The file that is updated is OLEPRO32.DLL. This is a Microsoft DLL and should not cause any problems; however, we recommend that you backup this file prior to installing the test program as a precaution.

Network Press MCSE Study Guide Sampler

Preview sample chapters from Sybex's best-selling line of MCSE study guides. From the four core requirements to the most popular electives, you'll see why Sybex MCSE Study Guides have become the self-study method of choice for thousands seeking MCSE certification.

Transact-SQL Commands Listing

An indispensable listing of the most commonly used Transact-SQL commands, organized by the items that they affect (in .PDF format).

NOTE: The Adobe Acrobat Reader 3.0 must be installed on your computer in order to view PDF file. We have included a copy of the Acrobat Reader with this CD for your convenience.

Microsoft *Train_Cert Offline* Web Site and *Internet Explorer 3*

Look to Microsoft's *Train_Cert Offline* web site for a snap-shot of Microsoft's Education and Certification web site. Offline will provide you with all of the information you need to plot your course for MCSE certification. You'll need to run Internet Explorer 3.0 to access all of the features of the Train_Cert offline web site, so we've included a free copy with this CD.

NOTE: Please consult the README file located in the root directory of the CD for a more detailed description of the CD's contents.

For a complete listing of all the Microsoft Exam Objectives, see the inside back cover.

MCSE: SQL Server 6.5
Administration Study Guide

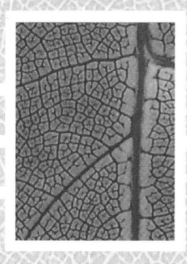

MCSE: SQL Server® 6.5 Administration Study Guide

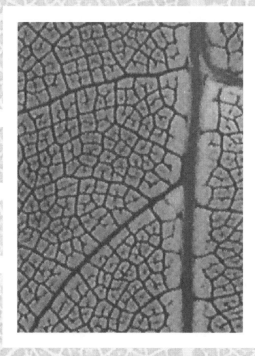

Lance Mortensen,
Rick Sawtell, and
Michael Lee

San Francisco • Paris • Düsseldorf • Soest

Associate Publisher: Guy Hart-Davis
Acquisitions Manager: Kristine Plachy
Acquisitions & Developmental Editor: Neil Edde
Editor: Marilyn Smith
Project Editor: Davina Baum
Technical Editor: Richard Waymire
Book Designer: Patrick Dintino
Graphic Illustrator: Andrew Benzie
Electronic Publishing Specialist: Bill Gibson
Production Coordinator: Eryn L. Osterhaus
Indexer: Matthew Spence
Companion CD: Molly Sharp and John D. Wright
Cover Designer: Archer Design
Cover Illustrator/Photographer: FPG International

Screen reproductions produced with Collage Complete.

Collage Complete is a trademark of Inner Media Inc.

Library of Congress Card Number: 97-80468
ISBN: 0-7821-2172-1

Manufactured in the United States of America

10 9 8 7 6 5 4 3 2 1

November 1, 1997

Dear SYBEX Customer:

Microsoft is pleased to inform you that SYBEX is a participant in the Microsoft® Independent Courseware Vendor (ICV) program. Microsoft ICVs design, develop, and market self-paced courseware, books, and other products that support Microsoft software and the Microsoft Certified Professional (MCP) program.

To be accepted into the Microsoft ICV program, an ICV must meet set criteria. In addition, Microsoft reviews and approves each ICV training product before permission is granted to use the Microsoft Certified Professional Approved Study Guide logo on that product. This logo assures the consumer that the product has passed the following Microsoft standards:

- The course contains accurate product information.
- The course includes labs and activities during which the student can apply knowledge and skills learned from the course.
- The course teaches skills that help prepare the student to take corresponding MCP exams.

Microsoft ICVs continually develop and release new MCP Approved Study Guides. To prepare for a particular Microsoft certification exam, a student may choose one or more single, self-paced training courses or a series of training courses.

You will be pleased with the quality and effectiveness of the MCP Approved Study Guides available from SYBEX.

Sincerely,

Holly Heath
ICV Account Manager
Microsoft Training & Certification

MICROSOFT INDEPENDENT COURSEWARE VENDOR PROGRAM

Software License Agreement: Terms and Conditions

To all the MCSE students and their families, and all the time, energy, and expense spent in pursuit of the MCSE. We hope you will agree that it was worth it.

Acknowledgments

Once again, thanks to the entire Sybex team: Neil Edde, for getting things going and always knowing what is going on; Davina Baum, for keeping track of all the little things; and Marilyn Smith, the best editor around. Richard Waymire, the technical editor, is a perfectionist (and it shows). Also thanks to Eryn Osterhaus, the production coordinator; Bill Gibson, the desktop publisher; and Matthew Spence, the indexer.

To Mike Lee and Rick Sawtell: It was a fun project—sure beats working for a living. Thanks for always being on time (if not early). Mike, we definitely need to work on more projects together. Rick, please don't get maimed or killed skydiving (if Neil and Davina only knew).

As always, thanks to Luann—you have great patience. More than once you found me playing computer games (Dark Reign this time) when deadlines loomed. Thanks for taking care of things while I hid in my office.

Bryce, Jessany, and Devin: Thanks for wrestling, teasing, and playing computer games with me. You kids are the cutest things around.

Lance Mortensen

Thanks, Lance and Mike, for keeping this project moving smoothly and for the excellent work you did on the book. Thanks, Davina, for the quips—your sense of humor helped us though those tough spots. You did a great job managing this project. Thanks, Neil, for all of the work you did to get this project off the ground and running. Thanks, Marilyn, for doing your magic with the word processor; turning our manuscripts into something legible and accurate. Thanks, Richard, for doing such a wonderful job with the technical editing. Your contribution has really made a big difference in the quality, content and usefulness of this book.

Thank you, Melissa, for working so hard and being so supportive while I worked all of those late nights on this book. No one could ask for a more wonderful and caring wife. It's time to renew our love affair and go on that vacation we keep putting off.

Thanks, Mom and Dad, for buying me that first computer and then giving me all of the support that I needed to continue with my education. Your guidance and care has opened opportunities in my life that I never dreamed possible.

Rick Sawtell

First and foremost, all my thanks and love go to my wife Raelynn who tolerated late nights and excessive neglect to complete this project, and to my son Myles who provided the needed diversions when I couldn't look at the monitor for another minute. The two of you are the light of my life. To my parents, all four of them, thank you for believing in me even when times were rough.

Thanks to Lance, Rick, and the whole gang at Sybex: Neil, Davina, Marilyn, Eryn, and Bill for giving me this opportunity and making it such a pleasure. You all work miracles and I appreciate all you have done. Lance and Rick, its been a privilege that I hope we can repeat in the future.

To Joey Taylor and Jon Hansen for being the best friends a guy could have. Thanks for your encouragement and support through the many years. Finally, many thanks to Michael Murphy and Bob Taylor for providing me with my first breaks in the fields of education and computers. I would not have been able to do this without any of you. I will always consider you my friends.

Mike Lee

Contents at a Glance

Table of Contents

Table of Exercises

Introduction

Whether you are just getting started or are ready to move ahead in the computer industry, the knowledge and skills you have are your most valuable assets. Microsoft, recognizing this, has developed its Microsoft Certified Professional (MCP) program to give you credentials that verify your ability to work with Microsoft products effectively and professionally. The Microsoft Certified Systems Engineer (MCSE) certification is the premier MCP credential designed for professionals who support Microsoft networks.

This book has been certified by Microsoft to help you prepare for the System Administration for Microsoft SQL Server 6.5 Certification Exam. Here, you will find the information you need to acquire a solid foundation in the field of SQL Server administration and to take a big step toward MCSE certification.

Is This Book for You?

If you want to become certified as an MCSE, this book is for you. The MCSE is *the* hot ticket in the field of professional computer networking. Microsoft is putting its weight behind the program, so now is the time to act. This book will start you off on the right foot.

If you want to be a capable Microsoft SQL Server administrator, this book is also for you. You'll find clear explanations of the fundamental concepts you need to grasp, as well as straightforward instructions on how to set up, maintain, and troubleshoot SQL Server systems. This book is designed to not only prepare you for the MSCE exam, but to also be a valuable addition to your library after you have passed the exam.

What Does This Book Cover?

Think of this book as your guide to Microsoft SQL Server administration. It begins by covering the most basic of SQL Server concepts, including an introduction to SQL Server, its platform (Windows NT), and its version of the SQL language (Transaction SQL). The following chapters cover the topics you need to know for the exam and in your day-to-day work as a database administrator:

- Installing and configuring SQL Server

- Using the SQL Server utilities to administer your system

- Creating and managing databases and users

- Setting up database security

- Backing up and restoring databases

- Automating maintenance tasks

- Managing, copying, and moving data

- Setting up replication

- Tuning SQL Server performance

- Troubleshooting SQL Server

Throughout each chapter, you will find hands-on exercises that take you step by step through the various tasks. At the end of each chapter, there are practice questions to test your knowledge of the topics covered in that chapter. You will find the answers to those questions in Appendix A.

We have also provided several appendices with additional information that you may find useful in your work as a SQL Server system administrator. Appendix B is about SQL Server and ODBC (Open Database Connectivity). Appendix C covers SQL Server and the Internet. In that appendix, you will learn how to include SQL Server data in your Web pages. Appendix D is a handy reference to commonly used Transaction SQL (the version of the SQL language used by SQL Server) commands. At the back of the book, you'll find a glossary of terms related to SQL Server and database administration.

How Do You Become an MCSE?

Attaining MCSE status is a serious challenge. The exams cover a wide range of topics and require dedicated study and expertise. Many who have achieved other computer industry credentials have had trouble with the MCSE. This is, however, why the MCSE certificate is so valuable. If achieving MCSE status were easy, the market would be quickly flooded by MCSEs and the certification would quickly become meaningless. Microsoft, keenly aware of this fact, has taken steps to ensure that the certification means its holder is truly knowledgeable and skilled.

To become an MCSE, you must pass four core requirements and two electives. Most people select the following exam combination for the MCSE core requirements for the Windows NT 4.0 track, which is the most current track:

Client Requirement

70-73: Implementing and Supporting Windows NT Workstation 4.0

or

70-63: Installing and Supporting Windows 95

Networking Requirement

70-58: Networking Essentials

Windows NT Server 4.0 Requirement

70-67: Implementing and Supporting Windows NT Server 4.0

Windows NT Server 4.0 in the Enterprise Requirement

70-68: Implementing and Supporting Windows NT Server 4.0 in the Enterprise

For the electives, you have about ten choices. Three of the most popular electives are:

70-53: Internetworking Microsoft TCP/IP on Microsoft Windows NT 3.5x/4.0

70-26: SQL Server Administration

70-76: Implementing and Supporting Microsoft Exchange Server 5.0

For a complete description of all the MCSE options, visit Microsoft's Microsoft's Training & Certification Web site at www.microsoft.com/Train_Cert.

This book is a part of a series of MCSE study guides, published by Network Press (Sybex), that covers the core requirements and electives—the entire MCSE track.

Where Do You Take the Exams?

You may take the exams at any of more than 800 authorized testing centers around the world. For the location of a center near you, call (800) 755-EXAM (755-3926). Outside the United States and Canada, contact your local Sylvan or Microsoft office.

To register for a Microsoft Certified Professional exam:

1. Determine the number of the exam you want to take.

2. Register with Sylvan by calling 1-800-755-3926. At this point you will be asked for advance payment for the exam.

3. Make sure you arrive to the testing center on time. You will need to bring two photo IDs with you.

At this writing, the exams are $100 each. Exams must be taken within one year of payment. You can schedule exams up to six weeks in advance or as late as one working day prior to the date of the exam. You can cancel or reschedule your exam if you contact Sylvan at least two working days prior to the exam. Same-day registration is available in some locations, although this is subject to space availability. Where same-day registration is available, you must register a minimum of two hours before test time.

When you schedule the exam, you'll be provided with instructions regarding appointment and cancellation procedures, ID requirements, and information about the testing center location.

What the SQL Server Administration Exam Measures

The System Administration for SQL Server 6.5 Certification Exam covers concepts and skills required for the support of SQL Server 6.5. It emphasizes the following areas:

- SQL Server hardware and software requirements

- Installing SQL Server

- Configuring SQL Server

- Creating databases and their devices

- Creating and managing transaction logs

- Backing up databases

- Backing up transaction logs

- Creating SQL Server users

- Managing database security

- Tuning SQL Server

- Data replication

- Troubleshooting

Microsoft publishes a list of objectives that the test will cover. In this book, we have made it easy for you to find the information associated with each exam objective. Before the relevant discussion, you will see:

Microsoft *Exam* *Objective*

Objective listed here.

 Exam objectives are subject to change at any time without prior notice and at Microsoft's sole discretion. Please visit Microsoft's Training & Certification Web site (www.microsoft.com/Train_Cert) for the most current exam objectives listing.

Tips for Taking the SQL Server Administration Exam

The exam focuses on fundamental concepts relating to Microsoft SQL Server operation. It can also be quite specific regarding how SQL Server administrative tasks are performed. This exam is often perceived as one of the more difficult of the Microsoft Certified Professional tests. Careful study of this book, along with hands-on experience with the operating system, will be especially helpful in preparing you for the exam.

Here are some general tips for taking the exams successfully:

- Arrive early at the exam center so you can relax and review your study materials, particularly tables and lists of exam-related information.

■ One student, upon exiting the test, remarked, "This test must have been written by lawyers." In other words, questions are often worded so that, while more than one answer looks correct, only one answer is actually the right one.

■ Read the questions carefully. Don't be tempted to jump to an early conclusion. Make sure you know *exactly* what the question is asking.

■ Don't leave any unanswered questions. They count against you.

■ When answering multiple-choice questions you're not sure about, use a process of elimination to get rid of the obviously incorrect questions first. This will improve your odds if you need to make an educated guess.

■ Because the hard questions will eat up the most time, save them for last. You can mark any questions to make them easy to find, and then move forward and backward through the exam.

■ Many participants run out of time before they are able to complete the test. Once your time is up, you cannot go on to another question; however, you can remain on the question you are on indefinitely. If you are unsure of the answer to a question, you may want to choose one of the answers, mark the question, and continue. When you are almost out of time, go to a question you feel you can figure out—given enough time— and work until you think you've got it right.

■ This is not simply a test of your knowledge of Transaction SQL commands, but on how it is used to administer SQL Server 6.5 on Windows NT. You will need to know how to use the Transaction SQL language *and* the graphical utilities to perform your administrative tasks.

How to Use This Book

This book can provide a solid foundation for the serious effort of preparing for the System Administration for SQL Server 6.5 exam. To best benefit from this book, you might want to use the following study method:

1. Study a chapter carefully, making sure you fully understand the information.

2. Complete all hands-on exercises in the chapter, referring to the chapter so that you understand each step you take.

Each of the hands-on exercises is clearly labeled with a number (based on the chapter and its order within that chapter, such as Exercise 2.3, for the third exercise in Chapter 2) and title stating the goal of the exercise. Within the exercises, we have used two conventions: text you should enter is in boldface type, and menu selections are denoted with a ➢ symbol. For example, you may be instructed to select Start ➢ Programs ➢ Command Prompt and enter `makepipe`.

3. Answer the practice questions at the end of the chapter. (You will find the answers to these questions in Appendix A.)

4. Note which questions you did not understand, and study those sections of the book again.

5. Note the exam objectives; you will most likely get at least one question on each objective.

6. Before taking the exam, try the practice exams included on the CD that comes with this book. They will give you a good idea of what you can expect to see on the real thing, although the actual exam is usually more difficult than the practice tests.

To learn all the material covered in this book, you will need to study regularly and with discipline. Try to set aside the same time every day to study, and select a comfortable and quiet place in which to do it.

Although we would love to guarantee that you will pass the test on the first try, we can't (you wouldn't really want us to give you the actual test questions and answers, would you?). Microsoft is proud of the fact that the tests are difficult. If you fail the test the first time you take it, don't get discouraged—keep on trying. If you work hard, you will be surprised at how quickly you learn this material. Good luck.

What's on the CD?

The CD contains several valuable tools to help you study for your MCSE exams:

- The Microsoft *Train_Cert Offline* Web site provides an overview of Microsoft training and certification programs and the process of becoming an MCSE.

- The exercise questions and answers from each of the chapters in this book are included in a simple-to-use exam preparation program.

- The custom scripts are flat ASCII files that have a .SQL extension for use in the exercises in two chapters.

- The *Common Transact-SQL Commands* appendix is included on the CD in a fully searchable, indexed Acrobat Reader format.

How to Contact the Authors

You can e-mail Lance, Rick, or Mike at the following addresses:

Lance Mortensen	LMSQL@aol.com
Rick Sawtell	Quickening@msn.com
Mike Lee	MLee@apeleon.net

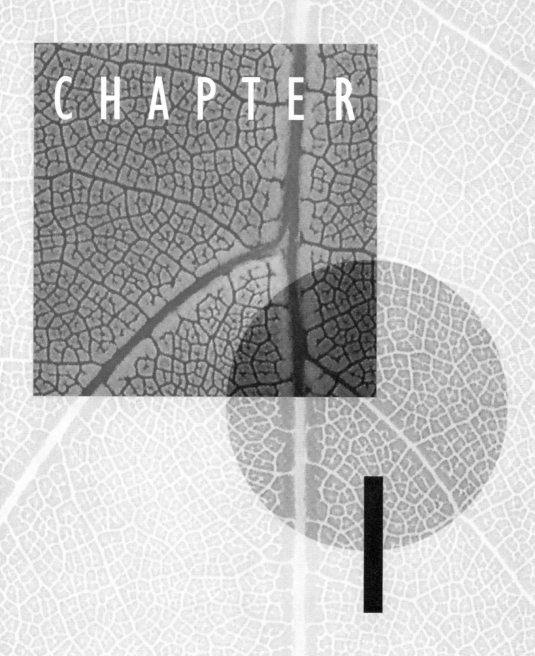

CHAPTER

1

Introduction to SQL Server 6.5 and
Relational Databases

SQL Server is a client/server-based relational database management system that runs on Windows NT Server or Windows NT Workstation, and it is included in Microsoft's BackOffice suite. In this chapter, we provide an introduction to SQL Server 6.5 and also to some important database-management concepts.

We will start with some background material on SQL Server and Windows NT. We will then look at what defines a client/server environment. Our next topic will be types of databases and what they contain. Finally, we'll go over the tasks of the SQL Server developer and the tasks of the SQL Server administrator.

Some Background on SQL Server and Windows NT

Microsoft has energized the database market with the release of SQL Server for Windows NT. This version's price and performance have allowed many companies to downsize from mainframes to networks based on personal computers. More than two million copies of Microsoft's SQL Server have been sold since it was first introduced. Currently, SQL Server is installed in approximately 37 percent of the companies that use some kind of database server.

SQL Server is one of the cornerstones of Microsoft's strategy for its BackOffice suite (Microsoft's line of client/server support applications). Every company has data, and almost every program generates even more data. The paperless office needs to store its data somewhere—usually in some kind of data server. SQL Server is an excellent data server, designed to provide great flexibility for your database storage and applications.

Before you administer a SQL Server system, you need to understand its native language and history, as well as how it works with Windows NT.

History of the SQL Language

Back in the 1970s, IBM invented a computer language designed specifically for database queries. This language was called SEQUEL, for Structured English QUEry Language. IBM released SEQUEL into the public domain, where it soon became known as SQL. This is why you can pronounce it either as "sequel" or by its initials, "S-Q-L."

Over time, the language has been expanded so that it is not just a language for queries, but can also be used to build databases and manage security of the database engine. Currently, there are various versions of the SQL language in use. Microsoft SQL Server uses a version called Transact-SQL or T-SQL, both of which stand for Transaction SQL.

The Transact-SQL language can be divided into two generic categories of commands:

- Data-manipulation commands, also known as the Data Definition Language (DDL), are used to define the database, tables, and other objects that have to do with the management of the structure of the database.

- Data-management commands, also known as Data Management Language (DML), are used much like the original commands of the SQL language. With these types of commands, you can manipulate, add to, or delete data in the database, as well as run queries.

History of Microsoft's SQL Server on Windows NT

Microsoft initially worked with Sybase Corporation on a version of a SQL server system for OS/2. When Microsoft abandoned OS/2 in favor of its new network operating system, Windows NT, it decided to enhance the SQL server engine from Sybase and help modify the code for Windows NT. The resulting product was Microsoft SQL Server 4.0 for Windows NT, which stabilized at 4.21.

Over time, Microsoft took over more and more responsibility for the development of SQL Server, until version 6.0, when Microsoft was in complete control of the software. Sybase engineers continued developing their database engine to run on Windows NT (Sybase version 10), while Microsoft developers continued enhancing SQL Server 6.0 (now 6.5). Sybase continues to develop its product for Windows NT, while Microsoft's next version of SQL Server is expected to be released sometime in late 1998.

Introduction to Windows NT

Microsoft started developing Windows NT in 1990, when it became obvious that running a 16-bit version of Windows on top of MS-DOS just wasn't giving the performance and security that businesses needed. Windows NT 4.0 was released in 1996, and NT 5.0 is due in the second half of 1998.

Windows NT is a 32-bit operating system that has been designed with a familiar user interface (basically the same as the Windows 95 interface). One way to look at Windows NT is that it is much like a mainframe operating system under the hood, but the user interface is a friendly Desktop. Windows NT has both server and client properties; that is, it can simultaneously function as a network server and as a client on the network. We'll talk more about client/server systems in the next section.

Windows NT comes in two versions:

- A Workstation version that is primarily used on desktop and laptop computers, but can act as a server for up to ten simultaneous connections at a time

- A Server version that is primarily used as a file/application server that theoretically can have thousands of simultaneous users connected to it

Windows NT is the ultimate general-purpose server. You can add functionality to the base server by installing services. SQL Server 6.5 is implemented as a set of services on either Windows NT Workstation or Windows NT Server.

You can obtain the latest news about SQL Server 6.5, and even download a 120-day trial of SQL Server, from Microsoft's Web site: www.microsoft.com\sql.

What Is Client/Server?

Microsoft's SQL Server is a client/server database engine. SQL Server is the server part of the client/server equation.

Client/server can be defined as an application that is split into at least two parts: one part runs on a server, and the other part runs on client computers, or workstations. The server side of the application provides security, fault-tolerance, performance, concurrency, and reliable backups. The client side provides the user interface and may contain items such as reports, queries, and forms.

In older, non-client/server database systems, the work is not shared between the server and workstation machines. For example, suppose that you have a 10MB database stored on your network server. With a non-client/server application, when a client opens the database and runs a query, all 10MB are downloaded to the client, and then the query is processed at the client computer. Figure 1.1 illustrates how these older database systems worked.

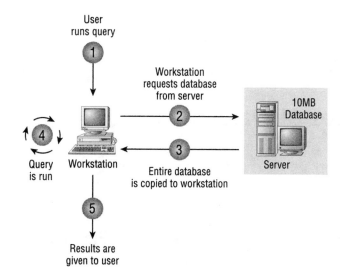

In contrast, when a query is run on a client/server system, the server searches the database, and then sends back to the client just those rows that match the search conditions. Figure 1.2 illustrates how a client/server database system works. This not only saves bandwidth on your network, but it is often faster than having the workstations do all of the work (as long as the server is a powerful enough machine).

F I G U R E 1.2

In a client/server application, the server and workstation share the work.

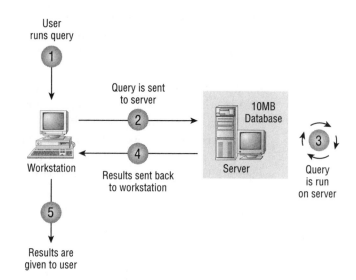

Types of Databases

A database can generally be thought of as a collection of related data. However, that data can be structured in various ways, and the database can be designed to store historical data or changing data.

Relational Databases versus Flat-File Databases

In earlier database products, a database was usually one file—something like payroll.dbf for a payroll-related file or patients.dbf for a doctor's office. When all of its information is stored in a single file, and the information is accessed sequentially, the database is considered a *flat-file database*. A flat-file database resembles a spreadsheet, because it is all contained in one "page" or file. dBASE, Access, and other personal computer databases are examples of flat-file databases. Although flat-file databases are relatively easy to set up, they are more difficult to maintain if they hold complex data.

A *relational* database is composed of tables, which contain related data. The process of organizing data into tables in a consistent and complete format is referred to as *normalizing* the database.

Before you implement your database design, you should start with a fully normalized view of your database. Normalization of relational designs is a complex topic, which won't be addressed in this book. You can refer to other books that are devoted to this topic.

In a relational database management system (RDBMS), such as SQL Server, a database is not necessarily tied to a file; it is more of a logical concept that is based on a collection of related *objects*. A database in SQL Server not only contains the raw data, it also contains the structure of the database, the security of the database, and any views or stored procedures related to that particular database.

Objects in a Relational Database

A SQL Server database is composed of different types of objects. The following are some of the more common types of objects used in a database:

Object	Description
Table	A table contains rows, columns, and the actual raw data.
Column	A column is part of the table and holds the data.
Row	A row is not a separate object, but rather a complete set of columns within a single table. It is a logical construct, not a physically implemented object like the other items discussed here.
Datatype	Various datatypes, such as character, numeric, and date, can be used in columns. However, a column can hold data of only a single datatype.
Stored procedure	A stored procedure is a set of Transact-SQL statements combined to perform a single task or set of tasks. This object is like a macro, in that Transact-SQL code can be written and stored under a name. By invoking the name, you actually run the code.
Trigger	A trigger is a stored procedure that activates when data is added, edited, or deleted from a table. Triggers are used to ensure that tables linked by keys stay internally consistent with each other. For example, an automobile dealer's database might include a trigger that makes sure that every time a car is added, the assigned salesperson actually exists.

Object	Description
Rule	A rule is assigned to a column so that data being entered must conform to standards you set. For example, rules can be used to make sure that the state in a person's address is entered in uppercase and that phone numbers contain only numbers.
Default	A default is assigned to a column so that if no data is entered, the default value will be used. For example, you might set a default for the state code to the state where most of your customers reside, so the default can be accepted for most entries.
View	A view is similar to a stored query. Rather than rewriting the query every time you want to run it, you can use the view instead. A view usually either excludes certain columns from a table or links two or more tables together. A view appears very much like a table to most users.

Some of these common database objects are illustrated in Figure 1.3.

FIGURE 1.3

Some common database objects

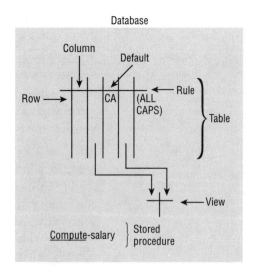

Data Warehousing versus Transaction Processing

There are two general categories that databases fall into:

- Databases designed for storage and querying of historical data. These are often referred to as *data-warehousing or decision-support systems.* The main focus of data-warehousing systems is the ability to quickly query existing data and perform complex analyses, usually looking for patterns or other relationships that are difficult to locate during day-to-day operations of a company.

- Databases designed for activities that involve live, continually changing data. This type of database activity is referred to as *OLTP,* or *online transaction processing.* In this case, the flexibility to expand and edit the database is the main focus.

Although these types of databases may appear to be the same at first glance, they are basically exact opposites. Data warehousing emphasizes reading the database with long-running transactions; OLTP emphasizes writing to the database with very quick transactions.

SQL Server makes a great server for both OLTP and data-warehousing types of databases. However, if your company is using both OLTP and decision-support databases, you may want to consider using two SQL Server machines—one for each function—in order to get optimal performance.

Another related (and rapidly growing) use of databases is to put the data into a Web page and publish it either internally on an intranet or to the public on the Internet. Again, the same basic types of databases are used: data warehousing if the data on the Web page is for historical reporting purposes or OLTP if the customer can order items from the Web page. Currently, most of the data is historical, or static, but that will change as the security and tools for transaction processing across the Internet improve.

Tasks of a SQL Server Developer

A SQL Server developer is responsible for designing, programming, and populating the database. The developer's responsibilities can be summarized as follows:

- Analyze the business situation to see what type of system is required. Is it a new system or an upgrade? Is it is a small company at one location or a big corporation with multiple locations?

- Design the database, tables, and all objects. In the design process, the developer identifies objects and relationships and how those all fit together as logical entities, which are then translated into physical tables (normalized). The developer must then plan for the application design, including reports and queries, as well as other pieces, including access to Web pages.

- Design the security for the SQL Server system and for the individual databases. Implementing security is covered in Chapter 7.

- Design any data-replication scenarios. Replication, including scenarios and implementation, is covered in Chapter 11.

- Program the database, tables, and all objects. This involves working with the Transact-SQL language and is covered in Microsoft's SQL Implementation class and test (not in the System Administration for Microsoft SQL Server test, which is the focus of this book).

- Program the initial security of the database. For example, the designer may plan how the users will be placed in groups to help administer database security. Creating groups is covered in Chapter 6.

- Design the user interface, reports, and update screens. This is the front end of the system and will probably have the most impact on the users.

- Test the design, interface, reports, and update screens.

- Populate the database with live data from legacy systems, and prepare the database to receive new data.

- Hand the project over to the administrator with appropriate documentation and training.

Microsoft has two separate exams related to SQL: one test is designed for the system administrator (which is the focus of this book), and one is designed for Transact-SQL programmers (called the Implementation test). The duties of the developer are not covered in detail in this book. We will concentrate on the tasks of the system administrator and provide the information you need to pass the System Administration for Microsoft SQL Server 6.5 exam.

Tasks of a SQL Server Administrator

A SQL Server administrator is usually responsible for the day-to-day administration of the database. The administrator takes over where the programmer left off. In many companies, the lines between administrator and developer may become quite blurred, and the same person may be doing tasks related to both roles.

Microsoft **Identify system administrator functionality.**
✓ Exam
Objective

Exam objectives are subject to change at any time without prior notice and at Microsoft's sole discretion. Please visit Microsoft's Training & Certification Web site (www.microsoft.com/Train_Cert) for the most current exam objectives listing.

The administrator's duties can be summarized as the following:

- Back up the databases (see Chapter 8).

- Restore the databases when necessary (see Chapter 8).

- Manage the databases (see Chapters 5, 9, and 10).

- Set up and manage users for SQL Server (see Chapter 6).

- Manage security for new users and existing users (see Chapter 7).

- Set up and manage tasks, alerts, and operators (see Chapter 9).

- Manage the replication environment (see Chapter 11).

- Tune the SQL Server system for the optimal performance (see Chapter 12).

- Troubleshoot any SQL Server problems (see Chapter 13).

You will be learning how to accomplish the tasks of a SQL Server system administrator throughout this book.

Summary

Microsoft's SQL Server is a client/server-based relational database management system (RDBMS), which uses Transact-SQL as its dialect of the SQL language. Its ever-increasing popularity makes learning SQL Server 6.5 a wise career decision.

A *client/server* database is an application that is divided into a part that runs on a server and a part that runs on workstations (clients). The server side provides security, fault-tolerance, performance, concurrency, and reliable backups. The client side provides the user interface.

A *relational* database is composed of tables, which contain related data. The process of dividing a database into related tables is called *normalization*.

SQL Server developers have the responsibility to design and implement the databases. Designing a good database starts with understanding the client's requirements for the database. The data can then be grouped into related tables. SQL Server administrators have the responsibility for the day-to-day tasks of maintaining and managing the databases. SQL Server administration involves backing up databases and restoring them when necessary, setting up and managing users, managing database security, managing the replication environment, tuning the database system, and troubleshooting any problems that arise.

Exercise Questions

1. SQL Server is part of Microsoft's Office Suite.

A. True

B. False

2. SQL Server is part of Microsoft's BackOffice Suite.

A. True

B. False

3. Which of the following is a database object? (Choose all that apply.)

A. Table

B. Index

C. Rule

D. Default

4. Which role is responsible for backing up databases?

A. The database administrator

B. The database developer

C. Database users

D. The Windows NT administrator

5. Who is responsible for ongoing database security?

A. The database administrator

B. The database developer

C. Database users

D. The Windows NT administrator

6. Who is responsible for ongoing SQL Server optimization?

A. The database administrator

B. The database developer

C. Database users

D. The Windows NT administrator

7. What is the process of breaking related information into tables called?

A. Fragmentation

B. Database design

C. Normalization

D. Tablizing the data

8. Data warehousing emphasizes fast reads.

A. True

B. False

9. Online transaction processing (OLTP) emphasizes fast reads.

A. True

B. False

10. When a query is run in client/server computing, who actually runs the query?

A. The client

B. The server

C. Both the client and the server

D. Neither; a middleware piece runs the query

11. SQL Server is an example of which kind of a database system?

    A. Flat-file

    B. 3-D

    C. RDBMS

    D. DB2

12. Data in relational databases is organized into what format?

    A. Fields

    B. Files

    C. Reports

    D. Tables

CHAPTER

2

Installing SQL Server 6.5

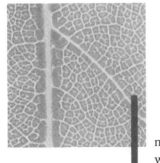

nstalling SQL Server is not a complex task, but there are several areas where a little foresight can prevent potential disasters down the road. For example, if you make the wrong choice about which character set to install, remedying the situation requires dropping (deleting) all of your databases, reloading them with information, and rebuilding your indexes.

In this chapter, you will learn how to correctly install SQL Server 6.5 in the Windows NT 4 environment. The first part of this chapter deals with the tasks you should complete before you begin the installation process. First, you must make sure that your system meets at least the minimum hardware and software requirements for SQL Server 6.5. You will also need to make an informed decision on the type of file system to use, FAT or NTFS. Another preparation task is setting up the SQL Executive account.

The next part of this chapter covers the actual installation process, which includes choices about your network libraries, character sets, and sort orders, as well as other options. Then you will learn about installing the client software for SQL Server on MS-DOS, Windows 3.*x*, and 32-bit Windows platforms (Windows 95 and Windows NT). The final sections deal with starting and stopping the SQL Server service and troubleshooting SQL Server setup problems.

Configuring Windows NT 4.0 for SQL Server 6.5

The first step in installing SQL Server is to make sure that you have the appropriate hardware and software installed. SQL Server can be installed on any platform that Windows NT runs on (DEC Alpha-AXP, Intel *x*86, MIPS, and Power PC). SQL Server 6.5 requires Windows NT 3.51 or later, running on a 486 or better CPU.

Microsoft ✓ ***Exam*** ***Objective*** **Configure Microsoft Windows NT for SQL Server installations.**

As with most Microsoft products, the bigger and faster your platform, the better SQL Server will run. This book will focus on the Intel *x*86 platform, but you can apply the information here to SQL Server installations on other platforms.

Hardware and Software Requirements

Table 2.1 summarizes the minimum hardware and software requirements for installing and running Microsoft SQL Server 6.5. The following sections discuss RAM, hard disk space, file system, and disk subsystem requirements in more detail.

Microsoft ✔ *Exam Objective*

Configure SQL Server for various memory scenarios.

TABLE 2.1

Minimum Hardware and Software Requirements for SQL Server 6.5

Component	Minimum Requirement
Platform	i486 or later, Power PC, MIPS, DEC Alpha-AXP
RAM	16MB, 32MB for replication
Operating system	NT 3.51 or later
File system	FAT or NTFS
Hard disk	60MB, additional 15MB for SQL Server Books Online

RAM and Hard Disk Space Requirements

One of the most important decisions that you will be making concerns what hardware to use to maximize SQL Server's performance. As a minimum, SQL Server 6.5 requires 16MB of RAM and 60MB of hard disk space. If you are planning on replicating information to other SQL Server machines (as discussed in Chapter 11), you must have at least 32MB of RAM installed.

SQL Server Books Online is an invaluable resource and should be placed online somewhere in your environment. Books Online takes up an additional 15MB of hard disk space if you do a full installation; 1MB of hard disk space is required if you want to run Books Online from the CD-ROM. Running Books Online from the CD-ROM is a little less convenient, but it's a decent alternative if disk space is at a premium.

SQL Server Books Online encompasses all of the books that normally ship with Microsoft SQL Server, but in an electronic format. Books Online takes advantage of the original TechNet style interface, complete with a search engine for key words and phrases, bookmarks, and the ability to copy and paste from within it.

File System and Disk Subsystem Requirements

You can install SQL Server on either FAT or NTFS partitions. We recommend using NTFS partitions for both security and fault tolerance (transaction tracking and hot fixing).

More important than the file system is the disk subsystem that you select. You should select a disk subsystem with the degree of fault tolerance that you desire, while maintaining or improving your overall system performance. For critical applications, you may want to take advantage of a hardware implementation of the RAID 5 disk subsystem. A RAID 5 subsystem writes files across multiple hard disks and multiple partitions in what are called *stripes*. It also keeps track of the information contained in each piece of the stripe with a parity checksum. A RAID 5 system offers advantages in two areas:

- Disk access is faster because more than one disk controller is reading information at a time.

- Because of the striping with parity, if you lose a single hard disk, you will not lose any information. The hard disk can be replaced and then rebuilt from the parity information and data from the other drives.

A hardware version of RAID 5 is expensive, but when you need that level of fault tolerance and performance, it's the best choice. For those who can't afford a hardware version, or don't need the highest level of fault tolerance, there is the alternative of implementing a software version of a RAID 5 array using Windows NT's disk striping with parity. You can also use Windows NT mirroring to make exact replicas of your information.

You should create your stripe sets and mirrors before you install SQL Server. These fault-tolerance features are discussed in a bit more detail in Chapter 8. For instructions on using these Windows NT features, refer to the Windows NT Resource Kit and *MCSE: Windows NT Server Study Guide.*

Where Should You Install SQL Server?

Before you decide on which server you should install SQL Server, you should understand SQL Server's security options, because these may affect your choice of an installation location. SQL Server has three security modes: standard, integrated and mixed. Here, we'll provide an overview of SQL Server login security. We will discuss these topics in greater detail in Chapter 6.

Standard Security

The standard security mode forces SQL Server to do its own account authentication, rather than having the Windows NT Security Accounts Manager (SAM) database (also referred to as the *directory database*) do it. The standard security mode does not require any additional network libraries to be loaded, but it does require that you create login IDs and passwords internal to the SQL Server machine. These IDs and passwords will be placed into the SQL Server system table named syslogins, to be used for authentication.

The standard security mode is useful for environments where Windows NT is not used for authentication, or environments where SQL Server does not have access to domain accounts through trust relationships. (A trust relationship occurs when Domain A has resources that it would like users located in Domain B to have access to—Domain A can trust Domain B to validate those users, and the users in Domain B will be able to "see" the resources located in Domain A.) For example, if you are working in a Novell NetWare environment, all the network security is being handled by NetWare; therefore, you must use standard security for SQL Server, because there is no Windows NT domain to authenticate users logging in.

In a Novell NetWare environment, you could create local accounts for all of your users on the Windows NT Server machine that is running SQL Server. However, this causes problems because users now have multiple network user IDs. A workaround is to use the DSMN (Directory Service Manager for NetWare) software, which will synchronize accounts between the NetWare bindery and the Windows NT SAM database.

The default security that is installed with SQL Server is standard security. Once you have successfully installed SQL Server, you can change your security mode, as explained in Chapter 6.

Integrated Security

When your environment has a Windows NT machine doing authentication, you can use the integrated security mode. This can greatly simplify administration by using Windows NT's SAM database for validation of SQL Server logins. There are a couple of requirements for using integrated security:

- You must install either the named pipes and/or multi-protocol network libraries on both the clients and the SQL Server machine.

- The SQL Server machine must have access to the Windows NT SAM database, either locally or through a trust relationship.

To implement integrated security, you (or the network administrator) simply add the user accounts to the SAM database (directory database) through the Windows NT User Manager for Domains tool and assign the appropriate rights, privileges, and groups. You (as the SQL administrator) could then use the SQL Security Manager tool to "map" those Windows NT SAM accounts into the SQL Server syslogins table. When users who have a mapping into SQL Server log in to Windows NT, they are automatically logged in to both Windows NT and SQL Server.

Mixed Security

Mixed security is useful for environments where you have a mixed group of clients. For example, suppose that your organization uses a single SQL Server machine to support databases for both the Accounting department and Sales department. The Accounting department people are being validated by a Novell NetWare server, and the Sales department people are being validated by a Windows NT Server machine in a trusted domain. In this type of setup, you can use either mixed security or standard security.

Mixed security allows logins to SQL Server to be authenticated by either the Windows NT SAM database or directly by SQL Server. If you are in a trusted domain and are using either named pipes or multi-protocol network libraries on both the client and the SQL Server machine, then SQL Server will look for a valid Windows NT ID that has been mapped into SQL Server. If there is one, you will be logged in with it. If SQL Server can't find a Windows NT ID, SQL Server will attempt to log you in with the ID that you supplied.

Choosing an Installation Server

After reviewing all of this information, where should you install SQL Server? Primary domain controllers (PDCs) and backup domain controllers (BDCs) are not the best choices for installation, because they are using valuable CPU cycles, memory resources, and network bandwidth to conduct authentication and replication tasks. You should install SQL Server on a machine that is not busy with these operations—the more system resources you dedicate to SQL Server, the better it will perform.

Finally, if you are running SQL Server in a multi-domain environment, you should place SQL Server on a server that has access to domain accounts through a trust relationship. If you do not, you will not be able to implement integrated security, and will be forced to rely on standard security.

Setting Up a SQL Executive Service Account

The SQL Executive account is used by the SQL Executive service, which is a suite of utilities that includes replication, task, event, and alert managers. You can use these utilities to streamline the administration of SQL Server and to distribute information throughout your enterprise (see Chapter 9 for more details about tasks, alerts, and events).

Microsoft
Exam
Objective

Configure SQL Executive to log on as a service.

To create the SQL Executive account, you set up a regular Windows NT user account using Windows NT's User Manager for Domains tool. You then add the new account to the local Administrators group. You finish up by giving the account the advanced user right of Log on as a Service. To create your own SQL Executive account, follow the steps outlined in Exercise 2.1.

NOTE The exercises in this book assume that you are using Windows NT 4.0. If you're running NT 3.5x, the procedures will still work, but you will need to start programs using standard NT 3.5x techniques.

EXERCISE 2.1

Creating a SQL Executive Account

1. In Windows NT, start the User Manager for Domains tool by choosing Start ➢ Programs ➢ Administrative Tools ➢ User Manager for Domains.

2. Select User ➢ New User. The New User dialog box (shown below) appears.

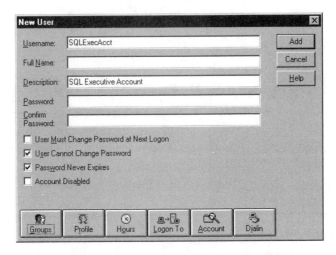

3. In the Username field, enter **SQLExecAcct**.

4. In the Description field, enter **SQL Executive Service Account**.

5. In the Password field, enter a password (this account will have Administrative privileges).

6. Clear the checkbox for User Must Change Password at Next Logon.

7. Check the Password Never Expires checkbox.

8. Check the User Cannot Change Password checkbox.

9. Click on the Groups button to add your account to the Administrators group.

10. Double-click on the Administrators group entry. Your Group Memberships dialog box should look similar to the one shown below.

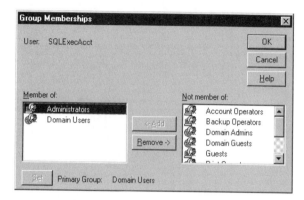

11. Click on OK to return to the New User dialog box.

12. Click on the Add button to add this account.

13. Click on the Close button to close the New User dialog box.

14. To give the account the advanced right Log on as a Service, select Policies ➤ User Rights.

15. Click on the Show Advanced User Rights checkbox in the lower-left corner. Then click on the drop-down list box and choose the Log on as a Service right, as shown below.

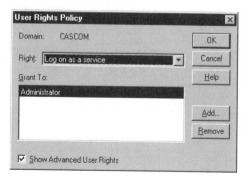

16. You will notice that your SQLExecAcct is not listed in the Grant To list. To add this user, click on the Add button to display the Add Users and Groups dialog box.

17. To add your SQLExecAcct, click on the Show Users button. Then scroll down through the list of accounts and double-click on SQLExecAcct. It should now be listed in the lower box, as shown below.

18. Click on OK to close the Add Users and Groups dialog box.

19. Now your account is listed in the middle section of the User Rights Policy dialog box. Click on OK to close this dialog box.

20. Close the User Manager for Domains utility.

When you create your SQL Executive account, remember to give it the following characteristics:

- Set the User Cannot Change Password option.

- Set the Password Never Expires option.

- Add the account to the local Administrators group on the computer where SQL Server is installed.

- Grant the Log on as a Service right.

A Pre-Installation Checklist

Here is a summary of the tasks you should take care of before you install the SQL Server software:

- Make sure that you have enough hard disk space for SQL Server, as well as for any additional databases your system requires and SQL Server Books Online.

- If you are going to be using striping with parity (RAID 5) or disk mirroring, set that up before you install SQL Server.

You cannot use network disk locations (non-local hard disks) for the normal operation of SQL Server. You can use network directories for backups, however.

- If you are going to be using integrated or mixed security, place your SQL Server on a machine that has access to user accounts through trust relationships. You should not install SQL Server on a domain controller (a PDC or BDC).

- Create an account for the SQL Executive service. The SQL Executive service is made up of a group of SQL administration managers that can take care of automating your server. The service includes managers that can handle alerts processing, tasking, event processing, and replication. For the SQL Executive service to have network access, which is required to perform many of these functions, it needs a logon account that has been granted the Log on as a Service right.

- Apply the latest NT Service Pack to your Windows NT machine before you begin your installation. At the time of this writing, NT Service Pack 3 is available.

You can find the latest Service Packs for Windows NT on the TechNet CDs or obtain them from the Microsoft Web site (http://www.microsoft.com/ NTServerSupport/Content/ServicePacks/Where.htm) or the FTP site (ftp:// ftp.microsoft.com/bussys/winnt/winnt-public/fixes/). Look for the NT4sp3_i.exe file. We strongly recommend that you read the README.TXT file associated with the Service Pack *before* you install it.

Installing SQL Server 6.5

$\mathbf{S}$QL Server 6.5 ships with two package configurations: a standard edition and a workstation edition. The workstation edition ships with the Program Developers Kit (PDK), which is useful to developers who wish to know which dynamic link library (DLL) functions are available and what they do. Both configurations come on CD-ROM and include SQL Server Books Online, as well as all of the graphical tools and utilities. The only significant difference between the two packages is the available licensing options. The standard edition allows you to configure as many licenses as you have purchased in either a Per-Server or Per-Seat format. In the workstation edition, you are allocated one server license and up to 15 individual connections from a single computer, which cannot be changed.

After you have decided on which Windows NT machine to install the SQL Server software, its role in your environment, the hardware, the file system, and the flavor of SQL Server (standard or workstation) to use, the next step is to begin the installation process itself.

For information about upgrading to SQL Server 6.5 from a previous version, see Chapter 10.

The SQL Server installation process can be broken down into nine major steps, which are described in detail in the following sections:

- Begin the setup process.

- Choose a licensing option.

- Select an installation path.

- Choose the Master database device.

- Choose where to install SQL Server Books Online.

- Select a character set and sort order.

- Select network support.

- Select auto-start options for the SQL Server services.

- Choose the SQL Executive logon account.

If you are using the SQL Server 6.5 CD-ROM, you will be installing from the \i386 directory. This is the Intel implementation of SQL Server. You can also install from the Microsoft BackOffice CD-ROMs. SQL Server 6.5 is on the second CD-ROM in the set. Browse to the Sql65 directory and then to the I386 subdirectory.

Beginning the Setup Process

To begin the setup process, double-click on the SETUP.EXE program. The location of this file depends on which CD-ROM set you are installing from. If you are using the BackOffice CD-ROM, this file will be hidden. To view it, go to either Explorer or My Computer, and choose Options from the View menu. In the Options dialog box, choose the View tab, and then select the Show All Files option, as shown in Figure 2.1. Click on OK when you are finished. You should now be able to see the SETUP.EXE file.

FIGURE 2.1

Choose the Show All Files option in the View tab of the Options dialog box to view hidden files.

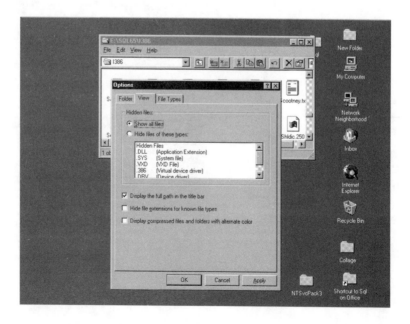

If you are installing from the SQL Server 6.5 CD-ROM, navigate to the \i386 directory and double-click on the SETUP.EXE program there. You will notice that SQL Server has support for \Alpha for DEC-Alpha-AXP computers, \MIPS for MIPS-based computers, and \PowerPC for IBM PowerPC computers.

When you start the SETUP.EXE program, the Welcome to Setup dialog box appears, as shown in Figure 2.2. Click on the Continue button to proceed with your installation. In the next dialog box, shown in Figure 2.3, enter your name, company name, and product ID (located on the jacket of the CD-ROM) in the appropriate fields. Only the Name field is required; however, you might wish to provide the company name and product ID for future reference.

WARNING Microsoft will not provide you with technical support if you do not have a valid product ID.

FIGURE 2.2

The SQL Server Setup Welcome dialog box

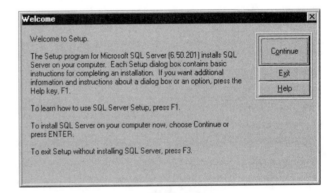

FIGURE 2.3

Add your name, company name, and product ID.

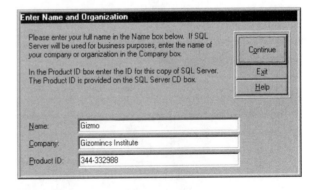

Next, you see the Microsoft SQL Server 6.5 Options dialog box, as shown in Figure 2.4. If SQL Server 6.5 is not currently installed on your system, three options will be available in this dialog box: Install SQL Server and Utilities, Upgrade SQL Server, or Install Utilities Only. Choose Install SQL Server and Utilities, and then click on Continue.

F I G U R E 2.4

The SQL Server 6.5 Options dialog box

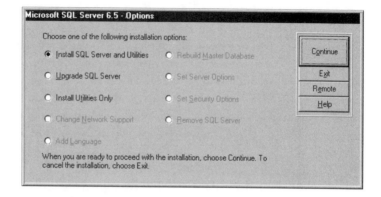

Choosing a Licensing Option

The Choose Licensing Mode dialog box appears next, as shown in Figure 2.5. The licensing method used in SQL Server 6.5 is the same as that used for Windows NT. Your licensing choices are Per Server or Per Seat.

F I G U R E 2.5

The Choose Your Licensing Mode dialog box

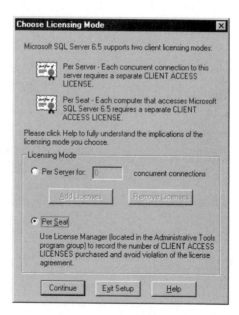

The appearance of the Licensing dialog box depends on the operating system that you are using. Your screen may look slightly different than the one shown in Figure 2.5.

The best way to describe the differences between Per Server and Per Seat licensing is to use an example. With a Per Server license setup, you may install SQL Server anywhere in your enterprise. You must then buy client licenses for that one particular server. If you decide to put another SQL Server machine somewhere in your enterprise, every client that you wish to give access to that second instance of SQL Server must have an additional client license to that SQL Server. In contrast, with a Per Seat license setup, you buy a single client license that will give you access to any or all servers in the enterprise.

If you do not know which license option to set your server up with, you should choose the Per Server option. With the Per Server option, you have a one-time, one-way option to change to the Per Seat licensing mode.

After you select your licensing mode, click on Continue to move on in the Setup program.

Setting Your Installation Path

The SQL Server Installation Path dialog box appears next, as shown in Figure 2.6. This is where you tell the installation program the drive and directory on which you want to install SQL Server. The default SQL Server installation directory is \MSSQL on the root of the first drive that has sufficient hard drive space available (in many cases, the C: drive). Accept the default drive and path, or enter other ones, and then click on Continue.

F I G U R E 2.6

Choose your SQL Server installation path and drive.

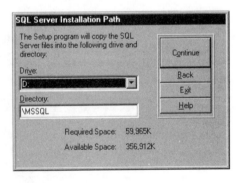

SQL Server needs at least 60MB of hard disk space, and an additional 15MB if you want to install SQL Server Books Online.

Choosing the Master Database Device

The next dialog box to appear is named Master Device Creation, as shown in Figure 2.7. The Master device, also referred to as the Master database device, is a hard disk file in the SQL Server directory structure that stores several critical system databases. The Master device is used by SQL Server to control the operation of SQL Server.

FIGURE 2.7

Select the size and location of the Master database device.

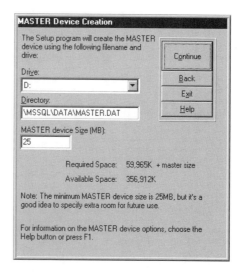

By default, the Master device is stored as \MSSQL\DATA\MASTER.DAT on the same drive that MSSQL was installed (as specified in the previous dialog box). The minimum size of the Master device is 25MB. Once you have chosen the location and size of your Master device, click on the Continue button.

You may wish to increase the size of the Master device from its default value of 25MB to 30MB or 35MB. This will ensure that you have some extra growing room in the event that you wish to extend the system databases.

Installing SQL Server Books Online

The SQL Server Books Online dialog box appears next, as shown in Figure 2.8. You are given three options:

- Install and copy Books Online onto the hard disk.
- Install and run Books Online from the CD.
- Do not install Books Online.

FIGURE 2.8

SQL Server Books Online installation options

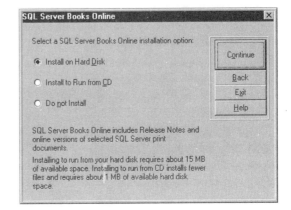

The SQL Server Books Online feature is an excellent resource and should be installed on at least one of the SQL Server machines in your enterprise. If you choose to install and run Books Online from the CD, you will need 1MB of hard disk, and the CD-ROM must be available to the server when users attempt to access information. Make your selection and click on Continue.

We recommend installing SQL Books Online onto your hard disk because this will give you the fastest access. If you don't have the additional 15MB of hard disk space required by Books Online to spare, then you might want to reconsider using that system for SQL Server (or at least consider increasing its hard disk capacity).

Choosing Character Sets and Sort Orders

The Installation Options dialog box appears next, as shown in Figure 2.9. This dialog box allows you to select the character set, sort order, and network support options for SQL Server. You can also select whether or not you want to automatically start SQL Server when the system is booted, as well as whether or not you want the SQL Executive service to automatically start at boot time.

FIGURE 2.9

The Installation Options dialog box

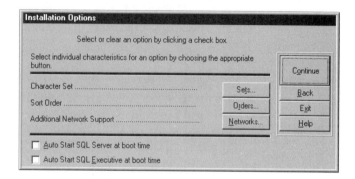

The character set (code page) and sort order options are two of the most important decisions that you must make during your installation. Both choices impact the compatibility and performance of your SQL Server system.

WARNING   If you need to change the character set or sort order after you have installed SQL Server, all of your databases must be rebuilt and all of your data must be reloaded.

Choosing the Character Set

When you choose a character set, you are informing SQL Server which characters it should recognize. Of the 256 characters contained in each character set, the first 128 characters are the same throughout the various code pages. The last 128 characters, also known as extended characters, are different.

Click on the Sets button to select a character set. The Select Character Set dialog box, shown in Figure 2.10, presents you with some of the available choices.

The three most common character set options are ISO 8859-1 (the default for SQL Server 6.5), code page 850 Multilingual (the default for SQL Server 4.21), and code page 437 U.S. English.

FIGURE 2.10

Character set choices

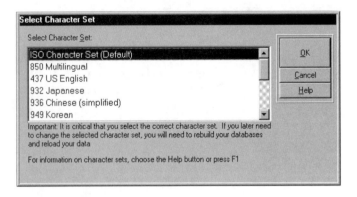

ISO 8859-1 is also referred to as Latin 1, ANSI, or just the ISO character set. It is the most portable of these three choices, since it is the same character set used by Sybase SQL Server for Unix and Digital's VMS operating system; using it for SQL Server allows you to maintain compatibility with these platforms. The ISO character set is also compatible with the character set used by Microsoft Windows operating systems. Since you must use the same character set on both the client and the server in order to make use of the extended characters, Microsoft recommends leaving ISO as the default character set in most situations.

Code page 850 Multilingual provides all of the characters necessary for most written languages in North America, South America, and Europe. This character set might be especially useful for companies with an international presence, especially in North and South America, where several different languages are in use.

Code page 437 U.S. English is the most commonly used character set in the United States. The extended characters provide additional graphics characters. You might need to choose this code page if your database application uses these extended graphics characters as data. However, this requirement is uncommon, and you probably are better off leaving the default ISO character set.

Click on OK in the Select Character Set dialog box after you have selected your character set.

Choosing a Sort Order

The sort order option tells SQL Server how to collate, store, and present data. The sort order and character set options are interrelated. The sort order options that are available depend on the character set that you have chosen. The most important sort order descriptions include the following:

- Dictionary order specifies that database and table information be sorted like that of a dictionary.

- Binary order sorts the data based on the binary value of the character represented.

- Case-sensitive order takes case into consideration; therefore, *A* and *a* are not the same and are ordered accordingly.

If you choose a case-sensitive sort order, nearly everything you do in SQL Server will be case-sensitive. For example, when you refer to column names and tables, you must use propercase.

- Case-insensitive order treats *A* and *a* as the same value; therefore, the sort does not need to go beyond basic alphabetizing.

Your front-end application needs to be aware of the sorting method used for your back-end program to ensure that your program accommodates this sorting and storage method. For example, if you choose a case-sensitive sort order for the back-end program, then your developers and your users must enter information in the appropriate case.

From the Installation Options dialog box, click on the Orders button. The sort order selections available for the ISO 8859-1 character sets are shown in Figure 2.11. Click on OK when you have selected a sort order.

FIGURE 2.11

The sort order you choose can impact the performance of SQL Server as well as its compatibility with your front-end application.

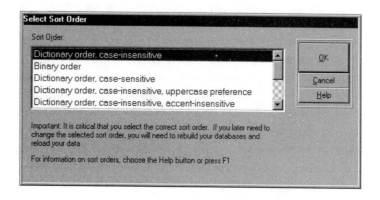

Adding Network Support

SQL Server supports several network library protocols for client/server communication. You can load multiple Net-Libraries during installation.

Microsoft ✓ **Exam** **Objective**

Load multiple Net-Libraries.

Click on the Networks button in the Installation Options dialog box to view the list of network protocols that you can install, as shown in Figure 2.12.

F I G U R E 2.12

You have many network protocol options.

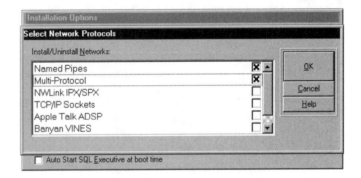

In order to use integrated security (described earlier in this chapter), you must select the Named Pipes and/or Multi-Protocol options as your Net-Library. When you choose Named Pipes, the default path used by SQL Server is \\computer_name\pipe\sql\query.

Multi-protocol is a great feature that is available in SQL Server 6.5. As its name suggests, multi-protocol allows SQL Server to communicate over any interprocess communication (IPC) mechanism. It also provides support for integrated security. Multi-protocol takes advantage of remote procedure calls (RPCs) to pass information between the client and server, and therefore may run a little slower than using named pipes.

Only named pipes and/or multi-protocol will allow you to use integrated security on your SQL Server system. Named pipes is the default protocol and must be used to install SQL Server. Although the Setup program provides named pipes as an option you may select, if you try to remove it, you will get an error message.

Other network protocols supported by SQL Server include NWLink (for compatibility with Novell NetWare's IPX\SPX), TCP/IP using Windows Sockets, Banyan Vines SPP (for compatibility with StreetTalk), AppleTalk ADSP (for use with Apple Macintosh clients), and DECNet Sockets (from Digital Equipment Corporation).

Choosing Auto Start Options

The last two options in the Installation Options dialog box are Auto Start SQL Server at Boot Time and Auto Start SQL Executive at Boot Time. Setting these options enables SQL Server to automatically restart itself in the event of a power outage or server reboot.

If your SQL Server system is mission-critical (it must always be up and running), you should select these two checkboxes. However, if you don't choose them during initial installation, you can set up auto start for the SQL Server and/or SQL Executive services later, either from within SQL Enterprise Manager or from the Windows NT Services Control Panel (see Chapter 4 for details on configuring auto start and other server options). When you're finished making your selections in the Installations Options dialog box, click on Continue.

Configuring the SQL Executive Logon Account

As explained earlier in the chapter, your SQL Executive account is used by the SQL Executive service, which is a set of administrative utilities. Before you begin the SQL Server installation process, you should have created this Windows NT user account with the User Manager for Domains utility (see Exercise 2.1). By creating a special service account that will be used exclusively by the SQL Executive service for authentication, you ensure that the password and permissions for that particular account are never modified and that the account will always be available for the SQL Executive service.

Microsoft Exam Objective

Configure SQL Executive to log on as a service.

After you've clicked on Continue in the Installation Options dialog box, the SQL Executive Log On Account dialog box appears, as shown in Figure 2.13. In this dialog box, you specify the SQL Executive account and password that will be used by the SQL Executive service to get its rights and permissions for access to the Windows NT server.

FIGURE 2.13

Specify the Executive log on account you created under Windows NT here.

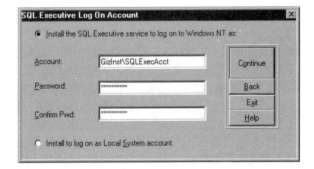

NOTE

The default account in this dialog box is the account that you are currently logged on as. Make sure that you delete that portion of the text and replace it with the SQL Executive logon account. If you do not specify an account here, the SQL Executive services will log on using the LocalSystem account, which will not allow the SQL Executive to participate in network-related functions (like replication).

Completing the Installation Process

Enter the account information and click on Continue. The file-copy process will now begin. Following the copy process, the SQL Server Setup program will create the Master device and the other required devices and databases. Entries will also be made to the Windows NT Registry. (We'll discuss all of the items added during SQL Server installation in Chapter 3.) Once your installation is complete, you should reboot Windows NT.

NOTE

The file-copy portion of the SQL Server setup process can take from 10 minutes to as long as 45 minutes.

Installing the SQL Server 6.5 Client Software

The client software that you will be able to install depends on the type of operating system on your client machine. SQL Server comes with both 16-bit and 32-bit client utilities.

Microsoft
✓ *Exam*
Objective

Install client support for network protocols other than named pipes.

If you are using 16-bit MS-DOS-based client software, you will be able to install only the 16-bit command-line utilities:

- BCP, the bulk copy utility

- ISQL, the query utility

- READPIPE, which is used for testing named pipes

- ENDDBLIB, which turns off TSRs (terminate-and-stay resident programs)

If you are using 16-bit MS Windows (Windows 3.*x*), you will be able to install the 16-bit command-line utilities listed above, as well as the 16-bit GUI (graphical user interface) utilities:

- ISQL/W, the Windows-based query utility

- SQL Client Configuration, which includes DB-Library, Net-Library, and other client configuration options

If you are using a 32-bit Microsoft Windows operating system (Windows 95 or Windows NT), you will be able to install all of the 16-bit utilities listed above, plus the following:

- SQL Enterprise Manager, a graphical management tool

- SQL Trace, which allows you to monitor and record SQL Server activity

- SQL Server Web Assistant, which allows you to create SQL-based Web pages

- Microsoft Query, a graphical tool used to create SQL statements

The following sections describe how to install the client utilities. See Chapter 4 for an overview of what these utilities do and how to use them.

Installing to 16-bit MS-DOS-based Operating Systems

If you are going to be installing to MS-DOS-based systems, you must do all of the work by hand. You should create a \SQL\BIN directory (or any other path that makes sense to you) on your machine and then copy all of the files from the \Clients\MSDOS directory on the CD-ROM.

When you are running MS-DOS, it can have only one Net-Library loaded at a time. You should add lines to your AUTOEXEC.BAT file to run the appropriate client Net-Library. Included on the CD are DBNMPIPE.EXE for use with named pipes, DBMSSPX.EXE for use with Novell's IPX/SPX, and DBMSVINE.EXE for use with Banyan Vines.

Installing to 16-bit Windows Operating Systems

To install the client utilities on a Windows 3.x machine, navigate to the \Clients\Win16 directory and run the Setup program. The Setup program will create a new directory called \MSSQL\BIN, configure the chosen default Net-Library, create the SQL Server Tools program group, add icons, and then copy all of the necessary files and DLLs to the BIN directory. Appropriate entries will also be added to your WIN.INI file.

If you are going to be using ODBC-based applications, you can install the ODBC drivers that come on the SQL Server CD-ROM. They are located in the \Clients\Win16\ODBC directory. However, we have found these files to be dated in general and suggest you search the Web for the latest and greatest versions.

Check out the Microsoft site at http://www.microsoft.com/odbc/ for the latest ODBC drivers. Also, see Appendix B for more information about SQL Server and ODBC (Open Database Connectivity).

Installing to 32-bit Operating Systems

When you have a 32-bit operating system like Windows NT or Windows 95, you can install all of the client software, including the 16-bit and 32-bit utilities. Simply navigate to the appropriate directory on your SQL Server CD-ROM (\i386 for Intel-based machines) and run the Setup program.

The Setup program will create an \MSSQL\BINN directory and an \MSSQL\Install directory if you decided to add SQL Server Books Online to a particular client. The Setup program will also create the SQL Server Tools program group and add the icons for the utilities you've selected. Finally,

Setup will copy the DB-Library and Net-Library DLLs to the appropriate system directory on your machine. New entries will also be added to your Windows Registry.

Starting and Stopping SQL Server

With SQL Server's tight integration with Windows NT (which is the topic of the next chapter), Microsoft has designed SQL Server to run as a set of Windows NT services. This design enables you to start, stop, and pause SQL Server services from five different locations: the Services Control Panel, a command prompt, SQL Service Manager, SQL Enterprise Manager, and Server Manager.

The two SQL Server services that we are concerned with here are the Microsoft SQL Server service (MSSQLServer) and the SQL Executive service (SQLExecutive). The MSSQLServer Service enables you to control whether or not SQL Server is running and accepting new logon and transaction requests. The MSSQLServer service has three states:

Started   When the SQL Server service is started, SQL Server will respond to queries and process requests.

Stopped   When the SQL Server service is stopped, SQL Server will not respond to or process requests.

Paused   When the SQL Server service is paused, queries can be processed and the currently logged on users can function normally, but no new users will be allowed to log in. If you are currently logged in to SQL Server and then log off, you will not be allowed to log back in until the SQL Server service has been started again.

The SQL Executive service allows for event scheduling, alert notification, and other management functions. The SQL Executive service only has two states: started and stopped.

Starting and Stopping SQL Server from the Services Control Panel

By using Windows NT's Services Control Panel, shown in Figure 2.14, you can stop, start, or pause the SQL Server service or stop or start the SQL Executive service. Simply open the Services Control Panel (by choosing Start ➤ Settings ➤ Control Panel and double-clicking on the Services icon), highlight the desired service, and click on the Start, Stop, or Pause button.

FIGURE 2.14

You can stop and start the
MSSQLServer and
SQLExecutive services
from Windows NT's
Services Control Panel.

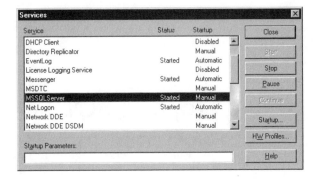

Another feature available from the Services Control Panel is startup options. To add temporary command-line startup options to the MSSQLServer service or SQLExecutive service, click on the Startup button. In the Service dialog box, shown in Figure 2.15, you can select the service account that will be used at startup. This can be useful if you did not create a special account for the SQL Executive to use and you would like to add one now (see Exercise 2.1, earlier in this chapter). After you add a new account through the User Manager for Domains utility, you can go to the Services Control Panel, click on the Startup button, and specify the new account to be used. The options at the top of the Service dialog box let you specify how the service starts up; you can choose whether it is Automatic, Manual, or Disabled.

FIGURE 2.15

Click on the Setup button
in the Services Control
Panel to set startup
options for your services.

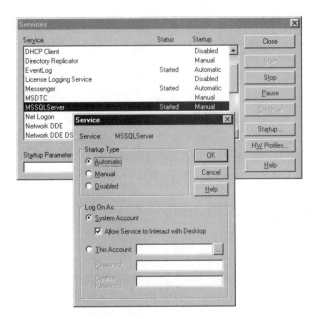

Starting and Stopping SQL Server from Server Manager

You can also use the Server Manager utility to start and stop your SQL Server and SQL Executive services.

To start Server Manager, select Start ≻ Programs ≻ Administrative Tools ≻ Server Manager. Click on the server of your choice, and then choose Computer ≻ Services. This will bring up the Services Control Panel (Figure 2.14), which works as discussed in the previous section.

Starting and Stopping SQL Server from a Command Prompt

From a command prompt, you can use the NET STOP and NET START commands, followed by the name of the appropriate service, MSSQLServer or SQLExecutive, to start and stop these services. For example, to start the SQL Server service from the command line, type the following command:

```
C:\ > NET START MSSQLServer
```

To see which services are currently running, type **NET START** without specifying any parameters.

Starting and Stopping SQL Server with SQL Service Manager

Using SQL Service Manager is probably the most intuitive method you can use to control your SQL Server services. To access SQL Service Manager, select Start ≻ Programs ≻ Microsoft SQL Server 6.5 ≻ SQL Service Manager. This brings up the SQL Service Manager window, as shown in Figure 2.16.

FIGURE 2.16

SQL Service Manager can be used to start, pause, and stop the SQL Server, SQL Executive, and the DTC (Distributed Transaction Coordinator) services.

SQL Service Manager shows the server and service in the top two drop-down list boxes, with a traffic light below to indicate the state of the service. The green light denotes that the service is currently running, the yellow light shows that the service is paused, and the red light indicates that the service is stopped. By double-clicking on the appropriate light, you can start, stop, or pause the selected service.

Starting and Stopping SQL Server from SQL Enterprise Manager

Another way to control the state of services is through SQL Enterprise Manager. However, before you can administer SQL Server using Enterprise Manager, you must first register the server in it. Follow the steps in Exercise 2.2 to register your SQL Server in SQL Enterprise Manager.

To start, pause, or stop a server registered in SQL Enterprise Manager, right-click on the server and then choose the appropriate option from the context menu, as shown in Figure 2.17. You will be able to do this once you have registered your server (Exercise 2.2)

F I G U R E 2.17

You can start and stop the SQL Server services from SQL Enterprise Manager.

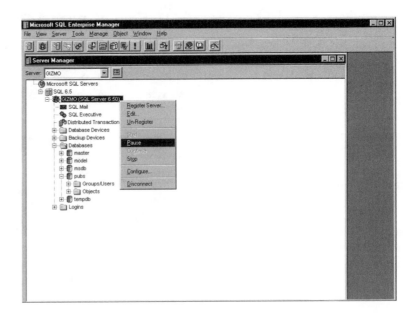

EXERCISE 2.2

Registering SQL Server in SQL Enterprise Manager

1. Make sure that the MSSQLServer service has been started.

2. Start SQL Enterprise Manager by selecting Start ➤ Programs ➤ Microsoft SQL Server 6.5 ➤ SQL Enterprise Manager.

3. The first time you start SQL Enterprise Manager, you will see the Register Server dialog box, as shown below. Enter your computer's name in the Server text box. (If you are not sure what your computer's name is, go to the Networks Control Panel, which will show your computer's name.)

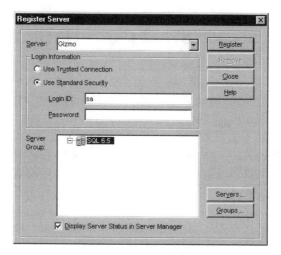

4. In the Login ID text box, type in **sa**, which is the default SQL Administrator ID. SQL Server installs with the default security setting of standard. This account has no restrictions on what it can do in the SQL Server environment.

5. Leave the Password field blank.

6. Click on the Register button. Your server will now show up in SQL Enterprise Manager, under the SQL 6.5 Server group.

Starting SQL Server as an Application

In the event that you are having problems starting SQL Server as a service, it is possible to start SQL Server as an application instead of as a service. To do this, you execute the following command from the command prompt:

SQLSERVER

If you run SQL Server as an application instead of a service, SQL Server will write to the screen all of the error messages that normally are written to the SQL Server error log (as well as writing them to the log). We will cover this in more detail in Chapter 13, which is about troubleshooting problems with SQL Server.

Troubleshooting Your Installation

Troubleshooting your SQL Server setup can be a daunting task at times, but there are some relatively simply steps you might take.

Microsoft ✓ ***Exam*** ***Objective***   **Locate information relevant to diagnosing a problem.**

The following are some techniques that you can use for troubleshooting your SQL Server setup:

- Check the SQL Server error log.

- Check the Windows NT Application log by using the NT Event Viewer.

- Check the output (*.OUT) files in the \MSSQL\Install directory.

- Test the named pipes.

Checking the SQL Server Error Log

If you have completed your installation (or it didn't complete successfully) and you are trying to determine why your SQL Server machine is not working properly, your first stop should be the SQL Server error log. The SQL Server error log writes SQL Server audit and error information to a file called ERRORLOG located in the \MSSQL\Log directory. You can view this error log either through a text file editor (like Notepad) or through SQL Enterprise Manager. A new error log is created each time you stop and restart the MSSQLServer service. Previous logs are archived using a six-log rotation, with the oldest logs being replaced with the next oldest logs.

To view the SQL Server error log from SQL Enterprise Manager, register your server if you have not done so already (Exercise 2.2), and then attach to your server. Expand the server by clicking on the + symbol next to the server name. You should see a red squiggly line next to your server when you are attached to it. From the Server menu, choose Error Log. You should now see a display similar to the one shown in Figure 2.18.

FIGURE 2.18

You can check the SQL error log for SQL Server setup problems.

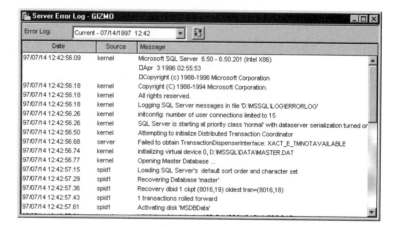

Checking the Windows NT Application Log

You can take a look at the Application log portion of the Windows NT event log by using the NT Event Viewer. The NT Event Viewer lists most of the events that are written to the SQL Server error log, and you may also see events of other applications that post messages to the Windows NT Application log. Each event is labeled with its severity: informational, warning, or error. You can use the time stamp, severity, and source of the error to help determine if the event had an impact on your SQL Server setup. Exercise 2.3 demonstrates the use of the NT Event Viewer.

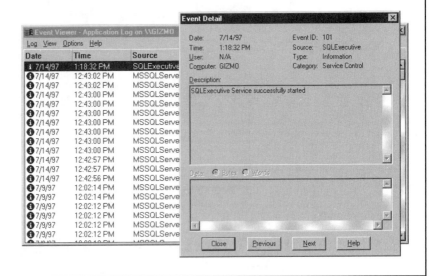

EXERCISE 2.3

Troubleshooting SQL Server with the NT Event Viewer

1. To start the NT Event Viewer, select Start ➢ Programs ➢ Administrative Tools ➢ NT Event Viewer.

2. The default log to be viewed is the System log. To change to the Application log, select Log ➢ Application.

3. If you see any red stop signs with a source of SQLExecutive or MSSQLServer, as shown below, double-click on those items to gather more information.

Checking the Output Files

During the installation of SQL Server, output (*.OUT) files are written into the \MSSQL\Install directory by the installation script files. The output file that is usually of most importance is that of the last script to execute.

When you're looking at your installation output files, it is best to sort them by date and time, either from Explorer or at a command prompt. If you're working from the command prompt, you can display the files sorted by date and time by using the following command in the \MSSQL\Install directory (the /od switch is for order by date):

```
C:\MSSQL\Install> dir *.out /od
```

Testing Named Pipes

SQL Server will always use named pipes for installation purposes. You can make use of the MAKEPIPE and READPIPE utilities to ensure that communication can be established between a client and the server for installation purposes, or just to test the named pipes. Exercise 2.4 demonstrates the use of the MAKEPIPE and READPIPE utilities.

EXERCISE 2.4

Testing the Named Pipes Protocol

1. To test the named pipes protocol, you will need a client and a server. On the server, go to a Command Prompt window by selecting Start ➢ Programs ➢ Command Prompt.

2. At the command prompt, enter **makepipe**.

3. You should now see:

   ```
   Making PIPE:\\.\pipe\abc
   read to write delay <seconds>:0
   Waiting for Client to Connect. . .
   ```

The server is waiting for a client to try to use the named pipe.

4. From a client machine, or from the same server (in a different Command Prompt window), enter the following:

   readpipe /S<*servername*> /D<*string*>

   For example, if your server's name is Gizmo and you want to send the message "testing123" to the named pipe, enter:

   readpipe /Sgizmo /Dtesting123

You should get something like this in response on the client machine:

   ```
   SvrName:\\Gizmo
   PIPE: :\\Gizmo\pipe\abc
   DATA: :Testing123
   Data Sent: 1 Testing123
   Data Read: 1 Testing123
   ```

EXERCISE 2.4 (CONTINUED FROM PREVIOUS PAGE)

On the server machine, you should see something similar to this:

```
Waiting for client to send . . . 1
Data Read:
Testing123
Waiting for client to send . . . 2
Pipe closed
Waiting for Client to Connect. . .
```

5. To close the pipe, close the Command Prompt window.

Summary

SQL Server is a big software package, and we covered a lot of information in this chapter about installing it.

We began with the administrative details that need to be taken care of before you begin the installation process. These include making sure that your system meets the minimum hardware and software requirements for SQL Server. We explained that having enough RAM and hard disk space is essential, and that you should probably install SQL Server on an NTFS partition for the added security. (We will discuss SQL Server memory configuration in detail in Chapter 12.)

We then discussed where to install SQL Server. This included brief descriptions of the three different security modes: integrated, standard, and mixed. We also suggested that you install SQL Server on a server that has access to domain accounts through a trust relationship rather than on a primary or backup domain controller (PDC or BDC).

The final preparation step was setting up a SQL Executive account, which is used by the SQL Executive service.

Then we moved to the actual SQL Server 6.5 installation process. We emphasized the importance of choosing the right character set and sort orders. A mistake choosing either of those two options will force you to rebuild your databases and reload the information. We also mentioned the network libraries (Net-Libraries) available. Remember, if you want to use integrated security, you must have either named pipes or multi-protocol network libraries installed with SQL Server. We finished with a discussion of configuring the SQL Executive to log on as a service. The SQL Executive account allows the SQL Executive to log on to the system and perform administrative functions on the server.

Next, we covered installing the SQL Server 6.5 client software. SQL Server comes with both 16-bit and 32-bit client utilities. We described how to install the utilities on MS-DOS-based operating systems, Windows 3.*x* systems, and Windows 95 and NT systems.

After the installation instructions, we described how to start and stop SQL Server services from the Windows NT Control Panel, Server Manager, the command prompt, SQL Service Manager, and SQL Enterprise Manager.

We then talked about some techniques for troubleshooting SQL Server setup problems, including checking the SQL error log, the Windows NT Application log, and the output (*.OUT files). We finished that section with a short exercise that illustrated using the MAKEPIPE and READPIPE utilities to test named pipes.

Exercise Questions

1. Where should you install SQL Server?

   A. Onto a PDC or BDC—the server will have direct access to domain accounts and will therefore run much more quickly

   B. Onto any machine in the enterprise with access to the domain accounts directly or through a trust relationship (preferably not a PDC or BDC)

   C. Onto any machine in the enterprise that is running TCP/IP, because this is the default protocol for most machines

   D. Onto any machine that is not a member of a domain—because the machine is not involved in any domain-related activities, it will run much more efficiently

2. Which of the following if changed would force you to rebuild your databases and reload all of your data? (Choose all that apply.)

A. The character set

B. The Net-Library

C. The SQL Executive logon account

D. The sort order

3. Which of the following can be used to start and stop SQL Server? (Choose all that apply.)

A. The Services Control Panel

B. The command prompt

C. SQL Service Manager

D. SQL Enterprise Manager

4. When installing the client software, the client's operating system is of no concern and all of the components get loaded onto every client.

A. True

B. False

5. What platforms can SQL Server be installed on? (Choose all that apply.)

A. Intel 486 and later

B. MIPS

C. DEC Alpha

D. PowerPC

6. When installing SQL Server onto an Intel $x86$ machine, which subdirectory is used?

A. \Intel

B. \Macintosh

C. \X86

D. \i386

7. What is the minimum amount of RAM needed to install and run SQL Server?

A. 12MB; 24MB for replication

B. 16MB; 32MB for replication

C. 24MB; 32MB for replication

D. 32MB; 48MB for replication

8. What is the SQL Executive logon account used for?

A. By the MSDTC to distribute transactions for the SQL Executive service

B. By the SQL Executive managers to log on to SQL Server and perform automation tasks, alerts processing, event firing, and replication

C. By the MSSQLServer service to log on to SQL Server and perform automation tasks, alerts processing, event firing, and replication

D. By Windows NT to log on to SQL Server and place all error messages in the NT Event Viewer

9. You have one SQL Server in your enterprise and you are planning on adding two more in the next month. Which licensing option would best suit this environment?

A. Per Server—by using the Per Server licensing option, you can add as many servers as you want in the enterprise and you do not need to purchase any more client licenses

B. Per Seat—by using the Per Seat licensing option, you have a one-time one way upgrade to a Per Server client license

C. Per Seat—by using the Per Seat licensing option, you can add as many servers as you want in the enterprise, and you do not need to purchase any more client licenses

D. Per Server—by using the Per Server licensing option, you have a one-time one way upgrade to a Per Seat client license

10. What is the minimum and default size of the Master database device?

A. 20MB

B. 30MB

C. 25MB

D. 35MB

11. In an MS-DOS environment, you may install only a single network client in the AUTOEXEC.BAT file.

A. True

B. False

12. In a Windows 3.*x* (16-bit) environment, you may install only a single network client. The network client options will be found only in the *.INI files.

A. True

B. False

13. In a Windows 95 or Windows NT environment, you may install multiple network clients. The network client options will be found in the Windows Registry.

A. True

B. False

14. What happens when you pause SQL Server?

A. The entire SQL Server is paused, and everyone who was using SQL Server is disconnected until the SQL Server is started again

B. The entire SQL Server is paused, and everyone who was using SQL Server continues to process normally but new connection requests are denied

C. Only the users currently connected to SQL Server are paused; their work is halted and they are disconnected

D. Only the users currently connected to SQL Server are paused; their work is halted, but they are not disconnected, and once the SQL Server is restarted, they will resume their processing

15. Which of the following will start the SQL Server service from a command prompt?

A. SQLSERVR.EXE

B. MSSQLServer

C. NET START SQLSERVR.EXE

D. NET START MSSQLServer

16. Which of the following will start the SQL Executive service from a command prompt?

A. SQLEXEC.EXE

B. MSSQLExecutive

C. NET START SQLEXEC.EXE

D. NET START SQLExecutive

17. Where could you look for troubleshooting information if your installation did not proceed properly? (Choose all that apply.)

A. SQL Server error log

B. NT application log

C. *.OUT in the \MSSQL\Install directory

D. \MSSQL\SQLInstError directory

18. You wish to install support for the Banyan Vines client on an MS-DOS-based machine. Which of the following will you load in the AUTOEXEC.BAT file?

A. DBMSPIPE.EXE

B. DBMSVINE.EXE

C. DBMSSPX.EXE

D. DBMSTCP.EXE

CHAPTER

3

SQL Server and Windows NT

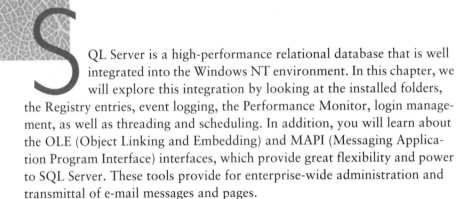

QL Server is a high-performance relational database that is well integrated into the Windows NT environment. In this chapter, we will explore this integration by looking at the installed folders, the Registry entries, event logging, the Performance Monitor, login management, as well as threading and scheduling. In addition, you will learn about the OLE (Object Linking and Embedding) and MAPI (Messaging Application Program Interface) interfaces, which provide great flexibility and power to SQL Server. These tools provide for enterprise-wide administration and transmittal of e-mail messages and pages.

We will also look at what was installed with SQL Server, including the default databases, devices, login IDs, and stored procedures. In the final section of this chapter, you will learn about the various ways that you can get help with SQL Server: through the Help system in SQL Enterprise Manager, the SQL Books Online feature, and the help available with stored procedures.

SQL Server Integration with Windows NT

SQL Server is tightly integrated with the Window NT environment. In the following sections, we will look at the various ways that this integration is implemented.he first step in installing SQL Server is to make sure that you have the appropriate hardware and software installed. SQL Server can be installed on any platform that Windows NT runs on (DEC Alpha-AXP, Intel x86, MIPS, and Power PC). SQL Server 6.5 requires Windows NT 3.51 or later, running on a 486 or better CPU.

Microsoft
✓ *Exam*
Objective

Identify how SQL Server is integrated with Windows NT.

Exam objectives are subject to change at any time without prior notice and at Microsoft's sole discretion. Please visit Microsoft's Training & Certification Web site (www.microsoft.com/Train_Cert) for the most current exam objectives listing.

Here are the points of Windows NT/SQL Server integration:

- SQL Server folders are installed under Windows NT.

- SQL Server adds entries to the Windows NT Registry.

- SQL Server uses the Windows NT event log for SQL Server event logging.

- With SQL Server installed, you can use the Performance Monitor to watch vital SQL Server statistics.

- With integrated security, you can map a Windows NT login ID into SQL Server.

SQL Server Folders Added under Windows NT

SQL Server installs its files into the default directory \MSSQL on the drive that you specified during your installation process. Table 3.1 lists the folders that are created and what they contain.

T A B L E 3.I SQL Server Folders	**Folder**	**Contents**
	\MSSQL\Backup	Default folder to store backup devices for both databases and transaction logs
	\MSSQL\BIN	16-bit utilities and DLLs
	\MSSQL\BINN	32-bit utilities and DLLs
	\MSSQL\CharSets	All character sets and their associated sort orders
	\MSSQL\Data	Default folder to store database devices, as well as the Master device (MASTER.DAT)
	\MSSQL\Install	Installation scripts, files needed by the Setup program, and any installation output files (useful for troubleshooting an installation—search for *.OUT files)

TABLE 3.1 (cont.) SQL Server Folders	Folder	Contents
	\MSSQL\Log	Default folder to store SQL Server error logs (up to six error logs may be present, in an FIFO rotation)
	\MSSQL\ReplData	Working folder for the SQL Server replication process
	\MSSQL\SNMP	Working folder for SNMP (Simple Network Management Protocol) files
	\MSSQL\SQLOLE\Samples	Sample OLE interfaces into SQL Server
	\MSSQL\Symbols	DLLs used for generating stack dumps and traces

Windows NT Registry Entries for SQL Server

SQL Server will add entries in two different places in your Windows NT Registry. Since you are installing Microsoft software, most of the default startup options will be added to this Registry key:

\HKEY_LOCAL_MACHINE\SOFTWARE\Microsoft\MSSQLServer

Because SQL Server and the SQL Executive run as services, they will also have entries under the Services section of your registry. You can check on those entries in these keys:

\HKEY_LOCAL_MACHINE\SYSTEM\CurrentControlSet\ Services\MSSQLServer

\HKEY_LOCAL_MACHINE\SYSTEM\CurrentControlSet\ Services\SQLExecutive

Microsoft ✓ *Exam Objective*

Locate where Windows NT Registry entries for SQL Server are stored.

To view Registry entries, you can use the REGEDT32 (Registry Editor) utility that ships with Windows NT. Exercise 3.1 guides you through the process of starting and viewing the SQL Server entries in the Registry.

EXERCISE 3.1

Viewing SQL Server Registry Entries

1. To start REGEDT32, select Start ➤ Run to display the Run dialog box.

2. In the Open field, type **REGEDT32**, as shown below, to open the Registry Editor.

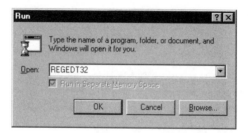

3. Locate the HKEY_LOCAL_MACHINE key. Then drill down through the SOFTWARE key (expand the key by double-clicking on the **+** symbol), then through the Microsoft key, and finally to the MSSQLServer key. You should see something similar to the listing shown below.

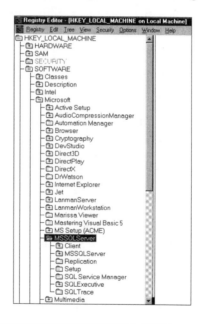

Tampering with the Registry is a potentially dangerous activity and could result in a nonfunctioning NT Server if you make improper changes. You should use the utilities in the Control Panel (or other utilities that modify the Registry, such as SQL Enterprise Manager) to make adjustments to your Registry whenever possible.

SQL Server Event Logging in the Windows NT Event Log

Windows NT adds records to the Windows NT event log rather than showing user error messages on the screen. You can see the entries in the NT event log by using the NT Event Viewer utility. The Event Viewer tracks three types of information in three different logs:

System log   Lists errors and events originating in the Windows NT kernel and drivers

Security log   Lists security breaches and audit information (such as successful logins)

Application log   Lists applications running on Windows NT that write messages to the NT event log

The NT event log in which SQL Server events are recorded is the Application log. The event log can track successful starts and stops of the SQL Server and SQL Executive services. It will also track errors that occur within SQL Server.

The Application log has three different priority levels, which you can see in the Event Viewer window shown in Figure 3.1:

- Informational messages are denoted with a blue icon with the letter *i* in it.

- Warnings are denoted by a yellow icon with the exclamation symbol (!) in it.

- Critical error messages are denoted by a red stop sign.

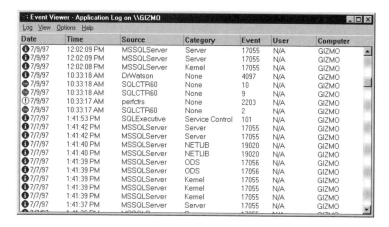

Follow the steps in Exercise 3.2 to use the NT Event Viewer to look at SQL Server information.

EXERCISE 3.2

Using the NT Event Viewer

1. To start the NT Event Viewer, select Start ➤ Programs ➤ Administrative Tools ➤ NT Event Viewer.

2. The first time that you run the NT Event Viewer, it will be displaying the System log. To view the Application log (where SQL Server events are stored), select Log ➤ Application.

3. To gather more information about a particular event, double-click on the event to display the Event Detail dialog box. The example below shows a SQL Server event with the Event ID 17055. The Description box indicates that SQL Server message 18109 occurred and that a database with an ID of 5 was successfully checkpointed and recovered.

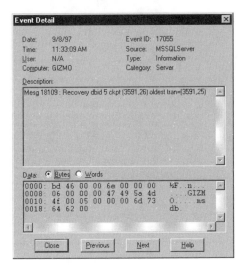

4. After you have reviewed the details, click on Close in the Event Detail dialog box.

5. Close the NT Event Viewer.

NT Scheduling, Threading, and Performance Services for SQL Server

SQL Server is integrated into Windows NT's scheduling and threading services. SQL Server is a multithreaded application. Each thread is scheduled based on its priority level and is then given CPU cycles. Because SQL Server is loaded as a service, its base priority (its lowest thread priority level) is automatically higher than most other applications, thus allowing it more frequent access to the CPU.

Installing SQL Server 6.5 also modifies how Windows NT handles performance for all applications on that particular Windows NT Server machine. SQL Server adjusts the Server Optimization property up one level, from the Maximize Throughput for File Sharing setting to the Maximize Throughput for Network Applications setting (SQL Server is considered a network application).

You can view the Server Optimization properties on the Services tab of the Windows NT Network Control Panel (select Start ➢ Settings ➢ Control Panel and double-click on the Network icon), as shown in Figure 3.2.

F I G U R E   3.2

The Services tab of the
Windows NT Network
Control Panel

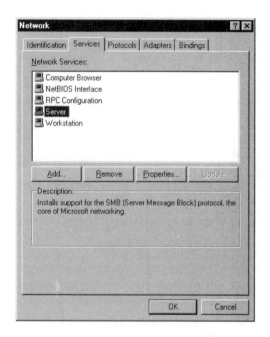

In the Services tab, select Server in the Network Services list, and then click on the Properties button. You will now see the Server Optimization properties, as shown in Figure 3.3.

F I G U R E   3.3

The Server Optimization
dialog box

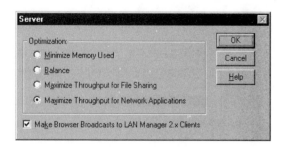

The options in this dialog box work as follows:

- The Minimize Memory Used option is used to allocate memory when you have ten or fewer network connections.

- The Balance option is used to support up to 64 network connections and is the default setting used for the NetBEUI software.

- The Maximize Throughput for File Sharing option gives as much memory as possible to the server to optimize file-sharing operations. This is useful for large networks where the primary purpose of your server is to centrally manage information.

- The Maximize Throughput for Network Applications option optimizes memory for distributed applications that do their own memory caching (like SQL Server). This is also useful for large networks.

Refer to your Windows NT Resource Kit for more information about the Network Control Panel.

The SQL Performance Monitor within the NT Performance Monitor

You can get up-to-the-second information about the performance of SQL Server through the SQL Performance Monitor. The SQL Performance Monitor provides settings for the Windows NT Performance Monitor. This tool can show you statistics on individual data items. These individual data items are called *performance counters*. Performance counters are grouped together into *performance objects*.

When you install SQL Server, the system automatically configures from six to eight performance objects related to SQL Server. These are listed in Table 3.2.

	Performance Object	Information Tracked
T A B L E 3.2 SQL Server Performance Objects	SQLServer	General information about the performance of the server
	SQLServer–Replication-Published DB	Replication transaction information

	Performance Object	Information Tracked
T A B L E 3.2 (cont.) SQL Server Performance Objects	SQLServer–User Defined Counters	User-defined counters, attached to the currently empty stored procedures sp_user_counter1 through sp_user_counter10
	SQLServer–Licensing	Licensing information
	SQLServer–Locks	Information about all locks currently in place
	SQLServer–Log	Transaction log information for all open databases
	SQLServer–Procedure Cache	Information about the procedure cache
	SQLServer–Users	Information about users

When you start the SQL Performance monitor (by selecting Start ➤ Programs ➤ Microsoft SQL Server 6.5 ➤ SQL Performance Monitor) while SQL Server (the MSSQLServer service) is running, you will see the default performance counters, as shown in Figure 3.4.

F I G U R E 3.4

The SQL Performance Monitor can be used to track statistical information about SQL Server.

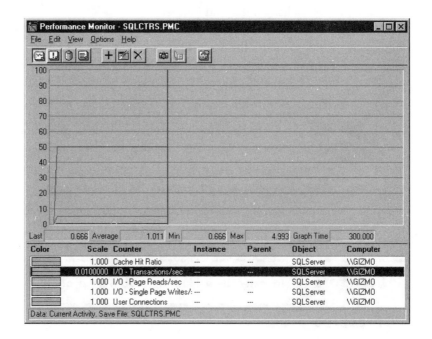

These default performance counters work as follows:

- The Cache Hit Ratio counter shows the percentage of time that a request was found in the data cache instead of being read from hard disk. This number should be as close to 100% as you can get it.

- The I/O Transactions/sec counter shows the number of Transact-SQL commands executed per second.

- The I/O Page Reads/sec counter shows the number of physical pages that are read per second. This number should be low for an optimized system.

- The I/O Single Page Writes/sec counter is the number of single page writes performed per second by SQL Server. This number should be low for an optimized system.

- The User Connections counter shows the number of configured user connections.

You can add more performance counters by clicking on the large plus symbol (+) on the toolbar or by selecting Edit ➢ Add to Chart. This brings up the Add to Chart dialog box. To add a counter, choose SQLServer in the Object drop-down list box, select a counter from the Counter list box, and click on the Add button.

If you want more information about a particular counter, select it in the Counter list box and click on the Explain button. You will see information in the Counter Definition box at the bottom of the Add to Chart dialog box, as shown in Figure 3.5.

The SQL Performance Monitor is discussed in greater detail in Chapter 12, which is about SQL Server performance and tuning.

Integrated Logon to NT and SQL Server

As we mentioned in Chapter 2, you can set up your system to use a single Windows NT user account to log in to both Windows NT and SQL Server.

Microsoft ✓ *Exam* *Objective* | **Identify the impact on SQL Server of integrated security.**

FIGURE 3.5

The Add to Chart dialog
box in the SQL
Performance Monitor

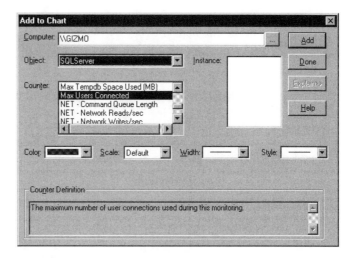

This type of logon has the following requirements:

- You must change your SQL Server security mode from its default value of standard security to integrated security.

- To use integrated security, you must have either named pipes and/or multi-protocol installed on the SQL Server as your network libraries.

Named pipes is the default protocol and is used to install SQL Server.

- You need to create your Windows NT user accounts and then use SQL Security Manager to "map" those IDs into SQL Server.

In Chapter 6, you will learn how to implement integrated security in order to have a single logon account for Windows NT and SQL Server.

What Was Installed?

If you open SQL Enterprise Manager (by selecting Start ➤ Programs ➤ Microsoft SQL Server 6.5 ➤ SQL Enterprise Manager) and expand SQL Server (by clicking on the + symbol next to your server), you will notice that there were a lot of items added during installation. Figure 3.6 shows the

Server Manager listing within SQL Enterprise Manager. Let's take a look at the components of your SQL Server installation, and also clarify SQL Server's integration with OLE (Object Linking and Embedding) technology.

FIGURE 3.6

The SQL Enterprise Manager with a single server expanded

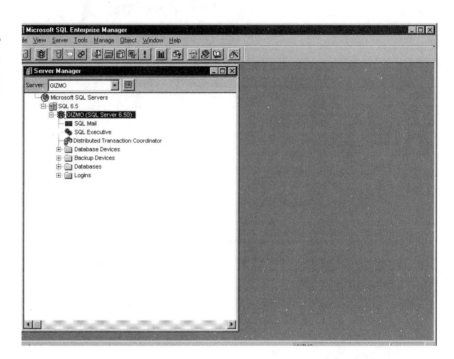

FIGURE 3.6

The SQL Enterprise Manager with a single server expanded

SQL Server and OLE

SQL Server has two main components: the database engine, which is named MSSQLServer, and the SQL Executive utilities, named SQLExecutive. These two components can be manipulated through an OLE interface called the SQL-DMO (Database Management Objects). All of these pieces collectively are called the SQL-DMF, or SQL Distributed Management Framework.

The SQL-DMF is made up of the following components:

SQL Enterprise Manager: A GUI (graphical user interface) tool used to centrally manager multiple SQL Server machines, regardless of their physical locations. SQL Enterprise Manager uses the SQL-DMO interface to interact with the core components of SQL Server (SQL Executive and the SQL Server Engine).

SQL-DMO (SQL Server Distributed Management Objects):   This interface exposes OLE automation objects that other programs can take advantage of to manipulate both the SQL Server Engine and the SQL Executive utilities.

SQL Executive: A service (SQLExecutive) that is made up of four utilities. These utilities bypass the OLE interface and work directly with the SQL Server Engine. There are managers for replication, tasking, event processing, and alert handling.

SQL Server Engine: The engine is also a service (MSSQLServer) and is the core of SQL Server. The engine handles all of the data processing.

These DMF components are illustrated in Figure 3.7.

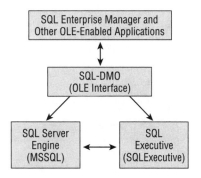

Default Components

The default components can be broken down into several logical categories: devices and databases, login IDs, stored procedures, and DBCC commands. Let's explore what makes up each of these components.

Devices

Devices are files on your hard disk that store your databases, transaction logs, and backups of your databases and transaction logs. They are simply disk space that is assigned to SQL Server. Devices normally reside in the \MSSQL\Data folder as <*filename*>.DAT. For example, the Master database device is called MASTER.DAT.

An individual device can store one or more databases and one or more transaction logs. When you installed SQL Server, you were asked for the location of the Master device. The Master device has a default size of 25MB. The Master device stores the Master, Model, Tempdb, and Pubs database, as illustrated in Figure 3.8.

FIGURE 3.8

The Master device stores the Master, Model, Tempdb, and Pubs databases.

The default devices are named Master, Msdbdata, Msdblog, and Diskdump. To view your default devices, follow the steps outlined in Exercise 3.3.

EXERCISE 3.3

Viewing the Default Devices

1. Start SQL Enterprise Manager by selecting Start ➢ Programs ➢ Microsoft SQL Server 6.5 ➢ SQL Enterprise Manager.

2. Expand your server by clicking on the **+** symbol.

3. Expand your Database Devices folder and your Backup Devices folders, as shown below.

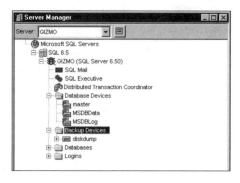

4. Note that your devices are listed as master, MSDBData, MSDBLog, and diskdump. Double-click on the master database device to see the Edit Database Device dialog box. Here you can see the databases on the Master device and a graph of their space usage. Move the mouse pointer over each of the databases, and you will see the size of the database at the bottom of the dialog box.

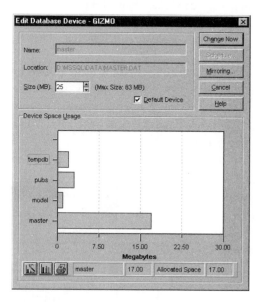

In the dialog box above, you can see that the Master database is 17MB. When you check the sizes of the other databases, you will see that Tempdb is 2MB, Pubs is 3MB, and Model is 1MB.

5. Click on Cancel to close the Edit Database Device dialog box.

6. To see what databases are located on the other devices listed in the Server Manager window, double-click on each device, view the Edit Database Device dialog box information, and click on Cancel when you're finished.

Databases

Now let's explore the default databases that were installed. Remember that an individual database can reside on a single device, or it can span multiple devices. A transaction log can be stored on the same device as your database or on multiple other devices.

A transaction log keeps track of every change that you make to a particular database. Think of the transaction log as check register. Every time you write a check, you place an entry in your check register. You will learn more about the structure of SQL Server databases and transaction logs in Chapter 5.

Every database in your system has its own components. These include groups/users and objects (tables, views, triggers, and so on).

When you expand your Databases folder in the Server Manager window of SQL Enterprise Manager, you will see a list of your databases, as shown in Figure 3.9.

FIGURE 3.9

You can manage your databases with the SQL Enterprise Manager.

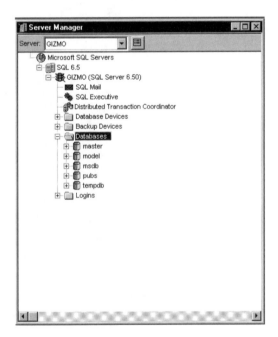

Let's look at the functions of the five default databases: Master, Model, Msdb, Pubs, and Tempdb.

The Master Database The Master database controls server-wide aspects of SQL Server. It tracks information about other databases and devices in your server. It also tracks user accounts, configuration information, system error messages, and system stored procedures. The Master database is sometimes called the *data dictionary*.

Table 3.3 lists some of the more important tables in the Master database that you, as a SQL Server administrator, should know about.

T A B L E 3.3

Some System Tables in the Master Database

Table	Contents
sysdatabases	Each database that has been created in SQL Server
sysdevices	Each device (database or backup) that has been created in SQL Server
syslogins	SQL Server login IDs
sysusages	Each portion of a device that has been allocated to a specific database or transaction log

For a complete listing of the Master database tables and their contents, see the "System Tables" section in SQL Server Books Online.

The Model Database The Model database is used as a template for all user-created databases. It contains the system tables required in each database. Each time you create a new database, the Model database's contents are copied into it.

You can add new tables and information to the Model database. When you create a new database after you've modified the Model database, the new database will reflect those changes. For example, if you add the guest user ID to the Model database, then all new databases that you create will automatically have a guest user account in them. Table 3.4 lists some of the more important system tables in the Model database.

	Table	Contents
TABLE 3.4 Some System Tables in the Model Database	sysalternates	User IDs that have been aliased to other database user IDs
	syscomments	Each default, rule, stored procedure, trigger, and view that has a Transact-SQL definition
	sysindexes	Each index, both clustered and nonclustered, that has been created on tables in this database
	syslogs	The transaction log for this database
	sysprotects	User permissions that have been granted or revoked
	sysusers	Each user and group that has been created in this database

Since all new databases are created from the Model database, what is the minimum size of a new database? If you guessed 1MB, you are correct. If you followed the steps in Exercise 3.3, you will have seen that the default Model database size is listed as 1.00MB.

The Msdb Database   The SQL Executive (SQLExecutive) service is a suite of utilities that works with the SQL Server Engine (MSSQLServer). These utilities include a task manager, an event manager, an alert manager, and a replication manager, which need to store information about the alerts, tasks, events, and replication tasks that they need to perform or have performed. This information is stored in the Msdb database. The Msdb database also includes information about system operators, including the e-mail addresses and/or pager numbers of the administrative personnel in charge of running this SQL Server machine.

The Msdb database spans two separate database devices. The database portion of the Msdb database resides on the Msdbdata device and is 6MB in size by default. Its transaction log resides on the Msdblog device and is 2MB in size by default. Table 3.5 lists some of the system tables located in the Msdb database.

TABLE 3.5	Table	Contents
Some System Tables in the Msdb Database	sysoperators	Administrative personnel information, including e-mail addresses and pager numbers
	sysalerts	User-defined alerts; SQL Server checks this table to determine whether or not to fire an alert
	systasks	User-defined tasks; SQL Server checks this table to determine when to run a scheduled task
	syshistory	Tracks whether or not a task was executed, including successes and failures and dates and times
	sysnotifications	All currently active alerts and their notification operator information (e-mail/pager)

Microsoft ✓ Exam Objective

Identify the capabilities of SQL Server when used with MAPI.

You may have noticed from looking at Table 3.5 that when a task or alert is fired, an operator can be notified. You can integrate SQL Server with any MAPI-compliant back-end service provider or post office. This includes Microsoft Exchange, MSMail, CC:Mail, Profs, and many others. Many mail packages allow an e-mail message to be generated and automatically sent to a pager. These pager addresses are also supported in SQL Server.

You will learn how to configure SQL Server to use the Microsoft Exchange Server and Windows Messaging profiles in Chapter 9.

The Pubs Database The Pubs database resides on the Master device. It is a sample database that Microsoft has provided to you as a learning tool. The Pubs database is a complete database that simulates the day-to-day activities of a book publisher. It is also the basis for many examples in the SQL Server manuals, SQL Server Books Online, and this book.

If you accidentally destroy your Pubs database, you can rebuild it by running the Instpubs.sql script, which is stored in the \MSSQL\Install folder. To run this script, open it inside the ISQL/W utility.

The ISQL/W utility allows you to run Transact-SQL queries. See Chapter 4 for details about using the ISQL/W utility.

The Tempdb Database   The Tempdb database resides on the Master device and is 2MB in size by default. It is used as a temporary storage location for variables and temporary tables, and as a general working storage location. For example, suppose that you have a large ad-hoc query, "Give me a listing of every widget between 2 inches and 5 inches that we sold in Los Angeles between 2:00 PM and 4:00 PM on the second Monday of every month for the last ten years, and put that information in descending order by year and then by widget size." To respond to this query, SQL Server needs to sift through much of your historical data to get the precise information and then to sort that information as requested in the ad-hoc query. The Tempdb database is the space that the system uses for this type of work.

The Tempdb is shared by all databases on SQL Server. Every time you stop and restart SQL Server, this database is destroyed and re-created. Since the Tempdb database is so volatile, and it may be used extensively, you could enhance SQL Server's performance by allocating more memory to the Tempdb database or by placing it in RAM.

Placing the Tempdb database in RAM is addressed in Chapter 12, which covers SQL Server performance and tuning.

Login IDs

To gain access to SQL Server, you must have a valid login ID. This ID is stored in the Master database, in the syslogins table. You can see the default login IDs that are assigned to SQL Server when it is first installed by expanding the Logins folder in the Server Manager window of SQL Enterprise Manager, as shown in Figure 3.10.

The probe Login ID   The probe ID may be used by the SQL Server Performance Monitor to gather relevant information. This is the case when you are using standard security. For integrated and mixed security, the SQL Server Performance Monitor will use the sa ID to probe for information about the performance of your server.

FIGURE 3.10

The default SQL Server login IDs are stored in the Logins folder.

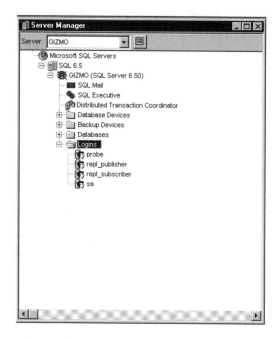

The repl_publisher and repl_subscriber Login IDs   These two IDs are used by the replication managers in SQL Executive to gather and publish or subscribe to replication articles and publications. (See Chapter 11 for information about replication.)

The sa Login ID   The sa (or SA, for SQL Server Administrator) ID is the default login ID for SQL Server. This ID has no restrictions on what it can do within the SQL Server environment. By default, anyone who has logged in to SQL Server will be able to use the SA account unless you make some modifications first. If you are using standard security, you should specify a password for the SA ID. With integrated security, anyone who is a member of the Windows NT Administrators group will be logged in as SA automatically. (See Chapter 6 for more information about setting up SA and other login accounts, as well as the various security modes.)

Since we are using standard security right now, let's assign a password to the SA account. Follow the steps in Exercise 3.4 to give SA a password.

EXERCISE 3.4

Assigning a Password to the SA Account

1. Start SQL Enterprise Manager by selecting Start ➤ Programs ➤ Microsoft SQL Server 6.5 ➤ SQL Enterprise Manager.

2. Expand your server by clicking on the **+** symbol, and then expand your Logins folder.

3. Double-click on the sa ID. This opens the Manage Logins dialog box, as shown below.

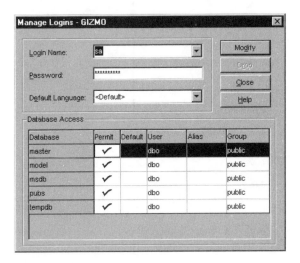

4. Select the Password text box and delete the current password. Type in your new password.

5. Click on the Modify button. You will be asked to confirm your new password, as shown below. Type in the same password again and click on OK. You will be given a confirmation dialog box that the password was successfully changed.

EXERCISE 3.4 (CONTINUED FROM PREVIOUS PAGE)

6. Click on OK to return to the Manage Logins dialog box.

7. Click on the Close button to close this dialog box and return to SQL Enterprise Manager.

You can use the system stored procedure sp_password to change a password. See Chapter 6 for details about using Transact-SQL statements to manage login and user accounts.

System Stored Procedures and DBCC Commands

Stored procedures and DBCC (Database Consistency Checker) commands are also installed with SQL Server.

Stored procedures are a Transact-SQL–based method of implementing many of the changes that you would like to make in SQL Server. For example, there are stored procedures to add login IDs, change passwords, add users to a database, add new groups to a database, and so on. The system stored procedures have a prefix of sp_ followed by the rest of the statement. System stored procedures are stored in the Master database. For example, the following is the stored procedure to get information about a database:

sp_helpdb <databasename>

DBCC commands are used to check the consistency and integrity of your database. These commands generally are used to gather information about the status of your database rather than to make changes to your database. For example, to report the percentage of available device space used by your transaction log, issue the following command:

DBCC SQLPerf(Logspace)

If you allocated 2MB on a device for your transaction log, and the transaction log is currently using 1.5MB, the DBCC command would report that 75% of your log space is currently used.

You can run stored procedures and DBCC commands from the ISQL or ISQL/W utility. (See Chapter 4 for more information about using these utilities to enter and execute stored procedures and DBCC commands.)

Getting Help in SQL Server

SQL Server has a very robust Help system. You can get help from several different sources:

- The Help menu in SQL Enterprise Manager

- SQL Server Books Online

- Individual stored procedures

SQL Enterprise Manager's Help Menu

Click on the Help menu in SQL Enterprise Manager to see the following choices:

Contents   An overview type of help on SQL Enterprise Manager's contents (see Figure 3.11)

Getting Started   A brief description of SQL Enterprise Manager

Transact SQL Help   A Transact-SQL reference library

Using Help   Help on how to use Help

Tip of the Day   A SQL Server tip of the day window

Search for Help On   The typical Windows-type Help system

SQL Server Books Online

The SQL Server Books Online feature is an electronic version of the manuals that come with your SQL Server package, and it will be an invaluable resource to you as a SQL Server system administrator. Figure 3.12 shows the opening

FIGURE 3.11

Microsoft SQL Enterprise
Manager Help Contents

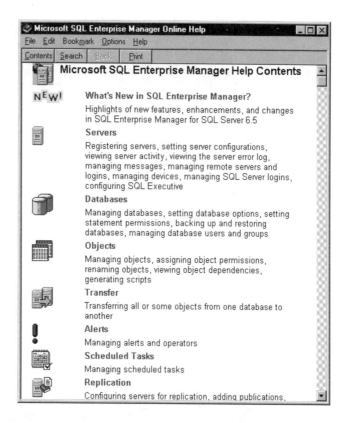

screen of SQL Server Books Online. In the left panel is a list of books. In the right panel is a particular piece of information that has been "explored" to. You can expand the different books, just as you can expand folders in SQL Enterprise Manager.

The big advantage of Books Online is the fully cross-referenced search engine, which is incredibly flexible and robust. You can even search for keywords throughout all of the books, or just a subset of books. Follow the steps outlined in Exercise 3.5 to learn about using SQL Server Books Online and its search engine.

FIGURE 3.12

The opening screen of
SQL Server Books Online

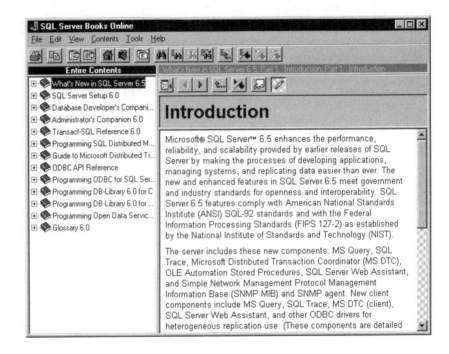

FIGURE 3.12

The opening screen of
SQL Server Books Online

EXERCISE 3.5

Using SQL Server Books Online

1. To start SQL Server Books Online, select Start ➤ Programs ➤ Microsoft SQL Server 6.5 ➤ SQL Server Books Online.

2. To find out about the Administrators Companion book, drill down through the Administrators Companion 6.0 book and the Before You Begin book, and then double-click on About the Administrators Companion page. You should see something similar to the window shown below.

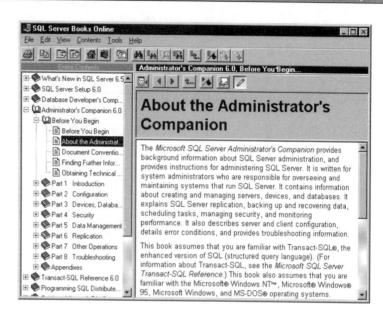

3. Let's perform a simple query. To make sure that we all get the same information, let's start at the top. To return to the contents list (Figure 3.12), click on the icon of the house or select Contents ≻ Home Screen.

4. Click on the icon of the large pair of binoculars or select Tools ≻ Query to display the Query dialog box, shown below.

EXERCISE 3.5 (CONTINUED FROM PREVIOUS PAGE)

5. In the Query box, type **Setup**, and then click on the Run Query button. The Query Results dialog box appears, as shown below. You can see that 272 topics were found.

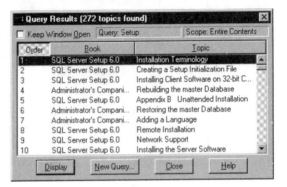

6. Select the first topic, which should be Installation Terminology, and then click on the Display button. Books Online displays the Installation Terminology page in the right panel. Notice that the left panel does not reflect any changes in location.

7. To see where this page fits within all of those books on the left, click on Sync Contents button (located in the upper-left corner of the right panel) or select Contents ➢ Sync Contents. You should now see a window similar to the one shown below.

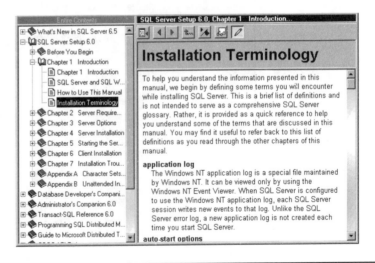

This Installation Terminology page is located in the SQL Server Setup 6.0 book, Chapter 1, last page.

8. To create a bookmark so that you can quickly return to the Installation Terminology page, click on the flag button located near the middle of the toolbar in the right panel or select Edit ➤ Bookmarks. Click on the Add button to create the bookmark, as shown below. Then click on Close to close the Bookmarks dialog box.

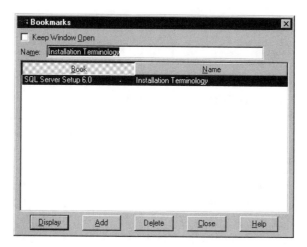

9. You can continue to experiment with finding information in Books Online. When you are finished, close Books Online.

For more information about how to use the SQL Books Online search engine, see Help in SQL Books Online.

Stored Procedure Help

You can get help on individual stored procedures in the ISQL utilities by running the following query:

```
EXEC sp_help <stored_procedure>
```

You can also get context-sensitive help on a stored procedure from within the ISQL/W utility. Simply highlight the stored procedure that you are interested in and press Shift+F1.

Summary

In this chapter, we discussed how SQL Server is integrated into the Windows NT environment. We first looked at the SQL Server folders added under Windows NT. We then examined the Windows NT Registry keys where SQL Server configuration information is stored. Remember that the MSSQLServer is located in \HKEY_LOCAL_MACHINE\Software\Microsoft\MSSQLServer.

Next, we saw how the Windows NT event log can log events and error messages from SQL Server. Remember that the NT Event Viewer breaks the log into three separate pieces, and that SQL Server information is recorded in the Application log.

You also learned that SQL Server is also integrated with Windows NT through its programming as a multithreaded application that receives CPU cycles through NT's threading and scheduling services. SQL Server also modifies the Server Performance property in Windows NT, upgrading if from a file server type system to a network application server.

Another way of integrating SQL Server and Windows NT is by mapping an NT Login ID into SQL Server. If you are using integrated security and have the network libraries of named pipes and/or multi-protocol installed, you can take advantage of mapping Windows NT user accounts into SQL Server. This allows your users to have a single Windows NT login account that will automatically log them in to SQL Server.

The next topic we covered was SQL Server and OLE. The two main components of SQL Server, MSSQLServer (the database engine) and SQLExecutive (the SQL Executive utilities) can be manipulated through an OLE interface called the SQL-DMO (Database Management Objects). In fact, SQL Enterprise Manager uses the SQL-DMO to communicate with the SQL Server and the SQL Executive services. Collectively, all of these components are referred to as the SQL-DMF (SQL Distributed Management Framework).

We then examined the default components that are installed with SQL Server. These include the default database devices of Master, Msdbdata, Msdblog, and Diskdump. The default databases that were installed include the Master, Model, Msdb, Tempdb, and Pubs databases. We also took a look at the default SQL login IDs and assigned a password to the SA account.

We finished up with a look at the help available for SQL Server, including the Help system in SQL Enterprise Manager, SQL Books Online, and stored procedure help.

Exercise Questions

1. What is the default folder for a SQL Server installation?

A. \MSSQLServer

B. \SQL65

C. \MSSQL

D. \SQLServer

2. In which folder are database devices saved by default?

A. \MSSQLServer\Data

B. \MSSQL\Data

C. \MSSQLServer\Devices

D. \SQLServer\Devices

3. A device can store what type of information? (Choose all that apply.)

A. Transaction logs

B. Databases

C. Database dumps (backups)

D. Transaction log dumps (backups)

4. The Master database device has which of the following databases on it? (Choose all that apply.)

   A. Master

   B. Model

   C. Msdb

   D. Tempdb

5. The SQL Executive utilities use which database?

   A. Master

   B. Model

   C. Msdb

   D. Pubs

6. The task manager, alerts manager, events manager, and replication manager make up which component of SQL Server?

   A. The MSSQLServer service

   B. The SQLExecutive service

   C. The server engine

   D. The MSSQL utilities

7. In which Registry key(s) will you find configuration information for SQL Server? (Choose all that apply.)

   A. \HKEY_LOCAL_MACHINE\Software\Microsoft\MSSQLServer

   B. \HKEY_LOCAL_MACHINE\Software\Microsoft\SQLExecutive

   C. \HKEY_LOCAL_MACHINE\SYSTEM\CurrentControlSet\Services\ MSSQLServer

   D. \HKEY_LOCAL_MACHINE\SYSTEM\CurrentControlSet\Services\ SQLExecutive

8. SQL Server error messages can be viewed in the SQL Server error log and which Windows NT application?

A. Windows NT Performance Monitor

B. Windows NT Network Control Panel

C. Windows NT Network Monitor

D. Windows NT Event Viewer

9. SQL Server is a multithreaded application. Which Windows NT kernel process gives the SQL threads CPU time?

A. Windows NT Threader

B. Windows NT Scheduler

C. Windows NT Network Service

D. Windows NT Local Application Service

10. SQL Server can be integrated with Windows NT logon security. What needs to be in place before this can happen? (Choose all that apply)

A. SQL Server must be running in integrated security mode, and the Windows NT user accounts must be mapped into SQL Server

B. SQL Server must be running in integrated security mode and the SQL Server login IDs must be mapped out to the Windows NT SAM database

C. You must be running any protocol other than named pipes because named pipes is used for SQL installation only

D. You must be running named pipes or multi-protocol

11. SQL Enterprise Manager uses which component of the SQL Distributed Management Framework (DMF) to communicate with SQL Server?

A. The SQL-DMO (Database Management Objects) or its OLE interface

B. It doesn't need any components; it works directly with the database engine and the SQL Executive utilities

C. The SQL Executive

D. SQL Enterprise Manager doesn't communicate with SQL Server at all

12. What is the default login ID to SQL Server?

A. Guest

B. SA

C. Probe

D. Administrator

13. You should be careful when you create passwords for your user IDs because they may be case-sensitive.

A. True

B. False

14. SQL Server Books Online is a fairly useless feature and just an excuse for Microsoft to quit printing books.

A. True

B. False

15. SQL Server can send e-mail messages to which of the following mail servers?

A. MS Exchange

B. CC:Mail

C. Profs

D. All the above and any MAPI-compliant mail provider

16. There are no restrictions on the SA account in SQL Server.

A. True

B. False

CHAPTER

4

Administering SQL Server 6.5

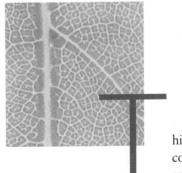

his chapter provides an overview of some of the utilities that come packaged with SQL Server. You have already worked with some of these utilities in previous chapters. For example, you've learned how to use SQL Enterprise Manager to start and stop SQL Server, and to view the default devices and databases that were installed with SQL Server. The SQL Enterprise Manager utility is so large and flexible that you will be presented with different aspects of its management capabilities in each chapter.

In this chapter, we will focus on creating and managing multiple servers and server groups with SQL Enterprise Manager. You will also learn how to modify the server options on any of the SQL Server machines that have been registered in SQL Enterprise Manager.

Configuring SQL Server clients is also an important task for database administrators. Making sure that your SQL Server clients are using the right network libraries and database libraries is crucial in troubleshooting client-related problems. You can do this through the SQL Client Configuration utility.

You will also learn about the ISQL and ISQL/W utilities, which are used to execute Transact-SQL statements. We will provide an overview of Transact-SQL, SELECT statements, stored procedures, and DBCC commands.

The last section of this chapter covers the SQL Trace utility, which allows you, as an administrator, to track connections and disconnections from SQL Server.

Creating Server Groups

Server groups are used to provide logical groupings for administrative purposes. You can set up server groups through SQL Enterprise Manager. You should create your server groups first, and then register your servers and place them in the newly created groups.

As explained in Chapter 2, before you can work with servers using SQL Enterprise Manager, you must first register each server in that utility (see Exercise 2.2).

Manage servers in the enterprise.

Exam objectives are subject to change at any time without prior notice and at Microsoft's sole discretion. Please visit Microsoft's Training & Certification Web site (www.microsoft.com/Train_Cert) for the most current exam objectives listing.

There are some rules that apply to creating server groups and registering your servers:

- Server groups can be created at the local server only. If you want the SQL Enterprise Manager utility running on other machines to have the same logical groups, you must go to each of those machines and repeat the same steps that you did with the first server.

- Group names must be unique at each server.

- You must also register the server at each server that is running SQL Enterprise Manager. You cannot do this remotely.

- SQL Server computer names can consist of only letters, numbers, and these characters: _ (underscore), # (pound sign), $ (dollar sign). You should avoid using the punctuation symbols because they have special meanings in the SQL Server environment.

- If you are not using integrated or mixed security, you must provide a valid ID and password for each server registered. You should use the SA account, because it gives you the most rights.

In Exercise 4.1, we will create server groups and subgroups. The two main groups will be for the Accounting department and the Sales department. The Sales department has two distinct pieces: inside sales and outside sales, so we will create subgroups for them. We will then register several SQL Server machines to fill in these groups. Finally, we will simulate a reorganization of the company and combine all of the Sales department servers under a single grouping.

In this exercise, you will be registering servers in your enterprise. If you have the servers available, go ahead and register them using their computer names. If you do not, you can still do this exercise, filling in the names of servers that do not really exist. Although you won't be able to connect to them or manage them, you can register them anyway. This way, you will learn the procedure for creating and managing server groups, which you can apply to any new servers you add to your enterprise.

EXERCISE 4.1

Creating and Managing SQL Server Groups and Servers

1. Start SQL Enterprise Manager by selecting Start ➢ Programs ➢ Microsoft SQL Server 6.5 ➢ SQL Enterprise Manager.

2. Select Server ➢ Server Groups, or right-click on the SQL 6.5 server group and choose New Server Group from the context menu, to display the Manage Server Groups dialog box.

3. To add the Accounting server group, in the Name box, enter **Accounting**. Make sure that the Top Level Group option button is selected, as shown below, and then click on the Add button.

4. To add the Sales server group, enter **Sales** in the Name box, make sure that the Top Level Group option button is selected, and click on Add.

EXERCISE 4.1 (CONTINUED FROM PREVIOUS PAGE)

5. To add the Inside subgroup, enter **Inside** in the Name box, click on the Sub-Group of option button, and select Sales in the lower box, as shown below. Then click on the Add button.

6. To add the Outside subgroup, enter **Outside** in the Name box, click on the Sub-Group Of option button, select Sales, and click on the Add button.

7. Click on the Close button to close the Manage Server Groups dialog box. Your Server Manager window should look similar to the one shown below.

8. To register the server in the Accounting group, select Server ➤ Register Server, or right-click on the Accounting group and choose Register Server from the context menu. This brings up the Register Server dialog box. Notice that your server groups are listed in the lower box.

EXERCISE 4.1 (CONTINUED FROM PREVIOUS PAGE)

9. In the Server box, type **AcctSvr** (the computer name of the Accounting server, which resides somewhere in the enterprise). Leave the Use Standard Security option button selected, and enter the Login ID as **SA**, as shown below. You also need to specify the password for the SA account that is on the AcctSvr. (In our example, this field is left blank.) Make sure that the Accounting group is selected in the Server Group list, and click on the Register button.

Since the AccSvr server used in this example doesn't really exist, the error message shown below appears. You can get this error message for several reasons. If you've entered the name of an existing computer, the most probable reason for this message is that there is a connectivity issue. Make sure that the SA account exists on the computer you named, that you have typed the correct password, and that the computer name is correct. (See Chapter 13 for more information about troubleshooting networking problems.)

10. Click on the Yes button to register anyway.

11. In the Register Server dialog box, repeat the procedure to register a server named **InSales,** placing it in the Inside subgroup of the Sales group. Then register two more servers, named **SalesA** and **SalesB,** placing each of them in the Outside subgroup.

12. Click on the Close button in the Register Server dialog box. Your Server Manager window should now look something like the one shown below.

A handy technique that you can use in SQL Enterprise Manager is drag-and-drop. You can easily move servers to different server groups by simply dragging them with your mouse and dropping them into their new place. For our example, let's say that the Sales staff has been reorganized from Inside Sales and Outside Sales groups into a single Sales group. Now we need to rearrange our server groups to match this reorganization.

13. In the Server Manager window, click on the INSALES server and drag-and-drop it onto the Sales group icon. This moves the INSALES computer out of the InSales group to the Sales group.

14. Drag-and drop the SALESA and SALESB servers onto the Sales group icon. When you are finished, your Server Manager window should look something like the one shown below.

15. To remove the empty Inside server group, right-click on it, choose Remove from the context menu, and then verify the deletion. Remove the Outside group in the same way.

Configuring SQL Server

After you've registered a server in SQL Enterprise Manager, you can configure it using that utility.

Configure servers in the enterprise.

To access the configuration settings in SQL Enterprise Manager, right-click on a server that is running SQL Server and choose Configure from the context menu, or choose Server ➤ SQL Server ➤ Configure. You'll see the Server Configuration/Options dialog box, as shown in Figure 4.1.

FIGURE 4.1

The Server Options tab of the Server Configuration/Options dialog box

This dialog box has four tabs: Server Options, Security Options, Configuration, and Attributes. The following sections describe the settings available on each of these tabs.

Setting Server Options

The settings on the Server Options tab allow you to specify general server options. The three text boxes at the top of the dialog box allow you to specify paths, as follows:

Root Directory   Specifies the path for the root folder containing the SQL Server files.

Master Database Path   Specifies the path and filename for the Master database device.

Error Log Path   Specifies the path and filename used for the SQL Server error log. SQL Server will keep a history of error logs up to six levels deep. If you do not want to have any SQL Server error logs, delete this entry (of course, deleting the error logs is not recommended).

The checkboxes control Auto Start options, Windows NT event logging, the Performance Monitor mode used for SQL Server, and the security mode of users when they run commands from the command prompt. These checkboxes work as follows:

Auto Start Server at Boot Time   Automatically starts the MSSQLServer service whenever Windows NT is booted.

Auto Start Executive at Boot Time   Automatically starts the SQLExecutive service whenever Windows NT is booted.

Auto Start Mail Client   Automatically starts the mail client when SQL Server is started.

Windows NT Event Logging   Logs SQL Server and SQL Executive events to the NT Application log. If you are going to be using alerts, you must select this option. Alerts fire only when an event is recorded in the NT Application log. (See Chapter 9 for more information about alerts.)

Performance Monitor Integration   Makes SQL Performance Monitor statistics available to Window NT's Performance Monitor utility. With the Direct Response Mode option selected, SQL Server performance statistics are gathered in a batch and then displayed. This mode provides better performance overall for SQL Server, but incurs a slight lag for information passed to the Performance Monitor. With the On Demand Mode option selected, SQL Server performance statistics are shown as they happen. You get real-time information about SQL Server, but you lose some performance overall due to the overhead.

xp_cmdshell–Use SQLExecutiveCmdExec Account for Non SA's Forces the user to run in the security mode of the client when the xp_cmdshell extended stored procedure is used. If it is not selected, the user will run in the context of the account running the MSSQLServer service, which can be very dangerous.

The xp_cmdshell extended stored procedure is used to run Windows NT Shell commands from within SQL Server batches. If the xp_cmdshell... option is not selected, your server's security is at risk. For example, while working in the security context of the account running the MSSQLServer service (when the xp_cmdshell... option is not selected), a user could run the SQL batch command xp_cmdshell 'DELTREE c:*.* /y' successfully. When the xp_cmdshell...option is selected, Windows NT's security prevents users from actually deleting anything that they did not have permissions on. This is not the least of the things users can do. With knowledge of the NET USER statements, users could add a new user ID and give that ID administrative privileges.

The Server Options tab also has three command buttons that lead to additional options:

Parameters Allows you to set SQL Server startup options.

Tape Support Allows you to specify how long SQL Server will wait before trying to read a tape drive. This gives you enough time to load a tape into a tape drive before SQL Server tries to read it.

Mail Login Allows you to specify parameters needed for starting the mail client. (See Chapter 9 for more information about setting up e-mail support.)

Setting Security Options

The settings on the Security Options tab of the Server Configuration/Options dialog box, shown in Figure 4.2, are grouped in three areas: Login Security Mode, Audit Level, and Mappings.

Here, you can specify the security mode you wish to use, a default login ID, and a default domain. (See Chapter 6 for more information about security modes and login IDs.) You can also specify the audit levels. These settings allow you to track both successful logins and login failures.

F I G U R E   4.2

The Security Options
tab of the Server
Configuration/Options
dialog box

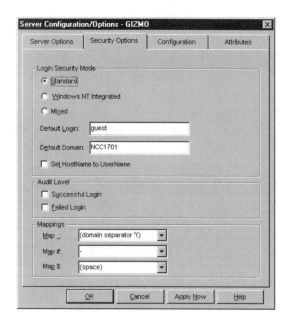

Windows NT supports IDs that use characters that are not recognized in
SQL Server. Those unrecognized characters can be mapped to characters that
are recognized by SQL Server. This is the purpose of the Mappings section of
the Security Options tab.

Setting Configuration Options

The Configuration tab of the Server Configuration/Options dialog box,
shown in Figure 4.3, allows you to make many configuration changes to SQL
Server. If you select a setting from the Current field, the Description box at the
bottom of the dialog box will tell you what the option does. For example, in
Figure 4.3, the Current field for the Allow Updates option is selected, and the
Description box says:

```
Specifies whether or not direct updates are allowed against
system tables. Users with appropriate permissions can update
system tables directly if this value is set to 1. Takes effect
immediately.
```

FIGURE 4.3

The Configuration tab of
the Server Configuration/
Options dialog box

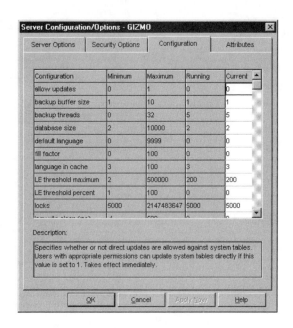

FIGURE 4.3

The Configuration tab of
the Server Configuration/
Options dialog box

There are options to change the fill factor, memory, locking, and many
other settings. There are even advanced options, which are listed in their own
dialog box. To view the advanced options, scroll down to the Show Advanced
Options field, change the value to 1, and click on OK (which will close the
dialog box). Then return to the Configuration tab of the Server Configuration/
Options dialog box to see the advanced options. The first item in the list is no
longer the Allow Updates option; it is now the Affinity Mask option. (See
Chapter 12 for more information about setting the options on the Configuration tab to tune SQL Server.)

Viewing Attributes

The Attributes tab of the Server Configuration/Options dialog box is shown in
Figure 4.4. This tab lists the values of attributes for this running instance of
SQL Server. It is for informational purposes only; you cannot make any
changes here.

FIGURE 4.4

The Attributes tab of the
Server Configuration/
Options dialog box

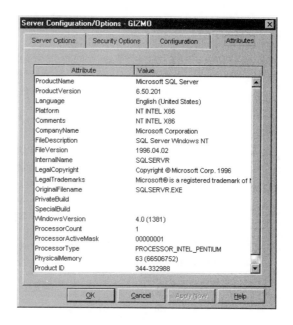

FIGURE 4.4

The Attributes tab of the
Server Configuration/
Options dialog box

Using SQL Server Utilities

Squad SQL Server comes with quite a few utilities, some of which we have already discussed in this book. Table 4.1 summarizes the utilities and their functions.

Administer servers in the enterprise.

TABLE 4.1

The SQL Server Utilities

Utility	Usage
BCP (Bulk Copy Program)	A command-line utility used for transferring information into and out of SQL Server.
CHKUPG65	A command-line utility used to check the compatibility between a current version of SQL Server and older user-defined databases that are being upgraded.

TABLE 4.1 (cont.) The SQL Server Utilities	**Utility**	**Usage**
	ISQL	A command-line utility that provides a query interface to SQL Server. You can run Transact-SQL statements, as well as stored procedures and DBCC commands. This utility is primarily used by administrators.
	ISQL_w	A utility that allows you to run all of the same commands that the ISQL command-line utility does. It has the advantage of having a Windows graphical user interface. This allows you to run multiple queries and view the results of multiple queries in their own separate windows.
	MAKEPIPE and READPIPE	Command-line utilities that can be used to verify that the named pipes protocol is working properly.
	Microsoft ODBC SQL Server Driver	A SQL Server ODBC (Open Database Connectivity) driver help file.
	Microsoft Query	A utility used to graphically create SQL statements for any ODBC-compliant data source.
	SQL Client Configuration	A utility used to configure SQL Server client network libraries. It also reports on the DB Library version that is in use for a particular client.
	SQL Distributed Management Objects	A help file that displays the SQL-DMO (Database Management Objects) framework, which is particularly useful to SQL Server application developers.
	SQL Enterprise Manager	A utility used to graphically manage nearly every aspect of one or more servers in your enterprise.
	SQL Performance Monitor	A utility used to capture statistical information about the performance of SQL Server.
	SQL Security Manager	A utility used to "map" Windows NT user accounts to SQL Server when SQL Server has been configured to run in integrated or mixed security mode.
	SQL Server Books Online	An electronic version of the SQL Server manuals, which contains a fully cross-referenced search engine.
	SQL Server Web Assistant	A utility used to create static Web pages of SQL Server data.

	Utility	Usage
TABLE 4.1 (cont.) The SQL Server Utilities	SQL Service Manager	A utility used to start, stop, and pause the SQL Server, SQL Executive, and Distributed Transaction Coordinator services.
	SQL Setup	A program used to upgrade SQL Server or to make other modifications to the system.
	SQL Trace	A utility used to monitor who is running what on SQL Server.
	SQLMaint	A utility used to create tasks that will take care of day-to-day administration of SQL Server. This includes automating backups, updating statistics, and rebuilding indexes. Information generated here can be sent out in a report locally, to a UNC path, or to an e-mail operator.
	SQLSERVR	An executable file used to start SQL Server from the command line. It has special options to start your server in a troubleshooting mode.

Using the SQL Setup Utility

You can use the SQL Setup utility to upgrade your version of SQL Server, change network support, add languages, rebuild the Master database, set server options, set security options, and remove SQL Server.

To run SQL Setup, select Start ➤ Programs ➤ Microsoft SQL Server 6.5 ➤ SQL Setup. You will be presented with a Welcome screen. Click on Continue to move to the next screen, which notifies you that SQL Server is already installed. Once again, click on Continue to move on. SQL Setup now displays the Microsoft SQL Server 6.5–Options dialog box, as shown in Figure 4.5.

FIGURE 4.5

The SQL Setup utility's Options dialog box

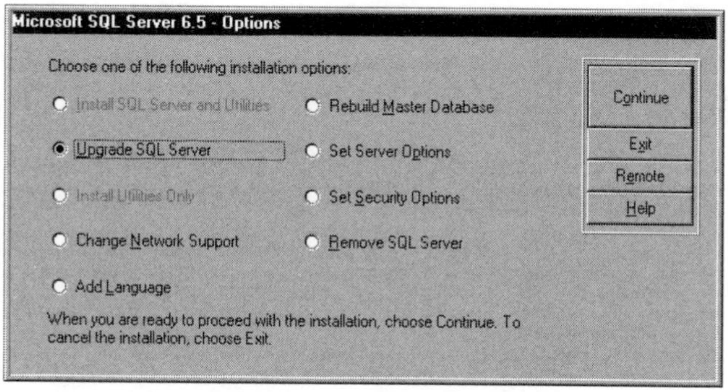

These options work as follows:

Upgrade Allows you to upgrade from a previous version of SQL Server.

Change Network Support Allows you to modify the current network clients.

Add Language Allows you to add a new language to SQL Server. You must have the SA password to do this.

Rebuild Master Database Re-creates the Master database.

You should not need to use this Rebuild Master Database option if you have created backups of your Master database. However, there are some instances where a disaster could force you to re-create the Master database using this option. If you re-create the Master database, you will need to recover all of your user-defined databases. See Chapter 8 for details on backing up and restoring databases.

Set Server Options Allows you to set server options (as you can from the Server Option tab of SQL Enterprise Manager's Server Configuration/Options dialog box—see "Setting Server Options").

Set Security Options Allows you to set the security used by SQL Server (as you can from the Security Option tab of SQL Enterprise Manager's Server Configuration/Options dialog box—see "Setting Security Options").

Remove SQL Server Removes SQL Server from your Windows NT server. It will also remove most of the Registry entries associated with SQL Server.

Choose an option and click on Continue. When you're finished, click on the Exit button. You will see another dialog box asking you whether or not you wish to exit to Windows NT. Click on the Exit to Windows NT button.

Using the SQL Client Configuration Utility

You can use the SQL Client Configuration utility to configure client network libraries and to report on which version of the DB Library the client is using. To run this utility, select Start ➤ Programs ➤ Microsoft SQL Server 6.5 ➤ SQL Client Configuration Utility. Its window has three tabs: DBLibrary, Net Library, and Advanced. The options on each of these tabs are discussed in the following sections.

DB Library Options

The DBLibrary tab, shown in Figure 4.6, offers only two DB Library configuration options:

Automatic ANSI to OEM   Automatically converts ANSI characters to OEM characters. Most clients will use the ANSI character set, but some may use their own OEM character sets.

Use International Settings   Allows your client to take advantage of international settings. This includes support for the money datatype and date/time datatypes.

The Version Statistics section reports the DB Library version, DB DLL version, location, date, and size.

F I G U R E   4.6

The DBLibrary tab in the SQL Server Client Configuration Utility window

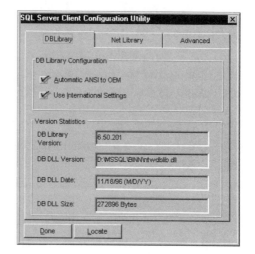

Net Library Options

The Net Library tab, shown in Figure 4.7, displays the current default network library configuration. In Figure 4.7, you can see that Named Pipes is listed as the Default Network. The network libraries on both the client and server must match for the client and server to communicate. The Version Statistics section reports the Net Library version, location, date, and size.

FIGURE 4.7

The Net Library tab in the SQL Server Client Configuration Utility window

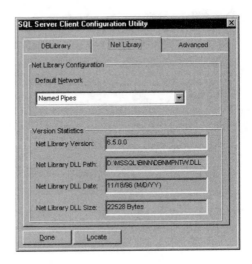

Advanced Options

In the Advanced tab, you can add new libraries to your client's configuration. This allows you to set up support for various network protocols for your network clients.

Microsoft ✓ *Exam Objective*	**Set up support for network clients by using various network protocols.**

To make modifications to your client configuration, you need to add information into the Client Configuration section. You can specify a server and the DLL you wish to load. In the example shown in Figure 4.8, the computer name is Gizmo, the DLL name is Named Pipes, and the Connection String field is left blank. If you need remote connections, you can enter a login string with your user ID and password in this field.

If you do not know where the DLL that you want to use is stored, click on the Locate button. This brings up the Locate Libraries dialog box, which lists where your network and database libraries are located on that machine, as shown in Figure 4.9.

When you are finished filling in the information, click on the Add/Modify button. Your new library will now be listed in the Current Entries field, as shown in Figure 4.10. When you are finished, click on Done to exit the utility.

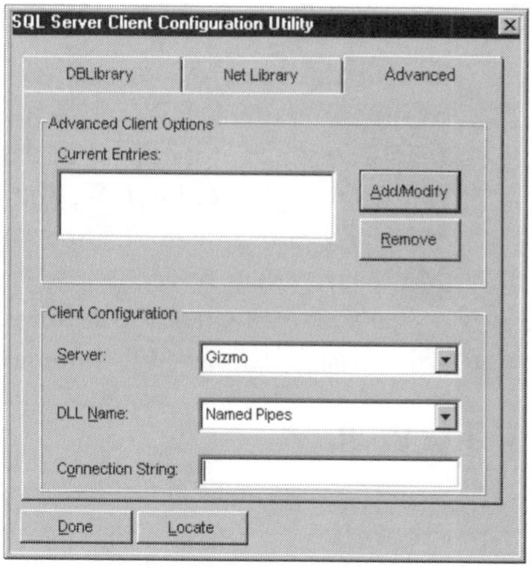

FIGURE 4.8

Adding client
configuration information
to the Advanced tab in the
SQL Server Client
Configuration Utility
window

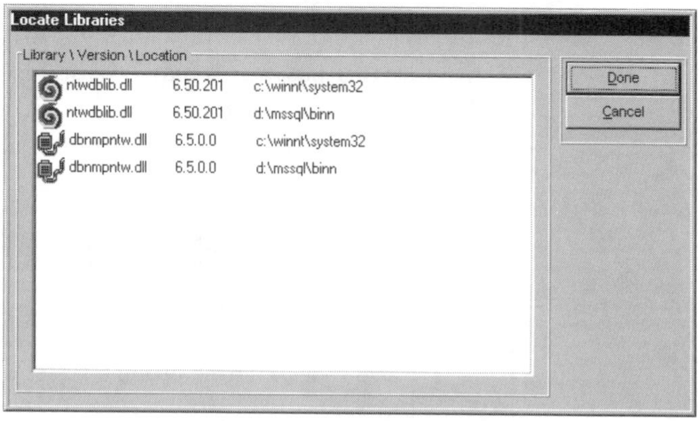

FIGURE 4.9

The Locate Libraries
dialog box

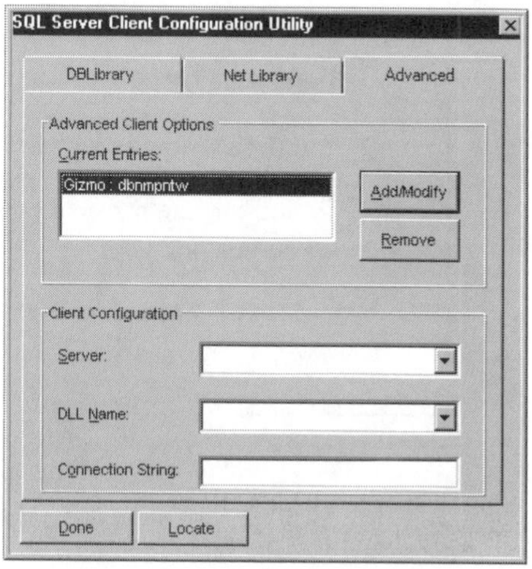

FIGURE 4.10

Adding the Named Pipes
library to a client

Using Transact-SQL and the ISQL Utilities

As explained in previous chapters, SQL Server uses the Transact-SQL version of the SQL language. You can run queries using Transact-SQL to manipulate the information stored in your databases. These queries can be created and run from the ISQL, ISQL/W, and MSQuery (Microsoft Query) utilities, and from program code in third-party programs like Microsoft Access or Microsoft Visual Basic.

Let's take a look at the utilities that come with SQL Server, and then review some basic Transact-SQL statements.

Using ISQL

You can run the ISQL utility from the command prompt. The command syntax is:

```
isql /U<user_id> /P<password> /S<servername>
```

If you do not supply a server name, you will be logged in to the local server. Remember that passwords may be case-sensitive.

To run a query, type it in, adding the word GO on a line by itself.

For a quick overview of the ISQL utility, follow the steps outlined in Exercise 4.2.

EXERCISE 4.2

Running the ISQL Utility

1. To go to a command prompt, select Start ➤ Programs ➤ Command Prompt.

2. From the command prompt, you must log in to SQL Server. Type the following command:

   ```
   isql /Usa /P
   ```

3. You should now see a command prompt that looks like this: 1>.

4. To find out the name of your SQL Server machine, enter the following commands:

   ```
   SELECT @@servername
   GO
   ```

5. You should see the results, which will look similar to:

```
--------------------
Gizmo
(1 row(s) affected)
```

6. Type in the following statements:

USE pubs

GO

SELECT * FROM authors

GO

You will quickly notice one of the major limitations of using the ISQL utility. Although you retrieved all of the information from the Authors table in the Pubs database, it scrolled past the top of your screen and word-wrapped in such a way that it is difficult to read. For this reason, you will find the ISQL/W utility much easier to work with.

7. To exit the ISQL utility and return to a command prompt, type the following:

```
Exit
```

8. To exit the command prompt, type the same command:

```
Exit
```

Using the ISQL/W Utility

You can run all of the same queries in ISQL/W as you can in the ISQL utility. The ISQL/W utility has the advantage of being an MDI (multiple document interface). This allows you to run multiple queries in separate windows, and then view the results in a separate window as well, so you can see the entire result set. In the Results window, you can scroll through the results and use cut, copy, and paste features. Another feature of the ISQL/W utility is its ability to retrieve and store SQL scripts.

There are two ways to start the ISQL/W utility:

- To start it as a stand-alone utility, select Start ➢ Programs ➢ Microsoft SQL Server 6.5 ➢ ISQL_w. When you use this method, you will need to log in by filling out the fields in the Connect Server dialog box, as shown in Figure 4.11.

FIGURE 4.11

You must log in to the
server to use ISQL/W as a
stand-alone utility.

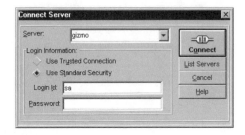

- To enter through SQL Enterprise Manager, select Tools ➤ SQL Query
  Tool or click on the SQL Query Tool icon (the one that looks like two
  mini-spreadsheets, one overlapping the other) on the toolbar. You will
  not need to log in again when you start ISQL/W from SQL Enterprise
  Manager.

Figure 4.12 shows the Query tab of the ISQL/W window. We've added
labels to identify the parts of the window. Its two other tabs are Results and
Statistics I/O.

FIGURE 4.12

The Query tab of the
ISQL/W window

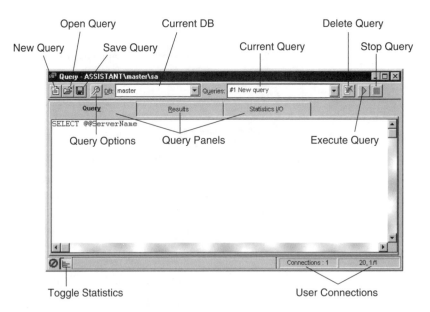

You can type your Transact-SQL statements directly into the Query tab. In Figure 4.12, you see the SELECT @@servername query that we ran from the command-line ISQL utility.

The buttons on the toolbar work as follows:

- The New Query button allows you to create a new query. It will increment the query count by one in the Current Query list box. It will also clear the window so that you start with a clean slate.

- The Open Query button allows you to browse for SQL scripts that you have saved. These SQL scripts are generally stored as ASCII text files with a .SQL extension. There are many prebuilt .SQL scripts that are used by the SQL Server installation process. These are stored in the \MSSQL\Install folder.

- The Save Query button allows you to save the current query as a .SQL ASCII text file.

- The Query Options button allows you to modify the query options (see SQL Server Books Online for information about the query options).

- The Delete Query button allows you to delete a query from the Current Query list box.

- The Execute Query button executes the query in the Current Query box.

- The Stop Query button lets you stop the processing of the current query.

Follow the steps in Exercise 4.3 to get an idea of how to use the ISQL/W utility.

EXERCISE 4.3

Using the ISQL/W Utility

1. Start ISQL/W by selecting Start ➤ Programs ➤ Microsoft SQL Server 6.5 ➤ ISQL_W (and log in), or from SQL Enterprise Manager, select Tools ➤ SQL Query Tool.

2. In the Query tab, enter the following:

    SELECT @@servername

3. Click on the Execute Query button (with the icon of a green arrow) or press Ctrl+E to execute the query. You should see the results in the Results tab, as shown below.

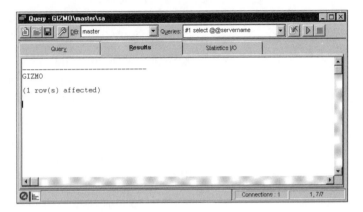

4. Click on the New Query button (on the far right of the toolbar). Notice that the Current Query list box shows that you are now working on Query #2.

5. Enter and execute the following query:

   SELECT @@version

The Results tab should show your current version. You may also notice that the Connections indicator on the status bar shows 2 connections.

6. Click on the Open Query button (the second one from the right on the toolbar) and browse to the \MSSQL\Install folder. From there, select the InstPubs.SQL script. This is a fairly extensive SQL script, which is used to create or re-create your Pubs database.

7. Before you run this script, make sure that you will be able to see some statistics as they are generated. Check that the Statistics icon on the left side of the status bar shows that toggle is on.

8. Execute the query. This query can take half minute to several minutes to run, depending on your system. If you look in the Current Query list box, the world icon will be spinning while the query is running. (You could stop the processing of this query by clicking on the Stop Query button, on the far right side of the toolbar.)

9. When the query has finished executing, click on the Statistics tab. You will see statistics that were generated during the running of this query, which should look similar to the window shown below.

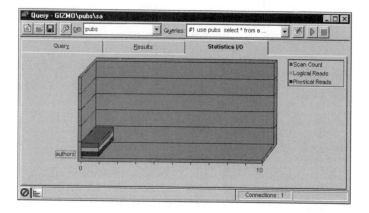

10. From the Current Query list box, select the first query you executed, and click on the Query tab. You will see your original query. You can look at the saved result set by clicking on the Results tab, or you can re-execute the query and view the new results (which in this case will be the same server name as before).

So far, we have been working with the Master database. In the next steps, we will use two different ways of switching to another database and running a query.

11. Click on the New Query button to start a new query. In the Query window, type the following:

```
USE pubs
SELECT * FROM authors
```

---

12. Execute this query. You will notice that the current database has been switched to Pubs. The result set should look similar to the window shown below.

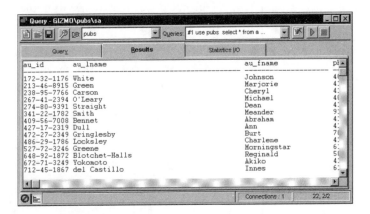

13. Click on the New Query button, and in the Current Database list box, select the Pubs database.

14. Enter and execute the following query:

    SELECT * FROM authors

You should see the same result set as you did in step 12.

15. Close the ISQL/W utility window or the Query Tool window in SQL Enterprise Manager.

Using Simple **SELECT** Statements

Now that you know how to use the ISQL utilities, let's take a look at the SELECT statement.

Although you will not see questions that are specific to SELECT statements on the MCSE exam, being able to read simple SELECT statements and understand what they do will be beneficial not only when you're taking the exam, but also in your work as a SQL Server system administrator.

The SELECT statement can be used to retrieve specific rows and columns of information from one or more tables in one or more databases. There are three basic components to every SELECT statement: SELECT, FROM, and WHERE. (Although the ISQL/W utility is not case-sensitive when you are using Transact-SQL statements, we will show the Transact-SQL keywords in upper-case for clarity.)

The syntax for a simple SELECT statement is:

```
SELECT <column_list>

FROM <table(s)>

WHERE <search_criteria>
```

One of the simplest SELECT statements is to select all columns from a single table. You use the * operator to do this, as in this example:

```
SELECT *

FROM authors
```

These statements select all columns and all rows from the Authors table, which would look something like this (the table has been edited to condense it):

au_id	au_lname	au_fname	phone	...
172-32-1176	White	Johnson	408 496-7223	
213-46-8915	Green	Marjorie	415 986-7020	
238-95-7766	Carson	Cheryl	415 548-7723	
267-41-2394	O'Leary	Michael	408 286-2428	
274-80-9391	Straight	Dean	415 834-2919	
341-22-1782	Smith	Meander	913 843-0462	
409-56-7008	Bennet	Abraham	415 658-9932	
427-17-2319	Dull	Ann	415 836-7128	
472-27-2349	Gringlesby	Burt	707 938-6445	
486-29-1786	Locksley	Charlene	415 585-4620	
527-72-3246	Greene	Morningstar	615 297-2723	
648-92-1872	Blotchet-Halls	Reginald	503 745-6402	

```
672-71-3249   Yokomoto      Akiko       415 935-4228

712-45-1867   del Castillo  Innes       615 996-8275

722-51-5454   DeFrance      Michel      219 547-9982

724-08-9931   Stringer      Dirk        415 843-2991

724-80-9391   MacFeather    Stearns     415 354-7128

756-30-7391   Karsen        Livia       415 534-9219

807-91-6654   Panteley      Sylvia      301 946-8853

846-92-7186   Hunter        Sheryl      415 836-7128

893-72-1158   McBadden      Heather     707 448-4982

899-46-2035   Ringer        Anne        801 826-0752

998-72-3567   Ringer        Albert      801 826-0752


(23 row(s) affected)
```

Specifying Columns   You can specify individual columns in the *column-list* parameter. This is sometimes called *vertical partitioning,* because you are selecting only certain columns. For example, if you wanted to get only the last name and first name of each author, you could run this query:

```
SELECT au_lname, au_fname

FROM authors
```

The result set would look like this:

```
au_lname                    au_fname
----------------            ---------------
White                       Johnson
Green                       Marjorie
Carson                      Cheryl
O'Leary                     Michael
........                     ........
Panteley                    Sylvia
Hunter                      Sheryl
McBadden                    Heather
Ringer                      Anne
Ringer                      Albert


(23 row(s) affected)
```

Specifying Rows   The WHERE clause is used to discriminate between rows of information. This is also known as *horizontal partitioning,* because you are selecting only certain rows of information. For example, if you wanted to get information on all authors that have a last name that begins with the letter *M,* you could run this query:

```
SELECT *

FROM authors

WHERE au_lname LIKE 'M%'
```

And the result set would look like this:

```
au_id          au_lname           au_fname          phone          ...
-----------    ----------------   ----------------  ------------
724-80-9391    MacFeather         Stearns           415 354-7128
893-72-1158    McBadden           Heather           707 448-4982

(2 row(s) affected)
```

Joining Information   For more complex queries, you can join information from two or more tables and then extract the results. For example, to find out which authors publish which titles, you would need to join the Authors table, Titleauthor table, and the Titles table, and then display results based on matching title IDs in the Authors and Titles table in a join table called Titleauthor. This query would look like this:

```
SELECT authors.au_lname, authors.au_fname, titles.title

FROM authors, titleauthor, titles

WHERE titleauthor.au_id = authors.au_id

AND titles.title_id = titleauthor.title_id
```

Your results would look like this:

```
au_lname       au_fname       title
-----------    ------------   -------------------------------------
Green          Marjorie       The Busy Executive's Database Guide
Bennet         Abraham        The Busy Executive's Database Guide
O'Leary        Michael        Cooking with Computers: Surreptitious
                              Balance Sheets
```

```
MacFeather      Stearns        Cooking with Computers: Surreptitious
                               Balance Sheets
Green           Marjorie       You Can Combat Computer Stress!
Straight        Dean           Straight Talk About Computers
del Castillo    Innes          Silicon Valley Gastronomic Treats
DeFrance        Michel         The Gourmet Microwave
Ringer          Anne           The Gourmet Microwave
........         .........     ...........
O'Leary         Michael        Sushi, Anyone?
Gringlesby      Burt           Sushi, Anyone?
Yokomoto        Akiko          Sushi, Anyone?

(25 row(s) affected)
```

Ordering Results   You can also order your result sets in either ascending (the default) or descending order. For example, if you wanted to list some author information in descending order by last name, you could run this query:

```
SELECT au_fname, au_lname

FROM authors

ORDER BY au_lname DESC
```

Your results would look like this:

```
au_fname                au_lname
-------------------     -------------------------------------
Akiko                   Yokomoto
Johnson                 White
Dirk                    Stringer
Dean                    Straight
........                ........
Cheryl                  Carson
Reginald                Blotchet-Halls
Abraham                 Bennet

(23 row(s) affected)
```

Using the MSQuery Tool

You can also create queries using the MSQuery tool. One of the nice features of the MSQuery tool is that you can visually create your queries and then cut and paste the Transact-SQL statements into your programs or into ISQL/W. You simply add the tables you wish to work with, and then drag-and-drop the fields that you want to include.

Follow the steps in Exercise 4.4 to get an overview of how the MSQuery tool works.

EXERCISE 4.4

Using the MSQuery Tool

1. Start the MSQuery tool by selecting Start ➢ Programs ➢ Microsoft SQL Server 6.5 ➢ MSQuery.

2. Select File ➢ New Query to display the Select Data Source dialog box.

3. Select LocalServer by clicking on the drop-down list, and add **-sa** to your login ID, as shown below

4. Click on the Use button. You will see the SQL Server Login dialog box.

5. Enter your password and click on OK to continue. You will now see the Add Tables dialog box, as shown below.

6. Use the Database drop-down list box at the bottom of the dialog box to switch from Master to Pubs. You will now see the tables in the Pubs database in the Table list box.

7. Select the Authors table and click on the Add button.

8. Select the Titleauthor table and click on Add. Then select the Titles table and click on Add.

9. Click on the Close button to close the Add Tables dialog box. You should see the Query window with the three tables you selected in the top pane, as shown below.

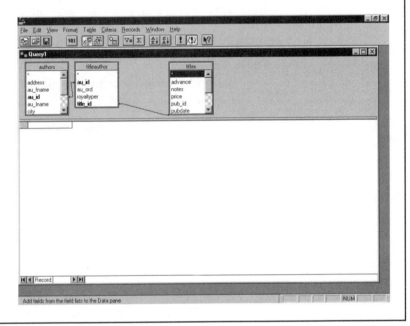

10. Drag-and-drop the au_fname field from the Authors table to the lower pane in the window. Then drag-and-drop the title field from the Titles table. Your screen should look similar to the one shown below.

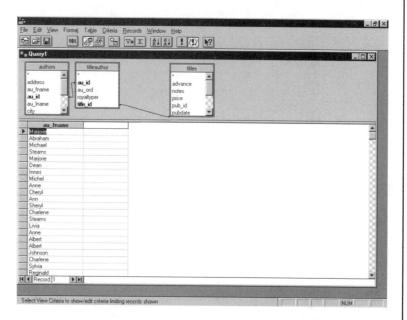

11. To view the SQL statement that you created, click on the SQL button on the toolbar. You should see something similar to the statement shown below.

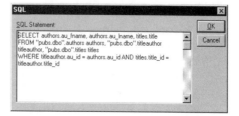

You can now cut and paste this SQL query into another application, such as Visual Basic or the ISQL/W utility. Although this was a relatively simple query, you can build extremely complex queries using the MSQuery tool.

Using Stored Procedures

As mentioned in the previous chapter, stored procedures are precompiled Transact-SQL statements that are stored on the SQL Server machine itself. There are three types of stored procedures:

- System stored procedures, which are shipped with SQL Server and are denoted with an sp_ prefix. These are typically found in the Master database.

- User-defined stored procedures, which you can create yourself. Only the SA can register user-defined stored procedures with the system.

- Extended stored procedures, which work outside the context of SQL Server and generally have an xp_ prefix. These are actually calls to DLLs.

Because stored procedures are precompiled, they run much more quickly and efficiently than regular queries do. The compiler doesn't need to figure out what it needs to do in order to run a stored procedure. The work order, or blueprint, is saved with the stored procedure. All SQL Server has to do is load the information and run it.

You can get help on the individual parameters that stored procedures require by running the stored procedure sp_help <*procedure_name*>.

You can run stored procedures from the ISQL utilities. For example, to find out information about all databases, run the following query:

```
EXEC sp_helpdb
```

Your results might look something like this:

name	db_size	owner	dbid	created	status
master	17.00 MB	sa	1	Apr 3 1996	logonchkpt.
Model	1.00 MB	sa	3	Apr 3 1996	nooptionsset
msdb	8.00 MB	sa	5	Sep 14 1997	logonchkpt.
Pubs	3.00 MB	sa	4	Apr 3 1996	logonchkpt.
Tempdb	2.00 MB	sa	2	Sep 15 1997	selectinto/bulkcopy
testpubs2	8.00 MB	sa	6	Sep 15 1997	log on chkpt.

Installing an Extended Stored Procedure

Earlier in the chapter, we mentioned the xp_cmdshell... option as one of the server options available through SQL Enterprise Manager's Server Configuration/Options dialog box (see "Setting Server Options"). This is an extended stored procedure, which passes information to the command shell. As with other stored procedures that are created and registered in the Master database, extended stored procedures can be registered only by the SA.

Microsoft ✓ *Exam* *Objective*	**Install an extended stored procedure.**

Extended stored procedures are generally created in C or C++ and then compiled into a DLL file. You should then place the DLL in the same folder as the other SQL Server DLL files. Once you have done this, you can execute the stored procedure sp_addextendedproc, which registers the function with the function and name of the DLL. The information will be stored in the syscomments and sysobjects tables as an extended stored procedure, with X as the object type. You must do this for each extended procedure defined in the DLL.

For example, if you have an extended procedure DLL called FROGGER.DLL, which has a function called Leap in it, you would execute the following stored procedure to register and install the extended procedure:

```
EXEC sp_addextendedproc 'Leap', 'Frogger.dll'
```

Using DBCC Commands

As mentioned in Chapter 3, DBCC commands are used to check the logical and physical consistency of your databases. DBCC commands report information about the state of your databases, rather than resolve problems. You should use stored procedures and Transact-SQL statements to fix any problems reported by DBCC commands.

As an administrator, you should become familiar with the DBCC commands. These can help you to more quickly and efficiently diagnose problems with SQL Server, as well as optimize your system. Here are a few DBCC commands that you should definitely know about:

DBCC CheckCatalog   Checks for consistency between system tables.

DBCC CheckDB   Checks all tables and indexes in a database to see that index pages are correctly linked to their data pages. It will also make sure that the indexes are in sorted order and that the information on each page is reasonable.

DBCC NewAlloc Makes sure that all pages in a database are correctly allocated and used.

DBCC SQLPerf(LogSpace) Reports on the currently used amount of transaction log space, expressed as a percentage.

DBCC SQLPerf(LRUStats) Reports on how your procedure and data caches are being used.

Using the SQL Trace Utility

You can use the SQL Trace utility to track logins and logouts to SQL Server. In addition, you can see which Transact-SQL statements are used and by whom.

Follow the steps in Exercise 4.5 to get an overview of the use of the SQL Trace utility.

EXERCISE 4.5

Using the SQL Trace Utility

1. Start the SQL Trace utility by selecting Start ➤ Programs ➤ Microsoft SQL Server 6.5 ➤ SQL Trace.

2. You will need to log in by filling out the fields in the Connect Server dialog box (see Figure 4.11, earlier in the chapter). Choose your server, enter your login id as **SA**, and supply a password if necessary. Then click on the Connect button when you are ready.

3. If this is the first time you have run the SQL Trace utility, you will be presented with the dialog box shown below, asking you whether or not you want to create a new filter. Click on Yes.

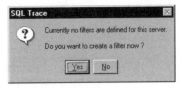

4. SQL Trace displays the New Filter dialog box, as shown below. Give your filter a name. Leave the default settings and click on the Add button to continue.

The New Filter dialog box includes capture options that you can select for your filter. If you click on the Events tab, you can select different events to track as well. For more information about the events and capture options, see SQL Trace Help.

5. Start the ISQL/W tool (see Exercise 4.3) and enter and execute the following query:

   USE pubs

   SELECT * FROM authors

6. Switch back to the SQL Trace utility. Your Filter window should look similar to the one that follows.

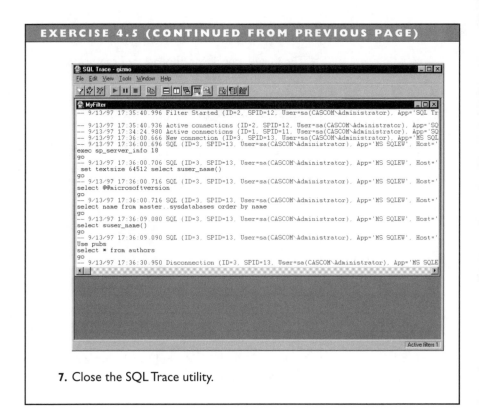

7. Close the SQL Trace utility.

Summary

In this chapter, we explored many of the utilities used for managing your servers and administering SQL Server. In addition, we presented an overview of the Transact-SQL language.

We began with a look at implementing and managing multiple SQL Server servers in different server groups. This included creating and dropping server groups, as well as registering new servers in the enterprise. You also learned that you can move individual servers from group to group by using drag-and-drop techniques.

The next section concentrated on configuring servers. This included a look at the SQL Enterprise Manager's Configuration/Options dialog box.

We then went over the use of the SQL Setup utility. With this utility, you can add new network libraries and languages to SQL Server. The SQL Setup utility can also be used to upgrade SQL Server or to rebuild the Master database.

The next utility we explored was the Client Configuration utility. With this utility, you can find out what network and database libraries are loaded on a client, as well as add client support.

We then turned to the ISQL and ISQL/W utilities. When you use either utility, you must supply a valid login ID and password. For the command-line version, remember that the switches are case-sensitive. The ISQL/W utility is a very robust application that you will use extensively in your SQL Server administrative tasks.

In the discussion of Transact-SQL, we explored the uses of the SELECT statement. You discovered how to vertically and horizontally partition tables and then sort your result set in either an ascending or descending fashion. You also learned how to run a simple query with multiple tables involved.

We then took a quick look at the MSQuery tool. If you do not know SQL, the MSQuery tool can be a useful crutch to help you quickly get up to speed on some of the Transact-SQL language constructs. This tool is generally more useful to developers than it is to administrators.

The next section covered stored procedures and DBCC commands. All of these statements can be executed from the ISQL utilities.

We finished up the chapter with a look at the SQL Trace utility. This tool can be used to track user interaction with your SQL Server. You can track logins and logouts and any SQL commands that were processed.

Exercise Questions

1. Which of the following is true regarding server groups? (Choose all that apply.)

   A. You can use drag-and-drop to move registered servers from group to group

   B. You can use drag-and-drop to move a server group to a subgroup

   C. You can use drag-and-drop to move server groups in SQL Enterprise Manager on machine A to SQL Enterprise Manager on machine B

   D. You can use the stored procedure sp_movesvrgrp to move server groups from machine A to machine B

2. Before you can administer a SQL Server machine in SQL Enterprise Manager, you must first register it and supply the proper login credentials, or use a trusted connection.

   A. True

   B. False

3. You can force a user who is working with the `xp_cmdshell` extended stored procedure into the security context of the client rather than the server by setting an option in the SQL Enterprise Manager's Server Configuration/Options dialog box.

   A. True

   B. False

4. The SQL Setup utility can be used to do which of the following? (Choose all that apply.)

   A. Add network libraries

   B. Add database libraries

   C. Install languages

   D. Rebuild the Master database

5. The SQL Client Configuration utility can be used to do which of the following? (Choose all that apply.)

   A. Add network libraries

   B. Add database libraries

   C. Configure languages

   D. Rebuild the Master database

6. The SQL Client Configuration utility needs to be run on only the server running SQL Server because all SQL Server clients get their configuration information from SQL Server itself.

   A. True

   B. False

7. Which of the following will start the ISQL command-line utility and log you in?

   A. `isql /Login sa /Pwd *****`

   B. `isql /Lsa /S`

   C. `isql /Usa /P`

   D. `sqlservr /Usa /P`

8. You can run any Transact-SQL command from the ISQL/W window, but you cannot run any DBCC commands from the ISQL/W window.

   A. True

   B. False

9. You can run any Transact-SQL command from the ISQL command line, but you cannot run any DBCC commands from the ISQL command line.

   A. True

   B. False

10. You can run multiple Transact-SQL commands, each in their own window, in the ISQL/W utility.

   A. True

   B. False

11. You can specify the database you wish to work with in the ISQL/W utility in which of the following ways? (Choose all that apply.)

A. Use the :USE *<databasename>* command in your SQL script

B. Click on the Databases list box and select your database

C. Just run the command—it will know which database you want to use

D. Drag-and-drop the database you wish to work with onto the ISQL/W window

12. What does the following Transact-SQL script do?

```
SELECT Employee.FirstName, Employee.LastName,
WorkInfo.YearsExp FROM Employees, WorkInfo WHERE
Employee.EmpID = WorkInfo.EmpID.
```

A. Displays all information in an employee record and all associated work information

B. Displays the first name and last name in an employee record, and if the employee has work experience, it will display that too

C. Displays all employees' first names and last names and their work experience where there are records that have a matching employee ID in the WorkInfo table

D. Displays all employees' first names and last names and their work experience whether or not they have a matching employee ID in the WorkInfo table

13. The ORDER BY clause in a Transact-SQL SELECT statement is used to change the default sort order from descending to ascending.

A. True

B. False

14. The MSQuery utility can be used to create complex Transact-SQL statements using a graphical interface.

A. True

B. False

15. The MSQuery utility allows you to cut and paste Transact-SQL statements into other applications.

   A. True

   B. False

16. The MSQuery tool is useful only for creating Transact-SQL queries to run in SQL Server.

   A. True

   B. False

17. What are the benefits of stored procedures? (Choose all that apply.)

   A. They are precompiled and therefore run more efficiently than normal queries

   B. They can be used in Transact-SQL batches

   C. They are not precompiled and therefore run more efficiently than normal queries, because the optimizer can look at the current conditions and make the necessary optimizations in real-time

   D. They are not used in Transact-SQL batches

18. The SELECT statement can be used to both horizontally and vertically partition a table.

   A. True

   B. False

19. Anyone can register an extended stored procedure.

   A. True

   B. False

20. DBCC commands generally fix problems in your databases, whereas stored procedures are used to report on the integrity of your database.

   A. True

   B. False

21. The SQL Trace utility can be used to view logins to SQL Server and to filter out Transact-SQL statements run by those logins.

   A. True

   B. False

CHAPTER

5

Managing Database Storage

aving SQL Server installed is no good to you whatsoever unless you have a place to store all of your data. After all, that is why you installed SQL Server in the first place. SQL Server stores database information in big files called *devices*. Once the devices are created, databases can be created inside these devices.

In this chapter, you will learn about SQL Server database storage structures, both the ones that you can create and manage and the ones that the system creates and manages. Next, we will discuss the procedures of creating and managing devices and databases, including creating databases on removable media. Then we will describe how to estimate the storage requirements of databases. Finally, you will learn how to create table and index database objects.

But before we get to the details about database storage components, let's go over the broader concepts of databases, database management systems, and relational database management systems.

Databases and Database Management Systems

A *database* is nothing more than a collection of individual pieces of data put into a format that makes it easy to query and maintain. A database can be as simple as a telephone book or as complex as the mainframe systems that hold government data about anything and everything. In fact, this book is a database of sorts—it contains the data that you need to pass the Microsoft SQL Server 6.5 System Administration exam.

A *database management system* (DBMS) is an environment specifically created for the purpose of working with databases. The term database management system usually refers to an electronic system or a computer program designed to work with databases. Microsoft Access and FoxPro are both examples of database management systems.

Microsoft SQL Server is one step beyond the traditional database management system. SQL Server belongs with a breed of database products known as *relational database management systems* (RDBMs). There are some fundamental differences between products like FoxPro and SQL Server. While many may argue that FoxPro and Access are relational database management systems, this is simply not the case. These database management systems do not support some of the most critical components of a pure relational database management system, such as true data and transactional integrity, and a server-side relational database engine.

What Is a SQL Server Database?

A database in SQL Server is a big container that holds data objects and other objects related to database management. Among the objects held in a SQL Server database are tables, views, stored procedures, rules, defaults, triggers, and user-defined datatypes. For an example, take a look at Figure 5.1, which shows the folders containing the objects in the Pubs database.

FIGURE 5.1

Viewing objects in the Pubs database in the Server Manager window of SQL Enterprise Manager

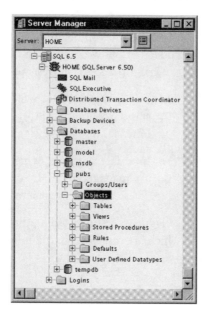

Although we just said that a database contains objects, this is not truly the case. In reality, the only objects stored inside databases are tables and indexes. Every object, no matter what type, is actually stored in a system table of some kind. In Chapter 3, you were introduced to the system tables that store catalog information about SQL Server. Some of these system tables actually store database objects.

For example, we stated before that a database contains stored procedures. To be more accurate, we should say that a database contains a system table that holds the definition of the stored procedures. The sysprocedures system table records an entry for every procedural object held in that database. The list of procedural objects is actually larger than just stored procedures alone; views, rules, defaults, and triggers are all procedural objects.

As another example, user-defined data types, which can be created by the owner of a database, are stored in the systypes system table of that database. No matter what the object, at some point, its definition is ultimately stored in a table. SQL Server's data storage architecture is formed around this basic premise.

SQL Server Data Storage Structures

Before you begin to create databases in SQL Server, it is important to understand how data storage structures are actually used.

Data storage structures can be grouped into two basic categories:

- External structures, which are those that you can see and affect with standard Transact-SQL commands. The SQL Server devices and databases fall under the classification of external structures.

- Internal structures, which are those that are hidden to some extent and are managed by SQL Server rather than the database administrator. These include all structures except for devices and databases.

Figure 5.2 shows a diagram of data storage structures in SQL Server 6.5, which are discussed in the following sections.

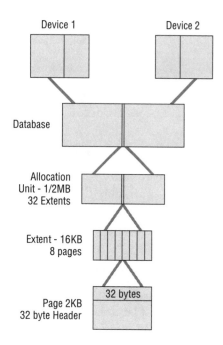

Devices: The Building Blocks

The device is the basic building block of SQL Server data storage. A device represents a preallocated amount of storage space, held in the form of a file or an entire disk partition. SQL Server stores information about devices in the sysdevices system table located in the Master database. There is only one sysdevices system table on a server on which SQL Server is installed, and that sysdevices table is part of the system catalog. Although the Windows NT operating system is responsible for actually doing the I/O operations, it does so under the direction of the SQL Server service. Windows NT sees the device as nothing more than a large file. SQL Server keeps track of all the information inside the device. Windows NT does not know or care about the actual contents of the device.

Here are some rules about SQL Server devices:

- Devices can be from 1MB to 32GB in size.

- A database can span multiple devices.

- The entire device does not need to be devoted to an individual database; a single device can hold pieces of multiple databases.

- A single SQL Server machine can hold up to 256 devices.

- Each device must be located on a local drive; a device cannot be created on a network share.

Databases: The Containers for Tables and Indexes

Databases are created on devices and are the structures where all tables and indexes are stored. Database information is stored in the sysdatabases system table of the Master database. SQL Server databases can be anywhere from 1MB to 1TB in size—large enough for even the most demanding data storage requirements.

The upper limit of 1TB (terabyte) for a database is due to the fact that a database cannot be broken into any more than 32 fragments. Each portion of a database that lies on a device is a fragment. Since devices can be up to 32GB (gigabytes) in size, the maximum size of a database is 32 fragments of 32GB, or 1TB.

Storing Databases on Devices

As explained in the previous section, a database can be hosted on many devices, but the entire device does not need to be devoted to an individual database. It is a common practice to put pieces of multiple databases such as transaction logs on a single device.

Since databases can exist on multiple devices and devices can host multiple databases, this creates a classic many-to-many relationship between databases and devices. A many-to-many relationship in a normalized database is resolved with a table containing the primary keys from the other two tables. This is also the case with databases and devices, as illustrated in Figure 5.3.

FIGURE 5.3

The relationship between databases and devices

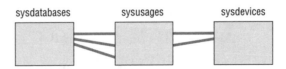

The three tables shown in the figure are constructed as follows:

- The sysdatabases system table holds one record for every database installed on the system.

- The sysdevices system table stores one line for every device on the system.

- The sysusages table stores one line for every fragment of a database stored on a device. This allows the system to maintain the many-to-many relationship.

The Transaction Log

There is another component of a database that is absolutely critical to the functionality and the fault tolerance of the database: the transaction log. The transaction log stores all the modifications that are made to the database. The transaction log functions as a write-ahead log. This means that the data modifications are actually made to the transaction log before they are made to the database.

There are three main purposes for the transaction log:

- To provide the necessary information to roll back transactions as a part of normal operations

- To provide for a physical depository for all cached data changes, thus enabling the possibility of automatic recovery and user-initiated recovery in the event of media failure

- To support incremental transaction log backups, thus reducing the need for full database backups whenever a backup is required

Let's look at each of these roles individually and see how the transaction log provides vital services to the database.

Standard Transactions A *transaction* is a set of data modifications that are issued in an "all-or-none" fashion. If an error occurs anywhere in a transaction, the entire transaction should be canceled. This is absolutely essential to maintaining data integrity.

For example, if you go to a teller at your neighborhood bank and turn over a pocketful of cash, you also want the balance in your account to be increased accordingly. This is a transaction with two distinct steps: The money is handed to the teller, and your account balance is increased. If there is an error in accomplishing either one of these steps, the entire transaction should be canceled. Any work that has been already accomplished by either party involved in the transaction should be immediately undone.

In the normal operating environment of SQL Server, transactions are constantly being issued against the server. All data modification activities that take place in SQL Server will happen in a transaction. There are two types of transactions that SQL Server will manage:

- An *implicit transaction* is automatically started by the server whenever a data modification takes place. There are three primary data-modification activities: insert, update, and delete. Each of these activities may affect more than one underlying record when it is executed. For example, a call for a searched update may affect 100 records in a 1000-record table. This update must be executed as an implicit transaction, because if any one of the 100 updates fails, the entire transaction should be canceled. SQL Server accomplishes this by writing a Begin Transaction record to the transaction log whenever a data modification is requested.

- An *explicit transaction* is started by the developer, usually to have a set of data modifications occur as a single transaction. For example, for transferring data from an active table to an archive table, a developer may write a script that deletes data from one table and inserts data into another. In order to ensure that these steps will occur as a single transaction, the developer prefaces the first modification request with an explicit Begin Transaction statement in the code. This will allow the developer to reverse all of the work done in the explicit transaction whenever an error occurs or to commit the transaction if no error occurs.

Regardless of the type of transaction, once a transaction begins, there are only two possible outcomes: Either the entire transaction will complete or the entire transaction will cancel. When a transaction completes, it is said to be *committed*. When a transaction is canceled, it is said to be *rolled back*.

To maximize SQL Server performance, an assumption is made that the majority of transactions will commit. To support this assumption, data changes are made to the database in cache after the entries are made to the transaction log. If the transaction is rolled back, all of the modifications to the database must be undone. This is where the transaction log comes in.

When a rollback is issued, the transaction log is used to undo all of the work that has been done to the database. This can be done because the transaction log contains enough information to completely reconstruct the database as necessary.

When a deletion occurs in a database, the entire deleted record is written to the transaction log so that is can be placed back into the database if needed. The same is true for an insertion; the entire inserted record is written to the transaction log so that the insertion can be reissued against the server if needed. For an update, what is written to the transaction log depends on what type of update occurs. The update mode depends on many factors, including the fields being updated, whether or not the total length of the record changes, and other considerations. Suffice it to say here that there is enough information written to the transaction log to reconstruct the effects of an update statement if necessary.

Support for Automatic Recovery   Another function that is supported by the transaction log is automatic recovery. Automatic recovery takes place whenever the server is started. During the automatic recovery process, each database on the server is evaluated for data integrity. The transaction log is an important part of this process.

Whenever a transaction commits on a database, the cached pages containing the committed transaction are immediately flushed to disk, providing a permanent record of the modification written to the database. Likewise, during the checkpoint process (a system process that flushes cached pages to disk), all modified pages, also known as *dirty pages*, are flushed from cache to disk, even if those pages contain work from uncommitted transactions. Those pages flushed during a checkpoint process will include both the data and the transaction log pages.

A *dirty page* is any page that has been altered since it was brought into cache or last flushed to disk. Dirty pages in cache represent the most current view of the data. It is very common for a user to read dirty pages from cache. This is not a violation of data integrity in any form and should not be confused with the concept of dirty reading, which is reading a page that is locked by another transaction, indicating editing in progress. Refer to Chapter 12 for more information about locking.

If the system were to have a failure between checkpoints that affected your drives, this would mean that there may be some data on disk representing an uncommitted transaction, which would disrupt data integrity. Also, you could have a situation where transaction log pages representing complete transactions have been flushed to disk, but the modified data pages remain in the cache. This may also be disruptive to data integrity.

The transaction log can solve this problem. During the automatic recovery process, the transaction log is read for every database, reissuing committed transactions against each database and rolling back any data from uncommitted changes made to the database. This process ensures data integrity in the event of a system failure, while also allowing the server to cache data for the purpose of efficiency. (See Chapter 8 for more information about the automatic recovery process.)

In the event that the disk containing the database device is lost, your saved backups along with the orphaned log on the transaction log device can be used to get you back to the exact point of the failure.

Backups   There may be times when a full database backup is neither needed nor desired. Between full database backups, you can make transaction log backups.

Transaction log backups are very different from full database backups in structure. A full database backup is a copy of every page of the database, including the transaction log. The backup is restored by copying the backup page by page back to the database. With a transaction log backup, the system is actually copying the pages of the transaction log that have been added since the last full database backup or transaction log backup. Since the transaction log backup represents a set of transactions, restoring a transaction log reapplies all of the transactions recorded in each log.

Although transaction log backups tend to be fairly compact, they can take a long time to restore to the server. It may take just as long to reissue the transactions against the server as it did to originally issue the transactions. Numerous accumulated transaction logs can take longer to restore than a database.

Transaction log backups eliminate the necessity of making a full database backup whenever you desire a point of recovery. Transaction log backups are also very compatible with other server activities and can be made even when users are still working in the database. (See Chapter 8 for more information about transaction log backups.)

Allocation Units: The Page Monitors

When a database is created, it is divided into *allocation units*. An allocation unit is a structure of 0.5MB in size. The purpose of the allocation unit is to provide a method of keeping track of which pages are allocated to which objects.

When an allocation unit is created, it is divided into 32 pieces called *extents*. The very first page of the first extent of the allocation unit is called the *allocation page*. The allocation page is responsible for keeping track of every extent in the allocation unit. Using this approach, the server does not need to read every single page of every allocation unit if it needs to find a free extent or page; it can simply query the allocation page of each allocation unit for information on the extents that it contains.

Allocation units affect the size of the database. Databases must be created and maintained in full allocation unit intervals. As an internal structure, all allocation units are the same 0.5MB in size. That is not something that you can control.

Since allocation units are 0.5MB in size, it would follow that the minimum incremental size of a database would be 0.5MB. While this is theoretically the case, the statement that is used to create a database will not accept noninteger values, thus forcing the actual minimum incremental size of the database to 1MB.

Extents: The Units for Tables and Indexes

An extent is a block of eight pages totaling 16KB in size. The extent is the basic unit of allocation for tables and indexes.

When a table or an index needs additional storage space, an extent is allocated to that object. A new extent will generally not be allocated for a table or index until all pages on that extent have been used. This process of allocating extents to objects rather than individual pages serves two purposes:

- The time-consuming process of allocation of pages is done in one batch rather than forcing each allocation to occur whenever a new page is needed.

- Allocating extents to objects forces the pages allocated to an object to be at least somewhat contiguous. If pages were allocated directly on an as-needed basis, it is quite likely that pages allocated to different objects would be next to each other in physical order. This arrangement would have a significant negative impact on performance during certain types of full table access.

Pages: The Common Denominator

At the most fundamental level, everything in SQL Server is stored on a 2KB page. There are many different types of pages, but every page has some things in common. Pages are always 2KB in size and always have a 32-byte header, leaving 2016 bytes of usable space on every page.

Types of Pages

There are five primary types of pages in SQL Server:

Data pages   These pages hold the actual rows for each table. Up to 256 rows can be placed on a data page. Although 2016 bytes are free for use on a data page, records are limited in length to no more that 1962 bytes. This is because rows cannot cross pages (with the exception of text and image data, which is not actually stored in the same page as the row that owns the data), and approximately 54 bytes are used for transaction log overhead in the transaction log entries. Transaction logs are held on standard data pages.

Index pages   These pages store the index keys and levels making up the entire index tree. Unlike data pages, there is no limit to the total number of entries that can be made on an index page. Index structure is discussed in detail in Chapter 12.

Allocation pages   The allocation page is the first page of the first extent of every allocation unit. The allocation page maintains information about the current allocation status of every extent in that allocation unit.

Text/image pages   These pages hold the actual data associated with text and image datatypes. When a text field is saved, the record will contain only a 16-byte pointer to a linked list of text pages that hold the actual text data. Only the 16-byte pointer inside the row is counted against the 1962-byte row size limit.

Distribution pages   Every index has a distribution page that tracks the distribution of values in that index. The distribution page is used by the query optimizer in choosing the most appropriate index for any given query request.

I/O and Locking on the Page Level

The page is the smallest unit of I/O in SQL Server. Every time data is read from or written to a database, this occurs in page units. Most of the time, this reading and writing is actually going back and forth between the data cache and disk. The data cache is divided into 2KB buffers, intended solely for the purpose of holding 2KB pages.

Creating and Managing Devices

Since nothing can be stored until a device is created, we will start by explaining how to create and manage devices.

When you create devices (and databases), you need to specify their size. Deciding how much storage space you need for your devices and databases requires some special considerations. This is particularly true for devices, because although you can later expand their size, you cannot make them smaller. Because you need to understand the processes of creating and managing devices and databases before you can estimate storage requirements with any accuracy, we talk about these processes first. For information about estimating the sizes of your devices and databases, see the section "Estimating Storage Requirements" later in this chapter.

Creating Devices

Creating a device is the process of reserving disk space for the exclusive use of SQL Server. Devices can be created as files or they can be created on unformatted disk space.

Microsoft ✓ *Exam* *Objective*   **Create a device.**

Exam objectives are subject to change at any time without prior notice and at Microsoft's sole discretion. Please visit Microsoft's Training & Certification Web site (www.microsoft.com/Train_Cert) for the most current exam objectives listing.

As with many database administration tasks, you can create a device using SQL Enterprise Manager or with a Transact-SQL statement. Only the SA has the authority to create devices, and this permission cannot be given to any other user.

Although you can create devices on raw partitions (unformatted disk space), there is little advantage to doing so. Furthermore, placing a device on a raw partition presents a disadvantage that could be important. The device-creation process will take less time if you use a raw partition, but once the device is created there will be little if any performance benefit. The disadvantage is that you will not be able to perform standard file system operations, such as copying, renaming, and so on, with the device.

Using SQL Enterprise Manager to Create Devices

You can create a device in SQL Enterprise Manager by using the New Database Device dialog box. The steps in Exercise 5.1 take you through the process of creating a device using SQL Enterprise Manager.

For information about starting and using SQL Enterprise Manager, see Chapter 4.

EXERCISE 5.1

Creating a Device Using SQL Enterprise Manager

1. Start SQL Enterprise Manager, connect to your server, and select Manage ≻ Database Devices to display the Manage Database Devices window, shown below. This window lists all of the devices that exist on this server.

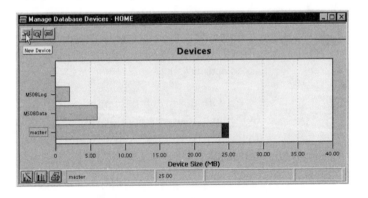

2. Click on the New Device button on the toolbar (the one with an icon of the disk drive with a yellow star, on the far left) to open the New Database Device dialog box, shown below.

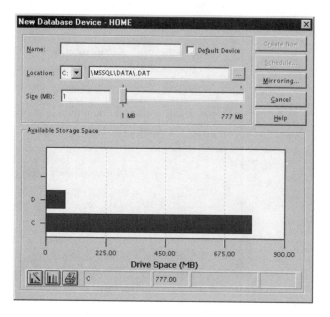

3. In the Name text box enter **SybexTestData**.

This is the name by which the device will be known internally on this installation of SQL Server. Whenever a device is referenced in Transact-SQL statements, this name will be used. The name can be from one to thirty characters in length. The first character can be an alphanumeric character, an underscore (_), the at sign (@), or the pound sign (#); the following characters can also include the dollar sign ($), but they cannot include the at sign.

4. Make sure that the Default Device checkbox is cleared.

A default device is the device that volunteers to host a database if no device is explicitly referenced when the database is created. Default devices are filled in alphabetical order.

5. Make sure that the filename appears in the Location box.

EXERCISE 5.1 (CONTINUED FROM PREVIOUS PAGE)

The default location is the Data subdirectory under the SQL Server installation directory. In SQL Server 6.5, this location is \MSSQL\DATA on your installation drive. If you wish, you can change the default location and specify a local drive and a path for the device. UNC names are not allowed; devices must be local drives and cannot be created on network shares.

6. Set the size to 5MB by entering **5** in to the Size text box or moving the slider. (It is usually easier to enter the value than to fiddle with the slider.)

Note that you can schedule the creation of this device for a later time if you wish by clicking on the Schedule button. Scheduling tasks is addressed in detail in Chapter 9.

7. Click on the Create Now button to create the device. Acknowledge the creation by clicking on the OK button in the message box that appears. You will see your new device listed in the Manage Database Devices window.

8. Close the Manage Database Devices window and return to the Server Manager window. Expand the Database Devices folder and check that the device has been created.

9. Using Windows NT Explorer, navigate to the location that you provided for your new device. You should see a file called SybexTestData.DAT. This is your new device. Minimize or close Windows NT Explorer and return to SQL Enterprise Manager.

WARNING Be cautious about how large you make your devices. Although you can expand a device later, you are not allowed to shrink a device. Disk space allocated to a device cannot be recovered without dropping and re-creating the device.

Using Transact-SQL to Create Devices

Another way to create devices is with Transact-SQL code. This approach allows a little more control over how the device is created, but it also requires you to do some mathematical conversions and remember some code. Depending on your situation, the added control may be worth the extra effort.

If you are planning to take the System Administration for Microsoft SQL Server 6.5. exam, it is important that you become very familiar with the Transact-SQL statements discussed in this book. The exam assumes that you have a thorough knowledge of both SQL Enterprise Manager and the Transact-SQL approaches to performing tasks.

Devices are created with the Transact-SQL command Disk Init. Here is its syntax:

```
DISK INIT
    NAME = 'logical_name',
    PHYSNAME = 'physical_name',
    VDEVNO = virtual_device_number,
    SIZE = number_of_2KB_blocks
[, VSTART = virtual_address]
```

The parameters of the Disk Init statement are used as follows:

NAME   The logical name of the device, or the name by which the device will be known inside the server. This parameter is the same as the logical name entered in the Name text box in SQL Enterprise Manager's New Device dialog box.

PHYSNAME   The filename for the physical file location on a local drive. This parameter is the same as the Location setting in SQL Enterprise Manager's New Device dialog box.

VDEVNO   The virtual device number of this device. SQL Server can host up to 256 devices per server. These devices are differentiated by their virtual device number. This number literally translates into the starting virtual page address for this device. Since a device can be up to 32GB in size, these virtual starting addresses are 32GB apart. This value can be any available device number between 1 and 255. Note that 126 and 127 are taken by the Msdb database devices, and 0 is taken by the Master database device.

SIZE   The size expressed in 2KB page units. You will probably think about database sizes in megabytes, so you may need to do a little conversion here. There are 512 2KB pages per megabyte.

VSTART   The specific virtual starting address that you wish to use for this device. This allows you to override the starting address implied through the virtual device number. This parameter is optional and should be used with extreme caution! You could work as a SQL Server database administrator for years and never need to use this parameter.

As you will note from the list of parameters above, there is one substantial difference between using SQL Enterprise Manager and Transact-SQL when creating devices. This difference is the virtual device number. In order to use Transact-SQL to create a device, you must first find out which virtual device numbers are available. You can obtain this information by using the system stored procedure sp_helpdevice. In Exercise 5.2, we will use this stored procedure to find available virtual device numbers, and then create a device using Transact-SQL.

You can start ISQL/W as a stand-alone utility from the Windows NT Desktop or from within SQL Enterprise Manager. For information about starting and using the ISQL/W utility, see Chapter 4.

EXERCISE 5.2

Creating a Device Using Transact-SQL

1. Start the ISQL/W utility.

2. Enter and execute the following statements:

   ```
   USE master
   EXEC sp_helpdevice
   GO
   ```

3. The results will list all of the devices currently installed on your system. Scroll all the way to the right in this window until you see the device_number column. This column lists all the virtual device numbers that are currently in use. Make a note of which numbers between 1 and 255 are free.

EXERCISE 5.2 (CONTINUED FROM PREVIOUS PAGE)

4. With a free virtual device number in hand, you are ready to create a device using Transact-SQL. Enter and execute the following statements (you may need to change the path or virtual device number if these parameters are not appropriate for your server):

```
USE master
DISK INIT
  NAME = 'SybexTestLog',
  PHYSNAME = 'C:\MSSQL\DATA\SybexTestLog.DAT',
  VDEVNO = 2,
  SIZE = 1024
GO
```

The Results window should return the following message:

```
This command did not return data, and it did not return any
rows
```

5. Close the ISQL/W utility and return to the Server Manager window in SQL Enterprise Manager.

6. To refresh the device list, right-click on the Database Devices folder and select Refresh from the context menu. You should see your new device in the Database Devices folder.

SQL Enterprise Manager will not automatically refresh the window when you use a Transact-SQL statement to create, drop, or modify an object. You will need to get in the habit of refreshing SQL Enterprise Manager (step 6 of Exercise 5.2) if you wish to see the results of the Transact-SQL code changes in the SQL Enterprise Manager window.

Expanding Devices

If you need more room on a device to accommodate additional databases or additional fragments of existing databases, you can expand your devices up to a final size of 32GB. There is no real cost associated with expanding existing devices, other than the possibility of disk fragmentation (which is usually only a major problem when the devices are created on FAT partitions). Because you can expand a device after you create it but not reduce its size, it is sometimes wise to be conservative in sizing a device when you create it.

Using SQL Enterprise Manager to Expand Devices

To expand a device with SQL Enterprise Manager, you simply edit the device to change the size setting. Exercise 5.3 guides you through the process of expanding a device with SQL Enterprise Manager. We will expand the Sybex-TestData device, which we created in Exercise 5.1, from 5MB to 7MB.

EXERCISE 5.3

Expanding a Device Using SQL Enterprise Manager

1. In the Server Manager window of SQL Enterprise Manager, expand the Database Devices folder.

2. Locate the SybexTestData device and double-click on it to display the Edit Database Device dialog box, as shown below.

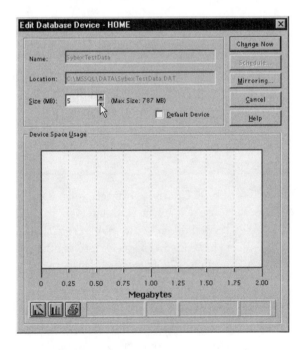

EXERCISE 5.3 (CONTINUED FROM PREVIOUS PAGE)

3. The Size box should contain 5, indicating a size of 5MB. Attempt to reduce the size of the device by clicking on the down arrow on the right side of the text box. You will not be able to change to a smaller number because SQL Server does not allow you to shrink an existing device.

4. Click on the up arrow next to the Size box to reset the value to **7**, so the size of the device is 7MB.

5. Click on the Change Now button to make your change.

6. Verify that the size has been changed by selecting Manage ➤ Database Devices. You should see that the SybexTestData device has been expanded to 7MB. Close the Manage Database Devices window.

As you saw in Exercise 5.3, you were prevented by the utility from shrinking the device. This is one of the advantages of using SQL Enterprise Manager. It will often prevent you from doing something that would result in a error.

Using Transact-SQL to Expand Devices

You can expand devices by using the Transact-SQL command `Disk Resize`. Here is its syntax:

```
DISK RESIZE
    NAME = logical_device_name,
    SIZE = final_size
```

The NAME parameter specifies the logical name of the device that was established when the device was created. The SIZE parameter specifies the final size of the device in 2KB page units.

You may have noticed the term DISK in this command and the previous Transact-SQL command described in this chapter. Whenever you see the word DISK in a Transact-SQL command, you are working with a device.

Follow the steps in Exercise 5.4 to expand a device using Transact-SQL. We will expand the SybexTestLog device, which we created in Exercise 5.2, from 2MB (1024 2KB pages) to 4MB (2048 2KB pages).

EXERCISE 5.4

Expanding a Device Using Transact-SQL

1. Start the ISQL/W utility.

2. Execute the stored procedure sp_helpdevice to verify the current size of the device (the size is listed in the Description column of the Result window).

3. Enter and execute the following statements to expand the device:

```
USE master
DISK RESIZE
  NAME = 'SybexTestLog',
  SIZE = 2048
GO
```

4. Execute the sp_helpdevice again to verify that the expansion has taken place.

5. Close the ISQL/W utility.

Dropping Devices

When devices are no longer needed, they can be dropped (deleted) from the server. Dropping a device removes the entry for that device from the sysdevices system table in the Master database. Devices cannot be dropped until they are empty. There can be no database fragments in a device when the device is dropped.

WARNING Although there are methods for recovering dropped devices, they do not work all of the time. You should be very careful about dropping devices, or be prepared to restore from a backup.

Using SQL Enterprise Manager to Drop Devices

The easiest way to drop a device using SQL Enterprise Manager is through the Server Manager window. Select the desired device in the Database Devices folder of the Server Manager and press the Delete key on the keyboard. You will be prompted to confirm the deletion; if you are sure that you wish to delete the device, click on the Yes button.

If you choose to delete a device that is not empty, SQL Enterprise Manager will prompt you to drop all databases that have any fragment on the device, as shown in Figure 5.4. If you choose to go ahead and delete the device, then the database or databases will be dropped automatically. Be aware that there is no way to delete just a portion of a database. If the device contains even a 1MB fragment of the database, then the entire database must be dropped if you wish to drop the device.

FIGURE 5.4

Deleting devices containing database fragments

When a device is deleted using SQL Enterprise Manager, this removes only the entry for that device in the sysdevices system table. It does not remove the file that was created by the operating system to hold the device information. You must delete the file manually before you can re-create the device using the same filename and location.

When you drop devices using SQL Enterprise Manager, be sure to delete the operating system file associated with that device. The disk space used by the device is not actually reclaimed until the file is deleted.

Using Transact-SQL to Drop Devices

You can drop devices from SQL Server using the `sp_dropdevice` system stored procedure. The parameters of this stored procedure include the logical name of the device and a flag called DELFILE that is used to delete the operating system file at the same time that the logical device is dropped. The syntax is as follows:

```
sp_dropdevice logical_name [, DELFILE]
```

Exercise 5.5 walks you through the process of dropping devices with and without the DELFILE flag, so that you can see the difference between the two approaches. We will drop the SybexTestData and SybexTestLog devices, which we created in Exercises 5.1 and 5.2.

EXERCISE 5.5

Dropping Devices Using Transact-SQL

1. Start the ISQL/W utility.

2. Enter and execute the following statements to drop the SybexTest-Data device:

   USE master

   EXEC sp_dropdevice sybextestdata

   GO

The Results window will indicate that the file was closed and the device was dropped.

3. Verify that the device was dropped by executing `sp_helpdevice`. The device should not appear in the list.

4. Verify the status of the associated file by using Windows NT Explorer to navigate to the folder containing the file. If you used the default setup location, this will be C:\MSSQL\DATA\. You should see the file SybexTestData.DAT in the directory. Delete this file and minimize Windows NT Explorer. Return to ISQL/W.

EXERCISE 5.5 (CONTINUED FROM PREVIOUS PAGE)

5. Enter and execute the following statements to drop the SybexTestLog device:

```
USE master
EXEC sp_dropdevice sybextestlog, DELFILE
GO
```

In this case, the Results window should indicate that the device was dropped and the file was deleted.

6. Verify that the device was dropped by executing sp_helpdevice.

7. Verify that the physical file was deleted by navigating to the folder that contained the file in Windows NT Explorer.

8. Close the ISQL/W utility.

Creating and Managing Databases

It's time to make a major shift in the way that you think about databases. We are going to take the word *file* out of our vocabulary. If you have worked with traditional desktop databases, everything is a file. In fact, these databases are often referred to as flat-file databases. This is because they lack the true relational advantages that a product like SQL Server can provide.

In SQL Server, the only file that is a part of data storage is the device, and once that device is created, we never refer to the file again. In fact, if you create your devices on raw partitions, there might not be a file at all! Sure, there are scripts that are saved as files, and even batch files that execute queries through ISQL, but these aren't actually part of the data store itself.

So what is a database if it is not a file? A database is a preallocated portion of a device that is available to tables and indexes in that database for extent allocation. Just as when you create a device, you must decide how large to make the database when it is initially created. You have the ability to expand databases after they are initially created, but you will pay a small price for doing so. You can also shrink databases, but there are some specific restrictions on how this can be done.

As when you create devices, you need to specify database sizes when you create them. For information about estimating the storage space you will need for your databases, see the "Estimating Storage Requirements" section later in this chapter.

In the following sections, we will look at creating, expanding, shrinking, and dropping databases. We will also look at how databases can be created on removable media, such as CD-ROMs or floppy disks.

Creating Databases

Creating a database is a process that allocates space for that database on the device of your choice. A database can be created on a single device, or fragments of a database can be located on multiple devices. Every database that is created will have a corresponding row in the sysdatabases system table. Each fragment of a database will enter a row in the sysusages table.

Microsoft ✓ *Exam* *Objective*	**Create a database.**

When creating a database, it is generally good practice to divide the database into at least two fragments: one for the data and another for the transaction log. There are several advantages to creating the transaction log on a separate device:

- When the transaction log is placed on a separate device, it can be backed up separately from the database. Transaction log backups are not allowed if the database and transaction log are created on a single device.

- If the transaction log is placed not only on a separate device but on a separate physical disk, this provides the greatest possible level of fault tolerance.

- When the transaction log is placed on a separate device, you can specify the log size explicitly. If the log and data are on the same device, they compete for space and will both fill up at exactly the same time.

Of the system databases that are created when you install SQL Server, only the Msdb database is divided between a data device and a log device. You can check existing databases to see if they have been divided in this manner. Exercise 5.6 will take you through this process.

EXERCISE 5.6

Identifying the Segmentation of a Database

1. In the Server Manager window of SQL Enterprise Manager, open the Databases folder and double-click on the Msdb database to display the Edit Database dialog box, as shown below. Notice that references are made to explicit sizes of the data portion and log portion of the database.

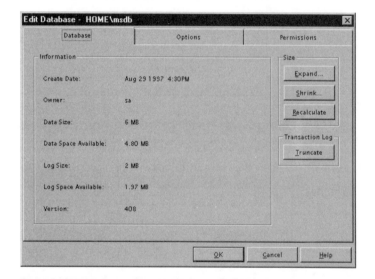

2. Close the dialog box, and then double-click on the Pubs database. The Edit Database dialog box for this database reports that the log and data portions share a device. Close this dialog box.

3. To retrieve the same information using Transact-SQL, start ISQL/W (choose Tools ➤ SQL Query Tool in SQL Enterprise Manager).

EXERCISE 5.6 (CONTINUED FROM PREVIOUS PAGE)

4. Enter and execute the following statements:

```
USE master
EXEC sp_helpdb msdb
GO
```

Notice that the fragments are data only and log only.

5. To see the information about the Pubs database, enter and execute the following statements:

```
USE master
EXEC sp_helpdb pubs
GO
```

This will report data and log fragments.

6. Close ISQL/W.

Using SQL Enterprise Manager to Create Databases

You can create databases in SQL Enterprise Manager by filling out the fields in the New Database dialog box. This dialog box not only allows you to create new databases, but it also provides easy access to the New Database Device dialog box, so that you can create a new device at the same time.

Exercise 5.7 takes you through the process of creating databases with SQL Enterprise Manager. In order to demonstrate the flexibility of this dialog box, we will create the devices for our new databases at the same time.

EXERCISE 5.7

Creating a Database Using SQL Enterprise Manager

1. In SQL Enterprise Manager, select Manage ➤ Databases to display the Manage Databases window. Click on the New Database button on the toolbar (on the far left) to display the New Database dialog box, as shown here.

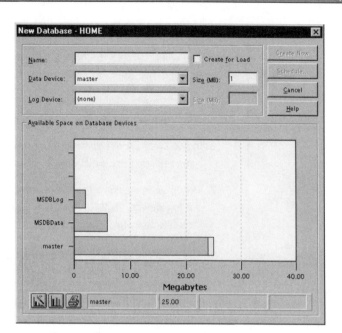

2. In the Name text box, type **SybexTestDB**.

The name you enter in the Name text box is the logical name by which this database is referred to internally. The name can be from one to thirty characters in length. The first character must be a letter; the following characters can include digits, the underscore character (_), the pound sign (#), and the dollar sign ($).

There are no physical name or location options. Instead, you identify which devices you wish to use to host this database. You can choose one data device and one log device, and specify the amount of space on those devices that you wish to use.

3. In the Data Device drop-down list box, select the <New> option to open the New Database Device dialog box. (You may need to scroll up in the list to see the <New> option.)

4. In this dialog box, create a 10MB device called **SybexTestData** (see Exercise 5.1). After you acknowledge the device creation confirmation, you will return to the New Database dialog box, with SybexTestData entered into the Data Device text box.

5. Reduce the size of this device to 4MB. You should see the bar in the graph below change color on 40 percent of its length.

6. In the Data Device drop-down list box, select the <New> option again and create a 6MB device called **SybexTestLog**.

7. When you return to the New Database dialog box, change the size of the log device to 2MB. The New Database dialog box should now look like the one shown below.

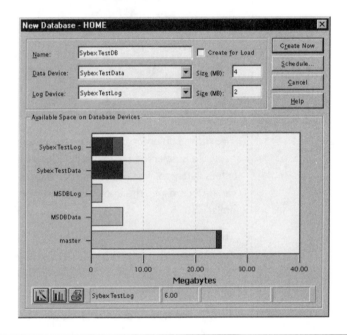

The For Load checkbox next to the Name box is a special option to be used when re-creating databases for the purpose of loading database backups. When this checkbox is selected, the database will be created with the status of loading and will be marked as DBO Use Only. This will prevent anyone else from getting access to the database until you have loaded the database and transaction log backups and turned off the DBO Use Only database option. We'll talk about the DBO Use Only option in more detail in Chapter 8, which covers backups.

8. Click on the Create Now button to create the database. You will now see your new database listed in the Manage Databases window. Close this window.

If you look very closely at your new database in the Manage Databases window, you will notice that a small amount of space (approximately 0.11MB) is marked as used. This space holds the system tables that are created automatically as the database is created.

Using Transact-SQL to Create Databases

The Transact-SQL approach to creating databases uses the same parameters as the New Database dialog box in SQL Enterprise Manager. You provide the size and device information, and can even include the For Load option if you wish. The command for creating a database is Create Database. It has the following syntax:

```
CREATE DATABASE database_name
[ON {DEFAULT | database_device} [= size]
   [, database_device [= size]]...]
[LOG ON database_device [= size]
   [, database_device [= size]]...]
[FOR LOAD]
```

Note the following considerations regarding the Create Database statement:

- The DEFAULT keyword can be used in place of a specific data device if you wish to place the database fragment on a default device. If there are multiple default devices, they are used in alphabetical order. In general, it is not a good idea to use default devices.

- A database can be spread across multiple data or log devices by using a comma between device parameters. Up to 32 fragments can be used for any given database.

- All sizes are indicated in megabytes, not 2KB pages.

As an example, to create a 12MB database called Mydb hosted on a 10MB data device called MyDataDev and a 2MB log device called MyLogDev, the statement would be written like this:

```
CREATE DATABASE mydb
    ON MyDataDev=10
    LOG ON MyLogDev=2
```

In Exercise 5.8, we will use a portion of the remaining space in the devices created in the earlier exercise to create a database called Pubs2.

EXERCISE 5.8

Creating a Database Using Transact-SQL

1. Start the ISQL/W utility.

2. To create the Pubs2 database, enter and execute the following statements:

```
USE master
CREATE DATABASE Pubs2
    ON SybexTestData=4
    LOG ON SybexTestLog=2
GO
```

EXERCISE 5.8 (CONTINUED FROM PREVIOUS PAGE)

The Results window will display the following information:

CREATE DATABASE: allocating 2028 pages on disk 'SybexTestData'

CREATE DATABASE: allocating 1024 pages on disk 'SybexTestLog'

3. Verify that the database was created properly be executing the following statements:

```
USE master
Exec sp_helpdb Pubs2
GO
```

The results should indicate a 6MB database divided between data and log portions.

Expanding Databases

If your database fills to capacity, you will need to expand the database before you will be able to add any more data. You also may need to add more capacity to your transaction log if you find that your transaction log is filling up before your scheduled log backups. To expand either the data or log portions of a database, you will need to add fragments to that database.

Microsoft ✔ *Exam* *Objective*   **Alter a database.**

When you expand a database, you are actually adding entries to the sysusages system table. This tables identifies which pages in the device are used for the database fragment. As stated earlier, a database can contain up to 32 fragments. These fragments can be added with either SQL Enterprise Manager or Transact-SQL code.

Using SQL Enterprise Manager to Expand Databases

The process of expanding a database in SQL Enterprise Manager is very much like the process of creating a database. The dialog box that you use to expand a database is almost identical to the one that you use to create a database.

In Exercise 5.9, we will expand the SybexTestDB database. We will add 1MB to both the data and transaction log portions of the database.

EXERCISE 5.9

Expanding a Database Using SQL Enterprise Manager

1. In the Server Manager window of SQL Enterprise Manager, expand the Databases folder.

2. Locate the SybexTestDB database and double-click on it to open the Edit Database dialog box.

3. Click on the Expand button in the Size section of the dialog box to open the Expand Database dialog box, as shown below.

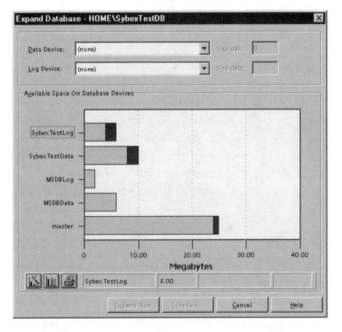

Notice that there are separate drop-down boxes for data devices and transaction log devices, just as in the New Database dialog box. This allows you to expand the data portion and/or the log portion of the database as necessary.

4. Open the Data Device drop-down list and select the SybexTestData device from the list. Notice that the log device that we created is not on this list. This is because this device is allocated for log storage on this database and cannot be used for data expansion. Change the size from 2MB to 1MB.

EXERCISE 5.9 (CONTINUED FROM PREVIOUS PAGE)

5. Select SybexTestLog from the Log Device drop-down. Change the size from 2MB to 1MB. The dialog box should look like the one shown below.

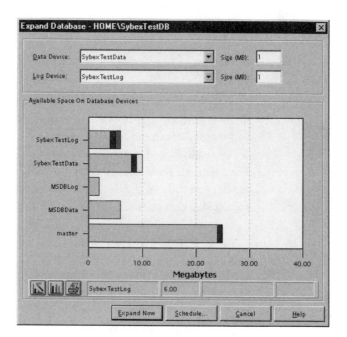

6. Click on the Expand Now button. You will return to the Edit Database dialog box. Confirm that the data portion has expanded to 5MB and the log to 3MB. Close the Edit Database dialog box by clicking on OK.

Using Transact-SQL to Expand Databases

SQL Enterprise Manager is extremely easy to use. So easy, in fact, that sometimes it hides the complexity of what is really happening to your database more than might be healthy. Expanding databases is a good example of this. Neither the dialog boxes with which you interact nor the reports that your receive from SQL Enterprise Manager really show you the fragmentation that has been created in your database. When using the Transact-SQL command, this fact is painfully clear.

To expand a database, use the `Alter Database` command. This command also allows you to expand the data or transaction log portions of your databases by providing the logical name of the device that you wish to expand. Here is its syntax:

```
ALTER DATABASE database_name
    [ON {DEFAULT | database_device} [= size]
    [, database_device [= size]]...]
    [FOR LOAD]
```

As you can see from the syntax, you can also expand multiple devices in a single statement. But notice that no distinction is made between data devices and log devices in the `Alter Database` syntax. The distinction is made in the device itself. If you expand a database on a device that already holds data fragments, then the expansion will result in an increase of storage capacity for the data portion of the database. In the same way, if you expand a database on a device that contains transaction log fragments, the storage capacity of the transaction log increases.

Another distinction here is that you specify additional space for the *size* parameter in *megabytes*. Remember that for device expansion, the Disk Resize statement uses a *final_size* parameter in 2KB pages. When you're expanding the database, it makes sense to use an incremental size rather than a final size for the database, since the result of the `Alter Database` statement is a new fragment written to the sysusages table. You are providing the size of that fragment, which is the incremental increase in the database size.

A good rule of thumb to remember is that whenever you work with devices, you will size them with 2KB pages. Databases always use megabytes as the unit of measure.

As an example, suppose that you wish to expand a database called Mydb to create an addition 5MB data fragment on a device called MyDataDev. This device currently holds other data fragments of this database. No log expansion is desired. You would use the following statement:

```
ALTER DATABASE Mydb
    ON MyDataDev=5
```

In Exercise 5.10, we will go through the process of expanding the Pubs2 database. We will add a 1MB fragment to both the data and log portions of this database.

EXERCISE 5.10

Expanding a Database Using Transact-SQL

1. Start the ISQL/W utility.

2. To verify the current size and fragmentation status of the Pubs2 database, enter and execute the following statements:

```
USE master
EXEC sp_helpdb Pubs2
GO
```

The Results window should report a 6MB database, divided as 4MB data and 2MB log.

3. Expand each of the database portions by 1MB by executing the following statements:

```
USE master
ALTER DATABASE Pubs2
  ON SybexTestData = 1,
  SybexTestLog = 1
GO
```

4. Verify the new size and fragmentation structure by repeating step 2. This time, the database size is reported as 8MB total, but the fragmentation structure is very different from what was reported in SQL Enterprise Manager. Four fragments are reported, two each for the data and log portions.

5. Close the ISQL/W utility.

The Effects of Database Expansion

Exercise 5.10 shows a little more clearly what is happening when you expand a database. It is not quite as nice and neat as it may look in SQL Enterprise Manager. You end up with fragmentation in your database, and fragmentation is something you may want to avoid.

There are some negative effects of fragmentation that you need to consider:

- The total number of fragments is limited to 32. It is possible to use up your allotment of fragments before you are finished increasing the size of the database.

- Fragmentation of this nature can have a negative impact on performance. It may force a query to jump wildly between the extents and allocation units of the database to retrieve the data needed to resolve the query. This is most often a problem when the query is reading every page in a table sequentially.

- It makes the process of recovering from a media failure more complex. When you are restoring a database backup into a newly created database, the new database must be created with exactly the same fragmentation structure as the original database. In our example, we now have an 8MB database. If we were to back up this database right now, restoring from that backup would not be a matter of simply creating an 8MB database with 5MB data and 3MB log portions. We would need to reconstruct the database with all four segments in exactly the same structure in order to successfully restore from the backup.

Obviously, some fragmentation cannot be avoided, and all fragmentation is not necessarily bad. In fact, you always want at least two fragments so that you can effectively divide data storage from log storage. However, you should strive to keep nonessential fragmentation to a minimum.

Another stored procedure, `sp_coalesce_fragments`, can also be used to eliminate some of the unnecessary fragmentation in a database. Here is its syntax:

```
sp_coalesce_fragments [DBNamePattern]
```

Shrinking Databases

If you have overstated the size of your database, it is possible to shrink that database by removing some of the unused space. Shrinking a database requires the alteration of the internal allocation structure. For this reason, you don't have much control over what shrinks and where it will take place.

When shrinking a database, you are allowed to remove only unused spaced back to the last allocation unit where data or log pages are present in the normal creation sequence. Figure 5.5 illustrates this with two examples. The gray portion of the bars represents used spaced, and the white portion shows unused space.

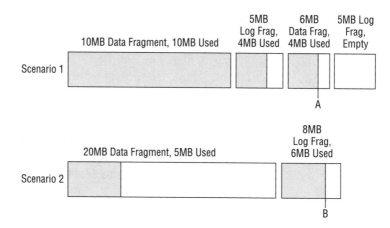

FIGURE 5.5

Shrinking databases

The first scenario shown in the figure involves a 26MB database. This database was originally constructed with a 10MB data fragment and a 5MB log fragment. Later, this was expanded to add 6MB to the data portion and 5MB to the log portion. The alterations were made in the order just cited. In this case, the smallest size that you can make this database is 19MB. You can shrink it to point A marked on this diagram, removing 5MB of log space and 2MB of data space. Even though there is an additional 1MB of unused space, this space is located before used space in the creation sequence, and therefore cannot be removed.

In the second scenario shown in Figure 5.5, a 28MB database is divided between a 20MB data fragment and an 8MB log fragment. These fragments represent the original creation of the database. No expansion has taken place. Although there is 15MB of unused space in the data fragment, this cannot be reclaimed because the transaction log stands as used space after the data fragment. The most that this database can be reduced in size is 2MB. This will be taken entirely from transaction log space, shrinking the database to point B in the diagram.

If you anticipate that you may need to shrink a large database after creation, it can be advantageous to create a moderate data portion and a full transaction log. Follow this by an additional data fragment. This will prevent the transaction log from standing in the way of the database reduction.

Using SQL Enterprise Manager to Shrink Databases

As when you expand a database, you go through SQL Enterprise Manager's Edit Database dialog box to shrink a database. Our sample database, Sybex-TestDB, has been constructed in such a way that the smallest size that it can be reduced to is 5MB. Follow the steps in Exercise 5.11 to shrink the Sybex-TestDB database.

EXERCISE 5.11

Shrinking a Database Using SQL Enterprise Manager

1. In the Server Manager window of SQL Enterprise Manager, locate the SybexTestDB database and double-click on it.

2. In the Edit Database dialog box, click on the Shrink button located in the upper-right corner. You will see a message saying that the database must be in single-user status before you can continue. If there is any other user connection to this database besides yours, this process will fail at this point.

3. Click on Yes to continue. The Shrink Database dialog box will appear. This dialog box shows the smallest possible size for the database and the current size.

4. Spin the current size down to 5MB, the smallest size allowed. Then click on OK.

5. In the Edit Database dialog box, verify that your database is currently configured with a 4MB data fragment and a 1MB log fragment. Then click on OK to close the dialog box.

Using Transact-SQL to Shrink Databases

Shrinking a database requires the deallocation of internal storage structures—allocation units. Whenever you need to manipulate internal storage structures, you must use a special set of commands. These commands are the DBCC (Database Consistency Checker) commands, which were introduced in Chapter 4. The DBCC command used to shrink a database is DBCC ShrinkDB. Here is its syntax:

```
DBCC ShrinkDB (database_name [, new_size [, 'MASTEROVERRIDE']])
```

When using this command, the size of the database is an optional parameter. If it is not supplied, the command will take no action on the database, but rather will return the smallest possible size to which the database can be reduced. The MSTEROVERRIDE parameter applies to the Master database. It prevents the logging of the fact that the Master database was shrunk. You must use this switch in order to shrink the Master database.

Just as when you reduce the size of a database using SQL Enterprise Manager, you must put the database in single-user status before using the DBCC command. Unfortunately, you need to do this yourself, rather than having the utility do it for you. Switching to single-user status is done with the system stored procedure sp_dboption.

The DBCC commands are covered in more detail in Chapter 13. The sp_dboption stored procedure is discussed in Chapter 12.

Follow the steps in Exercise 5.12 to shrink the Pubs2 database to its minimum size using Transact-SQL.

EXERCISE 5.12

Shrinking a Database Using Transact-SQL

1. Start the ISQL/W utility.

2. To set the database to single-user status, enter and execute the following statements:

```
USE master
EXEC sp_dboption Pubs2, 'single user', true
GO
```

You will be informed that the database has been changed to this status.

3. To find out the smallest possible size for the database, enter and execute the following statement:

```
USE master
DBCC ShrinkDB(Pubs2)
```

EXERCISE 5.12 (CONTINUED FROM PREVIOUS PAGE)

The Results window will show the current size of the database and the smallest possible size (both sizes are in 2KB pages). This smallest possible size is reported to the nearest allocation unit. Notice that the results also tell you which objects, if any, are preventing further reduction of the database.

4. Shrink the database to 5MB by entering and executing the following statement:

```
DBCC ShrinkDB(Pubs2, 2560)
```

5. Reset the status of the database back from single-user by entering and executing the following statements:

```
USE master
EXEC sp_dboption Pubs2, 'single user', false
GO
```

6. Verify the new database fragmentation by entering and executing the following statements:

```
USE master
EXEC sp_helpdb Pubs2
GO
```

You should see that the database is back down to two fragments from four, and these fragments are 4MB data and 1MB log.

7. Close the ISQL/W utility.

Dropping Databases

When you no longer need a database, you can drop it from your server, freeing device space for other database fragments. Only a DBO user of a database has the authority to drop that database.

Although the process is easy, remember that dropping a database is a permanent change. If you need to recover your database later, you will need to restore it from a backup.

Dropping a database is a simple task, both with SQL Enterprise Manager and Transact-SQL. In SQL Enterprise Manager, locate the database that you wish to drop in the Server Manager window, select the database, and press the Delete key. You will be asked to confirm the deletion, after which the database will be dropped. There is no physical file to delete, because the database is not held as a file. (Remember, we took the word *file* out of our vocabulary when we started this section!)

With Transact-SQL, you can drop a database by using the `Drop Database` statement. Here is its syntax:

```
DROP DATABASE database_name [, database_name...]
```

As you can see in the syntax, to drop multiple databases using a single statement, simply separate the database names with commas in a list.

As an example, if you wished to drop a database called Mydb, you would use this statement:

```
DROP DATABASE mydb
```

If a database is marked suspect, it may need to be dropped using the DBCC DBREPAIR command or the sp_dbremove system stored procedure. This process is covered in Chapter 13.

There are three databases that cannot be dropped: Master, Model, and Tempdb. You can drop the Pubs database if you wish, which will give you an additional 3MB in your Master device. The Msdb database can also be dropped, but this isn't recommended. This is because dropping the Msdb database renders the SQL Executive service and replication processes completely unusable. It will also cause errors to be reported whenever you do a backup or restore operation, because the system will attempt to write to some detail and history tables in the Msdb database.

Creating Databases on Removable Media

It has been said that we live in the information age. Information is all around us, and in very large quantities. SQL Server provides support for managing this vast information resource in the form of a very efficient mechanism for creating and distributing data on removable media, such as CD-ROMs. You can create databases on removable media and distribute this media. In this way, the databases can be installed on a server other than the one on which they were created.

Why a special consideration for creating databases on removable media? After all, can't you just copy the devices containing the database to the removable media? You can, but this is not as simple as it sounds.

In Chapter 3, we talked about system tables, and how some of these tables deal with security. These tables—sysusers, sysalternates, and sysprotects, along with a few others—are an integral part of the database and must be accessible for writing wherever the database is installed. It is unlikely that every installation of a removable media distribution will have exactly the same user base. This means that the data can exist on read-only media, but the system tables must be located on read-write media. Accomplishing this could be quite a feat, since the system tables and the data are usually integrated on the same fragments.

In reality, the data and system tables are actually stored on different segments in a database. The data is stored on a segment called *default*; the system tables are stored on a segment called *system*. You usually never see this, however, because both the system and data segments are normally found in every data fragment. You need to have a way to split up the segments across fragments so that the system tables can be moved to read-write media during installation.

A *segment* is a system- or user-created area of data storage that is dedicated to storing specific objects. Do not confuse the concept of a segment with a *fragment*. A fragment is an entry in the sysusages table. A segment is an entry in the syssegments table. Fragments usually contain one or more segments, and segments may be assigned to one or more fragments.

We have actually done this once before, with the transaction log. The transaction log is actually a system table called syslogs. This table is located in a segment called the *logsegment*. When we created a database with the transaction log on a separate device, we actually moved the logsegment from the data device and placed it on another device. We can do the same thing with the system segment.

To create a database with the system segment on another fragment, you must use Transact-SQL. There is no equivalent functionality in SQL Enterprise Manager. You use one system stored procedure to create the database and other stored procedures for packaging that database for distribution and installing the revised removable media database. There are five distinct steps to creating a database on removable media:

- Create the database using the stored procedure `sp_create_removable`.

- Create the database objects as usual.

- Certify that the database will be installable as a removable media database by using the stored procedure `sp_certify_removable`.

- Copy the database to the removable media for distribution.

- Install the database and bring it online.

Creating the Removable Media Database

Although the `Create Database` statement can create a database on a single device, the `sp_create_removable` stored procedure requires at least three devices, one each for the default, system, and logsegment segments. The syntax is as follows:

```
sp_create_removable dbname, syslogical, 'sysphysical', syssize,
loglogical, 'logphysical', logsize, datalogical1,
'dataphysical1', datasize1
[... , datalogical16, 'dataphysical16', datasize16]
```

The syntax requires a name for the database meeting standard object name requirements, and the logical names, path names, and sizes of the devices that will be used to hold the system tables, transaction log, and data. Up to 16 devices can be referenced for the data fragments if needed.

For example, a statement for creating a database for removable media distribution might look like this:

```
sp_create_removable mydb, sysdev, c:\mssql\data\systev.dat,
2048, logdev, c:\mssq\data\logdev.dat, 2048, datadev,
c:\mssql\data\datadev, 4096
```

This statement would create a database with a 2MB system segment, a 2MB logsegment, and a 4MB default (data) segment.

The `sp_create_removable` stored procedure creates the devices and the database for you. You do not create the devices in advance. Devices supporting removable media distribution databases must be created as files; they cannot be created on raw partitions.

Creating the Database Objects

After the database has been created, database objects are created in that database. Database objects include tables, indexes, views, and stored procedures. For details about creating database objects, see the "Creating Database Objects" section later in this chapter.

Certifying the Database

Certifying a database for removable media distribution is the process of ensuring that the database is able to be installed as a removable media database. In order to be certified, all objects must be owned by the DBO, and SA must be the DBO, since SA is the only user login known across all installations of SQL Server. The stored procedure used to certify a database is `sp_certify_removable`. Here is its syntax:

```
sp_certify_removable dbname [,AUTO]
```

If SA is not the DBO and there are users with permissions in the database, use the `AUTO` flag to allow SQL Server to remedy the situation. Specifically, the certification process does the following:

- Verifies that SA is the database owner and that DBO owns all objects in the database. If verification fails, this can be corrected with the use of the `AUTO` parameter.

- Verifies that there are no permissions granted to users of the database. If verification fails, this can be corrected with the use of the `AUTO` parameter.

- Checks the integrity of the devices upon which the database is built.

- Truncates the transaction log and moves the log to the system device.

- Drops the original device associated with the transaction log. The transaction log is not needed on a read-only database.

- Writes information needed for installation of the database to a file called \MSSQL\LOG\CertifyR_<*databasename*>.txt

The text file created by the `sp_certify_removable` stored procedure contains information that is required for the installation of this database once it is shipped. You may want to consider copying this file and installation instructions to the CD on which the database will be shipped.

Copying the Database for Distribution

Once the database has been certified, it can be copied to the distribution media. Since the devices that contain the database are created as files, you can simply copy the devices to the medium (for example, to the CD-ROM). The database itself will be installed directly from this medium.

Installing the Removable Media Database

There are two steps to the installation process: You must first install every device copied to your CD or other medium, and then you must bring the database online. The text file that was created at the certification step contains the information that the installation routine requires.

Installation   The installation is accomplished with the stored procedure sp_dbinstall. Here is its syntax:

```
sp_dbinstall database, logical_dev_name, 'physical_dev_name',
size,'devtype' [,'location']
```

Required arguments include the name of the database, the logical name of the device, the physical location of the device on the CD, the size of the device, and the type of the device (data or system). You can find this information in the text file created in the certification process.

The optional argument *location* is used if the contents of the device are to be copied to the read-write media. This will always be the case with the system device, because it allows the system device to be placed on disk while the data device(s) remain on the CD. Assuming that the CD drive uses a drive letter of E: and that the system device is in the root directory of that CD, the following statement would install the system device of the Mydb database to the local server:

```
sp_dbinstall mydb, sysdev, e:\sysdev.dat, 2048, system,
c:\mssql\data\sysdev.dat
```

WARNING   The sp_dbinstall stored procedure must be run for every device that you wish to install. If you do not install all of the devices, the database cannot be brought online. The location argument in not optional for the system device. This must be copied to the local drive.

Bringing the Database Online   Once the database has been installed, it is marked offline. You will need to bring the database online before your users can access it. This is accomplished with the stored procedure sp_dboption. One of the many database options you can set with this stored procedure is offline. To bring a database online, you set the offline option to FALSE.

For example, to bring a newly installed removable media database called Mydb online, use the following statement:

```
sp_dboption mydb, offline, FALSE
```

When you remove a removable media database from the system, it is very important that you first take the database offline. To take a database offline, use the sp_dboption stored procedure, and set the offline option to TRUE.

See Chapter 12 for more information about using sp_dboption and the rest of the database options you can set with this stored procedure.

Uninstalling the Database

If you wish to uninstall a database that was installed with the sp_dbinstall stored procedure, you cannot drop it as you would a normal database. Instead, you must use the stored procedure sp_dbremove, which will remove all references to the database in the system tables of the server. Here is its syntax:

```
sp_dbremove database[, dropdev]
```

If you use the optional parameter dropdev, this will also drop any references to the devices that were used for the database from the sysdevices system table. You will usually want to do this if the database is being removed from your system, since all of the devices were designed exclusively for that database. Note that the dropdev parameter does not delete the files associated with the devices; it removes only the entries for those devices in the system tables. The files must be deleted manually.

Estimating Storage Requirements

All storage space in SQL Server is preallocated, for both databases and devices. As you've learned in this chapter, devices can be expanded, but they cannot be reduced in size. Databases can be expanded and shrunk, but a fragmentation price is paid with expansion. When you shrink a database, you might not be able to recover the space where you actually want and need this space.

Microsoft
Exam
Objective

Estimate space requirements.

This poses an interesting dilemma for database administrators. How large should your databases and devices be? They need to be large enough to accommodate your data needs without excessive expansion, yet they must not be too large or this will simply become wasted space. When estimating storage requirements, you must go to the basic levels of data storage: the table and the index. Let's look at how you can estimate storage space based on the amount of room you will need for these objects.

Estimating Table Storage Requirements

Tables are really nothing more than templates specifying how data is to be stored and integrity is to be enforced. All data stored in a table must adhere to a datatype. There is a specific procedure that you can follow to estimate the space required by a table:

- Calculate the space used by a single row of the table.

- Calculate the number of rows that will fit on one page.

- Estimate the number of rows that the table will hold.

- Calculate the total number of pages that will be required to hold these rows.

- Calculate the number of extents that must be allocated to the table to hold the data.

- Calculate the number of megabytes required to hold the extents.

Calculating Row Size

Datatypes are of various shapes and sizes and allow you incredible control over how your data is stored. Table 5.1 lists some of the most common datatypes.

T A B L E 5.1 Common Datatypes	**Data Type Name**	**Description**	**Size**
	TinyInt	Integer from 0 to 255	1 byte
	SmallInt	Integer from -32,768 to 32,767	2 bytes
	Int	Integer from -2,147,483,648 to 2,147,483,647	4 bytes
	Real	1 to 7 digit-precision, floating point	4 bytes
	Float	8 to 15 digit-precision, floating point	8 bytes
	Smalldatetime	1/1/1900 to 6/6/2079, with accuracy to the minute	4 bytes
	Datetime	1/1/1753 to 12/31/9999, with accuracy to 3.33 milliseconds	8 bytes
	Smallmoney	4-byte integer, with 4-digit scale	4 bytes
	Money	8-byte integer, with 4-digit scale	8 bytes
	Char	Character data	1 byte per character

When calculating storage requirements for a table, you add up the storage requirements for each datatype in the table, plus an additional 4 bytes per row of overhead. This will give you the total space that is occupied by a single row. For example, if a table in a database has three fields defined as Char(10), Int, and Money, the storage space required for each row could be calculated as follows:

Char(10)	10 bytes
Int	4 bytes
Money	8 bytes
Overhead	4 bytes
Total	**26 bytes**

A row is limited to 4 bytes of overhead only when no variable datatypes have been used and no columns allow nulls. If variable-length columns are used or nulls are allowed, additional overhead must be added. The amount will depend on the datatype and number of columns.

Calculating Rows per Page

Once you have a number indicating the total bytes used per row, you can easily calculate the number or rows that will fit on a single page. Every page is 2KB in size and has a 32-byte header. This leaves 2016 bytes free for storing data. The total number of rows per page can be calculated as 2016 divided by the row size. The resulting value is truncated to an integer.

In our example, each row requires 26 bytes of space to store. We can calculate the rows per page as follows:

$$2016 \div 26 = 77.5$$

We then truncate this value to an even 77.

When calculating rows per page, there are some additional factors that you will need to consider:

- Only 256 rows can fit on a single page. If you have some very short rows, you may not be able to avoid having some wasted space in your pages.

- Rows can never cross pages. If there is not enough space on a page to complete the row, the row will be placed on the next page. This is why you need to truncate the result of your calculation.

- The number of rows that can fit on one page may also depend on a fill factor that is used for the clustered index. A fill factor is a way of keeping the page from becoming 100 percent full. If you use a fill factor, this may reduce the amount of space used on a page when the index is built.

As an example of the effect of a fill factor, if a clustered index was built on our table with a fill factor of 75, this means that the data will be reorganized so that the data pages are only 75 percent full. Therefore, instead of 2016 bytes free on each page, you are allowed to use only 1512 bytes. The reason for a fill factor is to provide room inside the data pages for additional insertions. This means that the space may be used eventually.

Estimating the Number of Rows for the Table

You need to know your data to estimate how many rows your table will eventually hold. When you make this estimate, consider how large you expect your table to grow. As much as possible, allow for this growth in your estimates. If you don't, you might not have enough physical disk space and will need to purchase more disk drives.

Calculating the Number of Pages Needed

Estimating the number of pages you will need is another simple calculation, as long as you have reliable estimates of the rows per page and the number of rows you expect the table to hold. To calculate the number of pages, you divide the number of rows in the table by the number of rows per page, and then round the result up to the nearest integer.

In our example, we calculated that 77 rows would fit in a single page of the table. If we expected this table to eventually hold 100,000 records, the calculation would be:

$$100,000 \div 77 = 1298.701$$

And we would round the value to 1299 pages.

Calculating the Number of Extents Needed

After you calculate the number of pages, you can determine the number of extents that must be allocated to this table to hold this data. Since all space is allocated in extents, you again need to round up to the nearest integer when calculating extents. Remember that there are eight 2KB pages per extent. To calculate the number of extents required, you simply divide the number of pages by eight.

For our example, we estimated that we needed 1299 pages for our table. Our extent calculation would be:

$$1299 \div 8 = 162.375$$

And we round the value to 163 extents.

Calculating the Number of Megabytes Required

Since a megabyte can store 64 extents, to calculate how many megabytes you need for the table, you divide the number of extents you came up with by 64 to come up with the minimum number of megabytes for the table. Add a little bit of extra space "just in case," and you are ready to proceed to the next table.

In our example, we estimated 149 extents. Our megabyte calculation would be:

149 ÷ 64 = 2.4MB

You may wish to add a little bit extra to your estimate in case you underestimated. The amount that you should add depends on the likelihood that this database will grow past your estimated boundaries, and if so, by how much.

Estimating Index Storage Requirements

Indexes in SQL Server are stored in a B-Tree format. This means that you can think of an index as a large tree. You can also think of an index as a table with a pyramid built on top of it. The main concept to understand is that for every index, there is a single entry point: the root of the tree or the apex of the pyramid. Figure 5.6 shows an illustration of a common index structure.

F I G U R E 5.6

A B-Tree index structure

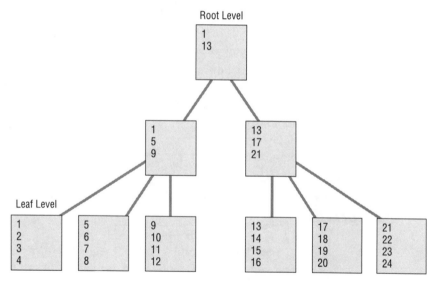

To estimate the size of the leaf level of an index, you can follow a procedure similar to the one used for estimating the storage requirements of a table (described in the previous section). Although the process is very similar, there are a few issues that are important to consider:

- You are adding the datatypes of the index keys, not the data rows.

- There is no 256-row limit to an index page.

- Clustered indexes use the data page as the leaf level. There is no need to add more storage for a clustered index leaf level.

The toughest part of estimating the size of an index is estimating the size and number of levels that you will have in your index. While there is a fairly long and complex series of calculations to determine this exactly, it is usually sufficient to add an additional 35 percent of the leaf-level space estimate for the other levels of the index.

For example, if we assume that we have index entries that take up about 20 bytes of space each, 100 entries would fit on an index page. If there are 2000 rows in the table, it would take 200 pages to store the leaf level of the index. Adding 35 percent of this estimate to consider the levels of the index would give us a total of 270 pages for this index.

Creating Database Objects

Although you will probably not be responsible for the creation of some of the more advanced database objects, such as stored procedures, views, and triggers, you should understand the process of creating tables and indexes. These may be tasks that you are called upon to perform as a database administrator.

Microsoft ✓ *Exam* *Objective*	**Create database objects.**

You can create tables and indexes with either SQL Enterprise Manager or Transact-SQL statements. Here, we will focus on using SQL Enterprise Manager, because it allows you to create your tables and indexes in a "point-and-click" fashion, eliminating the need to write a lot of code.

Creating Tables

You can create a tables in SQL Enterprise Manager by using the Manage Tables window. This window allows you to name fields, set data types, and specify field lengths. You can also define a primary key and configure column properties, such as nullability. The Manage Tables window for the Authors table in the Pubs database is shown in Figure 5.7.

FIGURE 5.7

The structure of the
Authors table in the Pubs
database shown in the
Manage Tables window

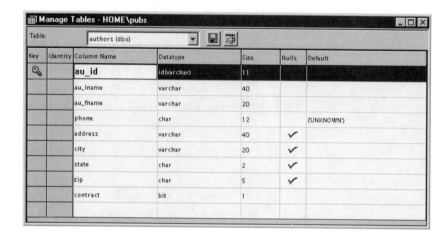

Key	Identity	Column Name	Datatype	Size	Nulls	Default
🔑		au_id	id(varchar)	11		
		au_lname	varchar	40		
		au_fname	varchar	20		
		phone	char	12		(UNKNOWN')
		address	varchar	40	✓	
		city	varchar	20	✓	
		state	char	2	✓	
		zip	char	5	✓	
		contract	bit	1		

In Exercise 5.13, we will create a table in the SybexTestDB database called
Customers.

EXERCISE 5.13

Creating a Table with SQL Enterprise Manager

1. In the Server Manager window of SQL Enterprise Manager, select the
SybexTestDB database.

2. Select Manage ➤ Tables to display the Manage Tables window.

3. In the Column Name box on the first line, enter **CustID**.

4. Click in the Datatype box and select Int from the list.

5. Click in the Nulls box. Make sure that there is no blue checkmark in
this box. If one is present, click on the box again to clear it.

6. Click in the Column Name box on the next line and enter **CustName**.
Set the datatype as Char and size at 20. This will allow you to enter 20
characters in this field. Do not allow nulls (make sure that there is no
checkmark in the Nulls field).

7. On the next line, add the column named **Address1**, with a datatype
of Char and a size of 25.

8. On the next line, add the column named **Address2**, with a datatype of Char and a size of 25. Click in the Nulls box to put a checkmark in this field (to allow nulls).

9. On the next line, add the column named **City**, with a datatype of Char and a size of 15.

10. On the next line, add the column named **State**, with a datatype of Char and a size of 2

11. On the next line, add the column named **Zip**, with a datatype of Char and a size of 5. Your window should now look like the one shown below.

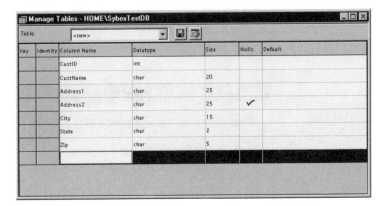

12. To add a primary key, click on the button with the green plus sign at the top of the window. This will open the advanced features window. Make sure that the Primary Key/Identity tab is selected. In the Primary Key section, choose CustID as the primary key and set the Type option button to Non-Clustered, as shown below. This will build a unique nonclustered index to enforce the primary key.

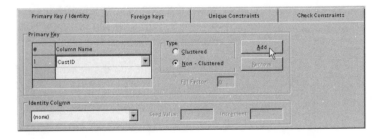

13. Click on the Add button. This will put an icon of a key in the Key field next to the CustID column.

14. Click on the Save Table button on the toolbar (the one with the icon of a floppy disk) of the Manage Tables window.

15. When you are prompted for a table name, enter the name **Customers**. Then close the window. You should now see the Customers table in the list of tables associated with the SybexTestDB database.

Creating Indexes

Indexes are used to speed up data access. For example, if your users select information by state very frequently, you might want to add an index on the State column of your table to speed the process of extracting the data.

All indexes can be placed into one of two categories:

Clustered   Each table is allowed one clustered index. This index is the actual sort order for the data in the table.

Non-Clustered   Nonclustered indexes consist of a list of ordered keys that contain pointers to the data in the data pages. Numerous nonclustered indexes can be created, but these occupy more space than clustered indexes.

You can create indexes in SQL Enterprise Manager by using the Manage Indexes dialog box. Follow the steps in Exercise 5.14 to create a clustered index for the Customers table we created in Exercise 5.13.

Creating an Index Using SQL Enterprise Manager

1. Select the SybexTestDB from the Server Manager window in SQL Enterprise Manager.

2. Select Manage ➤ Indexes to display the Manage Indexes dialog box. Our only table is the Customers table. The index enforcing the primary key will be displayed in the dialog box.

3. To add a new index, open the Index drop-down list in the upper-right portion of the dialog box and select New Index from the list.

4. In the Index box, enter the index name **idxState**.

5. In the list of available columns, click on State, and then click on the Add button in the center of the dialog box.

6. In the Index Attributes section, click on the checkbox for Clustered.

Notice that the bottom portion of the dialog box shows an estimation of the size and number of levels of the index based on your index specifications and the current data in the table. Your completed dialog box should resemble the one shown below.

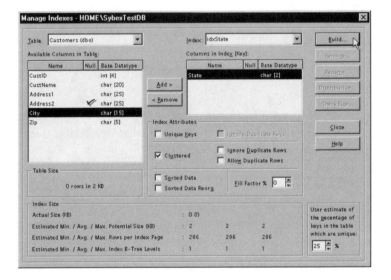

7. Click on the Build button to create the index.

8. Choose Execute Now when you are prompted for a schedule, and then close the dialog box.

Although you may create indexes as a database administrator, one of your more common tasks will be rebuilding existing indexes. When indexes become fragmented or if you need to re-create a fill factor for your indexes, you will need to rebuild the index. You can rebuild indexes from the Manage Indexes dialog box. You will notice that after the index has been created, the Build button changes to the Rebuild button. Use this to rebuild your indexes when necessary.

Summary

There is much more to data storage in SQL Server than meets the eye. SQL Server data storage structure is more than just a file or a collection of files. It is an entire internal architecture designed for one purpose alone—to allow you to extract and modify your data as quickly and efficiently as possible.

As you learned in this chapter, data storage in SQL Server is very well organized into its component pieces. We distinguished between external and internal storage structures. Allocation units, extents, and pages are all internal structures. You have little control over how these objects are allocated. When a table needs an additional extent allocated, an internal algorithm is used to determine where this extent will be located. It is not your option. On the other hand, devices and databases are both external structures. You can control the sizes and locations of these objects.

The rest of this chapter was devoted to creating and managing the external structures. You learned how to create and manage devices and databases. Then we discussed an approach for estimating the size of needed data storage. Finally, you learned how to create two basic database objects: tables and indexes.

Exercise Questions

1. Which of the following system tables is used to store information about the relationship between databases and devices?

   A. sysdatabases

   B. sysdevices

   C. sysusages

   D. sysfragments

2. How large can a device in SQL Server be?

   A. 32MB

   B. 32GB

   C. 32TB

   D. There is no limit to device size

3. How many fragments can a SQL Server database contain?

   A. 2

   B. 3

   C. 32

   D. There is no limit to the number of fragments that a SQL Server database can contain

4. All of the databases created on a SQL Server share a common transaction log.

   A. True

   B. False

5. What is the basic unit of I/O in SQL Server?

   A. Record

   B. Page

   C. Extent

   D. Allocation unit

6. What is the basic unit of database allocation?

   A. Page

   B. Extent

   C. Allocation unit

   D. Database space can be allocated with any unit of granularity

7. What is the basic unit of table or index allocation?

   A. Page

   B. Extent

   C. Allocation unit

   D. Table and index space can be allocated with any unit of granularity

8. What is the unit of measure for the Size parameter when using the Disk Resize statement?

   A. Incremental change in 2KB pages

   B. Final size in 2KB pages

   C. Incremental change in megabytes

   D. Final size in megabytes

9. What is the unit of measure for the Size parameter when using the Alter Database statement?

   A. Incremental change in 2KB pages

   B. Final size in 2KB pages

   C. Incremental change in megabytes

   D. Final size in megabytes

10. Which stored procedure is used to find out what virtual device numbers are available?

   A. sp_vdevno

   B. sp_virtual_device

   C. sp_helpdb

   D. sp_helpdevice

11. How much space is available for data in a data page?

   A. 1962 bytes

   B. 2016 bytes

   C. 2048 bytes

   D. 2KB

12. Which command is used to shrink a device?

    A. sp_shrinkdevice

    B. sp_changedevice

    C. DBCC ShrinkDevice

    D. You cannot shrink a device

13. You have used the statement sp_dbremove mydb, dropdev on the database Mydb, a removable media database. What will be the result?

    A. Only the database will be removed from the system

    B. The database and the devices will be removed from the system

    C. The database and devices will be removed and any physical files will be deleted

    D. The database will be brought offline; all references to the database and devices will remain in the system tables

14. You are estimating the storage requirements for a table defined with the following fields: Char(15), Int, Float, Char(10). How many bytes will be used to store each row assuming no fields allow nulls?

    A. 35

    B. 37

    C. 39

    D. 41

15. If a row requires 34 bytes of space to store, how many rows can be placed on a page with a fill factor of 80?

    A. 60

    B. 59

    C. 48

    D. 47

CHAPTER

6

Managing User Accounts

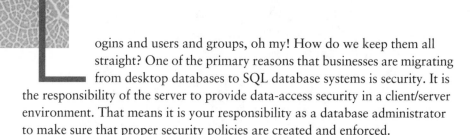

ogins and users and groups, oh my! How do we keep them all straight? One of the primary reasons that businesses are migrating from desktop databases to SQL database systems is security. It is the responsibility of the server to provide data-access security in a client/server environment. That means it is your responsibility as a database administrator to make sure that proper security policies are created and enforced.

In this chapter, we will look at managing secure access to a SQL Server system. We will begin with an explanation of how SQL Server security works. Then we will go into detail about the processes of creating and managing logins, users, and groups. Finally, we will look at the three security models available for SQL Server: the standard, integrated, and mixed security models. These models provide flexible ways to authenticate your users to SQL Server.

How SQL Server Security Works

When a user accesses a SQL Server database, the ultimate goal in most cases is to access a database object, such as a table, view, or stored procedure. Before the user can gain access to the object, the user must be properly authenticated. This authentication happens at three distinct stages: the server, the database, and the object itself.

The Authentication Stages

You can think of the access authentication stages as a series of three gates. Before you can get to your ultimate goal, you must pass through each gate. That would be easy enough if the gates were unlocked and unguarded, but this is not the case. Each gate has a gatekeeper whose job it is to keep you out unless you can provide the proper keys to let you through. Let's look at each of these gates and see how they form SQL Server security.

Security at the Server

The first gatekeeper is the SQL Server service itself. At this gate, you must provide a login and a password in order to get access to the server. This login information is held in the syslogins system table located in the Master database.

The syslogins system table is part of the system catalog, and it is found only in the Master database. This table holds the server login IDs, login names, and encrypted passwords, as well as other types of information. As you will see later, every user who gains access to the server can select from the system tables; however, only the SA login has the authority to select the password column from the syslogins table. Even though this field is encrypted, this column-level permission provides added protection against intrusion into your SQL Server database. Additionally, only the SA login has the authority to add, delete, or modify login information.

If you can provide a valid login and password to the server, you will be granted access to server resources. As you continue to the next gatekeeper, you will take with you your login ID.

Security at the Database

The second gatekeeper is the database whose resources you wish to access. When you come to this second gate, the gatekeeper checks your login ID to see if it is in the lists of logins that are allowed to access that database. There are two lists to check:

- The database checks the list of database users. This is the sysusers system table, stored in each individual database. The sysusers system table stores the login ID of every user that is allowed access to the database, along with a username that the login will be assigned when it passes through the gate. The login ID that each user carries from the first gate is compared against this list. If there is a match, then that login is allowed access to the database and is tagged with the username stored in the table.

- The database may check the list of aliases. An alias is essentially a mapping of an existing username to a login ID. This allows multiple logins to access a database under a single username. Aliases are also held in a system table, called sysalternates, stored inside each individual database.

A login can access a database under only a single username, either as the actual user or as a login aliased as that user. For this reason, every login will have at most one entry in either the sysusers or sysalternates system table and will never have an entry in both.

The login name for the server and a username for a database may be the same. This is not a requirement but is often the case, because it simplifies maintenance.

Occasionally, the gate will be left wide open. When a guest account has been created for the database, any login who is able to authenticate to the server can request access to all the database resources. We'll discuss the guest account in more detail later in this chapter.

Security at the Database Object

After obtaining a valid username from the second gatekeeper, the database uses this name to allow access to individual resources inside the database. The username becomes an identification card that is presented every time access is requested to a desired object.

For example, if a user wishes to execute a stored procedure, the list of permissions for that procedure will be checked for that user. If the user has execute permissions on that stored procedure, then the request is granted; otherwise, the request is denied. We'll cover the details of database objects and permissions in Chapter 7.

How Database Groups Fit into the Security Model

We have left one concept out of this discussion—the database group. A group is a collection of one or more users that have similar data access needs. To simplify the process of assigning object permissions, users with similar needs can be consolidated into *groups*. Assigning permissions to the group grants those permissions to all members of the group.

Groups, like users, are stored in the sysusers system table of every database. Groups are database-specific. If you want to have the same groups in every database, you must create those groups separately for each database.

To include identical groups in many databases, create these groups in the Model database before you create your user databases. Since every new user database is a copy of the Model database, this will place those groups in every new database that is created.

Every user is already a member of one group: the Public group. In addition to the Public group, a user also can be a member of only one other group. This is a departure from the traditional network security model, where a user can be a member of many groups, and that user will inherit the least restrictive permissions of their entire group membership. This means that for your SQL Server system, you must plan your group setup very carefully.

The Levels of Security

SQL Server's approach to security may seem odd at first, especially if you are an experienced network administrator, but there are reasons why it is designed this way. The most important reason is that this security model provides a high degree of control over each aspect of your security implementation. Users have access to only those areas of the server that you, as the database administrator, wish them to have. You can set permissions for individual tables down to even the column level if this is necessary.

Microsoft Exam Objective

Differentiate between a SQL Server login and a SQL Server user.

Exam objectives are subject to change at any time without prior notice and at Microsoft's sole discretion. Please visit Microsoft's Training & Certification Web site (www.microsoft.com/Train_Cert) for the most current exam objectives listing.

Let's take another look at each of the SQL Server levels of security and discuss why SQL Server behaves the way it does.

The Login

The login provides server access. There are only two classes of logins: the SA login and everyone else. When SQL Server is installed, by default, SA is the owner of every database on the server. The SA user bypasses all security checks, so that user has full control over everything that goes on at that server. Even if another login is later given ownership of a database, or another login creates a database, SA will still have an implied alias as the owner and can still exercise full control.

Every login other than SA must be granted specific rights to do anything on the server. These rights must be granted by SA or the owner of a database.

The User

A username is local to each database. There are two classes of users in a SQL Server database: the database owner (DBO) and regular users. The DBO controls all of the activities and rights in the database. As stated earlier, the SA is often the DBO for many databases. It is also quite common to have different people acting as DBO for different databases on the same server. This is why DBO must be distinguished at the database level, not at the server level. A DBO in one database may have no rights whatsoever in another database on the same server.

You may also have more than one user in a database who needs to act as DBO. This situation can be handled through the use of an alias. While there is only one login in each database mapped to the username DBO, there can be many others who have no username of their own and actually access the database aliased as DBO. Figure 6.1 illustrates how this relationship might work.

FIGURE 6.1

The relationship between logins and usernames in SQL Server

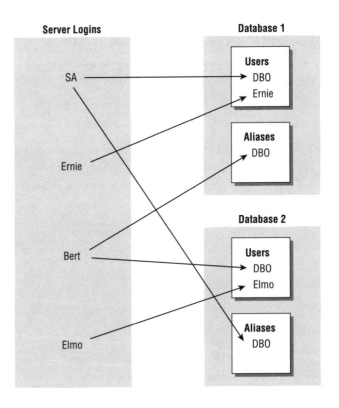

The example in Figure 6.1 includes four logins: SA, which is the administrative login, and three standard logins—Ernie, Bert, and Elmo. Database 1 gives access to the SA login through the user DBO. Notice that Ernie also has a username (Ernie) in this database. Bert does not have a username in Database 1. When Bert accesses Database 1, the database aliases him to the DBO user. He can do anything that DBO can do. Elmo cannot access Database 1 at all, because he does not have a username in that database.

Database 2 also allows access to the SA login; however, this time, SA has an alias to DBO rather than actually being DBO. SA will always have an implied alias of DBO if SA is not the actual DBO user. This alias will be managed by SQL Server. You do not need to explicitly create the DBO alias for the SA login, and since the alias is implied, you will not see SA in the sysalternates table.

The DBO of Database 2 is Bert. Elmo can also access Database 2 under the username Elmo. In this scenario, Ernie does not have a username in Database 2 and cannot access that database.

At this point, groups do not play a role in the security model. Groups are intended as a mechanism to consolidate permissions. Usernames are associated with the group in which they belong, but this group identification is used as permissions and checked on database objects, not as the login attempts to access the database. You create groups to make it easier to set up and maintain object permissions.

Creating and Managing Logins

Now that you understand how SQL Server security works, we will look at the mechanics of creating and managing logins. By creating a login, you are adding an entry to the first gatekeeper's (the server's) list. This information will be stored in the syslogins system table held in the Master database.

Viewing the Login List

The SQL Enterprise Manager can provide extensive information about logins. You can view the login list in the Server Manager window, which appears when you open SQL Enterprise Manager. Simply expand the Logins folder to view the list of current server logins, as shown in Figure 6.2. Notice that the logins themselves are not directly associated with any particular database. In fact, Server Manager shows the logins at the same level as databases and devices. This is appropriate, since the login is also a server-level object.

FIGURE 6.2

The login list in the Server Manager window

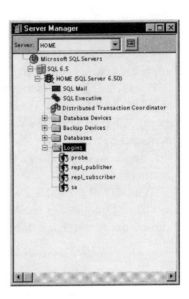

As you can see in the list shown in Figure 6.2, four logins are created automatically during the installation process:

probe The probe account is used to allow administrative processes to access SQL Server resources when SQL Server is using standard security. For example, the Windows NT Performance Monitor utility gathers SQL Server statistics through the probe account, and reports the counters and values you have requested. We'll discuss standard security in more detail later in this chapter.

repl_publisher When you're using SQL Server replication, the repl_publisher account is used by the replication processes on the distribution server to connect to a database and replicate transactions that it gathered from the publishing server. The replication process is discussed in detail in Chapter 11.

repl_subcriber The repl_subscriber account allows a subscribing server to connect to a publishing server and execute stored procedures during the replication process.

sa The sa account is the System Administrator (SA) login account. The assigned administrator logs in to SQL Server with this account to perform all administrative functions.

In addition to these four default login accounts, you can create as many other accounts as you need to control access to your server. Any accounts that you create will also appear in the login list in the Server Manager window.

Microsoft
✓ *Exam*
Objective

Create a login ID.

To create a login, you can use either SQL Enterprise Manager. which provides a very flexible interface, or you can use Transact-SQL statements. We will look at both approaches in the following sections.

Using SQL Enterprise Manager to Create Logins

To create a login account with SQL Enterprise Manager, you simply access the Manage Logins dialog box and enter the login name and password. SQL Enterprise Manager assigns the numerical login ID automatically. Creating a login account adds an entry to the syslogins table in the Master database.

The steps in Exercise 6.1 take you through the process of adding a login account using SQL Enterprise Manager (see Chapter 14 for details on how to work with SQL Enterprise Manager).

EXERCISE 6.1

Creating a Login Account with SQL Enterprise Manager

1. Start SQL Enterprise Manager.

2. Select Manage ➢ Logins to display the Manage Logins dialog box.

3. Type the login name and password in the appropriate text boxes. For our example, enter the name **Ernie** in the Login Name text box and the password **ernie** in the Password text box. Then click on the Add button.

EXERCISE 6.1 (CONTINUED FROM PREVIOUS PAGE)

You should see three changes in the dialog box: a series of asterisks has been entered into the Password box, a checkmark has been inserted into the Default column of the Master database in the Database Access section, and the Add button has changed to the Modify button. Your dialog box should look like the one shown below.

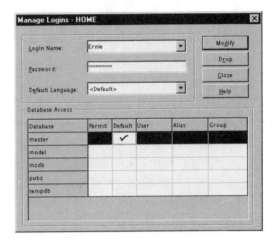

If you want to create another login account at this time, you can click on the arrow next to the Login Name field and select New Login from the drop-down list. The entries will be cleared, and you can add another login name and password. Just be sure to click on the Add button after entering new login information in the dialog box. If you select New Login from the list box without first clicking on Add, the information that you entered will be discarded without warning

You can continue this process until all of the logins have been added. In this example, we will add only one new login account, so we will close the Manage Logins dialog box now.

4. Click on the Close button to close the dialog box.

5. Expand the Logins folder in the Server Manager window and verify that the login account for Ernie has been added.

Using Transact-SQL to Create Logins

The system stored procedure used to create logins is `sp_addlogin`. Here is the syntax (the parameters within square brackets are optional):

```
sp_addlogin login_id [, passwd [, defdb [, deflanguage]]]
```

These parameters are used as follows:

login_id   The login name that you wish to add to the server. This is the only required parameter.

passwd   The password that you wish to assign to the login. If this parameter is not provided, the password will be null.

defdb   The default database of the login. The default database is the database that a login will be using immediately after authentication to the server. This should be the most common database used by that login. If this parameter is not provided, this value defaults to the Master database.

deflanguage   This allows a login to be associated with a specific language if more than one language is installed on the server. If this parameter is not provided, this value defaults to the default language of the server, typically US_English. (This parameter corresponds to the Default Language field in SQL Enterprise Manager's Manage Logons dialog box.) Most servers have only one language installed.

Exercise 6.2 takes you through the steps of adding a login account using Transact-SQL.

EXERCISE 6.2

Creating a Login Account Using Transact-SQL

1. Start the ISQL/W utility.

2. For our example, we will add a login account for Bert, specifying only the login ID and password. Enter and execute the following statements:

```
USE master
Exec sp_addlogin 'Bert', 'bert'
Go
```

EXERCISE 6.2 (CONTINUED FROM PREVIOUS PAGE)

3. Close ISQL/W.

4. In the Server Manager window in SQL Enterprise Manager, right-click on the Logins folder and select Refresh from the context menu. You should now see Bert in the login list.

For this exercise, you can start ISQL/W from within SQL Enterprise Manager or as a stand-alone utility. See Chapter 4 for details on how to work with ISQL/W.

Modifying and Deleting Login Accounts

After you've created a login account, you can modify its password, default database, and default language. The only attribute that can't be modified later is the login name. In general, the most common attribute that you will modify is the login account password. Any user with a login account can change his or her own password, but only the SA can change the password of another login account.

If you want to disallow someone's access to SQL Server, you will need to delete that person's login account from the login list. Unlike Windows NT, SQL Server has no mechanism for simply disabling a login account. The login account must be deleted completely if the individual is to be prohibited from accessing the server. Only the SA has the authority to delete login accounts from the server.

You will not be allowed to delete a login account that owns a database or any objects inside a database.

You can modify and delete login accounts from SQL Enterprise Manager or by using the Transact-SQL language, as explained in the following sections.

Using SQL Enterprise Manager to Modify and Delete Logins

In SQL Enterprise Manager, you can modify an existing login account at any time by returning to the Manage Logins dialog box. Select Manage ➤ Logins from the SQL Enterprise Manager menu. From the Login Name drop-down list box, choose the login account that you wish to modify. Make the necessary changes in the appropriate text boxes, and then click on the Modify button.

The simplest way to delete a login account is to select the login from the login list in the Server Manager window and press the Delete key. You will then be asked to confirm the deletion. After this confirmation, the login will be removed from the syslogins table.

Using Transact-SQL to Modify and Delete Logins

Using Transact-SQL to modify login accounts is more complex than using SQL Enterprise Manager's Manage Logins dialog box. In the dialog box, you can make all of your changes in one place. With the Transact-SQL language, there is a different stored procedure for every attribute of the login that you wish to change: `sp_password`, `sp_defaultdb`, and `sp_defaultlanguage`.

Changing a Password   To change the password associated with a login, use `sp_password`. Here is the syntax of this procedure:

```
sp_password old, new [, login_id]
```

This stored procedure requires the user to enter the old password for verification before the new password is entered. The password change will always affect the currently logged-in user. The only exception is the SA user, who can use the *login_id* optional parameter to change a password for another user. The steps in Exercise 6.3 demonstrate how the SA can change the password for a user account.

EXERCISE 6.3

Changing a Password Using Transact-SQL

1. Start the ISQL/W utility.

2. For our example, we will add a new login account and then change the password for that account. Add a new user named Elmo by entering and executing the following statements:

```
USE master
EXEC sp_addlogin 'Elmo'
Go
```

---

3. Verify the addition by executing the following query:

```
USE master
SELECT * FROM syslogins
GO
```

4. Scroll to the right of the results. You will see a login named Elmo with a null password.

5. Change the password for the Elmo user by executing the following statements:

```
USE master
EXEC sp_password null, 'Elmo', 'Elmo'
GO
```

6. Verify this change by executing the following query and looking at the results. You should see an encrypted password for Elmo.

```
USE master
SELECT * FROM syslogins
GO
```

7. Close ISQL/W.

Changing a Default Database   To change the default database associated with a login, use the stored procedure sp_defaultdb. Here is its syntax:

```
sp_defaultdb login_id, defdb
```

For example, if you wish to set the Pubs database as the default database for the Elmo login account, execute the following statements:

```
USE master

EXEC sp_defaultdb Elmo, pubs

Go
```

Changing a Default Language You can change the default language only if there are multiple languages installed on the server and a user wishes to see system messages and dialog boxes in a language other than the system default. In most cases, there will be only one language installed on the server, and that language is the default.

Installing multiple languages on the server makes it possible for the server to display all system messages and dialog boxes in that language. The multiple languages installed do not affect the character set and sort order.

You can change the default language for a user by using the stored procedure sp_defaultlanguage. Here is its syntax:

```
sp_defaultlanguage login_id [, language]
```

For example, if you want to change the default language for Ernie to French and the French language options are installed on the server, you can execute the following statements:

```
USE master

EXEC sp_defaultlanguage Ernie, French

GO
```

Of course, this won't work on your server unless you actually do have the French language options installed on it.

Dropping a Login Account You can delete (or drop) a login account from the server by using the sp_droplogin stored procedure. The syntax is as follows:

```
sp_droplogin login_id
```

This action will remove the login from the syslogins system table. If the login has the username of DBO in any database or owns an object in any database, this procedure will fail. The steps in Exercise 6.4 show how to drop a login account from the server.

EXERCISE 6.4

Dropping a Login Using Transact-SQL

1. Start the ISQL/W utility.

2. Enter and execute the following query to return a list of current logins:

   ```
   USE master
   SELECT name FROM syslogins
   GO
   ```

3. Verify that the login account that you want to delete appears in this list. For this example, we will drop the Bert login account by executing the following statements:

   ```
   USE master
   EXEC sp_droplogin Bert
   GO
   ```

4. Verify that the login was dropped by executing the query in step 2 again. Bert should no longer be in the list.

5. Close ISQL/W.

Creating and Deleting Groups

When you're planning database access, it is likely that you will want to include groups in your strategy. When you assign permissions to a group, every member of that group will have the permissions that you specify unless you override group permissions at the user level. This can make the process of managing permissions much easier. Here, we will cover the process of creating groups. In the next chapter, we will describe how to assign permissions to the groups you have created.

We will first discuss some considerations that you should address when planning groups. Then we will look at the physical process of creating and deleting groups with both SQL Enterprise Manager and Transact-SQL.

You may be wondering why we chose to discuss groups before discussing the topic of users. After all, a group is nothing more than a security context inside of which you place your users. Most books take the approach of discussing users before groups; however, in actual implementation, you usually create groups before you create users—sometimes even before creating login accounts. For this reason, we have chosen to break with tradition and follow a natural progression. We will discuss creating groups before going into the details of creating user accounts.

Planning Groups

Most network operating systems allow you to create multiple groups, give these groups specific permissions, and then associate a user with as many groups as necessary to ensure that the proper permissions are maintained for that user. In SQL Server, the concept is the same—by adding groups, permissions are assigned at the group level rather than at the user level. However, as mentioned earlier in the chapter, there is one major difference: SQL Server allows a user to be a member of only one other group besides Public. Although this may appear to be a serious restriction, in practice, it merely changes the way that you plan for group access to your database.

Rather than creating groups by functional area, you should create SQL Server groups with common data-access needs in mind. For example, the secretaries and engineers in your company may have completely different functional responsibilities, but their data-access needs might be very similar. They may both select from the same tables, insert the same types of data, and modify the same records. If this is the case, a group could be created for secretaries and engineers.

Of course, all of this planning should occur at the pad-and-pencil stage, long before you start adding groups to the database. If you add groups "on the fly" without proper planning, the organization of your group structure will very quickly become far too complex and difficult to maintain.

Viewing the Group List

Unlike login accounts, which are server-level in scope, groups are local to every individual database and are stored in the sysusers system table of each database. To see the list of groups currently stored in any database, expand that database in the Server Manager window, as shown in Figure 6.3.

F I G U R E 6.3

Viewing groups in the
SybexTestDB database

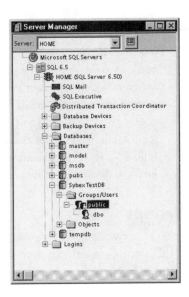

As you can see in Figure 6.3, there is only one group stored in the Sybex-
TestDB database: the Public group. The Public group is created automatically
when the database is created, and every user is automatically a part of the
Public group. Also, as you see in the figure, there is only one user in this database: DBO. This DBO user is currently a member of the Public group and no
other group.

Using SQL Enterprise Manager to Create and Delete Groups

Since groups are database-specific, you must first select the appropriate database in the Server Manager window before you start the process of group creation. Otherwise, you may accidentally create groups in a database other than
the one that you intended.

To create a group with SQL Enterprise Manager, you simply access the
Manage Group dialog box, choose the New Group option, and enter the
name for the group. The steps in Exercise 6.5 take you through the process
of creating groups with SQL Enterprise Manager.

The remaining exercises in this chapter assume that you have done the exercises in Chapter 5. If this is not the case, you will need to complete those
exercises before you continue.

EXERCISE 6.5

Creating a Group with SQL Enterprise Manager

1. In the Server Manager window of SQL Enterprise Manager, open the Databases folder and select SybexTestDB from the list of databases.

2. Select Manage ➢ Groups to display the Manage Groups dialog box. You should see the DBO user in the lower-left list box in this dialog box.

3. Open the Group drop-down list. You will see the Public group and an option for New Group.

4. Select New Group from the list. In the Group text box, enter the group name. For our example, enter **Monsters**.

5. Click on the Add button. Your new group is added, as shown below.

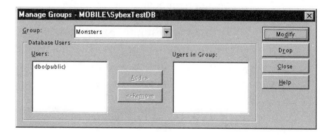

6. Click on Close to close the Manage Groups dialog box. In the Server Manager window, you should now see the Monsters group added to the list of groups for the SybexTestDB database. This group does not yet have any members.

After you create a group, you cannot make any modifications to it. If you wish to change a group name, you must delete the group and then re-create it.

To delete a group by using SQL Enterprise Manager, select the group from the list of groups in the appropriate database in the Server Manager window and press the Delete key. You will be prompted to confirm the deletion of this group.

NOTE

Deleting a group by using SQL Enterprise Manager does not drop any of the users associated with that group. All users are members of the Public group, which cannot be deleted. When you delete a group that you created, you will still see any users that were members of that group in the list of users associated with the Public group.

Using Transact-SQL to Create and Drop Groups

As explained earlier, there are no options associated with a group. It is really nothing more than a security shell. This makes the list of stored procedures for working with groups a short one: sp_addgroup and sp_dropgroup.

You can create groups with the sp_addgroup stored procedure. Here is its syntax:

sp_addgroup *groupname*

Before executing the stored procedure, it is imperative that you use the appropriate database first (such as with the statement USE sybextestdb), or else you may add the group to the wrong database. The steps in Exercise 6.6 take you through the process of creating a group using Transact-SQL.

EXERCISE 6.6

Creating a Group Using Transact-SQL

1. Start the ISQL/W utility.

2. To verify the current group list, enter and execute the following statements:

   USE sybextestdb
   EXEC sp_helpgroup
   GO

3. You should see the Monsters group (created in Exercise 6.5) and the Public group in the output. For this example, add a new group called NonMonsters by executing the following statements:

   USE sybextestdb
   EXEC sp_addgroup NonMonsters
   GO

EXERCISE 6.6 (CONTINUED FROM PREVIOUS PAGE)

4. Verify the addition of the group by executing the statements in step 2 again. You should now see NonMonsters in the list of groups.

5. Close ISQL/W.

To delete a group, use the stored procedure sp_dropgroup. Here is its syntax:

```
sp_dropgroup groupname
```

Unlike when you use SQL Enterprise Manager, you cannot drop a group with Transact-SQL unless the group is empty. If the group has members, the stored procedure will fail. To remove members from a group, you can delete the user or transfer the user to another group (such as Public). Working with user accounts is discussed in the next section.

Creating and Managing Users

The user is the basic component in database security. A login account simply allows or denies access to the server itself; a username is the login's passport into a database. Without the username, the login would have no entry into the database and no security context for the objects inside the database.

In the following sections, we will look at the process of adding, managing, and deleting users from a database. As with the other tasks covered in this chapter, you can work with users either through SQL Enterprise Manager or by using Transact-SQL. We will look at both approaches.

Because the users are database-level objects, the permissions to work with users are granted to the DBO user. Since the SA login will always have an implied alias as DBO, this login also has full permissions to work with users.

Viewing User Information

Creating a user adds an entry into the sysusers system table for a login ID. This allows that login to access the resources in the database. The sysusers table is held locally in every database and provides some critical information about how the user is allowed to interact with database resources. Figure 6.4 shows the contents of the sysusers table for the SybexTestDB database.

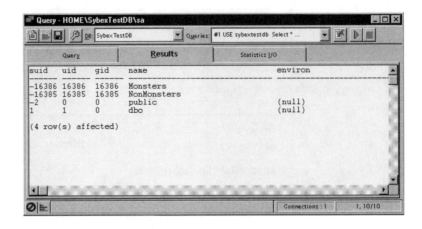

As you can see in Figure 6.4, the sysusers table includes three ID values; each specifies specific attributes of the user:

suid   This is the server user ID or the numerical ID associated with the login. This value "maps" a login to a username in the database.

uid   This is the user ID value, which is the numerical value representing this user within the database. When permissions are set, they make reference to the uid value.

gid   This is the group ID value, which is actually the uid of the group to which this member belongs. Notice that for the groups themselves, the gid and the uid are the same value.

The name is listed in the table strictly for your convenience so that you have a human-readable value that refers to the uid used by the system internally. The environ column in the table is reserved by the system, and it is currently not being used in the example shown in Figure 6.4.

Microsoft ✓ ***Exam Objective***   **Add a database user.**

When you create a user, all of this information is written to a record in the sysusers table. You simply provide a username and the login account to which you wish this user to map. You can also specify a group for the user when you create the user. The uid will be inserted automatically by the system.

Using SQL Enterprise Manager to Create Users

There are two ways to create users with SQL Enterprise Manager: through the Manage Users dialog box or through the Manage Logins dialog box.

Using the Manage Logins dialog box offers two primary advantages:

- You can work with numerous database mappings from the same dialog box.

- You can create logins and usernames from the same dialog box.

Both methods are described in the following sections.

Using the Manage Users Dialog Box to Create a User

Because the username is local to the database, you must first select the appropriate database in the Server Manager window before accessing the Manage Users dialog box.

Follow the steps in Exercise 6.7 to create a user through the Manage Users dialog box. In this example, we will add the username Elmo. This user is mapped to the login Elmo and is a member of the Monsters group.

In our example, the username is the same as the login. Although this is not a requirement, a smart administrator will do this whenever possible because it makes the database easier to maintain. The DBO user is a good example of a username that is different from the login.

EXERCISE 6.7

Creating a User with SQL Enterprise Manager's Manage Users Dialog Box

1. In the Server Manager window of SQL Enterprise Manager, select the SybexTestDB database.

2. Select Manage ➢ Users to display the Manage Users dialog box.

3. Enter **Elmo** in the User Name text box, select Elmo from the Login drop-down list, and select Monsters from the Group drop-down list. Your dialog box should look like the one below.

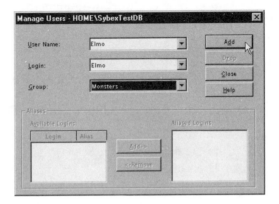

4. Click on the Add button.

5. Click on Close to close the Manage Users dialog box.

6. In the Server Manager window, drill down to the groups in the Sybex-TestDB database. You should now see Elmo in the Monsters group.

Using the Manage Logins Dialog Box to Create a User

As mentioned earlier, the Manage Logins dialog box can be an extremely logical place to work with users, because you can perform several tasks from this dialog box.

We worked with this dialog box earlier in the chapter, when we created logins with the SQL Enterprise Manager. In that section (Exercise 6.1), we ignored the lower portion of this dialog box. Now you will see how you can use that area to add a username. The steps in Exercise 6.8 take you through the Manage Logins dialog box once again. In this example, we will create a login for Cookie and add a username to a database based on that login.

EXERCISE 6.8

Creating a User with SQL Enterprise Manager's Manage Logins Dialog Box

1. In SQL Enterprise Manager, select Manage ➤ Logins to display the Manage Logins dialog box.

2. In the Login Name text box, enter the name **Cookie**, and in the Password text box, enter the password **cookie**.

3. We'll add this user to the Monsters group in the SybexTestDB database. In the lower section of the dialog box, click on the Permit box for the SybexTestDB database.

4. Click in the Group box of the SybexTestDB database to activate the drop-down list. Select the Monsters group from the list. The dialog box should look like the one shown below.

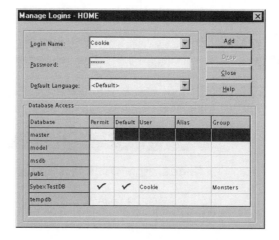

5. Click on the Add button to create the login and the database user.

6. Confirm the password, and then click on Close to close the dialog box.

7. Verify that the login was created by expanding the Logins folder in the Server Manager window.

8. Verify that the user has been created by viewing the Monsters group of the SybexTestDB database.

Using Transact-SQL to Create Users

You can add users to databases with the stored procedure sp_adduser. This stored procedure uses the following syntax:

```
sp_adduser login_id [, username [, groupname]]
```

These parameters are used as follows:

login_id   The login ID being mapped to this user. This is the only required parameter.

username   The name with which you will associate the mapped login in this database. If this parameter is not provided, the value will default to the same value provided for the *login_ID* parameter.

groupname   This parameter can be use to immediately assign the user to a group. If this parameter is not provided, the user will remain a member of the Public group but not be associated with any user-defined group.

Be sure to add logins before attempting to add users with sp_adduser. The procedure will not allow you to add a login and a user at the same time.

Follow the steps in Exercise 6.9 to add a user with Transact-SQL statements.

EXERCISE 6.9

Creating a User with Transact-SQL

1. Start the ISQL/W utility.

2. To verify current users, enter and execute the following code:

   ```
   USE sybextestdb
   EXEC sp_helpuser
   GO
   ```

3. In this example, we will create a user in the SybexTestDB database for the Ernie login and assign that user to the Monsters group. Enter and execute the following statements:

   ```
   USE sybextestdb
   EXEC sp_adduser Ernie, Ernie, Monsters
   GO
   ```

EXERCISE 6.9 (CONTINUED FROM PREVIOUS PAGE)

4. Verify that the Ernie username has been added correctly by executing the statements in step 2 again.

5. Close ISQL/W.

Modifying Group Membership

As the jobs or data-access needs of your users change, you may find it necessary to change their group associations. You can add or delete (drop) group members by using either SQL Enterprise Manager or Transact-SQL.

Microsoft ✓ *Exam Objective*   **Add and drop users for a group.**

When you consider a user's movement between groups, keep in mind that a user is always a member of the Public group, whether or not that user is also a member of a user-defined group.

Using SQL Enterprise Manager to Modify Group Membership

To reassign a user to another group through SQL Enterprise Manager, you use the Manage Logins dialog box (choose Manage ➤ Logins from the menu). Choose a login from the Login Name drop-down list and activate the Group box for whichever database you wish to modify group membership. Figure 6.5 shows this process. After you're finished reassigning the user to another group, click on the Modify button.

 WARNING Be sure to click on the Modify button after you have reset the options for each login. If you close the dialog box or continue to another login without clicking on the Modify button, your changes will be discarded without warning.

If you wish to drop a user from a group without reassigning that user to another group, make the user part of the Public group. As you've learned, all users are always members of the Public group. When you explicitly assign a user to the Public group, you revoke all group membership other than Public.

FIGURE 6.5

Modifying groups with the
Manage Logins dialog box

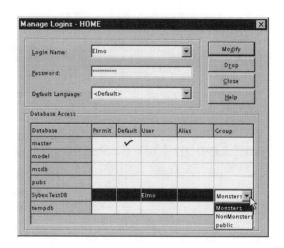

FIGURE 6.5

Modifying groups with the
Manage Logins dialog box

Using Transact-SQL to Modify Group Membership

To change group membership with Transact-SQL, you use the *sp_changegroup* stored procedure. Here is its syntax:

sp_changegroup groupname, username

In this procedure, the *groupname* parameter represents the group to which you wish to assign membership for that user. If the Public group is referenced in this parameter, any group membership other than public is revoked from that user.

Follow the steps in Exercise 6.10 to modify group membership for the Ernie user account. Ernie is currently a member of the Monsters group. Of course, we know that Ernie is not a monster, so his group membership must be modified.

EXERCISE 6.10

Modifying Group Membership Using Transact-SQL

1. Start the ISQL/W utility.

2. To verify current group membership for the Ernie account, enter and execute the following statements:

   USE **sybextestdb**

   EXEC **sp_helpuser Ernie**

   GO

EXERCISE 6.10 (CONTINUED FROM PREVIOUS PAGE)

3. Ernie should currently be a member of the Monsters group (accomplished in Exercise 6.9). To change Ernie's membership to the NonMonsters group, enter and execute the following statements:

```
USE sybextestdb
EXEC sp_changegroup NonMonsters, Ernie
GO
```

4. To verify that the change of group has taken place, execute the statements in step 2 again. Ernie should now be a member of the NonMonsters group.

5. Close ISQL/W.

Before you can drop a group using sp_dropgroup, the group must be empty (without any members). To remove members from a group, execute the sp_changegroup procedure for every user in the group, transferring their membership to another user-defined group or to Public. After this is done, you can drop the group.

Dropping Usernames from Databases

If a user with a login account no longer needs to access the resources for a particular database, you will want to remove that person's username from the database. You can do this with SQL Enterprise Manager or Transact-SQL.

Users can be dropped only if they own no objects inside of the database. If a user owns an object inside the database, the object must be deleted before the user can be dropped from that database. We'll discuss object ownership in Chapter 7.

Using SQL Enterprise Manager to Drop Users

There are several ways to drop users from a database with SQL Enterprise Manager:

- The easiest method is simply to select the username in the Groups/Users folder of the database in the Server Manager window and press the Delete key. You will be asked to confirm this deletion.

- You can use the Manage Users dialog box. Select Manage ➤ Users, choose the username from the drop-down list, and click on the Drop button.

- You can use the Manage Logins dialog box. Select Manage ➤ Logins, and then remove the checkmark in the Permit column of the database from which you wish to remove the username. This will allow you to remove or restructure all of the usernames for that login account if desired. After you're finished making changes, click on the Modify button to save the changes.

All three of these methods have the same effect. Your choice of which to use depends on which interface you prefer for working with the users. Using the Manage Logins dialog box is often easier if you need to restructure a number of options for a single login account.

Using Transact-SQL to Drop Users

You can remove users from a database by using the sp_dropuser stored procedure. Here is its syntax:

```
sp_dropuser username
```

For example, if the DBO of the SybexTestDB database wished to drop the Ernie user from the database, the following statements would be executed:

```
USE sybextestdb

EXEC sp_dropuser Ernie

GO
```

Before you remove a user from a database, make sure that the correct database is being used. Otherwise, you might drop a user with the same name from a database that he or she still needs to access.

Transferring Database Ownership

Another modification you may need to make is to transfer ownership of a database from one login account to another login account. A typical example is the SA login. Only the SA has permission to create databases. The SA login can transfer this permission to another user, but it is strongly recommended that this not be done. Instead, the SA can create the needed databases and subsequently transfer the ownership of these databases to another login account.

As you will remember, the username for the SA login is DBO in every database that the SA login creates. When transferring ownership of a database to another user, SA literally assigns the username of DBO in that database to another login account. The SA login will retain an implied alias as DBO in that database, so SA does not need to actually give up any control over the database.

A login can have only one username or one alias in a database. If you wish to transfer ownership of a database to a login who already has a username or alias in that database, you must first drop the username or the alias.

Unlike most of the other tasks discussed in this chapter, changing ownership of a database can be done only through Transact-SQL. There is no equivalent functionality in SQL Enterprise Manager.

Transferring ownership of a database is accomplished with the stored procedure sp_changedbowner. Here is its syntax:

```
sp_changedbowner login_id [, true]
```

You must be using the database for which you are transferring ownership before executing the stored procedure. The login_id parameter represents the login name that will receive ownership of the database. An optional flag is provided to allow aliases and their permissions to be transferred to the new owner. If the true flag is used, all logins currently aliased as DBO will retain their aliases and permissions in the database after the transfer of ownership. If this flag is not used, all aliases to DBO in the database will be dropped after the change in ownership.

The steps in Exercise 6.11 take you through the process of transferring ownership of a database to a user who already has a username in the database. In the exercise, you will first drop the username and then transfer database ownership.

EXERCISE 6.11

Transferring Database Ownership

1. Start the ISQL/W utility.

2. Verify current ownership of the database be entering and executing the following statements. The results of this query should show the login ID as the DBO user in the database.

   ```
   USE sybextestdb
   EXEC sp_helpuser DBO
   GO
   ```

3. We will assign ownership of this database to the Elmo login. The Elmo login already has a username in this database. Drop this username by executing the following statements:

```
USE sybextestdb
EXEC sp_dropuser Elmo
GO
```

4. Transfer ownership of the database to the Elmo login by executing the following statements:

```
USE sybextestdb
EXEC sp_changedbowner Elmo, true
GO
```

5. Verify that ownership has been transferred by executing the statements in step 2 again. This time, you should see that the Elmo login has been associated with the DBO username.

6. Close ISQL/W.

Working with Aliases

When you want a group of logins to share functional responsibility in a database, you have the option of using aliases. An aliased user has exactly the same rights and authorities as the user whose username is used as the alias.

For example, suppose that you have a group of users that you wish to act as DBO users. They each need to have the authority to create and drop objects, back up and restore databases, and perform other administrative tasks. Some of these permissions can be transferred readily, but others, such as the permission to restore databases and transaction logs, must stay with the DBO. Certain permissions cannot be transferred to other users. There are additional problems with the DBO giving extensive permissions to users in a database. These will be discussed in more detail in Chapter 7.

The advantage of using an alias in this situation is that no permissions actually need to be transferred. When a login that is aliased as DBO accesses the database, the database treats that user as if he or she were the actual DBO user. There are no limits placed on the functional ability of that user. In addition, any actions that the user takes will be treated as if they were performed by the DBO. If the aliased user creates a table in the database, the owner of the table will be DBO.

Aliases, like usernames, are local to the database. They are stored in the sysalternates system table. This system table is checked when a login attempts to access a database and an entry is not found for that login in the sysusers system table.

Aliases must always refer to a username that already exists in the database. If you have a group of logins that you wish to be aliases to a user account, you must create the user account first. One of the logins will be referenced as the actual user; the remainder can be aliased to that username.

Creating an alias is simply the process of mapping a login account to an already existing user account. This allows the login to access the database as the user to which the alias refers. You can create aliases through SQL Enterprise Manager or with Transact-SQL.

Using SQL Enterprise Manager to Create Aliases

The most efficient way to create an alias for a user account using SQL Enterprise Manager is through the Manage Logins dialog box. Exercise 6.12 takes you through the steps.

EXERCISE 6.12

Creating an Alias with SQL Enterprise Manager's Manage Logins Dialog Box

1. In SQL Enterprise Manager, select Manage ➢ Logins to display the Manage Logins dialog box.

2. Choose the login from the Login Name drop-down list and verify that the login has been permitted into the database that you wish to modify. For this example, choose the Ernie login and verify that a checkmark appears in the Permit column for the Pubs database.

3. Select the Alias column for that database. You will be presented with a list of valid users. Choose the user for which you are creating the alias. For this example, choose the DBO user, as shown below. You may need to clear the contents of the User cell before you are allowed to set an alias.

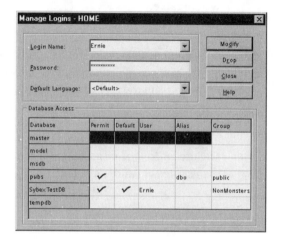

4. Click on the Modify button to save the change.

5. Click on Close to close the Manage Logins dialog box.

Using Transact-SQL to Create Aliases

You can use the sp_addalias stored procedure to add aliases for a database. The syntax for this procedure uses the login name and the aliased username, as follows:

```
sp_addalias login_id, username
```

For example, to add an alias as DBO for the Ernie login in the Pubs database, use the following statements:

```
USE pubs

EXEC sp_addalias Ernie, DBO

GO
```

When adding aliases using Transact-SQL, remember that a login can have either a username or an alias, but not both. If the login that you wish to map with an alias already has a username in the database, you must drop the username for that login before the alias can be created.

Using a Guest User Account

If you wish to allow any user who can access the server to have limited access to your database, you can create a guest user account. You can configure this account with very restrictive permissions to allow all server logins some basic access into a database.

To add a guest user, execute the sp_adduser stored procedure, as follows:

```
EXEC sp_adduser guest
```

If you remember from our earlier discussion, when this stored procedure is executed with a single parameter of a login ID, that login ID is mapped to a username of the same name. This would imply that for the statement above to execute properly, there would need to be a login of guest and that login would be mapped to the guest username in the database. However, SQL Server treats the guest username as a special situation. When adding a guest username to a database, no login mapping is explicitly created.

Figure 6.6 shows the results of executing a sp_helpuser query on the guest account in the Pubs database. As you can see in this listing, no login mapping has been created for the guest account.

FIGURE 6.6

The results of a query on the guest user in the Pubs database

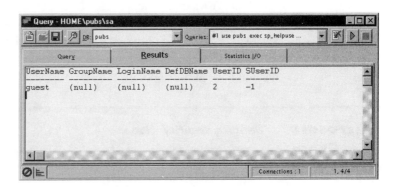

The guest user was created automatically by the SQL Server installation program when the Pubs, Tempdb, Msdb, and Master system databases were installed. (Note that you cannot remove the guest user from the Master database.) Absent from this list is the Model database. Since the Model database is the template for every new user database, the guest user has not been added to this database, giving you the option of adding a guest user to your databases at your own discretion. If you wish your database to support guest access, you must create the guest user after you create the database. This prevents a potential security hole of unknowingly having guest access to a database.

Using SQL Server Security Modes

Up to this point, we have discussed how SQL Server authenticates users to the server independently of the Windows NT environment. This approach is called *standard security*. When a user logs in to a Windows NT server, that user is still required to authenticate inside SQL Server if he or she wishes to access SQL Server resources. This requires two logins.

Another security approach that can be used is called *integrated security*. Integrated security is also sometimes called *trusted security*. This is because, in the integrated security mode, SQL Server trusts the authentication of logins to Windows NT, thus eliminating the need for multiple logins. The connections that are made to SQL Server by using Windows NT account information for authentication are called *trusted connections*.

However, some clients cannot make trusted connections to a SQL Server machine. A Macintosh client, for example, can connect to a Windows NT server but is not able to establish a trusted connection to SQL Server. Other clients may be using network libraries other than named pipes and multiprotocol. For these situations, and any other where a trusted connection is not desired, SQL Server supports *mixed security*.

Microsoft ✓ ***Exam*** ***Objective*** | **Set up a security mode.**

In the following sections, we will discuss the three security modes used by SQL Server: standard, integrated, and mixed. You will learn when it makes sense to use a particular mode and how to implement each type of security.

The security modes discussed in this section relate only to server access. Only the behavior of the first gatekeeper, the SQL Server machine, can be modified by using these security modes.

Implementing Standard Security

When SQL Server is installed, it is initially configured for standard security. In the standard security mode, SQL Server is responsible for authenticating all users to the server without any assistance from the operating system. The fact that a user is able to authenticate to the Windows NT server is irrelevant from the perspective of SQL Server. When a user attempts to access SQL Server, that user is forced to provide a SQL Server login and password to get past the first gatekeeper.

Everything that we have discussed so far in this chapter with regard to login accounts has been based on the assumption that you are using a standard security implementation. We have covered the two basic steps for implementing the standard security mode:

■ Create login IDs for every user who should have access to SQL Server.

■ Create usernames for these login IDs in the database to which access is desired.

Verifying Your Security Mode

You can verify the current security mode in use by checking the Security Options dialog box in SQL Enterprise Manager. Follow the steps in Exercise 6.13 to check that your server is currently running under standard security.

The security mode option is not dynamic. If you make any changes to the security mode, you must stop and restart the MSSQLServer service for the changes to take effect.

EXERCISE 6.13

Verifying the Current Security Mode

1. In SQL Enterprise Manager, select Server ➤ SQL Server ➤ Configure to display the Server Configuration/Options dialog box.

2. Click on the Security Options tab.

3. In the Login Security Mode section of the dialog box, you will see three option buttons, one for each of the three security modes. Verify that the Standard option button is selected, as shown below. If it is not selected, make that choice now.

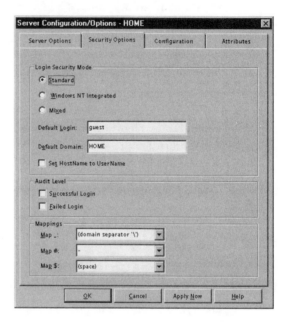

4. Click on the OK button to close the Server Configuration/Options dialog box.

Testing Standard Security

You can test standard security by attempting to log in under a login name that has not been added to the server. The steps in Exercise 6.14 will take you through the process of testing standard security on the server.

EXERCISE 6.14

Testing Standard Security

1. Start the ISQL/W utility.

2. Choose File ➤ Connect to display the Connect Server dialog box.

3. Check that the Login Information option in the Connect Server dialog box is set to Use Standard Security.

4. Enter the login ID of **Ernie** and a password of **ernie**. The dialog box should look like the one shown below.

5. Click on Connect. Ernie has just been authenticated by SQL Server. Notice that the title bar of the window indicates that you have authenticated as the Ernie login.

6. Choose File ➤ Disconnect to drop the connection.

7. Select File ➤ Connect again. This time, enter a login ID of **Grover**, leave the password null, and click on Connect.

8. The login attempt will fail. Click on the OK button on the failure message box, and then click on Cancel in the Connect Server dialog box.

9. Close ISQL/W.

In this exercise, you saw that you were able to connect to SQL Server only after you provided a valid login ID and password. This is the case no matter what your Windows NT Server login may be. You could be logged in to Windows NT as Administrator, and you still would not be able to connect to SQL Server without providing a valid SQL Server login ID and password.

Using Trusted Connections with Standard Security

Although integrated security will not support standard connections, standard security will support trusted connections if a trusted connection is requested from the client. It is actually very common for system processes and some ODBC (Open Database Connectivity) applications to request trusted connections even when the security mode is set to standard. The steps in Exercise 6.15 demonstrate how to use trusted connections with the standard security mode.

EXERCISE 6.15

Using a Trusted Connection with Standard Security

1. Verify that you are logged in to Windows NT as Administrator. If this is not the case, log out of Windows NT and log back in as Administrator.

2. Start ISQL/W and choose File ➤ Connect.

3. In the Connect Server dialog box, set the Login Information option to Use Trusted Connection.

4. Click on the Connect button. You should be authenticated to SQL Server. If you look in the title bar of the Query window, you should see that you are logged in to SQL Server as SA.

5. Close ISQL/W.

In Exercise 6.15, you requested a trusted connection to SQL Server even though the security mode was set to standard security. This is why you were not required to enter any authentication information. You connected to the SQL Server as SA because you were logged in to Windows NT as Administrator. Windows NT Administrators have default mappings to SA for trusted connections.

Implementing Integrated Security

With the integrated security mode, SQL Server will trust the Windows NT Server authentication as valid and either connect or deny connection to SQL Server based on the Windows NT identification of the user.

Microsoft Exam Objective

Identify the impact on SQL Server of integrated security.

You can use a strict integrated security model, in which only trusted connections are allowed. Trusted connections can be made to SQL Server from the following clients:

- Windows NT Server or Workstation clients

- Windows for Workgroups clients

- Windows 95 clients

- Microsoft LAN Manager clients running Microsoft Windows or MS-DOS

- Windows 3.1 clients on Novell NetWare systems

> **WARNING**
>
> Trusted connections are allowed on only named pipes or multi-protocol sessions. No other SQL Server Net-Library may be used. Consider this fact when planning your client access and installing Net-Library components.

When SQL Server gets a server authentication request while running under integrated security, one of three possible connections can be made:

Standard User   If SQL Server has a valid mapping of the Windows NT user account to a SQL Server login account, then that user is authenticated under the mapped ID. The mapping is done with a utility called SQL Security Manager.

SA User   If no valid mapping exists to a SQL Server user, the Windows NT login is checked to see if it has Windows NT Administrator authority or has been mapped to SQL Server SA authority. If this is the case, the Windows NT user will be authenticated as SA. This mapping is also done with SQL Security Manager.

Guest   If you wish, you can also add a guest login to the server to allow authentication for individuals who do not meet either of the criteria above. The name of this login account can be specified in the Security Options tab of the Server Configuration/Options dialog box.

Integrated security provides access to the server only. If you want the users to have access to database resources, you must add their usernames in each database. The login ID that you use for the username mapping is the same as the user's Windows NT login ID.

There are many benefits of using Windows NT integrated security. The first is that you are not required to authenticate to SQL Server whenever you wish to make a connection. This can eliminate much duplicated effort and frustration on the part of your users.

Another advantage of integrated security is that SQL Server security can be managed from the operating system level. This means that you may not need two administrators, both the network administrator and the database administrator, to manage login security. The database administrator may be freed for other tasks.

Although there are advantages, there are also disadvantages and barriers to using integrated security. The single most prohibitive barrier is that integrated security is allowed on only named pipes and multi-protocol connections. If you are using any other network libraries, you will not be able to support integrated security.

Another disadvantage is that unless the database administrator also has full administrative authority on the network, only the network administrator will be able to secure database access.

Changing to Integrated Security Mode

Implementing integrated security requires you to change the security mode of SQL Server, add some mappings from the Windows NT groups, and add users to SQL Server groups. Here are the four main steps involved in changing to integrated security:

- Organize your Windows NT accounts. It is much easier to map Windows NT groups to SQL Server accounts than to deal with individual NT user accounts. You might consider creating two groups: one for NT users who will receive SA authority and another for NT users who will access SQL Server as standard users.

- Map Windows NT groups and users to SQL Server. Using the Security Manager utility, you can give Windows NT groups and users mappings to SQL Server. When you map a user who will connect to SQL Server with standard user authority, this process creates the SQL Server login ID in the server for you.

- Reset the SQL Server security mode.   In the Security Options dialog box, change the option selection from standard to integrated security. This will disallow any non-trusted connections.

- Stop and restart SQL Server.   Since the change in security mode is not dynamic, the MSSQLServer service must be restarted for the change to take effect.

The steps in Exercise 6.16 take you through the process of implementing integrated security.

EXERCISE 6.16

Implementing Integrated Security

1. Create two new Windows NT groups using the User Manager for Domains tool. Name these groups **SQLUsers** and **SQLAdmins**.

2. Create two new Windows NT user accounts using the User Manager for Domains tool. For this example, give the account names as **Grover** and **Oscar**. Leave the passwords null. Clear the User Must Change Password at Next Logon checkbox. Select the Password Never Expires checkbox. (These options are for ease of demonstration; your own password options may be different.)

3. Assign Grover to the SQLAdmins group and Oscar to the SQLUsers group.

4. Open SQL Security Manager by selecting Start ➤ Programs ➤ Microsoft SQL Server 6.5 ➤ SQL Security Manager.

5. Enter your server name and log in as SA.

6. Select View ➤ Sa Privilege. You should see that the Administrators group has been granted SA authority.

7. Select Security ➤ Grant New, select SQLAdmins from the list of groups, and click on Grant. Click on OK in the message box acknowledging the action, and then click on Done. You have just granted SA authority to the SQLAdmins group.

8. Select View ➤ User Privilege. No Windows NT users or groups currently have user privileges.

EXERCISE 6.16 (CONTINUED FROM PREVIOUS PAGE)

9. Select Security ➢ Grant New, and then select SQLUsers from the list. Notice that option for adding login IDs for the members of the group is checked. Leave this option selected. The second checkbox gives you the option of adding usernames in a database for members of this group. Leave this option cleared. Click on Grant.

10. You will now see a report indicating how many login IDs were added. This action should report two: one for Oscar and possibly one for Administrator, who is also a member of the SQLUsers Group. Click on Done in this report window, and then click on Done in the Security dialog box.

11. Close Security Manager by selecting File ➢ Exit.

12. To change the security mode setting in SQL Server, start SQL Enterprise Manager and select Server ➢ SQL Server ➢ Configure. Click on the Security Options tab. In the Login Security Mode section of the dialog box, set the security mode to Windows NT Integrated and click on OK.

13. Stop and restart the server for the new security mode to take effect.

Testing Integrated Security

If you followed the steps in Exercise 6.16, you have just configured your server for integrated security. At this point, you will no longer need to enter any authentication information to connect to your SQL Server. Test your new security mode by following the steps in Exercise 6.17.

WARNING   When using integrated security, you may discover that your Windows NT login names use characters that are not valid characters in SQL Server. Characters such as the domain separator, the hyphen, and ampersand can be mapped to valid SQL Server characters in the Security Options tab of the Server Configuration/Options dialog box. SQL Server automatically maps some invalid characters for you. Learn these default mappings for the exam!

EXERCISE 6.17

Testing Integrated Security

1. Verify that you are logged in to Windows NT as Administrator. If this is not the case, log out and log back in to Windows NT as Administrator.

2. Start the ISQL/W utility and choose File ➤ Connect to display the Connect Server dialog box. Check that the Login Information option in the Connect Server dialog box is set to Use Standard Security.

3. Without entering a login ID or password, click on the Connect button. You should be connected to SQL Server as SA. Normally, this action would fail, but since you are using integrated security, you log in through a trusted connection.

4. Close ISQL/W. Log out of Windows NT and log back in as Oscar. Remember that the Oscar Windows NT user was mapped to user privileges in SQL Server.

5. Open ISQL/W. Verify that Use Standard Security is selected in the Connect Server dialog box and enter **sa** as a login ID. Enter the SA password if one exists. Click on the Connect button. You should be connected to SQL Server as Oscar. Again, because you enabled integrated security, you are given a trusted connection no matter what type of connection you actually requested.

6. Close ISQL/W and log out of Windows NT as Oscar. Log back in to Windows NT as Administrator.

Implementing Mixed Security

Mixed security is the perfect solution when trusted connections are preferred but standard connections must be supported. Although standard security supports trusted connections, they must be requested specifically. Integrated security does not support standard connections in any form. Mixed security provides the best of both worlds.

When a SQL Server is running in mixed security mode, if it is possible for a trusted connection to be made (based on the rules of mixed security), then a trusted connection will be granted. If a trusted connection cannot be made (usually because the user entered a SQL Server login that conflicted with that user's Windows NT login), then the server reverts back to standard security, checking the syslogins system table for a login ID for that user. If the user can be authenticated at this level, a standard connection will be granted. If not, the connection will be denied.

You can implement mixed security by implementing both integrated and standard security on the same system, as described in the previous sections. Then you set the SQL Server security mode to Mixed by using SQL Enterprise Manager's security options settings (select Server ➤ SQL Server ➤ Configure and click on the Security Options tab). Create mappings for users who need to access the server through trusted connections. Add login accounts to SQL Server for users who will make standard connections.

Summary

In this chapter, you learned all about login security. We explored the three levels of security in SQL Server and discussed the three access authentication stages—through the server, database, and database object.

We then examined the processes of creating and managing logins, groups, and users. You learned how to accomplish these tasks by using both SQL Enterprise Manager and Transact-SQL statements. Whether you choose to use SQL Enterprise Manager or Transact-SQL for these tasks, managing login security in SQL Server is quite intuitive once you learn the rules. If you have a well-designed security plan, you should be able to extend the boundaries of server access without much effort. Always consider how you will grow, and managing security will be much easier.

In the final sections of this chapter, we covered the three security modes supported by SQL Server: standard, integrated, and mixed. You learned how each of these modes works and how to implement them on your SQL Server system.

Exercise Questions

1. Which system table holds information about login IDs?

A. sysusers

B. syslogins

C. sysprotects

D. sysalternates

2. Which system table holds information about user aliases?

A. sysusers

B. syslogins

C. sysprotects

D. sysalternates

3. There can only be one user acting as the database owner in a database.

A. True

B. False

4. Which of the following security modes support standard connections? (Choose all that apply.)

A. Standard

B. Integrated

C. Mixed

D. None of the above

5. Which of the following security modes support trusted connections? (Choose all that apply.)

A. Standard

B. Integrated

C. Mixed

D. None of the above

6. Which Transact-SQL stored procedure is used to change ownership of a database to another user?

   A. sp_defaultdb

   B. sp_helpdb

   C. sp_changedbowner

   D. sp_addalias

7. Which of the following login IDs is not created during SQL Server installation?

   A. guest

   B. repl_publisher

   C. sa

   D. probe

8. An SA user attempts to transfer ownership of a database to another login and this action returns an error. What might be the problem?

   A. The login is accessing the database under a standard connection

   B. The login has an entry in the sysalternates system table in that database

   C. The SA does not have the authority to do the transfer of ownership; only the DBO has this authority

   D. The database is corrupt and must be repaired before the transfer of ownership can take place

9. When using the Transact-SQL stored procedure sp_addlogin, if a password is not provided when the login is created, what will be the password for the new login?

   A. null

   B. "password"

C. The same as the login name

D. The value provided in the Default Password text box of the Security Options dialog box

10. The SA is attempting to drop a group from a database using sp_dropgroup. This statement fails on execution. What might be the problem?

A. One of the users in the group owns an object in the database; the group and its users can't be deleted with sp_dropgroup if any user owns any objects

B. The SA does not have authority to drop groups from a database; only the DBO has that authority

C. The group is empty and deleting it would have no effect

D. The group is not empty and you cannot drop a group with members

11. The DBO is attempting to drop a login from the server using sp_droplogin and the attempt fails. What might be the problem?

A. The DBO does not have authority to drop logins; only the SA has that authority

B. The login owns an object in a database and cannot be dropped until the object is dropped

C. The login is part of a group and must be removed from the group before the login can be dropped

D. Logins can be dropped only through SQL Enterprise Manager

12. A user can be a member of how many groups including Public?

A. 1

B. 2

C. 3

D. 4

13. After ownership of a database was transferred from SA to another user, all users who used to be able to access the database under DBO aliases report that they can no longer access the database at all. What went wrong?

    A. The database ownership was transferred with SQL Enterprise Manager; this is a known bug in SQL Enterprise Manager

    B. When the `sp_changedbowner` stored procedure was called, the true flag was not included, indicating that existing aliases were to be maintained

    C. Nothing went wrong—it is not possible to retain aliases to DBO during ownership transfer

    D. The users who were formerly aliased as DBO already had usernames in the database, and aliases cannot be maintained unless these usernames are dropped

14. Which of the following Transact-SQL statements will drop the Grover user from the Monsters group?

    A. `sp_dropgroup Monsters, Grover`

    B. `sp_helpgroup Grover, Monsters`

    C. `sp_transfergroup null, Grover`

    D. `sp_changegroup public, Grover`

15. When are trusted connections established under mixed security?.

    A. Always

    B. Never

    C. Whenever possible

    D. Only when requested

CHAPTER

7

Managing Database Security

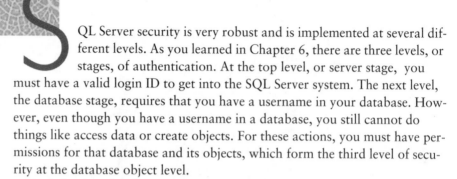

QL Server security is very robust and is implemented at several different levels. As you learned in Chapter 6, there are three levels, or stages, of authentication. At the top level, or server stage, you must have a valid login ID to get into the SQL Server system. The next level, the database stage, requires that you have a username in your database. However, even though you have a username in a database, you still cannot do things like access data or create objects. For these actions, you must have permissions for that database and its objects, which form the third level of security at the database object level.

Each database has its own independent permissions. In this chapter, we will explore the two different types of user permissions: statement and object. You will also learn about the database security hierarchy, which delineates who has what permissions and who can grant or revoke those permissions to others.

When you grant permissions to others, you create chains of ownership. These ownership chains can become complex and tricky. You will learn how to predict the permissions needed by users at different locations within the ownership chains.

Permissions can be granted to database users as well as database groups. The way in which these permissions are enforced in SQL Server 6.5 has changed from previous versions. In the final part of this chapter, we will discuss those differences.

Database Permissions

To create objects and access data, you must have *permissions*. There are two main types of permissions: statement permissions and object permissions. With statement permissions, you can create database objects, such as tables and views. With object permissions, you can view and modify data in those database objects.

Statement Permissions

Statement permissions allow you to use certain statements in a database. These permissions are generally related to the creation of database objects. Table 7.1 lists the statement permissions.

	Statement	Can be Granted by
TABLE 7.1 Statement Permissions	Create Database	Only the SA
	Create Default	SA or DBO
	Create Procedure	SA or DBO
	Create Rule	SA or DBO
	Create Table	SA or DBO
	Create View	SA or DBO
	Dump Database	SA or DBO
	Dump Transaction	SA or DBO

When you use a Create statement to create an object, you become the DBOO (database object owner), and then can grant or revoke all object permissions on that object.

Only the SA can grant All statement permissions, and only to a DBO. This is because only the SA can grant the Create Database statement permission.

Object Permissions

Object permissions generally allow users to manipulate data that a database object controls. For example, to view the data in a table, you must first have Select permission on that table. If you want to run a stored procedure, you must first have Execute permission on that stored procedure.

Object permissions can be granted by the SA or the DBOO. Table 7.2 lists the object permissions and which objects they affect.

	Permission	Allows	Objects Affected
TABLE 7.2 Object Permissions	Delete	Delete data from object	Table, view
	Drop *<object>*	Remove an object	Default, table, procedure, rule, view
	Execute	Run a stored procedure	Stored procedure
	Insert	Add new data to object	Table, view
	References	Create a foreign key reference	Table, column
	Select	View data in object	Table, view, column
	Update	Modify data in object	Table, view, column

Tables have additional objects attached to them, like indexes and triggers. Table permissions are listed in Table 7.3.

	Permission	Allows
TABLE 7.3 Implied Table Permissions	Alter Table	Add columns to a table
	Create Index	Create an index
	Create Trigger	Create a trigger
	Drop Index	Delete an index
	Drop Table	Delete a table
	Drop Trigger	Delete a trigger
	Truncate Table	Delete all information in a table, but keep the table schema intact
	Update Statistics	Update the statistical information stored in the indexes on a table

Although you can grant permissions on columns, it is not recommended, because any Transact-SQL statement that touches that table must check permissions on each column. Rather than grant permissions on columns, you should create a view on the required columns and then assign permissions to that view. This way, permissions are checked only once on the entire view rather than on each column.

The Database Permission Hierarchy

The permissions system incorporated into SQL Server 6.5 recognizes four types of database users:

- The lowest member of the hierarchy is the database user.

- The next level is the DBOO (database object owner).

- Above the DBOO is the DBO (database owner).

Above all is the SA (system administrator).

Microsoft ✓ *Exam* *Objective*	**Implement various methods of securing access to data.**

Exam objectives are subject to change at any time without prior notice and at Microsoft's sole discretion. Please visit Microsoft's Training & Certification Web site (www.microsoft.com/Train_Cert) for the most current exam objectives listing.

Database User Permissions

Database users are at the bottom of the heap. They get no respect! By default, a database user has no permissions on any objects with the exception of system tables. A database user has Select permission on system tables.

Database Object Owner Permissions

When a database user creates an object, he or she becomes a DBOO and is automatically granted all object permissions (see Table 7.2) on that object. All other users (including the DBO but excluding the SA) are denied any permissions on that object unless the DBOO grants permissions to them. This means that a DBOO may create objects that the DBO cannot use.

The DBO can still gain access to that object by impersonating that user and then granting the DBO permissions. This is accomplished using the SetUser statement. For example, suppose that Lisa, a database user, has created a view called LisaView1. Lisa has not given the DBO any permissions on LisaView1. The DBO could run the following statement and then impersonate Lisa:

```
SetUser Lisa
```

As Lisa, the DBO could then grant all permissions on LisaView1 to the DBO. In this fashion, the DBO can still retain control over the objects in the database.

Database Owner Permissions

DBOs have full permissions in their databases. This includes the ability to back up and restore (using the DUMP and LOAD statements) databases and their transaction logs. Table 7.4 lists the permissions available to a DBO that can be granted to others. Table 7.5 lists the permissions that a DBO has but cannot grant to others.

	Statement	Function	Objects Affected
TABLE 7.4 Permissions a DBO Can Grant to Others	Create *<object>*	Creates those objects in the database	Default, procedure, table, view, and rule
	Dump *<object>*	Backs up a database, transaction log, or table	Database, transaction, and table

	Statement	Function	Objects Affected
TABLE 7.5 Permissions That a DBO Cannot Grant to Others	Alter Database	Allows the DBO to resize the database	None
	Checkpoint	Issues a checkpoint in the database	None
	Drop Database	Deletes a database	None

	Statement	Function	Objects Affected
TABLE 7.5 (cont.) Permissions That a DBO Cannot Grant to Others	Load <*object*>	Restores a backup of the database or transaction log	Database, transaction
	Grant	Gives a user the ability to grant permissions on the DBO's object to others	None
	Revoke	Revokes the ability of a user to grant permissions on my object to others	None
	SetUser <*username*>	Impersonates a database user	Any valid database user
	DBCC <*statements*>	Database consistency checker statements (note that some statements are reserved for the SA)	Any valid database user

DBOs can use the Alter Database statement only if they have the Create Database permission granted to them by the SA.

SA Permissions

There are no restrictions on what the SA can do in SQL Server. The SA is automatically granted all permissions, and can grant most of those permissions to others.

Microsoft Exam Objective

Identify system administrator functionality.

In addition to the permissions listed in Tables 7.1 and 7.2, the SA has some permissions that cannot be granted to others. Table 7.6 lists these permissions.

TABLE 7.6	Permission	Allows
Permissions That Only the SA Can Use	Add/Drop *extended stored procedures*	Add or drop extended stored procedures
	Disk {Init, Mirror, Refit, Reinit, Remirror, Unmirror}	Perform device-related tasks
	Kill	Stop a process (but not a system process; you cannot kill a system process)
	Reconfigure	Reconfigure SQL Server
	Shutdown	Shut down SQL Server
	DBCC *<statements>*	Use Database Consistency Checker statements (note that some of these can be granted to the DBO)

Managing Permissions

As with many of the tasks covered so far in this book, you can grant and revoke permissions in two ways—by using SQL Enterprise Manager or by using Transact-SQL statements.

Microsoft ✓ Exam Objective

Grant and revoke permissions.

In the following sections, we will look at granting and revoking statement permissions by using SQL Enterprise Manager and Transact-SQL, and then at the methods for granting and revoking object permissions.

Granting and Revoking Statement Permissions

In the SQL Enterprise Manager utility, you can easily manage statement permissions through the database management controls. With Transact-SQL, you use the appropriate syntax of the GRANT and REVOKE statements.

Using SQL Enterprise Manager to Manage Statement Permissions

You can grant and revoke statement permissions through SQL Enterprise Manager's Edit Database dialog box. Figure 7.1 shows the Permissions tab of this dialog box.

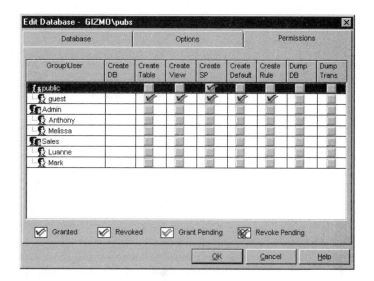

As you can see in Figure 7.1, there are no permissions currently set for any of the users or groups in the Pubs database. Follow the steps in Exercise 7.1 to grant and test some permissions using SQL Enterprise Manager.

You should run the /script7.sql script from the ISQL/W utility to create the login IDs and users needed to complete this exercise. Or, if you prefer, review that script and then implement the necessary changes to your database yourself (see Chapters 5 and 6).

Microsoft ✓ *Exam* *Objective*

Implement various methods of securing access to data.

EXERCISE 7.1

Granting and Revoking Statement Permissions Using SQL Enterprise Manager

1. Start SQL Enterprise Manager.

2. Connect to your server and drill down to the Pubs database.

3. Right-click on the database and choose Edit from the context menu.

4. Click on the Permissions tab. You should see Melissa under the Admin group and Mark under the Sales group.

5. Click on the Create View checkbox for Melissa and for Mark. Mark and Melissa should now have a green checkmark, indicating that the grant is pending.

6. Click on OK. The permissions will be added to the sysprotects table in this database.

7. Return to the Permissions tab of the Edit Database dialog box.

8. To revoke Mark's permission, click on his Create View permission. It should now have a red circle around the checkmark.

9. Click on OK. The permission will be revoked, and the sysprotects table will be updated appropriately.

10. To test the permissions, start the ISQL/W utility as a stand-alone program (by selecting Start ➤ Programs ➤ Microsoft SQL Server 6.5 ➤ ISQL_w).

11. In the Connect Server dialog box, choose the Use Standard Security option, enter your login ID as **Melissa**, and leave the Password box blank, as shown below.

12. Click on Connect. Your Query window should look similar to the one shown below. Note that the title bar reflects that you are logged in as Melissa.

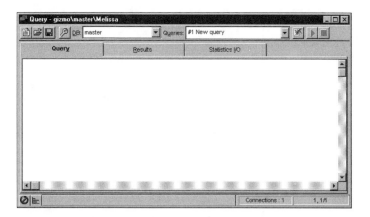

13. Enter and execute the following query to create a view:

```
USE pubs
GO
CREATE VIEW MelissaView1 AS
SELECT * FROM authors
```

EXERCISE 7.1 (CONTINUED FROM PREVIOUS PAGE)

The Results window should show:

> This command did not return data, and it did not return any rows

This means that you successfully created the view.

14. Select File ➢ Connect. This time, log in as **Anthony** (with Use Standard Security selected and no password). You should now have two separate Query windows open—one for Anthony and one for Melissa—as shown below.

15. Enter and execute the following query to create a view for Anthony:

```
USE pubs

GO

CREATE VIEW AnthonyView1 AS

SELECT * FROM employees
```

You should receive an error message that states the following:

> Msg 262, Level 14, State 1
>
> CREATE VIEW permission denied, database pubs, owner dbo

16. Close the ISQL/W utility.

Using Transact-SQL to Manage Statement Permissions

You can grant and revoke permissions using the Transact-SQL commands GRANT and REVOKE. Here is the syntax used for statement permissions:

GRANT {ALL | *statements* }

TO {PUBLIC | *users* }

REVOKE {ALL | *statements* }

TO {PUBLIC | *users* }

The *statements* parameters that you can specify are those that are listed in Table 7.1. The *users* parameter can be users (separate usernames with commas) and/or groups. For example, to grant the Create View permission to Luanne and Mark, you could run the following query as either the SA or the DBO:

USE pubs

GRANT CREATE VIEW

TO Luanne, Mark

You should get the following response:

This command did not return data, and it did not return any rows

You cannot grant permissions to both the group Public and to individual users in the same GRANT statement.

In Exercise 7.2, we will go through the procedure to revoke statement permissions from the Sales group using Transact-SQL.

EXERCISE 7.2

Using Transact-SQL to Revoke Statement Permissions

1. Start SQL Enterprise Manager and drill down to the Pubs database.

2. Right-click on the Pubs database and choose Edit from the context menu.

---

3. Click on the Permissions tab to view the current permissions.

4. If Luanne does not have the Create View permission, give it to her now (click on her Create View checkbox to place a green checkmark there). Then click on OK to close the Edit Database dialog box.

5. Start ISQL/W and enter and execute the following query:

```
USE pubs
GO
REVOKE ALL
FROM Luanne
```

You should get the following results:

```
This command did not return data, and it did not return any
rows
```

6. Close ISQL/W.

7. Return to the Permissions tab in SQL Enterprise Manager's Edit Database dialog box to view the permissions that Luanne now has. The checkmark should be gone from the Create View box.

Granting and Revoking Object Permissions

In SQL Enterprise Manager, object permissions are handled through their very own dialog box. With Transact-SQL, you use the appropriate syntax of the GRANT and REVOKE commands.

Using SQL Enterprise Manager to Manage Object Permissions

To grant or revoke object permissions in SQL Enterprise Manager, you need to select the database and then choose Permissions from the Object menu. The Object Permissions dialog box has two tabs:

- The By Object tab shows all users' permissions on the specified object, as shown in Figure 7.2.

- The By User tab shows all of the object permissions associated with the specified user or group, as shown in Figure 7.3.

F I G U R E 7.2

The By Object tab of the
Object Permissions
dialog box

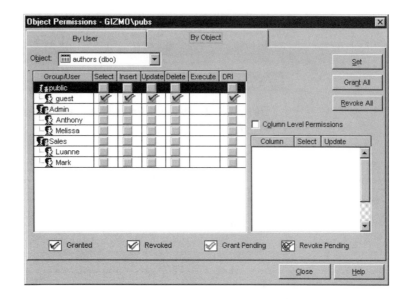

F I G U R E 7.3

The By User tab of the
Object Permissions
dialog box

Follow the steps in Exercise 7.3 to grant object permissions. We will begin this exercise by having Melissa attempt to select from MelissaView1 (which we created in Exercise 7.1).

EXERCISE 7.3

Granting Object Permissions Using SQL Enterprise Manager

1. Start the ISQL/W utility and log in using standard security and the login ID **Melissa** (no password).

2. Enter and execute the following query:

   ```
   USE Pubs
   GO
   SELECT * FROM MelissaView1
   ```

   You should get the following results:

   ```
   Msg 229, Level 14, State 1
   SELECT permission denied on object authors, database
   pubs, owner dbo
   ```

   This shows that the DBO never gave Melissa permission to select from the Authors table. So let's grant her that permission now.

3. Do not close the ISQL/W utility. Switch to SQL Enterprise Manager.

4. Drill down to the Pubs database and select it.

5. Select Object ➤ Permissions. Make sure that the By Object tab is selected.

6. In the Object list box, make sure that authors (dbo) is selected. You should now see the permissions for this object.

7. Click on the Select checkbox for Melissa to put a checkmark in the checkbox for that permission.

8. Click on the Set button to set the permission.

9. Click on Close in the Object Permissions dialog box and switch back to ISQL/W.

10. Rerun the query from step 2 above. The view should now return information in the Results window.

Using Transact-SQL to Manage Object Permissions

As with statement permissions, you can use the Transact-SQL GRANT and REVOKE statements to grant and revoke object permissions. Here is the syntax for object permissions:

```
GRANT {permissions}
ON {object}
TO {users}
[WITH GRANT OPTION]

REVOKE [GRANT OPTION FOR]{permissions}
ON {object}
FROM {users}[CASCADE]
```

For example, the following statements grant permissions on the Authors table to Melissa:

```
GRANT SELECT, INSERT, DELETE
ON authors
TO Melissa
```

The GRANT and REVOKE statements have two additional options when they are used for object permissions: WITH GRANT OPTION and CASCADE.

When a database object owner (this includes the DBO) grants permission on an object to another user with the WITH GRANT OPTION, the other user can then grant those same permissions to others. For example, if the DBO granted Melissa Select and Insert permissions on the Authors table with the WITH GRANT OPTION, Melissa could then grant Select and Insert permissions to Anthony, like this:

```
GRANT SELECT, INSERT
ON authors
TO Anthony
```

If Melissa was not given the WITH GRANT OPTION permissions, she could not pass on the permissions to others.

As you can see, the use of WITH GRANT OPTION can potentially cause problems, as the DBO begins to lose control over who has access to the object that he or she owns. This is where the CASCADE option comes into play. If the DBO simply revoked permissions on the Authors table from Melissa, like this:

```
REVOKE SELECT, INSERT
ON authors
FROM Melissa
```

Anthony would still have the permissions that Melissa granted him, and that the DBO may or may not know about. To revoke permissions from Melissa as well as from anyone Melissa granted permissions to, you can use the CASCADE option, like this:

```
REVOKE SELECT, INSERT
ON authors
FROM Melissa
CASCADE
```

Understanding Ownership Chains

With all of these permissions flying around, you will be creating what are called *ownership chains*. It is important for you to understand broken and unbroken ownership chains, and how SQL Server checks permissions.

Broken and Unbroken Ownership Chains

Let's keep working with user Melissa for our ownership chain example. Suppose that Melissa owns a table and then she creates a view based on her table. By doing so, she has created an *ownership chain*. This ownership chain has only one object owner. Figure 7.4 illustrates what has just happened.

FIGURE 7.4

An unbroken ownership chain

Melissa could grant Select permission to Mark on her view. When Mark attempts to select from MelissaView1, permissions would be checked on MelissaView1 as shown in Figure 7.5.

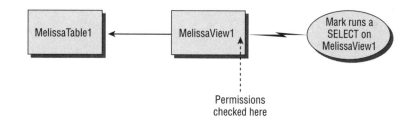

FIGURE 7.5

Permissions are checked only once in an unbroken ownership chain.

Microsoft
✓ *Exam*
Objective

Predict the outcome of a broken ownership chain.

If Mark created a view based on Melissa's view, this now becomes a *broken ownership chain*, because different users own objects within the permission chain. If Mark granted permissions to Luanne on his view, permissions would be checked on MarkView1 for Luanne and on MelissaView1 for Luanne, as illustrated in Figure 7.6.

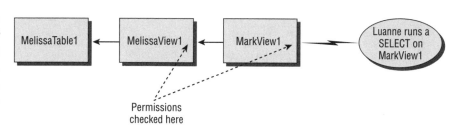

FIGURE 7.6

Permissions are checked every time ownership changes in a broken ownership chain.

If Luanne has Select permission on both MarkView1 and MelissaView1, then she could select successfully from MarkView1. If anywhere in the permission chain, Luanne does not have permission where permissions are checked, then she would not be able to select from MarkView1. Permissions are checked *every* time ownership changes. This doesn't seem too bad at first glance, but take a look at Figure 7.7 to see what could happen if you let your database developers create dependent objects as needed.

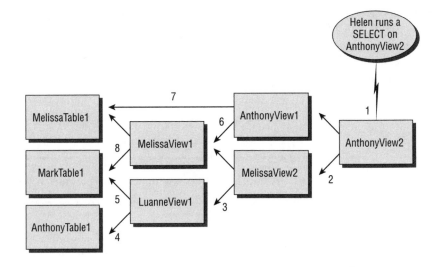

Figure 7.7 illustrates a complex broken ownership chain. Can you tell where permissions would be checked for user Helen? If you guessed the following, you would be correct, since each break in ownership must have a permission check:

- AnthonyView2

- MelissaView2

- LuanneView1

- AnthonyTable1

- MarkTable1

- MelissaView1

- MelissaTable1

One of the best ways to avoid this problem is to alias your database developers as DBO. In this manner, the DBO is the owner of all objects that are created by the aliased developers. This means that you do not have a break in the ownership chain, and permissions will be checked only once.

How Permissions Are Checked on Views

Permissions on views are checked when the view is used, not when it is created. This means that a database user could create a view based on a table that he or she does not have access to and then grant permissions on that view to another user. When the other person uses that view, the permissions will be checked both on the view itself and on any dependent objects where there is a break in ownership. If the user has permissions on all the dependent objects, then he or she will be able to use the view.

Permission Precedence

The permission precedence in SQL Server 6.5 is radically different from the implementation in previous versions SQL Server. We'll first examine the SQL Server 6.0 (and earlier) permission precedence, and then look at the SQL Server 6.5 implementation.

SQL Server 6.0 Permission Precedence

In SQL Server 6.0, the last permission to be set took precedence. The easiest way to understand this is through a couple of examples. The following scenarios assume that Rosa is a user who is a member of the Sales group as well as the Public group.

Scenario 1   The SA revokes object permissions from Rosa. The SA then grants object permissions to the Sales group. Would Rosa still have access? Yes, because the last permission set was to the Sales group, of which Rosa is a member.

Scenario 2   The SA grants object permissions to Rosa. The SA then revokes object permissions from the Public group. Would Rosa still have access? No, because the last permission set was to the Public group, of which Rosa is a member.

SQL Server 6.5 Permission Precedence

Thankfully, the permission precedence system was altered in SQL Server 6.5 to be ANSI compliant. You no longer need to worry about the last permission set. In version 6.5, the user permissions take precedence over the group permissions, which in turn take precedence over the Public group permissions. Let's take a look at a few scenarios. Here, we assume that Rosa is a user who is a member of the Sales group as well as the Public group.

Scenario 1   The SA revokes object permissions from Rosa. The SA then grants object permissions to the Sales group. Would Rosa still have access? No, because the more specific individual permissions on Rosa were revoked.

Scenario 2   The SA grants object permissions to Rosa. The SA then revokes object permissions from the Public group. Would Rosa still have access? Yes, because the explicit individual permissions on Rosa were granted.

Scenario 3   The SA grants object permissions to the Public group. The SA then revokes object permissions from the Sales group. Would Rosa have access? No, because the more specific Sales group permissions take precedence over the Public group permissions.

Summary

In this chapter, you learned about the robust security model that has been designed into SQL Server 6.5. We concentrated on the third level of database security—user permissions. Each database in SQL Server 6.5 has its own independent permissions. We looked at the two different types of user permissions: statement and object. Remember statement permissions give you the ability to run particular statements, and object permissions are used to manipulate data through the database objects. You also learned that statement permissions cannot be granted to others.

In the next section, we discussed the database hierarchy. We looked at the permissions available to the most powerful user, the SA, down through the low-level grunts (database users).

You then learned about chains of ownership. These are created when you grant permissions to others on objects that you own. As you add more users and they create dependent objects, you create broken ownership chains, which can become complex and tricky to work with. You learned how to predict the permissions needed by users at different locations within these ownership chains. You also learned that to avoid the broken ownership chains, you can alias your developers as the DBO.

Permissions can be granted to database users as well as database groups. The order in which these permissions are enforced has changed from SQL Server 6.0 to SQL Server 6.5. You learned that in earlier releases of SQL Server, the last permission modified was the permission that was enforced. In version 6.5, there is a specific precedence that begins with the user, then the groups, and finishes with the Public group. Remember that everyone is a member of the Public group.

Exercise Questions

1. Which of the following users can perform these tasks: `Disk {Init, Mirror, Refit, Reinit, Remirror, Unmirror}`? (Choose all that apply.)

   A. SA

   B. DBO

   C. DBOO

   D. Database user with permissions

2. Which of the following users can perform these tasks: `Shutdown, Reconfigure, Kill`, add and drop extended stored procedures? (Choose all that apply.)

   A. SA

   B. DBO

   C. DBOO

   D. Database user with permissions

3. Anyone can issue the `Kill` statement.

   A. True

   B. False

4. Only the SA can `Kill` a system process.

   A. True

   B. False

5. A DBO can use the `Alter Database` statement when which of the following is true? (Choose one.)

   A. The DBO is the SA

   B. The DBO has the Create Database permission in addition to the Alter Database permission

   C. Neither A nor B

   D. Both A and B

6. If a user in a database has created an object, and has not given permissions on that object to the DBO, the DBO can still access the object by using the `SetUser` statement.

   A. True

   B. False

7. Statement permissions can be granted to others.

   A. True

   B. False

8. You should grant permissions on individual columns in a table because this is much more efficient than granting permissions on a view.

   A. True

   B. False

9. Database users are always a member of which group?

   A. Users

   B. Everyone

   C. Public

   D. The World

10. If you grant Tanisha permissions and then later revoke permissions from the Sales group of which Tanisha is a member, Tanisha will *not* have access.

    A. True

    B. False

11. If James creates a table, and then James creates a view on his table and gives Laura permission on his view, Laura can select data from the view.

    A. True

    B. False

12. James creates a table, and then James creates a view on his table and gives Laura permission on his view, and Laura creates a view based on James's view and then gives Amanda permissions on her view. Where will permissions be checked? (Choose all that apply.)

    A. On Laura's view

    B. On James's view

    C. On James's table

    D. Permissions will not be checked

13. James can create a view on a table that he does not have access to because permissions on views are not checked until the view is run.

  A. True

  B. False

14. If you grant a permission with the `WITH GRANT OPTION` option, the grantee will be able to grant that permission to other users.

  A. True

  B. False

15. If you want to revoke permissions from grantees and anyone that they might have granted permissions to on your object, you can use the `REVOKE` statement with the `CASCADE` option.

  A. True

  B. False

CHAPTER

8

Backing Up and Restoring Databases

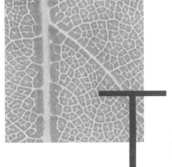

his chapter deals with a topic that is particularly critical to database system administrators. Here, we will look at the various options for protecting your data.

We will first review the ways that data corruption can occur and discuss the items you should consider in developing your backup plan. Then we will cover Windows NT's data-protection features, which allow you to set up mirrored, duplexed, or RAID drives.

Next, you will learn about SQL Server's automatic recovery of transactions. Then we will describe how to use SQL Server's backup features, including creating backup devices, backing up entire databases, and backing up transaction logs. Finally, we will look at the various ways to restore data.

Why Do Backups?

You may think that since you have fault-tolerant disk drives, you don't need to do backups. This is not true. Data corruption can come about in a variety of ways, including the following:

- Hard disk drive failure

- Hard disk controller failure

- Motherboard failure

- Power outage or spike

- Virus attack

- Accidental change or deletion of data

- Malicious change or deletion of data

Creating (and testing) regular backups is an integral part of any good administrator's maintenance plan. You never want to hear the words, "The hard drive is dead, and the backups are bad."

Developing a Backup Plan

Because you will probably be the one in charge of scheduling and verifying backups, you need to design a backup plan and implement that plan.

Here are some of the questions that you should consider in developing a backup plan for your SQL Server system:

- How often will the backups occur?

- To what medium will the backups be made?

- Who is responsible for the backups?

- How will the backups be verified?

- What are the policies for backing up non-logged operations?

- Will Windows NT's capabilities be used to help protect data?

- Will SQL Server be used to mirror database devices?

Each of these issues is discussed in the following sections.

How Often Will the Backups Occur?

A backup is a lot like a spare tire—you may never need it, but if you do, it is a lifesaver. The frequency of your backups is directly related to how much data you will lose if the system suffers a major catastrophe. If you back up only once a week on the weekends, any crash suffered late in the week could mean many days of data will be lost. Conversely, if you back up the transaction log every hour (with periodic full database backups), the most data you will lose will be a single hour's worth.

The following recommendations are general ones. Feel free to adjust them to accommodate your situation.

Database	How Often to Back Up
Master database	Schedule it for at least weekly backups, and perform a manual backup after major modifications to your databases, devices, or users.
Msdb database	Schedule it for weekly backups, and perform a manual backup after major changes to tasks, events, operators, or alerts.
Tempdb database	Don't bother backing it up, because it is automatically cleared every time SQL Server is stopped and started.
Model database	You should make a baseline backup of it, and then manually back it up if you modify it (which won't be very often, if ever).
Pubs database	Don't bother backing it up, because it is simply a sample database included so you can have live data to practice on. The only reason for backing it up would be to test your scheduling or restore procedures. You can always re-create this database using the Instpubs.sql script (in the Install folder).
User databases	Schedule these to be backed up at least every night. One option is to do an entire database backup every night. Another option is to do an entire database backup on the weekends, and back up just the transaction log on week nights. You can also schedule the log to be backed up during the day in case of failure, but backing up the entire database during production hours would probably be too slow and interfere with your users' work.

To What Medium Will the Backups Be Made?

SQL Server can back up databases to tape, a network share, a named pipe, the null device, a floppy disk, or a dump device (a file). If you are using a tape drive, it must be a model that is listed on the Windows NT Hardware Compatibility List (HCL), and it must be installed in the computer running SQL Server.

SQL Server and Windows NT use incompatible file formats for tape backups. You can use the same tape drive to perform both SQL Server and Windows NT backups, but make sure that you switch tapes for each operation. If you don't, the backup procedure will wipe out existing backup data from the other program.

Who Is Responsible for the Backups?

A very scary situation is when two co-administrators both think the other one took care of the backups. Have a plan for who is in charge. And don't forget to plan for what happens on that person's days off.

How Will the Backups Be Verified?

This section begs the question "Are backups of any worth if they can't be restored?" The whole purpose of backups is not to back something up, but to be able to restore it when necessary. Trusting your backups without verifying them is like trusting that your spare tire is in good condition—it *probably* is, but… .

One of the best ways to verify if your backups are working is to restore them to a separate computer. Not only does this verify the integrity of your backups, but it also helps prepare you in case you need to bring up a spare server quickly.

What Are the Policies for Backing Up Non-Logged Operations?

Most transactions are logged by SQL Server in the transaction log, however there are some transactions that are not logged. If you need to restore a database, any and all of the non-logged operations that happened since the last backup will be lost.

Non-logged operations include the following:

- Fast bulk copies when Select Into/Bulk Copy is enabled

- Select Into commands when Select Into/Bulk Copy is enabled

Bulk copies and the Select Into command are covered in Chapter 10.

The best way to avoid losing data about these operations is to back up the database before starting a non-logged operation. Then you will be able to restore the database to its state before that non-logged operation occurred.

Will NT's Capabilities Be Used to Help Protect Data?

The ultimate goal of designing and implementing a disaster-recovery plan is to plan for the protection of your data in case of a major catastrophe. Windows NT has several features that can protect data in case of hard drive failure, and do so in such a way that SQL Server will not even know that there has been a problem.

Disk Administrator is the Windows NT program used to create mirrored, duplexed, striped, and stripe with parity drives. For more information, see *MCSE: Windows NT Server Study Guide*, also published by Sybex.

Disk Mirroring

One option you have is to mirror the hard drive partitions so that all data writes are made to two separate, different physical hard drives. This setup is illustrated in Figure 8.1. In case of a hard drive failure, Windows NT simply uses the remaining hard drive until you replace the broken hard drive and mirror the disks again. Disk mirroring is transparent to SQL Server. You set up disk mirroring through Windows NT Disk Administrator, and then install SQL Server normally.

FIGURE 8.1

With disk mirroring, data writes are made to two physical hard drives.

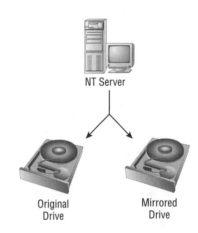

NT Server

Original
Drive

Mirrored
Drive

Disk Duplexing

Disk mirroring eliminates the hard drive as a single point of failure, but still uses only one hard disk controller card. If the controller happens to fail, then both the original and mirrored hard drives might contain corrupted data, or both disks might be unavailable. Disk duplexing attempts to avoid this problem by using two controller cards, as illustrated in Figure 8.2.

FIGURE 8.2

With disk duplexing, two controller cards are used.

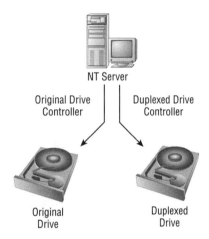

Disk duplexing is simply a fancier (and more reliable) way of doing disk mirroring. As with disk mirroring, you set up disk duplexing through Windows NT, and then install SQL Server normally on the duplexed drives. In case of either a controller or hard disk failure, Windows NT will use the remaining controller and drive until a replacement can be installed.

Make sure that you use SCSI drives, not IDE or EIDE drives, when you do your mirroring or duplexing. SCSI drives are independent, and a failure of one will not affect the others. IDE and EIDE drives are linked in a master/ slave relationship, where failure of one drive will probably stop the remaining drive from working.

Disk Striping

Windows NT supports the creation of a striped set, which is the fastest way you can set up your drives. Stripe sets run vertically across two or more physical drives, so that more than one hard drive participates in writing and reading data. This setup is illustrated in Figure 8.3.

FIGURE 8.3

With disk striping, multiple drives participate in writing and reading data.

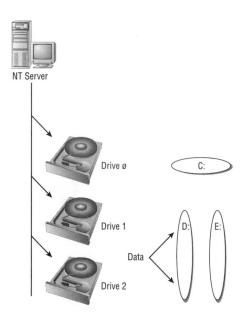

NT Server

Drive ø

C:

Drive 1

D: E:

Data

Drive 2

Striped drives write data in 64KB blocks, and then move to the next drive for the next block of data. To use stripe drives with SQL Server, create the striped set first through Windows NT, and then install SQL Server normally.

WARNING   Stripe drives have no redundancy built into them. If a hard drive within the stripe set fails, then data on the disks involved in the stripe set is lost. For data protection (at a cost of some speed and space) use striping with parity (RAID 5).

Disk Striping with Parity (RAID 5)

Windows NT supports stripe sets with parity drives, commonly referred to as RAID 5. When creating a stripe set with parity, Windows NT will create a parity or check bit that can be used to recover the data in case a hard drive fails. This parity bit is striped across the different drives. A parity bit works on the principle of $X + Y = Z$. If you know any two of the three variables, you can compute the missing variable.

Figure 8.4 shows a stripe set with parity, with all of the hard drives working. Figure 8.5 shows the same system, after the second hard drive has failed. Windows NT can reconstruct the second hard drive in memory, by using the parity bits and/or data spread across the remaining drives, as illustrated in Figure 8.6. After the failed hard drive is replaced, Windows NT can reconstruct the missing drive onto the new drive, and Windows NT regains its fault tolerance.

Although stripe sets with parity aren't as fast as a pure striped drive array, they do provide redundancy in case of hard disk failure.

F I G U R E 8.4

A stripe with parity (RAID 5) system

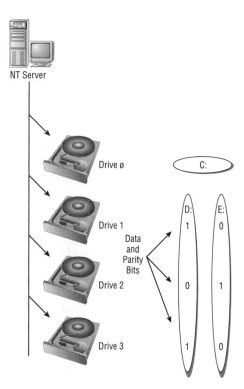

FIGURE 8.5

A single hard drive failure on a stripe with parity system

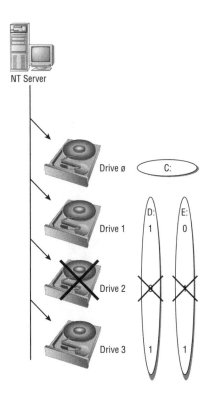

To use stripe set with parity with SQL Server, create the stripe set with parity through Windows NT, and then install SQL Server normally.

Some high-end servers support hardware-level RAID, and may even provide hot standby hard drives in case of failure. Hardware RAID is faster than the software RAID that Windows NT supplies, but it is also more expensive and may be proprietary. Most high-level servers from vendors such as Compaq and Hewlett-Packard contain some form of hardware-level RAID.

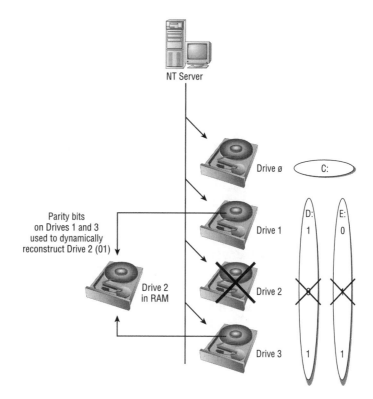

Reconstructing the lost drive with a stripe with parity system

Will SQL Server Be Used to Mirror Database Devices?

SQL Server adds another option that you can use to help maintain your data in case of hard disk failure. SQL Server allows you to mirror individual database devices (files). In case of a hard disk failure, SQL Server will use the remaining database device until the failed drive is replaced. In general, this is not a recommended solution.

SQL Server's Data-Protection Features

SQL Server provides both automatic database recovery and support for user-initiated backup and restore procedures. The automatic recovery feature protects databases from losing transactional integrity if the server is unexpectedly stopped. The manual recovery features allow you to restore databases and/or tables in case of equipment failure, user error, or other data-integrity problems. We'll cover the procedures for manual backups later in this chapter. The following sections explain some concepts related to database backup and recovery, and how SQL Server's automatic recovery feature works.

Understanding Transactions and Checkpoints

In order to understand backups and what part of the database is getting backed up when different commands are used, you need to know how transactions and checkpoints work.

A *transaction* is a logical set of one or more commands that need to be processed as a whole in order to make a complete unit of work. For instance, withdrawing cash from an automated teller machine is a transaction made up of two distinct parts: subtracting an amount from your account, and then delivering the cash to you. Figure 8.7 illustrates this example of a simple transaction. If any part of the transaction fails, a system that is designed correctly will cancel, or *roll back*, the entire transaction.

FIGURE 8.7

A simple transaction consisting of two steps

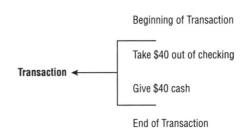

SQL Server treats each Transact-SQL statement as a separate transaction by default (but SQL programmers can establish the logical starting and ending points of a transaction with the key words BEGIN TRANSACTION and COMMIT TRANSACTION, respectively). If the transaction is interrupted, SQL Server will roll back the database to the state it was in before the transaction was started. The SQL program itself can be written to roll back a transaction by issuing a ROLLBACK TRANSACTION command at any time (such as when a user chooses the Cancel button).

SQL Server doesn't write every change to your database immediately. Instead, changes to your data are cached and eventually written to the database. Because cached data is vulnerable to power outages, SQL Server also logs each transaction in the transaction log. This way, SQL Server is providing the best of both worlds, by combining the speed of a cache with the data integrity of logged transactions.

SQL Server writes modified data to the database by periodically issuing a *checkpoint*. The DBO of a database may also issue a checkpoint at any time by running the command Checkpoint in the appropriate database.

Automatic Recovery of Transactions

Every time that SQL Server is restarted, SQL Server runs its automatic recovery feature, which is built into SQL Server and should not be disabled for normal servers.

Microsoft
✓ *Exam*
Objective

Identify how automatic recovery works.

Exam objectives are subject to change at any time without prior notice and at Microsoft's sole discretion. Please visit Microsoft's Training & Certification Web site (www.microsoft.com/Train_Cert) for the most current exam objectives listing.

SQL Server's automatic recovery feature ensures that the database is brought up to date, only completed transactions are put into the database, and partially done transactions are removed.

In Exercise 8.1, we will look at the SQL Server error log and examine the entry for the automatic recovery of the Master database. You can view the error log through SQL Enterprise Manager (see Chapter 4 for information about using SQL Enterprise Manager).

EXERCISE 8.1

Checking the Error Log for Automatic Recovery Entries

1. Start SQL Enterprise Manager, highlight the server, and select Server ➤ Error Log to open the error log.

2. Examine the log for transactions that were rolled forward. You should find an entry for the Master database, as shown in the portion of the log below, and you may see entries for all your user databases as well.

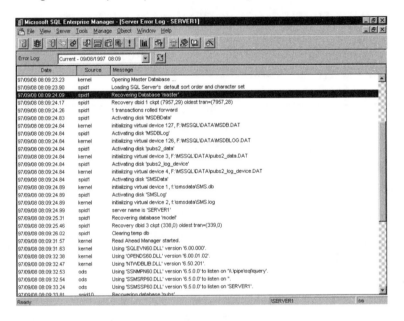

3. When you're finished viewing the error log, close its window.

The No Chkpt on Recovery option (which turns off automatic recovery) can be set per database. This is used for hot standby servers so they can stay in sync with their primary SQL Server machines.

Configuring Automatic Backup

You can adjust two attributes of SQL Server's automatic backup feature through SQL Enterprise Manager's Server Configuration/Options dialog box. To get to this dialog box, highlight the server, right-click on it, and choose Configure from the context menu. Alternatively, choose Server ➤ SQL Server ➤ Configure:

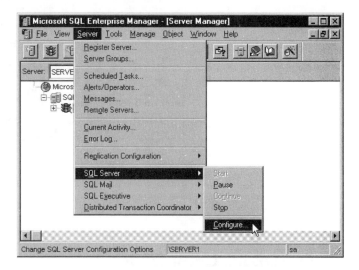

In the Server Configuration/Options dialog box, choose the Configurations tab. Two options here pertain to the automatic recovery feature:

- The Recovery Flags setting, when set to 1, provides a more verbose description of the recovery process.

- The Recovery Interval setting specifies the maximum amount of time (in minutes) that SQL Server will take to recover each database if there is a system failure.

The Configuration tab lists the minimum, maximum, running, and current settings for each configuration. When you click on a setting, its description appears at the bottom of the dialog box. Figure 8.8 shows the Configuration tab with an explanation of the Recovery Interval setting in the Description box.

FIGURE 8.8

In SQL Enterprise Manager, the Configuration tab of the Server Configuration/ Options dialog box contains settings related to automatic recovery.

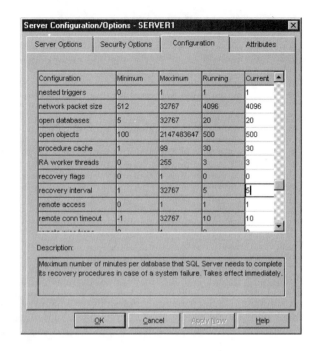

Configuration	Minimum	Maximum	Running	Current
nested triggers	0	1	1	1
network packet size	512	32767	4096	4096
open databases	5	32767	20	20
open objects	100	2147483647	500	500
procedure cache	1	99	30	30
RA worker threads	0	255	3	3
recovery flags	0	1	0	0
recovery interval	1	32767	5	5
remote access	0	1	1	1
remote conn timeout	-1	32767	10	10

Description:

Maximum number of minutes per database that SQL Server needs to complete its recovery procedures in case of a system failure. Takes effect immediately.

Running DBCC Commands

One of the more unpleasant features of SQL Server is that the backup routines are more tolerant of errors than the restore routines. Because of this, backup routines may appear to have worked, but the backups are actually worthless because they contain errors that cause the restore procedures to fail. Even worse, the restoration may appear to have succeeded, but then you find that the data isn't any good when you attempt to use it.

We've talked about DBCC (Database Consistency Checker) commands in the previous chapters. As you've learned, you can use these commands to check the database for errors. You should run these on a regular basis to ensure that the database is in perfect working order. For example, run DBCC CheckDB to check the database for errors, and DBCC CheckCatalog to check the system tables for allocation and corruption errors. (See Chapters 4 and 13 for some other useful DBCC commands.)

You may wish to use the WITH NO_INFOMSGS option of DBCC commands. It reduces the "chatty" behavior of DBCC commands so that you can see real errors instead of all the unimportant status messages.

The Database Maintenance Plan Wizard, which is discussed later in this chapter, not only allows you to run DBCC commands before a backup begins, but it also can be set to cancel the backup process if an error is found.

Backing Up Databases

SQL Server provides support for backing up an entire database or backing up just the transaction log for a database. Backing up the entire database is like doing a full backup of Windows NT Server computer; backing up just the log is similar to doing an incremental backup of your server.

Microsoft ✓ Exam Objective	Identify the functionality of dynamic backup.

SQL Server allows you to back up your databases dynamically (while they are in use), so that users can stay connected to the server while a backup is being run. When a database backup is started, SQL Server will first do a checkpoint of the database, thus bringing the database up to date by copying all completed transactions out of memory to the hard disks. SQL Server then "snapshots" the database, and backs up the entire database. If users are trying to update pages, they will be temporarily blocked by SQL Server, as it jumps ahead of the updates while the database is backed up.

Any transactions that were not completed when the backup started will not be in the backup, and they cannot be recovered if the database needs to be restored. Because of this, even though backups can be done during normal work hours, you will probably want to schedule some backups to occur outside regular work hours. Then you will have a better idea of what is in the backup and what didn't make it to the backup.

SQL Server backs up databases to a file called a backup device, or *dump device*. SQL Server comes with only a single device set up—the null device is configured as diskdump.

Anything sent to the null device (diskdump) is not saved anywhere. It is primarily used to test scripts.

Before you can start running backup procedures, you need to configure SQL Server backups by creating a backup device. Then you can back up the entire database or just the transaction log, schedule backups, view back up information, and use the Database Maintenance Plan Wizard to help automate your backup procedures. These topics are covered in the following sections.

Configuring SQL Server Backups

SQL has no built-in backup devices. You will need to create all of your backup devices and configure your backups in order to back up your databases on a regular basis.

Because SQL Server keeps the database devices (files) open while SQL Server is running, the databases are not backed up during regular Windows NT backups. You need to configure SQL Server's backups, because there are no default configurations to back up any of your databases! Once a backup has been made to a backup device, the backup device is closed, and it will be backed up during Windows NT backups.

In Exercise 8.2, we will attempt to rename the Master database device to demonstrate Windows NT's inability to back up an open database device.

This exercise will not be able to rename the Master database device as long as SQL Server is running. If your MSSQLServer service is not running, then the Master database device is like any other file and can be renamed. If this happens, simply rename it back before restarting the MSSQLServer service.

EXERCISE 8.2

Attempting to Rename the Master Database Device

1. In Windows NT Explorer, find the Master device. It will probably be in the \MSSQL\Data path and be called MASTER.DAT.

2. Right-click on the file and select Rename from the context menu.

3. Attempt to rename the file as **MASTER1.DAT**. You should get an error message like the following:

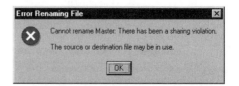

4. Click on OK to close the message box.

You can create a backup device either through SQL Enterprise Manager or by using Transact-SQL. Both methods are described in the following sections.

Using SQL Enterprise Manager to Create Backup Devices

It's easy to create backup devices using SQL Enterprise Manager. To create a backup device, simply right-click on the Backup Devices folder and choose the New Backup Device option from the context menu. This brings up the New Backup Device dialog box, in which you can enter the name and location of your backup device.

A backup device has the default extension of .DAT, although any extension will work. In our examples. we will change the extension for backup devices to .BAK to differentiate them from database devices (which also use the .DAT extension).

Microsoft ✓ *Exam* *Objective*

Create a dump device.

In Exercise 8.3, we will make backup devices for the Pubs, Pubs2, and Msdb databases, as well as the Pubs2 transaction log.

EXERCISE 8.3

Creating Backup (Dump) Devices Using SQL Enterprise Manager

1. From My Computer or Windows NT Explorer, create a new folder called **C:\SQL_Backups**.

2. Start SQL Enterprise Manager and open the Backup Devices folder.

3. Right-click and choose New Backup Device to display the New Backup Device dialog box.

4. In the Name field, enter **pubs_backup**.

5. In the Location field, enter **C:\slq_backups\pubs_backup.bak**.

In the Type section of the dialog box, leave the Disk Backup Device option button selected. The Tape Backup Device option is useful if you have a tape drive installed on your SQL Server machine. You can define a backup device that places the backup directly on tape. Your dialog box should look like the one shown below.

6. Click on the Create button.

7. Return to the New Backup Device dialog box. Enter **pubs2_backup** in the Name field, enter **C:\slq_backups\pubs2_backup.bak** in the Location field, and click on Create.

8. Return to the New Backup Device dialog box. Enter **msdb_backup** in the Name field, enter **C:\slq_backups\msdb_backup.bak** in the Location field, and click on Create.

9. Return to the New Backup Device dialog box and create a backup device for the Pubs2 transaction log. Name the device **pubs2_log_backup** and enter the location as **C:\sql_backups\pubs2_log_backup.bak**. Then click on Create.

10. Right-click and choose Refresh from the context menu to check that all the devices were created. Your screen should look similar to the one shown here.

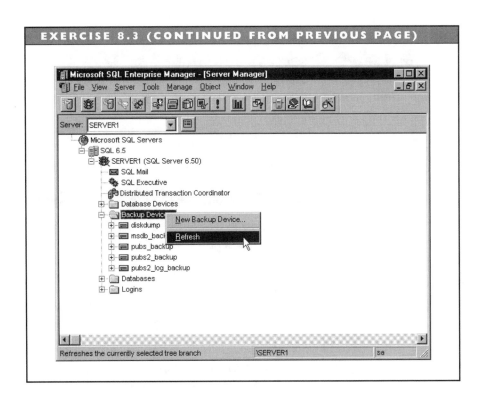

EXERCISE 8.3 (CONTINUED FROM PREVIOUS PAGE)

A backup device is mainly just a pointer that SQL Server remembers so that it knows where to put the backup file when the backup is actually done. Because of this, files are not created when a backup device is defined; they are created when a backup is first performed.

Using Transact-SQL to Create Backup Devices

You can also create backup devices by using the sp_addumpdevice system stored procedure. Here is its syntax:

```
sp_addumpdevice type, logicalname, path
```

The parameters specify the type of backup device you are creating, the logical name for the device, and the path to the file that will be created after the backup is completed.

SQL Server 6.0 referred to backup devices almost exclusively as *dump devices*, even in SQL Enterprise Manager, although the stored procedures haven't changed.

In Exercise 8.4, we will create a backup (dump) device for the Master database using `sp_addumpdevice`. (For information about starting and using the ISQL/W utility, see Chapter 4.)

EXERCISE 8.4

Creating a Backup (Dump) Device Using Transact-SQL

1. If you didn't already create a folder called C:\SQL_Backups (in Exercise 8.3), create that folder now.

2. Start the ISQL/W utility.

3. Enter and execute the following statement:

   sp_addumpdevice 'disk', 'master_backup', 'c:\sql_backups\master_backup.bak'

Your window should look similar to the one shown below.

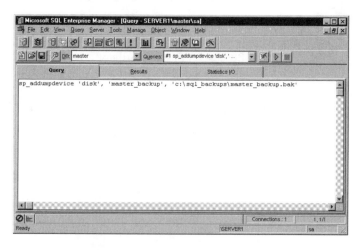

The results returned should say `'Disk' device added`.

EXERCISE 8.4 (CONTINUED FROM PREVIOUS PAGE)

4. In the Server Manager window of SQL Enterprise Manager, right-click on the Backup Devices folder and select Refresh from the context menu. You should see the master_backup device listed, as shown below.

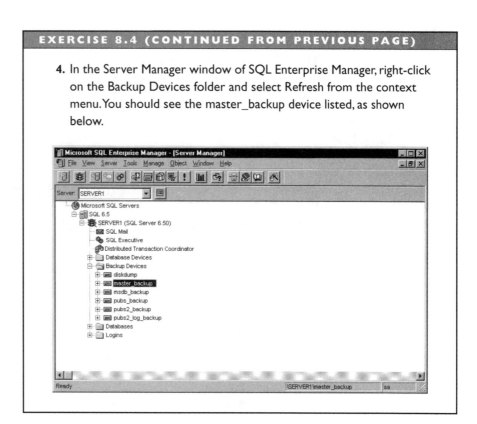

Backing Up the Entire Database

The actual process of backing up the database is relatively straightforward. SQL Server allows a database to be backed up to a single device or to multiple devices. When you create a back up across two or more devices, it is called a *parallel striped backup*.

Microsoft ✓ *Exam Objective*   **Perform a database dump.**

You can back up databases by using SQL Enterprise Manager or Transact-SQL. We will describe both methods, as well as how to do a parallel striped backup, in the following sections.

Using SQL Enterprise Manager to Back Up an Entire Database

Using SQL Enterprise Manager to back up databases is quite easy and intuitive. Follow the steps in Exercise 8.5 to back up the Pubs, Pubs2, Msdb, and Master databases.

You need to have already created backup devices for the databases (Exercises 8.3 and 8.4) before performing the backup.

EXERCISE 8.5

Backing Up Databases Using SQL Enterprise Manager

1. Start SQL Enterprise Manager and highlight the Pubs database.

2. Right-click and choose Backup/Restore from the context menu, or select Tools ➤ Database Backup/Restore to display the Database Backup/Restore dialog box.

3. In the Backup tab, select the Initialize Device checkbox in the Options portion of the dialog box (bottom left).

4. Highlight the pubs_backup device in the Backup Devices list on the right side of the dialog box, as shown below.

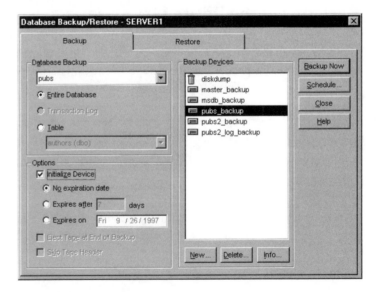

EXERCISE 8.5 (CONTINUED FROM PREVIOUS PAGE)

5. Click on the Backup Now button, and then click on OK in the Backup Volume Labels dialog box to accept the default volume labels. The Pubs database should take only a few seconds to back up.

6. After the backup completes, click on OK.

7. In the Database Backup/Restore dialog box, select the Master database, select the Initialize Device checkbox, select the master_backup device, click on Backup Now, and then click on OK. Click on OK after this database is backed up.

8. Repeat the procedure to select the Msdb database and back it up to the msdb_backup device.

9. Follow the same procedure to select the Pubs2 database and back it up to the pubs2_backup device.

10. Click on Close to close the Database Backup/Restore dialog box.

Using Transact-SQL to Back Up an Entire Database

You can use the Transact-SQL command Dump Database to back up databases. Here is its syntax:

```
Dump Database <databasename> to <backupdevice> (with init)
```

For example, to back up the Master database using the Transact-SQL command, start the ISQL/W utility and issue the following command:

```
Dump Database Master to master_backup with init
```

The results are shown in Figure 8.9.

FIGURE 8.9

The Result window after Dump Database to back up the Master database

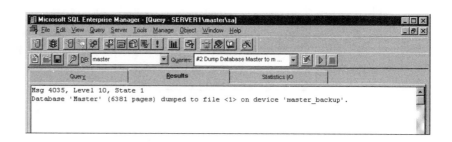

Performing Parallel Striped Backups

Using multiple devices to perform a parallel striped backup can make your backup operations more efficient. For example, a database that is backed up to tape may take an hour to back up. If you have three tape drives in the SQL Server machine and back up to all three devices simultaneously, the backup will take only about 20 minutes.

Microsoft ✓ ***Exam*** ***Objective***

Perform a striped backup.

Another feature of striped backups is that they don't need to be restored simultaneously. For example, if you had the backup set from the previous example (created by backing up to three tape drives simultaneously), you could restore to a SQL Server machine that has only one tape drive, by first restoring tape number 1, then number 2, and then the last tape.

In Exercise 8.6, we will perform a parallel striped backup of the Pubs database, using SQL Enterprise Manager.

EXERCISE 8.6

Performing a Parallel Striped Backup

1. Start SQL Enterprise Manager and create two new backup devices, named **pubs_a_backup** and **pubs_b_backup** (see Exercise 8.3).

2. Highlight the Pubs database, right-click, and choose Backup/Restore from the context menu.

3. In the Database Backup/Restore dialog box, select the Initialize Device checkbox in the Options portion of the dialog box.

4. In the Backup Devices list, highlight both the pubs_a_backup and the pubs_b_backup devices, as shown below. Use the Ctrl-click method (hold down the Ctrl key while you click with your mouse) to select more than one device.

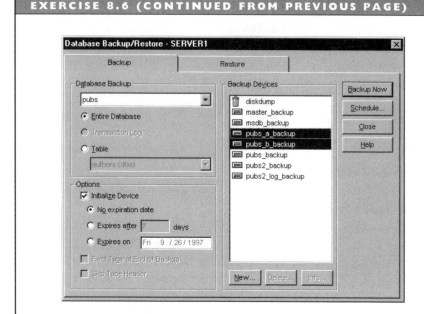

5. Click on the Backup Now button.

6. Click on OK to accept the default volume labels.

7. When the backup completes, click on OK, and then click on Close to close the Database Backup/Restore dialog box.

Backing Up Directly to a File

SQL Server 6.5 has the capability to back up databases directly to a file and restore directly from the file. When you use this method, you do not need to first specify a dump device.

You use a Transact-SQL command to back up directly to a file. The syntax is an extension of the Dump Database command:

```
Dump Database databasename to Disk='path\filename'
```

For example, to back up the Pubs2 database to a file named Pubs2.bak in the Dumps directory, use the following command:

```
Dump Database Pubs2 to Disk='C:\MSSQL\Dumps\Pubs2.bak'
```

Backing Up Transaction Logs

The transaction log for a database is a record of all of the transactions that have occurred in a database. One of the features of SQL Server is that the transaction log is truncated (cleaned out) only after a successful backup of the log using the Dump Transaction statement. Many companies have run SQL Server for two or three months with no problems, and then they suddenly find that no new transactions can be recorded because the transaction log is filled up.

Microsoft ✓ *Exam* *Objective*	**Dump a transaction log.**

The good news is that the transaction log will be cleaned out by SQL Server as part of a normal transaction log backup. The bad news is that SQL Server doesn't do this by default—all backups (and thus the cleaning or truncating of the log) must be configured by the administrator.

Backing up the full database does not affect the transaction log. You need to specifically back up the log to keep it cleaned out, or you may find yourself the recipient of the infamous 1105 error (transaction log full). Another advantage of backing up the transaction log is that it can be restored up to a certain point in time. For example, if you had a backup of the transaction log for Wednesday, and you discovered a major error occurred at 4:05 PM, you could restore the data up to 4:04 PM.

If the transaction log for a database is stored on its own backup device, the log can be backed up and restored separately from the database.

You can back up the transaction log through SQL Enterprise Manager or with Transact-SQL, as described in the following sections.

Using SQL Enterprise Manager to Back Up a Transaction Log

With SQL Enterprise Manager, you can back up just a database's transaction log through the Database Backup/Restore dialog box. In Exercise 8.7, we will add a new employee to simulate activity in the database, and then back up the log using SQL Enterprise Manager.

To complete this exercise, you need to have created the pubs2_log_backup device first (Exercise 8.3).

EXERCISE 8.7

Backing Up a Transaction Log Using SQL Enterprise Manager

1. Start SQL Enterprise Manager and select the Pubs2 database.

2. Select Tools ➤ SQL Query Tool and enter and execute the following statements:

   INSERT EMPLOYEE

   VALUES ('KRM52936F', 'Katie', 'R', 'Mortensen', DEFAULT, DEFAULT, DEFAULT, DEFAULT)

3. Highlight the Pubs2 database, right-click, and choose Backup/Restore from the context menu (or select Tools ➤ Database Backup/Restore) to display the Database Backup/Restore dialog box.

4. In the Database Backup section of the dialog box, select the Transaction Log option.

5. In the Backup Devices list, highlight the pubs2_log_backup device, as shown below.

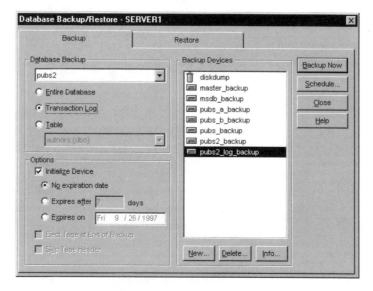

6. Click on the Backup Now button to start the backup procedure.

7. When the backup is complete, click on OK, and then click on the Close button in the Database Backup/Restore dialog box.

Using Transact-SQL to Back Up a Transaction Log

You can back up the transaction log by using the Dump Transaction command. Here is its syntax:

```
Dump Transaction database to device
```

For example, to back up the Pubs2 database to the pubs2_log_backup device, use the following command:

```
Dump Transaction pubs2 to pubs2_log_backup
```

This command not only backs up the log, it also removes all committed transactions (truncates it).

There are various switches that can be added to the Dump Transaction command to change the way the backup works:

truncate_only   This switch is used to only truncate (clean out) the log. For example, if you back up a database in its entirety every night, and you have no intention of ever using point-in-time recovery or recovering modifications made during a business day, maintaining a backup of the log would be redundant; however, the log still needs to be cleaned out.

no_log   This switch can be used as a last resort if the log becomes full. Normal backups of the log first make an entry in the log to record that the log has been backed up, and then the log is cleared out. If the log is completely full, the record of the backup cannot be made, so the backup fails and the log is not cleaned out.

no_truncate   This switch does the opposite of the truncate_only switch—it backs up the log without truncating or cleaning it out. The main purpose for this switch is to make a new backup of the transaction log when the database itself is too damaged to work. When you use this switch, only the log device is accessed, not the database device.

Another way to clear the transaction log if you do not wish to maintain transaction log backups is to use the Truncate Log on Checkpoint option for the database. You can do this through the Options tab of the Edit Database dialog box, as shown in Figure 8.10 (double-click on the database to display this dialog box).

In Exercise 8.8, we will simulate backing up a damaged database by using the Dump Transaction command with the no_truncate switch.

FIGURE 8.10

Setting a database to truncate the transaction log on each checkpoint

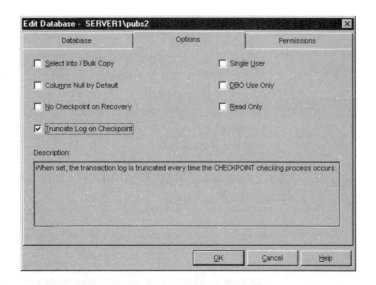

EXERCISE 8.8

Simulating the Recovery of Data from a Crashed Database

1. Stop SQL Server (the MSSQLServer service).

2. Navigate to the folder that is holding the database devices, and rename the pubs2_data.dat file to **pubs2_data.old**.

3. Start SQL Server.

4. Start SQL Enterprise Manager. Attempt to open the Pubs2 database (you shouldn't be able to open it).

5. Create a new backup of the log by starting ISQL/W and issuing the following command:

   `Dump Transaction pubs2 to pubs2_log_backup with no_truncate, no init`

6. Stop SQL Server.

7. Rename the pubs2_data.old file back to **pubs2_data.dat**.

8. Restart SQL Server.

Scheduling Backups

SQL Server has a built-in scheduling feature that allows you to set a recurring time for your backups. By scheduling backups, you are simply creating SQL Server tasks, which are handled by the SQL Executive service. (Creating, editing, and deleting tasks are covered in detail in Chapter 9.) You can schedule backups through SQL Enterprise Manager, either by using the Database Backup/Restore dialog box or by using the Server Manager's Database Maintenance Plan Wizard.

Using the Database Backup/Restore Dialog Box to Schedule Backups

You can easily schedule backups through SQL Enterprise Manager's Database Backup/Restore dialog box. In Exercise 8.9, we will schedule a backup of the Master database to occur nightly.

EXERCISE 8.9

Scheduling Backups with the Database Backup/ Restore Dialog Box

1. Start SQL Enterprise Manager and highlight the Master database.

2. Right-click and select Backup/Restore from the context menu (or select Tools ➢ Database Backup/Restore) to display the Database Backup/Restore dialog box.

3. Select the Initialize Device checkbox in the Options section of the dialog box.

4. Highlight the master_backup device in the Backup Devices list.

5. Click on the Schedule button.

6. Click on OK to choose a volume ID.

7. You may get a warning that the backup device contains previous data and that you will be overwriting that data. Click on OK to continue. The Schedule Backup dialog box appears. It contains a default task name, the Transact-SQL command that will be run, and options for scheduling, as shown here.

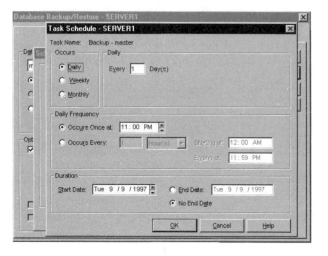

8. Click on the Recurring option button.

9. Click on the Change button to specify when the backup is to take place. The Task Schedule dialog box appears.

10. Set the backup to take place daily at 11:00 PM, as shown below.

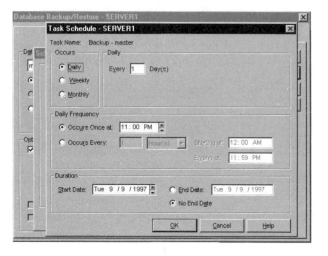

EXERCISE 8.9 (CONTINUED FROM PREVIOUS PAGE)

11. Click on OK in both the Task Schedule and Schedule Backup dialog boxes to save the task, and then click on Close in the Database Backup/Restore dialog box.

12. Check that the task has been scheduled by choosing Server ➤ Scheduled Tasks from the Server menu.

13. To run the task manually, highlight the task and select the Run Task button (the green one).

14. When you're prompted to confirm that you want to run the task, click on Yes, and then click on OK in the next dialog box. Your task has now been started.

15. Select the Refresh button (the one with an icon of a circle with two arrows) occasionally until the Last Run and Last Run Status fields show that the task has executed.

16. After the task completes, close the dialog box.

Using the Database Maintenance Plan Wizard

SQL Server 6.5 includes a Database Maintenance Plan Wizard, which does a great job of scheduling backups (and also performs optimizations). You can start this Wizard from Server Manager by clicking on the Wizard button on the icon bar (it's the icon on the right end).

The Database Maintenance Plan Wizard takes you through a series of dialog boxes, in which you accept the defaults or choose the other options and then click on the Next button to continue to the next step. When you run the Wizard, the first dialog box asks you to choose the database for which you want to schedule backups. The second Wizard dialog box contains settings grouped in Data Volatility and Data Growth sections, as shown in Figure 8.11.

F I G U R E   8.11

The Database
Maintenance Plan Wizard
asks you to describe the
data volatility and data
growth aspects of your
database.

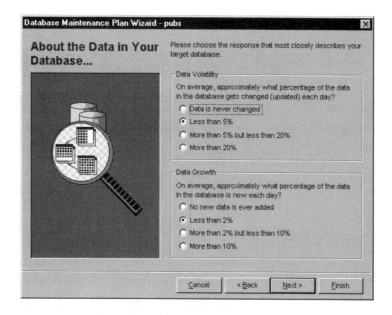

The next dialog box contains settings regarding data verification tests, and lets you select to run these tests daily or weekly. The Data Verification dialog box is shown in Figure 8.12. As you can see, all the test options are set by default and are recommended.

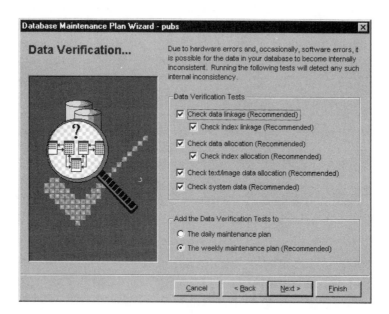

The Data Optimization dialog box appears next, as shown in Figure 8.13. Here you can select optimization options (both set by default and recommended) and have the optimizations run daily or once a week.

FIGURE 8.13

Setting data optimization options

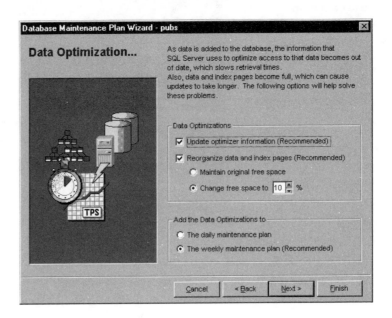

In the next dialog box, labeled Data Protection, you can select not to back up the database, to back up the database daily, or to back up the database weekly, as shown in Figure 8.14. There is also a checkbox that you can select to do the backup only if the data verification checks do not find any problems with the data. Choosing this option will ensure that, if any errors are encountered by the DBCC commands checking your data, the data will not be backed up.

In the Backup Destination dialog box, which appears next, the Wizard shows the default path and naming convention for the backup files, as well as a checkbox for setting the retention time for backup disk files. You can leave the default settings, shown in Figure 8.15, or change to another destination.

The Wizard will now allow you to set a day and time for the task to run. Figure 8.16 shows an example of scheduling a backup to run on Sundays at 11:45 PM.

FIGURE 8.14

Setting data protection (backup) options

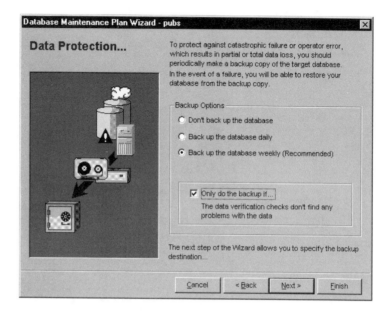

FIGURE 8.15

Setting the backup destination and file retention time

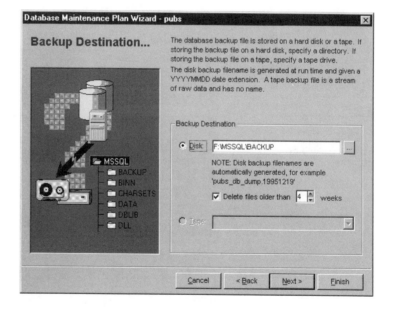

After you set the schedule, the Wizard shows you a summary of what you told it to do. Select Done to finish the creation of the task. Then you can choose whether or not to print a copy of the scheduled maintenance, and whether or not you want to run the task now.

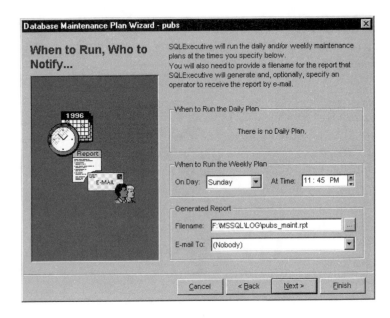

You can check your scheduled task by choosing Server ➤ Scheduled Tasks.
Figure 8.17 shows an example of a weekly backup task for the Pubs database
created through the Database Maintenance Plan Wizard. It is named pubs
Weekly Automated Maintenance.

Viewing Backup Device Information

There are several ways to get information about the backup devices and the dates and contents of the backups stored on them. You can use either SQL Enterprise Manager or Transact-SQL to view this information, as explained in the following sections.

Using SQL Enterprise Manager to View Backup Device Information

You can view the contents of backup devices in SQL Enterprise Manager in two ways: by opening the Backup Devices folder or through the Database Backup/Restore dialog box. In Exercise 8.10, we will use both methods.

EXERCISE 8.10

Examining Backup Devices Using SQL Enterprise Manager

1. Start SQL Enterprise Manager and open the Backup Devices folder.

2. Expand the master_backup device entry. You should see a list of all backups contained on that device, as shown in the example below.

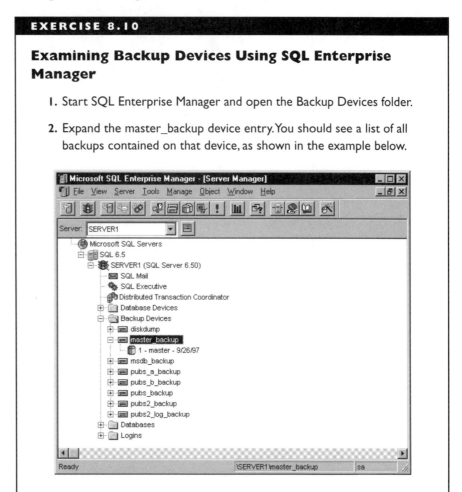

EXERCISE 8.10 (CONTINUED FROM PREVIOUS PAGE)

3. Right-click and select Backup/Restore from the context menu (or select Tools ➢ Database Backup/Restore) to display the Database Backup/Restore dialog box.

4. Highlight a backup device and click on the Info button (at the bottom of the dialog box). The Backup Device Information dialog box appears, as shown below. This dialog box contains details of the backup devices, including the backups and the dates of the backups.

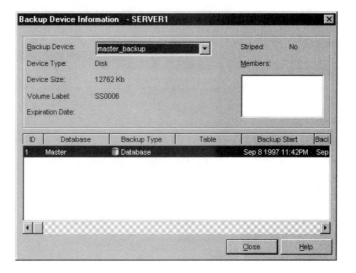

5. Click on Close in the Backup Device Information dialog box, and then click on Close in the Database Backup/Restore dialog box.

Using Transact-SQL to View Backup Device Information

The sp_helpdevice system stored procedure provides information about backup devices. When you use the system stored procedure by itself, you will see a list of all the devices, both database and backup, that are in SQL Server, as shown in the example in Figure 8.18.

FIGURE 8.18

Results of using
sp_helpdevice

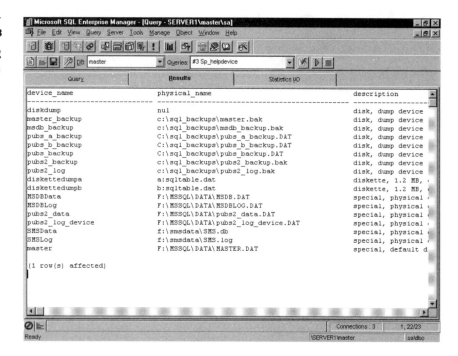

When you specify a particular device with sp_helpdevice, you will see details about that device. For example, to get information about the master_backup device, enter the following command:

```
sp_helpdevice master_backup
```

You should see something similar to the information shown in Figure 8.19.

FIGURE 8.19

Getting details about a
device with
sp_helpdevice
master_backup

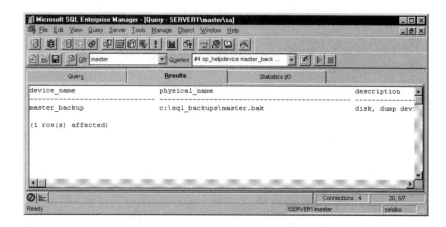

Restoring Databases

Before you restore a database from its backup, there are several steps you need to take. Your first task is to resolve the problem with the database, then you need to drop and re-create the affected databases and devices. Then you can proceed with the actual restore process.

Microsoft ✓ *Exam* *Objective* **Restore a corrupted database.**

Here are the steps for restoring a damaged database:

- Find and fix the cause of the failure.

- Drop all of the affected databases.

- Drop all of the affected devices.

- Re-create the affected devices.

- Re-create the affected databases.

- Restore the database from a database backup.

- Restore (or reapply) the transaction log (or logs) from the log backup (or backups).

- Change the database from DBO Use Only mode (if the Create for Load option was used)

Fixing, Dropping, and Re-creating

The steps to take before you restore a database from a backup involve troubleshooting and rebuilding your database structure. These topics are covered in detail in Chapters 5 and 13 and briefly summarized below.

Finding and Fixing the Cause of the Failure

First, you need to troubleshoot Windows NT and/or SQL Server to determine the cause of the failure. There are two basic reasons for determining the cause: the first is to fix the problem, and the second is to increase your chances of preventing it from happening again in the future.

Dropping the Affected Databases

Before the database can be re-created, it must first be dropped. The normal command, `Drop Database <databasename>`, expects to find the database before it drops it. If the database is completely destroyed, the command will not execute properly. Use the `DBCC DBREPAIR` command or the `sp_dbremove` system stored procedure to drop the affected database, because either of these will work even if the database is gone or corrupted beyond repair.

Dropping the Affected Devices

After a hardware failure or corruption of a device, the device must be dropped before it can be re-created. You can drop a device through SQL Enterprise Manager or with Transact-SQL. In SQL Enterprise Manager, simply highlight the device, right-click, and choose Delete.

The stored procedure to use is `sp_dropdevice`. Here is its syntax:

```
sp_dropdevice device1, device2...
```

The *device1, device2* parameters are the device names.

Re-creating the Affected Devices

After you have dropped any devices and databases that have been affected by the failure, you can re-create those devices.

Microsoft ✓ *Exam* *Objective*   **Re-create a lost device.**

SQL Server tracks databases by the amount of pages allocated on each device, and how those pages are used (data, indexes, transaction logs, and so on). Because of this, when you re-create devices to be used for the database, you need to make the new devices as similar to the originals as possible. For instance, if the original database was contained in the payroll.dat device file with a size of 100MB, and on the device called payroll2.dat with a size of 150MB, with the log on payroll_log.dat at 50MB, you should re-create these three devices with the same sizes (or larger).

Re-creating the Affected Databases

In order for the backup to be restored to the exact condition it was in originally, you will need to re-create the database with the same devices and sizes that were originally assigned, in the same order (including altering the databases as they were altered over time). See Chapters 5 and 13 for details on creating and troubleshooting databases.

You may want to use the Create for Load setting when creating your databases. To enable this setting, either check the For Load box in SQL Enterprise Manager, or add the keywords FOR LOAD if you're using Transact-SQL. Not only will it be faster to initialize the database, but the database can be used only to load backups. After the load is over, the database is set to DBO Use Only until you change the setting, as described later in this chapter.

Restoring the Database

You can quickly restore a database by using SQL Enterprise Manager. This is done through the Restore tab of the Database Backup/Restore dialog box.

Microsoft ✓ *Exam* *Objective*	**Load a database dump.**

The steps in Exercise 8.11 demonstrate how to restore databases. For this example, we will restore the Pubs and Pubs2 databases.

EXERCISE 8.11

Restoring Databases

1. In SQL Enterprise Manager, highlight the Pubs database, right-click, and choose Backup/Restore.

2. Select the Restore tab. You will see a history of all of the backups made to the Pubs database, even though some of the backups may have been overwritten.

3. Click on the From Device button, and then highlight the pubs_backup device. You will see a list of all of the backups held on that device, as shown here.

Restore From Device On Server - SERVER1

Destination Database: ⎡pubs⎤

Devices and Files:
- master_backup
- msdb_backup
- pubs_a_backup
- pubs_b_backup
- pubs_backup
- pubs2_backup
- pubs2_log_backup

Options
- ☐ Single Table
- ☐ Until Time   Fri 9 / 26 / 1997   06 : 54 AM

Restore Now
Add File...
Add Device...
Close
Help

Backup Information:

Restore	Backup Type	Database	Table	Backup S
◇	🗊 Database	pubs		9/26/97 6

4. Highlight the most recent backup and click on the Restore Now button. If you get a warning that the database is in use, you will need to find out who is using the database (select Server ➤ Current Activity), and either wait for them to finish or terminate their connection to the database.

5. Select the Pubs2 database and restore it in the same manner.

6. Click on OK, then Close in both dialog boxes.

WARNING   SQL Server wipes out the old database when you restore a backup of a database. There is no merging of the data.

Restoring the Transaction Log

When you restore a transaction log, you are actually reapplying all of the transactions just as they occurred. Transaction logs must be restored in the same order in which they were backed up. For example, if you have transaction log backups for each day of the week and Wednesday's backup is bad, you will be unable to load Thursday's or Friday's backups as well.

Unlike restoring the entire database, restoring transaction logs literally re-applies all of the transactions that took place between the time of the full database backup and the time of the backup of the transaction log.

In Exercise 8.12, we will restore the transaction log for the Pubs2 database and look at the results.

EXERCISE 8.12

Restoring a Transaction Log

1. In SQL Enterprise Manager, highlight the Pubs2 database, right-click, and select Backup/Restore.

2. Select the Restore tab.

3. Select From Device, and highlight the pubs2_log_backup device.

4. Click on Restore Now to start the restoration process.

5. Click on OK, then Close to close the dialog box.

Restoring Transaction Logs Up to a Certain Time

With SQL Server 6.5, you also have the capability to restore the transaction logs up to a certain point in time. To do this, select the Until Time checkbox in the Restore tab of the Database Backup/Restore dialog box and choose a date and time from which you would like to restore the log. Figure 8.20 shows an example. Here, although the transaction log contains data up to 1:28 PM, we will restore data only up to 12:30 PM.

Restoring Individual Tables

SQL Server 6.5 adds the ability to restore individual tables. This can be useful if you need to return to an earlier version of a table. In order to restore individual tables, the database must have the Select Into/Bulk Copy option enabled, and it should also be set to DBO Use Only.

F I G U R E   8.20

Restoring a transaction
log to a certain point in
time

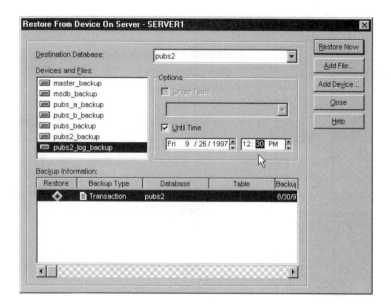

WARNING   Restoring tables that have referential integrity to other tables can cause your
data to become logically corrupted. For example, suppose that you needed
to restore the Clients table because all of the phone numbers had been
changed by mistake. If there were any new clients with pending orders added
after the backup, your Orders table would refer to a nonexistent client.

Follow the steps in Exercise 8.13 to restore an individual table. In this
example, we will restore a table in the Pubs database.

EXERCISE 8.13

Restoring a Table

1. In SQL Enterprise Manager, double-click on the Pubs database to display the Edit Database dialog box.

2. Choose the Options tab. Select the Select Into/Bulk Copy and DBO
   Use Only options. Click on OK to save the changes.

3. Right-click and select Backup/Restore to display the Database
   Backup/Restore dialog box.

4. Choose the Restore tab. Select From Device and highlight the pubs_backup device. Select the Single Table checkbox and choose the Employee table, as shown below.

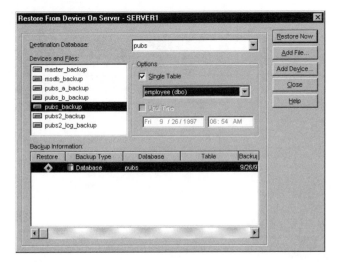

5. Click on Restore Now. Then answer Yes to both prompts.

6. Click on Close to close the dialog box.

Changing the Database from DBO Use Only Mode

As explained earlier in the chapter, if the database was originally created with the Create for Load option, after the database is loaded from a backup, it will be set to DBO Use Only. In order for ordinary users to access the database, you will need to turn off this database setting.

In Figure 8.21, the Pubs2 database is marked for DBO Use Only, which is denoted by its icon. To see what the Server Manager icons mean, display the Server Legend window (by clicking on the button next to your server name in the second row of the toolbar), which is also shown in Figure 8.21.

The DBO Use Only setting is on the Options tab of the Edit Database dialog box, as shown in Figure 8.22. To change a database back to one that all users can access, deselect this option.

F I G U R E   8.21

A database marked as
DBO Use Only

F I G U R E   8.21

A database marked as
DBO Use Only

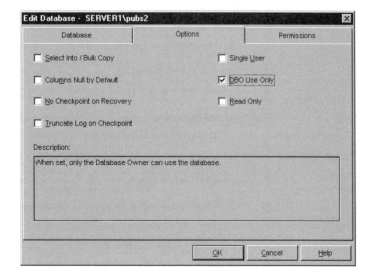

F I G U R E   8.22

The Options tab of the
Edit Database dialog box
has the DBO Use Only
setting.

Restoring the Master Database with a Valid Backup

Because the Master database contains most of the settings for SQL Server as a whole, restoring the Master database is not only more complicated, but it is also impossible to do accidentally. In order to restore the Master database, you must start SQL Server in single-user mode. You do this by starting the SQL Server program from the command prompt using the -m switch

When you rebuild the Master database, the Msdb database is also rebuilt (reset). You should restore the Msdb database from your most recent backups. If you do not, all of your scheduled jobs, alerts, and operators will disappear.

In Exercise 8.14, we will start SQL Server in single-user mode, and then restore the Master database from a backup.

EXERCISE 8.14

Restoring the Master Database

1. Stop SQL Server (the MSSQLServer service).

2. Open a Windows NT command prompt.

3. Start SQL Server from a command prompt by issuing the following command:

   SQLSERVR -m

4. Minimize the Command Prompt window.

5. Start SQL Enterprise Manager and expand your server. SQL Server will show a red stop light even though it is running.

6. Highlight the Master database, right-click, and choose Backup/Restore to display the Database Backup/Restore dialog box.

7. Select the Restore tab, highlight the master_backup device, and click on Restore Now.

8. After the Master database is restored, SQL Server should stop automatically. Return to the command prompt. It should be back to a regular C:\ prompt.

9. Restart SQL Server normally.

Restoring the Master Database without a Backup

If the Master database becomes corrupt and a current backup is not available, you can follow a procedure that will allow you to re-create the Master database so that your user databases reappear. The steps are as follows:

- Find and fix the cause of the failure. As with any other database failure, you will need to find and fix the hardware or software failure that caused the Master database to become corrupted.

- Rebuild the Master database. Use the SQL Server Setup program to rebuild the Master database.

Rebuilding the Master database does not fix the existing one. Instead, it re-creates a brand new Master database, just as if you reinstalled SQL Server.

- Run the Disk Reinit command for each device. The Disk Reinit command has the same syntax as the Disk Init command, but it is used to take an existing device and plug the specifications back into SQL Server. The exact parameters of the devices must be known. To help reconstruct the devices, you may want to print the specifications before you have a failure. Run sp_helpdevice to get details on the devices. You might also want to run sp_help_revdatabase. .

- Run the Disk Refit command. The Disk Refit command must be executed immediately after running the Disk Reinit commands. The Disk Refit command searches new devices for databases and plugs those specifications back into the sysusages and sysdatabases tables of the Master database. Note that you only run one Disk Refit command after you have completed all Disk Reinit commands.

- Re-create the settings for SQL Server. Because the rebuilt Master database holds all of the settings for SQL Server, all of the settings will be restored to their defaults. You will need to reconfigure SQL Server with its previous settings, and probably stop and restart SQL Server to have them take effect. (See Chapter 12 for details on changing SQL Server settings.)

- Re-create the users and security for each database. Because the rebuilt Master database will have only the default SQL logins, you will need to re-create all of the logins. (See Chapter 6 for details on setting up login accounts.)

- Restore the Msdb database. Rebuilding the Master database also rebuilds the Msdb database. Any tasks, alerts, and operators you have created will need to be re-created by hand if you don't have a current backup of the Msdb database.

Restoring a Database Directly from a File

If you backed up a database directly to a file using the `Dump Database` *databasename* to `Disk` command (as described earlier in the chapter), you can restore the database directly from this file.

The command to restore the database directly from a file is `Load Database`, with a from `Disk=` switch . For example, to restore a database using the Pubs2.bak file, use the following command:

```
Load Database Pubs2 from Disk='C:\MSSQL\Dumps\Pubs2.bak'
```

Summary

Preserving data under less than ideal situations is one of the primary responsibilities of a database administrator. We began this chapter with a discussion of several data-protection options. Windows NT provides some features that provide data protection, including disk mirroring, disk duplexing, and striping with parity (RAID 5 arrays). Although a pure striped drive does not provide any data protection, it is the fastest way to set up your drives.

We next looked at SQL Server's automatic recovery feature. This feature is run each time that SQL Server is restarted to bring the database up to date, with only completed transactions.

Then you learned about SQL Server's manual backup procedures. Because SQL Server database devices are locked when SQL Server is running, normal Windows NT backup procedures will not back up any data. The solution is to define backup (or dump) devices, which are files that contain a backup of databases and transaction logs. After the backup process is complete, the backup devices are closed by SQL Server, and they can be backed up normally by Windows NT.

After explaining how to create backup devices, we moved on to the actual backup process. You can perform backups through SQL Enterprise Manager or by using Transact-SQL commands. You can back up an entire database or just the transaction log. Backups can also be scheduled to happen on a regular basis. When you use SQL Enterprise Manager to schedule backups, it creates a SQL Executive task for the backups.

Finally, we discussed restore procedures. When you restore a database from a backup, all of the previous data and objects are deleted and replaced. When you restore a transaction log, the backup merely reapplies all of the transactions. Transaction logs can also be restored up to a certain date and time, making recovery from errors easier.

You learned that rebuilding the Master database resets it back to its new installation status, and you will need to reapply any changes you've made since you installed SQL Server. The Master database can be restored only while the database is running in single-user mode, which is done by loading SQL Server from the command prompt with the -m switch.

Exercise Questions

1. What is the Transact-SQL command to back up databases?

   A. Backup Database

   B. Dump Database

   C. Backup Device

   D. Dump Device

2. How do you edit a recurring (scheduled) backup? (Choose all that apply.)

   A. You can't—you must delete and re-create them

   B. From the Database/Tasks dialog box

   C. From SQL Executive/Tasks dialog box

   D. From the SQL Server/ Manage Scheduled Tasks dialog box

3. What is the Transact-SQL command to back up a transaction log?

   A. Dump Database /Log

   B. Dump Log

   C. Dump Transaction

   D. Backup Log

4. What does the no_log switch do on a transaction log backup?

   A. There is no such switch

   B. It removes committed transactions from the log without making a backup

   C. It makes a backup of the log without removing committed transactions

   D. It is a "last resort" switch for when the log has become full

5. What does the no_truncate switch do on a transaction log backup?

   A. There is no such switch

   B. It removes committed transactions from the log without making a backup

   C. It makes a backup of the log without removing committed transactions

   D. It is a "last resort" switch for when the log has become full

6. What does the truncate_only switch do on a transaction log backup?

   A. There is no such switch

   B. It removes committed transactions from the log without making a backup

C. It makes a backup of the log without removing committed transactions

D. It is a "last resort" switch for when the log has become full

7. What is the most efficient form of disk fault tolerance with six drives?

A. Stripe set

B. Mirror set

C. Duplex set

D. Stripe set with parity

8. Windows NT supports which of the following? (Choose all that apply.)

A. Mirroring

B. Duplexing

C. Striping

D. Striping with parity

9. What program allows you to do backups through a graphical user interface?

A. Transfer Manager

B. Backup Manager

C. SQL Security Manager

D. SQL Enterprise Manager

10. What is the Transact-SQL command to restore a database?

A. Restore Database

B. Run Database

C. Load Database

D. Undo Database

11. What is the Transact-SQL command to restore a log?

A. Restore Log

B. Load Log

C. Restore Transaction

D. Load Transaction

12. What is the switch that initializes a backup device?

A. with init

B. with format

C. overwrite

D. without protect

13. Which feature of SQL Server allows backups to run faster?

A. SCSI support

B. Striped backups

C. Mirror backups

D. Parallel striped backups

14. You can restore log files out of order.

A. True

B. False

CHAPTER

9

Tasks, Alerts, and Events

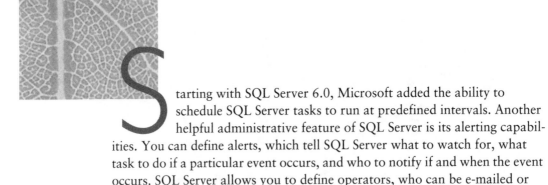

tarting with SQL Server 6.0, Microsoft added the ability to schedule SQL Server tasks to run at predefined intervals. Another helpful administrative feature of SQL Server is its alerting capabilities. You can define alerts, which tell SQL Server what to watch for, what task to do if a particular event occurs, and who to notify if and when the event occurs. SQL Server allows you to define operators, who can be e-mailed or paged to receive information about tasks and alerts.

The database that holds all of the tasks, alerts, and operators you've defined is the Msdb database. This database is installed by default, although there are no tasks or operators defined by default.

We will begin this chapter with a discussion of the Msdb database, including its system tables, as well as how to back it up and restore it. Next, we will cover the SQL Executive service, which is the overall controlling service for tasks, alerts, operators, and events.

Then we will explain how to create and manage alerts, operators, and tasks. You will learn how to set up each of these and how to make changes as necessary.

The Msdb Database

The Msdb database is a system database that is automatically created when you install SQL Server 6.0 and higher. The Msdb database contains tasks, alerts, and operators. The Msdb data portion of the database is contained on the MsdbData.DAT device; the MsdbLog.DAT device contains the log.

System Tables of the Msdb Database

You may recall from the discussion of system tables in Chapter 3 that there are five tables in the Msdb database that contain information about tasks, alerts, and operators.

Microsoft
Exam
Objective

Identify the role of the msdb database.

Exam objectives are subject to change at any time without prior notice and at Microsoft's sole discretion. Please visit Microsoft's Training & Certification Web site (www.microsoft.com/Train_Cert) for the most current exam objectives listing.

These tables maintain your tasks, alerts, and operators, as follows:

- The systasks table is the one that tracks the tasks that have been created. SQL Executive looks in this table for not only the task and what it entails, but also the schedule for the task. Doing a query on the systasks table shows information that is similar to what is displayed in the Manage Scheduled Tasks window of SQL Enterprise Manager (select Server ➤ Scheduled Tasks, or highlight SQL Executive, right-click, and choose Manage Scheduled Tasks).

- The sysalerts table holds all of the alerts that have been defined for the system. The individual columns list the SQL Server events that the SQL Executive service looks for, and what task to perform if the event is found.

- The sysoperators table holds all of the information about various operators and how they have been defined to SQL Server. E-mail addresses and paging numbers for each operator, as well as their hours of responsibility, can be defined. A fail-safe, or operator of last resort, can also be defined, in case there are no other operators available.

- The sysnotifications table relates alerts to the operators that will be notified if the alert is triggered.

- The syshistory table holds the history of attempted tasks. It maintains information about not only the success or failure of the task, but also how long the task took and when the task ran. You can access this table from SQL Enterprise Manager's Manage Schedule Tasks window, as explained later in this chapter.

Backing Up and Restoring the Msdb Database

Because the Msdb database contains all of your tasks, alerts, and operators, it should be backed up on a regular basis. Once a week should be sufficient. If you make a lot of changes to your tasks, alerts, or operators during the week, you may want to do a backup after you've made the changes.

The backup process for the Msdb database is the same as for any other database. You need to define a backup device for the Msdb database, and you will probably want to schedule a backup task to back up this database on a regular basis. (See Chapter 8 for details about backing up and restoring databases, as well as scheduling backup tasks.)

Msdb database backups are important because you may need to restore the Msdb database if you delete an important task, alert, or operator, or if the database gets corrupted. You can restore the Msdb database in the same way that you restore other databases: In SQL Enterprise Manager, highlight the database, select Backup/Restore from the context menu or Tools menu, choose a valid backup on the Restore tab, and click on the Restore Now button.

Rebuilding the Msdb Database

As mentioned in Chapter 4, if disaster strikes (you don't have a valid backup of the Master database, or you wish to change the character set or sort order), you may be forced to rebuild your Master database. You can do this through an option in the SQL Setup utility's Options dialog box. If you choose the Rebuild the Master Database option, the Setup utility rebuilds the Master database by deleting the current copy of the Master database, and creating a new one. The rebuilt Master database has all the default settings that existed when you initially installed SQL Server.

When you choose to rebuild the Master database, you also (without any warning or notice) rebuild the Msdb database as well. Like the rebuilt Master database, the rebuilt Msdb database has all the default settings that came with SQL Server installation. This means that not a single task or operator is defined. You will need to restore all of your Msdb data from a valid backup. If there is no valid backup, you will need to re-create your tasks, alerts, and operators by hand.

You can rebuild just the Msdb database by running the Instmsdb.sql, Web.sql, and Servmsgs.sql scripts from the Mssql\Install folder.

The SQL Executive Service

The SQL Executive service can be thought of as an optional helper service for SQL Server. Nothing it does is technically required to make SQL Server work, but it provides some valuable functions, so you will probably want to enable it.

Microsoft ✓ **Exam Objective**   **Identify the role of SQL Executive service.**

The SQL Executive service is in charge of finding and carrying out tasks and alerts, and notifying operators on the success and/or failure of those tasks and alerts.

Configuring the SQL Executive Service

The SQL Executive Service is installed by default. Although the SQL Setup program attempts to correctly configure the service for your system, it may not be entirely successful.

There are two main settings that are required for the SQL Executive service to work properly:

- A user account, with appropriate rights, should be assigned to the service.

- The service should be configured to start automatically (if it is set to manual, you will need to start it by hand every time you reboot your server).

While most services don't require a user account assigned to them in order to function correctly, services that go beyond the physical box and connect to other servers on the network (as the SQL Executive service may do) usually need a user account assigned to them. This is so they have an account to be authenticated with on the remote server. Otherwise, they connect with "null" security credentials, and by default will be denied access.

Setting Up the User Account

As explained in Chapter 2, you can set up your SQL Executive user account before you install SQL Server, and then configure the account correctly during the installation process. If you didn't do this at installation time, don't worry—you can still set up the account and configure it.

There are three parts to setting up the SQL Executive service user account: creating the user in Windows NT, giving the user appropriate rights, and assigning the user to the service. Here is the procedure:

- Create the user account using the Windows NT User Manager or User Manager for Domains utility, just as for any other user. Clear the User Must Change Password at Next Logon option, and check the Password Never Expires option. It may also be a good idea to set the User Cannot Change Password option.

- Give the user account appropriate rights. Make the user account for the SQL Executive service a member of the Administrators group, and also of the Domain Administrators group if you want that account to be usable on any and all SQL Server machines in the domain. Assign the Log on as a Service Right to this account. This right is in the Advanced Rights dialog box (choose User Rights from the User Manager for Domains Policies menu and check the Advanced Rights box). Add the account you've created to the list of accounts that already have this right by selecting Add, then pick the appropriate account from the list.

The Services Control Panel will usually assign the Log on as a Service right to a user account if it isn't already assigned.

- Assign the user to the service. The user account can be assigned to the SQL Executive in several different ways: during the initial installation (see Chapter 2), from the Services Control Panel, from Server Manager (by selecting Services from the Computer menu), and from SQL Enterprise Manager (by right-clicking on SQL Executive and selecting Configure from the context menu).

Starting the Service Automatically

As explained in earlier chapters, you can set SQL Server to start automatically, either by choosing this option during installation (see Chapter 2) or later, through the SQL Enterprise Manager's Server Configuration/Options dialog box (see Chapter 4). If you set auto start, the MSSQLServer service will start when the server boots; no one needs to be logged in in order to make things happen.

It makes sense that if you have SQL Server set to start automatically, then you should also set the SQL Executive service to start automatically. You can set this auto start option in the same way that you set auto start for the SQL Server service—during installation of SQL Server or through the Server Configuration/Options dialog box (Server Options tab).

Changing the SQL Executive Password

Occasionally, you may want to change the password assigned to the SQL Executive service (for example, after an employee who had access leaves). You'll need to change the password in two places:

- Change the password using Windows NT's User Manager for Domains.

- Change the password assigned to the SQL Executive service.

In the Windows NT User Manager for Domains utility, you change the password through the user's Properties dialog box. You'll need to replace the old password with the new one, and then confirm the new password.

Passwords, unlike usernames, are case-sensitive in Windows NT.

Once you have changed the password, you need to tell the SQL Executive service about the change. There are several ways to reconfigure the service: through the Services Control Panel, the Server Manager's Services option on the Computer menu, or SQL Enterprise Manager's SQL Executive Configure option (on the context menu).

Understanding Alerts, Tasks, and Events

The SQL Executive service is the overall controlling service for tasks, alerts, operators, and events. There are separate engines for tasks, alerts, and events, but the SQL Executive is the controlling service for these engines.

Microsoft
✓ *Exam*
Objective

Identify conceptual relationships among the Scheduler service, the msdb database, and the Windows NT event log.

Let's look at what happens to a common error before and after the SQL Executive service has been configured. Suppose that the Pubs2 database log fills up and generates an 1105 error (the standard error code generated for a full log). SQL Server's own internal error generator will create the 1105 error, but without SQL Executive to watch for and handle the error, the problem will need to be fixed by hand. And until you resolve the problem, the users will not be able to access the database. Figure 9.1 illustrates how errors are handled without tasks and alerts.

FIGURE 9.1

Flow chart of standard
SQL Server error
messages

With an alert and task predefined, the alert engine will be looking for the 1105 error in the Windows NT event log, and will be ready to trigger a backup task that will truncate (clean out) the log, as illustrated in Figure 9.2. Now when SQL Server generates an 1105 error, the alert engine finds it, and then acts on it by triggering the task. The database log is truncated, and users can resume using the database normally. If the backup failed to work, another error would be generated. At that point, the operator could be sent an e-mail message and/or paged.

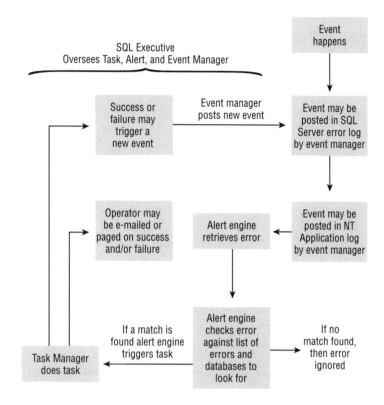

Creating and Managing Alerts

The SQL Executive, via the alert engine, looks in the sysalerts table in order to find which errors it should be looking for. By defining an alert, you are telling SQL Server which error codes to look for in the Windows NT event logs, and what action to take if an event is found.

Creating an Alert

Creating alerts is somewhat intuitive. Alerts can be based on a generic error message number, an error severity level, or an error happening in a specific database. There are several basic steps for setting up an alert:

- Define the error to look for.

- Optionally, define the database the error must happen in. An alert can filter error messages based on the database. For instance, an alert can be created that watches the Pubs database in case it fills up. This alert would operate only on the Pubs database; if any other database filled up, the alert wouldn't do anything.

- Define the task to perform. Alerts are usually created to perform a task when the alert condition is met. You can define a task that will run when the alert is triggered. Tasks can either run Transact-SQL statements or command-prompt programs such as BCP.EXE (covered in Chapter 10) or ISQL.EXE (covered in Chapter 3).

- Optionally, define who will be notified and how they will be notified. You can specify operators and whether they should receive an e-mail message and/or be paged when an alert is triggered. (See the "Creating and Managing Operators" section later in this chapter for details about setting up operators.)

- Activate the alert by selecting the Enabled box in the Edit Alert dialog box. This option is selected by default, but you can deselect it to temporarily disable an alert.

Microsoft ✓ *Exam* *Objective* **Set up alerts.**

Follow the steps in Exercise 9.1 to create an alert. In this example, we will set up an alert to watch for the log of the Pubs2 database to get full, and to back up the transaction log (thus clearing the log) if and when the alert is triggered.

EXERCISE 9.1

Creating an Alert

1. Start SQL Enterprise Manager and select Server ➤ Alerts/Operators, or highlight SQL Executive, right-click, and choose Manage Alerts/ Operators. You'll see the Alerts tab of the Manage Alerts and Operators window. You should see nine predefined alerts.

2. To add a new alert, click on the New Alert button on the toolbar (the one with an icon of a exclamation point, on the far left), as shown here.

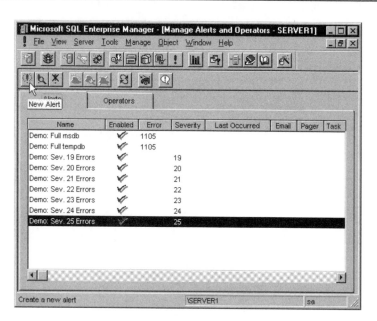

3. You'll see the New Alert dialog box. In the ID: New Name field, enter **Detect Full Pubs2 Transaction Log**.

4. In the Alert Definition section, select the Error Number option button and enter the number **1105** in the associated box. In the Database Name drop-down list box, choose Pubs2. Your dialog box should now look like the one below.

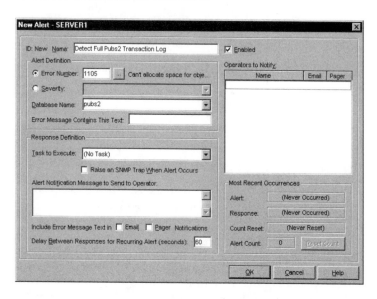

5. In the Task to Execute drop-down list box, choose New Task. This will open the New Task dialog box.

6. In the Name box, enter **Dump the Pubs2 log when an alert is triggered**.

7. In the Type drop-down list box, choose TSQL.

8. In the Command box, enter the following Transact-SQL statement:

   ```
   dump transaction pubs2 to pubs2_tl_backup
   ```

Your dialog box should look like the one shown below.

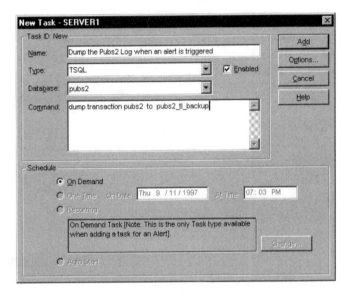

9. Click on Add in the New Task box.

10. Click on OK to save the alert. Your alert should now be listed with the default alerts.

Editing an Alert

After you've created an alert, you can easily make changes to it. Simply return to the Manage Alerts and Operators window, highlight the alert you want to change, and click on the Edit Alert button. In Exercise 9.2, we will edit the alert we created in Exercise 9.1.

EXERCISE 9.2

Editing an Alert

1. In SQL Enterprise Manager, select Server ➣ Alerts/Operators, or highlight SQL Executive, right-click, and choose Manage Alerts/Operators to display the Alerts tab of the Manage Alerts and Operators window.

2. Highlight the alert we added in Exercise 9.1, named Detect Full Pubs2 Transaction Log.

3. Click on the Edit Alert button on the toolbar (the one with an icon of an exclamation point with the magnifying glass, second from the left), as shown below.

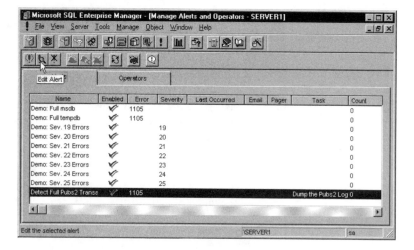

4. The Edit Alert dialog box appears, with all the settings you specified when you created the alert. Change the name to **Detect, dump and truncate full log for Pubs2**.

5. Click on OK to save your changes.

Editing and Creating SQL Server Error Messages

One of the "coolest" features of SQL Server is the ability to add your own error messages to the basic ones provided by SQL Server. You can call the new error message from within any Transact-SQL script or program by using the following command:

```
RaiseError error_number
```

You can then create alerts to watch for the error messages you have defined and notify you when the error is triggered.

You edit the posting of existing error messages to the Windows NT event log and create and edit new messages through the Alerts tab of the Manage Alerts and Operators window. In Exercise 9.3, we will edit an existing SQL Server error message so that it won't post to the Windows NT event log, and then create a new error message.

EXERCISE 9.3

Editing and Creating Error Messages

1. In SQL Enterprise Manager, select Server ➤ Alerts/Operators, or highlight SQL Executive, right-click, and choose Manage Alerts/Operators to display the Alerts tab of the Manage Alerts and Operators window.

2. Click on the Manage Messages button on the toolbar (the one with an icon of an exclamation point inside the bubble, on the far right), as shown below. The Manage Messages dialog box appears.

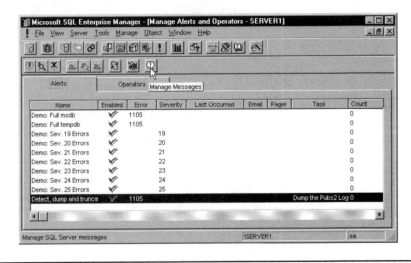

3. Enter **1105** in the Error Number box and click on the Find button on the right side of the dialog box. The 1105 message appears in the dialog box.

4. Double-click on the message, or click on Edit, to edit the message. The Edit Message dialog box appears, as shown below. Notice that the message cannot be edited, but the writing to the event log can be disabled (or enabled, if you have disabled this option).

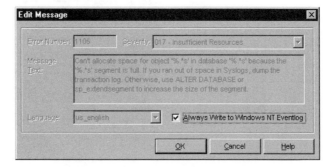

5. Click on Cancel in the Edit Message dialog box.

6. In the Manage Messages dialog box, click on the New button at the bottom of the dialog box.

7. Add a custom message to error number 50001: **This message triggered by Custom Application. Contact the Programmers**. Then check the Always Write to Windows NT Event Log box.

8. Click on OK, then Close to close the window.

9. To test the message, start the ISQL/W utility.

10. Enter and execute the following query:

```
raiseerror (50001,10,1)
```

The error message that you just created should appear in the Results window.

EXERCISE 9.3 (CONTINUED FROM PREVIOUS PAGE)

11. Open the Windows NT event log (select Programs ➢ Administrative Tools ➢ NT Event Viewer) and select Log ➢ Application to display the Application log. The message that you entered should appear.

12. Double-click on the message for more details. You should see the Event Detail dialog box with information about the error and your message, as shown below.

Forwarding Event Alerts

If you have more than one server running SQL Server, you can define a central server that will receive from other servers events for which you have not defined alerts. The server that receives these events is called an *unhandled event forwarding server*.

The server that is designated as the unhandled event forwarding server must exist or be created in SQL Enterprise Manager.

In Exercise 9.4, we will designate a server as the unhandled event forwarding server.

EXERCISE 9.4

Designating an Unhandled Event Forwarding Server

1. In SQL Enterprise Manager, select Server ➢ Alerts/Operators, or highlight SQL Executive, right-click, and choose Manage Alerts/Operators to display the Alerts tab of the Manage Alerts and Operators window.

2. Click on the Alert Engine Options button on the toolbar (the one with an icon of a car with an open hood, second to the right), as shown below. You will see the Fail-Safe tab of the Alert Engine Options dialog box.

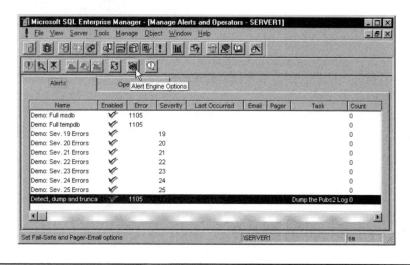

3. Choose New Forwarding Server (or you can pick a server already registered in SQL Enterprise Manager) from the drop-down list of the Server to Forward Events to window, and enter a server called **Server2**. SQL Enterprise Manager will warn you that it can't connect to Server2 and ask if you still want to register it (of course, you won't see this message if you actually do have a server called Server2); choose Yes. Server2 should now appear in the Server to Forward Events to box in the Fail-Safe tab, as shown below.

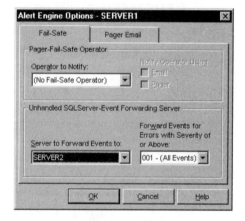

4. Because SQL Server can't connect to Server2, click on Cancel so that you don't save your changes. Of course, when you're actually designating an unhandled event forwarding server, you should click on OK to save your changes. (If you clicked on OK now, SQL Server would generate errors when it couldn't connect to Server2.)

5. Close the Manage Alerts and Operators window.

Creating and Managing Operators

SQL Server is MAPI-compliant, which means that SQL Server can send and receive e-mail. This gives you the ability to define operators and their e-mail addresses in SQL Server, and have SQL Server notify those operators about the success and/or failure of scheduled or triggered tasks and alerts.

SQL Server also supports many paging services and can be configured to page operators if an alert is triggered. These paging services depend on your e-mail system capabilities to decode an e-mail message in order to send a page message.

My favorite icon in SQL Server is the one for operators—the firefighter's hat! Those of you who are full-time administrators will know what I mean.

Enabling MAPI Support for E-mail

Different versions of Windows NT implement MAPI for services a bit differently. Windows NT 3.51 works quite well with SQL Server, but Windows NT 4.0 changed the way MAPI works with services to provide better security. Because of this, Service Pack 3 or later must be used with Windows NT 4.0 to allow MAPI to work with SQL Server and Windows Messaging (Microsoft Mail clients), although SQL Server and Exchange work without any Service Packs.

To install MAPI support for Windows NT 3.5, simply install Microsoft Mail support, create a user and password in the post office for SQL Server to use, and assign the user and password to SQL Server's e-mail user.

MAPI under Windows NT 3.5x has the problem of not wanting to start more than one session. In other words, if SQL Server has a MAPI session open and you start and stop the Microsoft Mail client, it may not restart—you must stop the MAPI session of SQL Server, start the Microsoft Mail client, and then restart the SQL Server MAPI session. The easiest way to do this is to stop and start the SQL Executive service.

There are five basic steps to installing MAPI support for Windows NT 4.0:

- Install the Windows Messaging services.

- Install Service Pack 3 for Windows NT 4.0

- Create a profile for the SQL Executive account using a valid post office user.

- Assign the SQL Executive account (or a new account with the same permissions) to the MSSQLServer service.

- Assign the profile to the SQL Mail portion of SQL Server.

You may need to reapply the Service Pack if you add any components from the original Windows NT 4.0 CD. You can find Service Pack 3 for Windows NT 4.0 on Microsoft's Web site (http://www.microsoft.com) or on TechNet. Use the Update command from the appropriate subdirectory (x386 for Intel-compatible computers) to install the Service Pack.

In Exercise 9.5, we will install support for MAPI for Windows NT 4.0 and SQL Server.

EXERCISE 9.5

Installing MAPI Support

1. Log in to Windows NT as the user you created for the SQL Executive account.

2. Make sure that the Windows Messaging services are installed by checking in the Control Panel. There should be an icon for Mail and Microsoft Mail Post Office.

3. If Messaging services are not installed, install them by going to the Add/Remove Programs Control Panel, selecting the Windows NT Setup tab, and choosing the Windows Messaging checkbox. Click on the Details button and verify that you have the Microsoft Mail and Windows Messaging services selected, as shown below.

4. Ensure that Service Pack 3 for Windows NT is installed by opening Windows NT Diagnostics (located in the Administrative Tools program group) and looking at the Version tab. If Service Pack 3 is installed, you should see this indicated, as shown below.

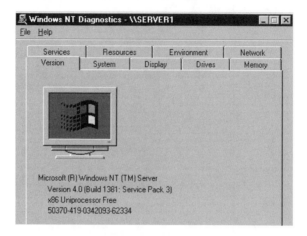

5. If the Service Pack is not installed, install it. You will need to reboot Windows NT after installing the Service Pack.

6. Set up a Microsoft Exchange profile for the SQL Executive service by first logging in as the user you created to support the service..

7. Ensure that there is an existing user in an existing post office for you to use. If you need to set up a post office, use the Microsoft Mail Post Office Control Panel to create a post office. Use the name **Admin** with a mailbox of **Admin**.

8. Create a post office user for SQL Server to use. For this example, set up a user named **server1** with a mailbox of **server1**, as shown below.

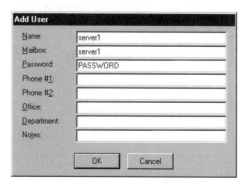

9. Create a profile by going to the Mail Control Panel, and choosing Add. This starts the Windows Messaging Setup Wizard.

10. You should have Microsoft Mail checked, as shown below. Click on Next to continue.

11. Enter or browse to the path to the post office, and then click on Next.

12. Choose Server1 as the user of the post office, and then click on Next.

13. Enter the password of the mailbox ("PASSWORD" is the default password).

14. Click on Next twice to save your personal folders to the local hard drive.

15. Click on Finish. The profile is called Windows Messaging Settings. Click on Close to close the dialog box.

16. To assign the profile to SQL Server, go to the Services Control Panel and set the MSSQLServer service to use the same account that the SQL Executive service uses, as shown below.

17. Stop and restart SQL Server.

18. Go to SQL Enterprise Manager (you may need to register your server again).

19. Highlight SQL Mail (under Server1), right-click, and choose Configure to open the SQL Mail Configuration dialog box.

20. In the Profile Name text box, enter **Windows Messaging Settings**, as shown below. Click on OK to save your changes.

EXERCISE 9.5 (CONTINUED FROM PREVIOUS PAGE)

21. Start the SQL Mail session by highlighting the Microsoft Mail icon, right-clicking, and choosing Start. The icon should turn green.

22. To have SQL Mail start automatically every time, run the SQL Setup program and select Set Server Options. Select the Auto Start Mail Client option, as shown below. Click on Change Options, and then click on OK to save your changes.

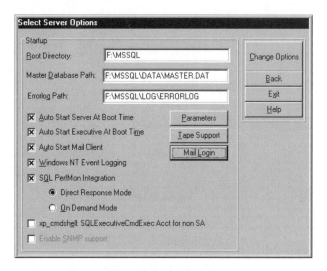

The process for configuring SQL Server for use with Exchange servers is basically the same: Set up a profile for the user account that SQL Server will be using that connects to an Exchange server, and assign that user and profile to SQL Server.

Creating Operators and Testing E-mail

To ensure that your MAPI support is configured correctly, you will want to send test messages to your operators. In Exercise 9.6, we will create an operator and test the ability of SQL Server to send messages to that operator.

EXERCISE 9.6

Creating an Operator and Testing E-mail

1. Log in to Windows NT as your normal account (not the SQL Executive account).

2. In SQL Enterprise Manager, select Server ➤ Alerts/Operators, or highlight SQL Executive, right-click, and choose Manage Alerts/Operators to display the Manage Alerts and Operators window.

3. Go to the Operators tab.

4. Click on the first firefighter's hat icon to set up a new operator.

5. In the Edit Operator dialog box, enter an operator name, such as **The NT Administrator**, and the e-mail name for the person you are logged in as, as shown below.

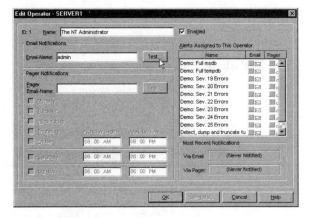

6. Click on the Test button to send mail to the user. SQL Server should report that the message was sent successfully.

7. Click on OK to save your new operator.

EXERCISE 9.6 (CONTINUED FROM PREVIOUS PAGE)

8. Minimize SQL Enterprise Manager, go to your Desktop, and start your Messaging client by double-clicking on the Inbox. You should have a message similar to the one shown below.

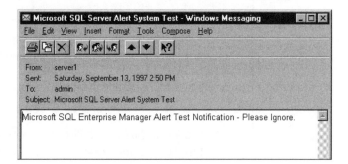

9. Close the Messaging client by selecting File ➤ Exit and Log Off from the menu.

Defining Fail-Safe Operators

After you've set up your operators, you can define their working hours and designate a fail-safe operator in case no other operators are on duty when an alert is triggered. In Exercise 9.7, we will define a fail-safe operator.

EXERCISE 9.7

Defining a Fail-Safe Operator

1. In SQL Enterprise Manager, select Server ➤ Alerts/Operators, or highlight SQL Executive, right-click, and choose Manage Alerts/Operators to display the Manage Alerts and Operators window.

2. Click on the Alert Engine Options button on the toolbar (the one with an icon of a car with an open hood, second to the right) to display the Fail-Safe tab of the Alert Engine Options dialog box.

---

3. In the Operator to Notify drop-down list box, select an operator you have already set up, as shown below.

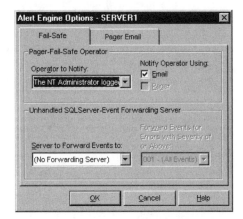

4. Click on OK to save your changes. The fail-safe operator should be indicated by a checkmark with a plus sign in the Operators tab.

Creating and Managing Tasks

Earlier versions of SQL Server (4.21a and earlier) could schedule backups, but that was the extent of their scheduling capabilities. Beginning with version 6.0, SQL Server's scheduling capabilities have been greatly expanded.

Microsoft ✓ *Exam Objective*

Schedule tasks.

In SQL Server 6.5, you can schedule tasks to run at regular intervals or when an alert is triggered. Replication tasks are also supported.

Types of Tasks

SQL Server supports five types of tasks:

TSQL tasks These tasks are written using Transact-SQL commands. They are often used to back up the database, rebuild indexes, and perform other various routine maintenance on database.

CmdExec tasks These tasks literally open a command prompt and run some sort of batch file or executable file. Common CmdExec tasks are those created by the Database Maintenance Plan Wizard or by the SQL Server Web Assistant.

Distribution tasks These tasks deal with replication and when the data is sent out to subscribing sites.

Logreader tasks These tasks deal with replication and when changed data is looked for.

Sync tasks These tasks deal with replication and keeping databases in sync.

Creating Tasks

The required elements of a task are the type, schedule, and command to be executed. There are various ways to create and schedule tasks.

Task Creation Methods

The following are the most common ways to create tasks:

- You can create your own tasks manually, through the Manage Scheduled Tasks window in SQL Enterprise Manager.

- You can let SQL Enterprise Manager create tasks for you. SQL Enterprise Manager can create certain tasks, the most common of which is the backup task. In Chapter 8 (Exercise 8.9), we used the SQL Enterprise Manager's Database Backup/Restore dialog box to create a backup task.

- The Database Maintenance Plan Wizard, which comes with SQL Server 6.5, can create tasks to handle routine maintenance and database backup. In Chapter 8, we explained how to create a backup task using the Database Maintenance Plan Wizard.

The Database Maintenance Plan Wizard creates a command prompt (CmdExec) task, not a Transact-SQL task. The task that is created starts a program called SQLMAINT.EXE, which was expressly written for SQL Server 6.5 maintenance.

- When you use the SQL Server Web Assistant to set up updates to a Web page that happen on a regular basis, it creates a recurring task. The SQL Server Web Assistant is covered in Appendix C.

- When you install and set up replication, various tasks are created to make replication work. Replication is covered in Chapter 11.

Task Scheduling Methods

Tasks can be scheduled in one of three ways:

- An on-demand task is one that is created for alerts. It is executed only if the alert triggers, or if you request the task to run interactively.

- A one-time-only task is usually created for a special purpose. It executes only once on its scheduled date and time.

- A recurring task happens on a regular basis. The task's frequency can be daily, weekly, or even monthly.

In Exercise 9.8, we will manually create a Transact-SQL task and schedule it as a recurring task. This new task will back up the Pubs database on a daily basis.

EXERCISE 9.8

Creating a Task Manually

1. In SQL Enterprise Manager, highlight SQL Executive, right-click, and choose Manage Scheduled Tasks, or select Server ➤ Scheduled Tasks. This opens the Manage Scheduled Tasks window.

2. Click on the New Task button on the toolbar (the one with an icon of a clock with a checkmark, on the far left), as shown below.

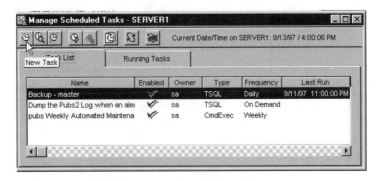

3. In the New Task dialog box, enter a name for the task, such as **Back up Pubs2 database every night**.

4. Make sure that TSQL is selected in the Type box.

5. In the Command box, enter the following Transact-SQL statement:

   `Dump Database pubs2 to pubs2_backup with init`

This will overwrite any old backups stored on that device.

6. Click on the Change button in the lower-right corner of the dialog box.

7. In the Task Schedule dialog box, select the Daily option button in the Occurs section.

8. Under Daily Frequency, select the Occurs Once at option button and set the time to 12:30 AM, as shown below.

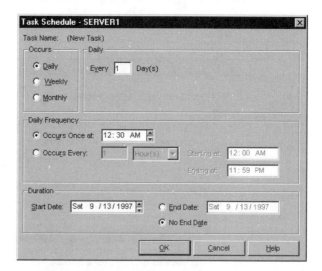

9. Click on OK in the Task Schedule dialog box, and then click on Add in the New Task dialog box to save the task. The task now appears in the list in the Manage Scheduled Tasks window.

Editing Tasks

You can modify tasks to change their name, type, command, or schedule. In Exercise 9.9, we will edit the task we created in Exercise 9.8 to change its schedule.

EXERCISE 9.9

Editing a Task

1. In SQL Enterprise Manager, highlight SQL Executive, right-click, and choose Manage Scheduled Tasks, or select Server ➢ Scheduled Tasks, to open the Manage Scheduled Tasks window.

2. Highlight the task we created in Exercise 9.8.

3. Click on Edit Task button on the toolbar (the one with an icon of a magnifying glass over a clock, second from the left) to open the Edit Task dialog box.

4. Click on the Change button in the lower-right corner of the dialog box.

5. In the Task Schedule dialog box, change the time of execution from 12:30 AM to 1:00 AM. Then click on OK.

6. Click on the Modify button in the Edit Task dialog box to save your changes.

Running Tasks Manually

Even if you have scheduled a task, you can run it manually at another time. In Exercise 9.10, we will run the task we created in Exercise 9.8.

EXERCISE 9.10

Running a Task Manually

1. In SQL Enterprise Manager, highlight SQL Executive, right-click, and choose Manage Scheduled Tasks, or select Server ➢ Scheduled Tasks, to open the Manage Scheduled Tasks window.

2. Highlight the task we created in Exercise 9.8.

3. Click on the Run Task button on the toolbar (the one with an icon of a clock and a green play arrow). Click on OK to confirm that you want to run the task.

4. If you are fast enough, you can switch to the Running Tasks tab and see the task as it is running (you may have to select the Refresh button to update the screen).

5. SQL Enterprise Manager will inform you when the task has finished running. Click on OK to close the message box.

Viewing Task History

A very helpful feature of SQL Enterprise Manager is that it keeps a record of each task's time of execution, as well as whether the task was successful or not. In Exercise 9.11, we will examine the history of the task that we ran in Exercise 9.10 to see if it was successfully completed.

EXERCISE 9.11

Examining the History of a Task

1. In SQL Enterprise Manager, highlight SQL Executive, right-click, and choose Manage Scheduled Tasks, or select Server ➤ Scheduled Tasks, to open the Manage Scheduled Tasks window.

2. Highlight the task we created in Exercise 9.8.

3. Click on the Task History button (the one with an icon of a clock and pieces of paper, third from the right) to display the Task History dialog box, as shown below.

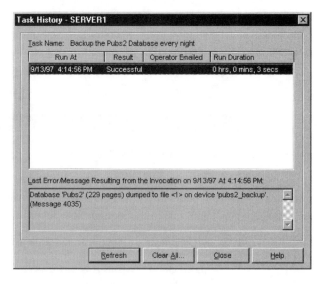

As you can see, the task is listed as Successful.

4. Click on Close to close the dialog box.

---

5. To see options for the size of the task history log, click on the Task Engine Options button on the toolbar (the one with an icon of a car with an open hood, second to the right) to display the Task Engine Options dialog box, as shown below. You can see that the default settings are a maximum of 1000 rows of history, with a maximum of 100 rows per task.

6. Click on Cancel to close the Task Engine Options dialog box.

Deleting Tasks

If you no longer need a task, you can easily delete it in SQL Enterprise Manager. In Exercise 9.12, we will delete the task we created in Exercise 9.8.

Deleting a Task

1. In SQL Enterprise Manager, highlight SQL Executive, right-click, and choose Manage Scheduled Tasks, or select Server ➤ Scheduled Tasks, to open the Manage Scheduled Tasks window.

2. Highlight the task we created in Exercise 9.8.

3. Click on the Delete Task icon on the toolbar (the one with an icon of a clock with a red slash through it, third from the left).

4. Click on Yes to confirm that you want to delete this task.

5. Close the Manage Scheduled Tasks window.

Summary

In this chapter, you learned about creating and managing alerts, operators, and tasks to help you with your administrative duties.

We first talked about the Msdb database, which holds all of the information for alerts, operators, tasks, and history of tasks. Because the Msdb database contains all of your tasks, alerts, and operators, you should schedule regular backups of this database.

Then we explained how the SQL Executive service is a helper service that oversees the automation of tasks inside SQL Server. You must configure SQL Executive correctly before any of your alerts, operators or tasks will work.

The rest of the chapter described how to set up alerts, operators, and scheduled tasks. Alerts can watch the Windows NT event log, and they can cause a task to execute upon finding predefined error messages. Alerts from multiple SQL Servers can be forwarded to a central server in order to make management of many servers easier.

Operators can be defined so that SQL Server can either e-mail and/or page the operator upon success and/or failure of tasks. SQL Server is MAPI-enabled, which is why it can send and receive e-mail.

Tasks can be defined that can not only run Transact-SQL statements, but also run command-prompt commands and replication tasks. Tasks can be run on a regular basis, on demand when an alert triggers, or only once.

Exercise Questions

1. What rights does the SQL Executive service account user need? (Choose all that apply.)

   A. Log on as a Service right

   B. Administrator group membership

   C. Backup Operators membership

   D. Server Operators membership

2. What is the API set that allows SQL Server to send and receive e-mail?

   A. TAPI

   B. EAPI

C. OLE

D. MAPI

3. Which database holds alert and task information?

　A. The Master database

　B. The Model database

　C. The Msdb database

　D. None—it is held in the Registry

4. How can you rebuild the Msdb database?

　A. You can't; you must reinstall SQL Server

　B. Run SQL Setup and choose Rebuild Master Database

　C. Run SQL Setup and choose Rebuild Msdb Database

　D. Stop and restart SQL Server; the Msdb database will be rebuilt automatically

5. Where do alerts look for errors?

　A. The Windows NT event Application log

　B. The SQL Server event log

　C. The Master database error log

　D. SQL Server sends errors directly to the alert engine

6. What kinds of tasks can be created? (Choose all that apply.)

　A. TSQL (Transact-SQL)

　B. CmdExec (Command Prompt)

　C. Replication

　D. Windows NT Kernel

7. You can create new error messages in SQL Server.

A. True

B. False

8. Alerts can be defined but not activated.

A. True

B. False

9. What is the operator of last resort called?

A. Weekend operator

B. Last-chance operator

C. Notification operator

D. Fail-safe operator

10. What is the central server that receives alerts from other SQL Server servers called?

A. Central alerter

B. Standardized alerter

C. Central control

D. Unhandled events server

11. Which of these four services is in charge of the others?

A. Alert Manager

B. Task Manager

C. SQL Executive

D. Event Manager

CHAPTER

10

Importing and Exporting Data

anaging data is one of the major tasks required of a SQL Server administrator. SQL Server provides various tools and utilities to help in the management of your data.

In this chapter, we will look at the various methods for transferring data into or out of your databases. We'll begin with SQL Enterprise Manager's transfer management interface. This interface lets you copy objects, data, and security from one database to another database.

Next, we'll look at BCP. BCP stands for Bulk Copy Program, which is a stand-alone program that can transfer large amounts of data into or out of a single table or view of a database.

Then we'll review the uses of database backups for data transfer. Backing up a database and then restoring it to a different database is a method of data manipulation that is both easy and relatively foolproof.

Another method for copying data is replication. Replication is the real-time synchronization of one or more tables of a database to another database. We'll take a brief look at the process here, and go into details in Chapter 11.

Still another method of data transfer is creating a removable media database. We'll go over the requirements and steps for using removable media databases.

Our final subject will be SQL Server's support for upgrading from SQL 4.2x to SQL Server 6.5. You can keep copies of both versions on the same server.

Transferring between Databases

T hrough SQL Enterprise Manager, you can transfer objects, security, and/or data from one database to another. When you use this method, the objects, data, and security in the original database are unaffected; they are copied to the receiving database, not actually moved.

SQL Transfer Manager was a separate program in earlier versions of SQL Server. In version 6.5, this function is incorporated into SQL Enterprise Manager.

Because new objects are being created, the user performing the transfer needs Select rights in the database being transferred, and DBO rights in the receiving database.

Also, both servers involved in the transfer need to be registered in SQL Enterprise Manager. You can register new servers when you set up the transfer.

Using the Transfer Management Interface

To start the transfer management interface in SQL Enterprise Manager, choose Tools ➤ Database/Object Transfer. This takes you to the Database/ Object Transfer dialog box. Figure 10.1 shows an example of this dialog box filled in to transfer all objects from the Pubs database to a database named Pubs_copy.

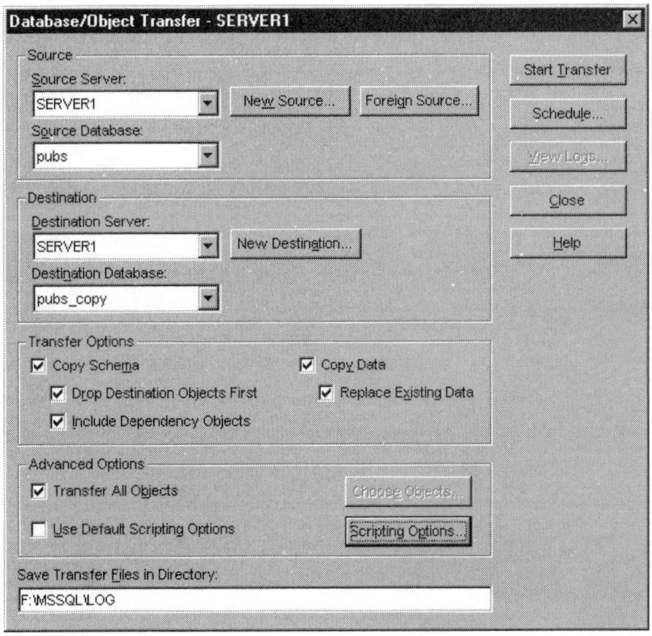

FIGURE 10.1

The Database/Object Transfer dialog box lets you select your source and destination database and set transfer options.

Database/Object Transfer - SERVER1

Source
Source Server:
SERVER1   New Source...   Foreign Source...
Source Database:
pubs

Destination
Destination Server:
SERVER1   New Destination...
Destination Database:
pubs_copy

Transfer Options
☑ Copy Schema   ☑ Copy Data
☑ Drop Destination Objects First   ☑ Replace Existing Data
☑ Include Dependency Objects

Advanced Options
☑ Transfer All Objects   Choose Objects...
☐ Use Default Scripting Options   Scripting Options...

Save Transfer Files in Directory:
F:\MSSQL\LOG

Start Transfer
Schedule...
View Logs...
Close
Help

In the Source section, you specify the source server and database, as follows:

Source Server Specifies the server that the data and objects will come from.

New Source Registers a new server.

Foreign Source Allows a Sybase server to be chosen as the source server.

Source Database Specifies the database that will provide the data and objects.

In the Destination section, specify the destination server and database, as follows:

Destination Server Specifies the server that you will be copying data and objects to.

New Destination Registers a new destination server.

Destination Database Specifies the database that data and objects will be copied into.

The Transfer Options and Advanced Options sections of the dialog box have settings that you let control the transfer operation:

Copy Schema Re-creates selected objects in the destination database.

Drop Destination Objects First Deletes the object (if it exists) from the destination database and then re-creates it.

Include Dependency Objects Copies over all objects that the selected object relies on.

Copy Data Specifies if the data will be copied to the destination database.

Replace Existing Data Specifies that all existing data will be deleted before the new data is copied over. If this option is not selected, the imported data will be appended to any existing data (if you didn't choose to drop the objects).

Transfer All Objects Re-creates every object in the destination database.

Choose Objects Specifies which objects will be re-created in the destination database. Clicking on this button opens the Choose Objects to be Transferred dialog box, as shown in Figure 10.2.

Use Default Scripting Options   Re-creates all objects, indexes, and security.

Scripting Options   Specifies which objects, indexes, and security will be re-created in the destination database. Clicking on this button displays the Transfer Scripting Options dialog box, as shown in Figure 10.3.

FIGURE 10.2

Selecting individual objects to be transferred

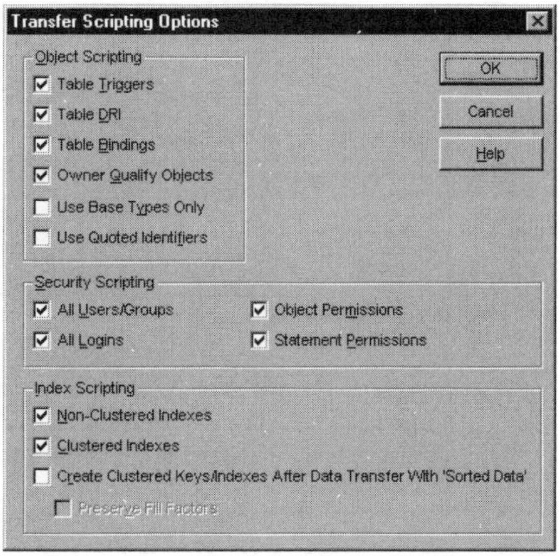

FIGURE 10.3

Selecting transfer scripting options

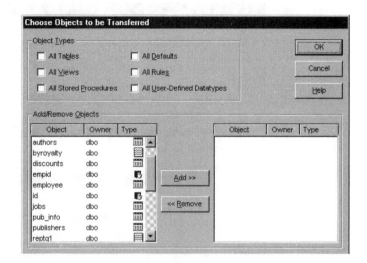

After you've completed the Database/Object Transfer dialog box, you can either start the transfer immediately, or click on the Schedule button to schedule the transfer to happen at a later time or set up a recurring schedule.

In Exercise 10.1, we will create a new database, transfer the Pubs data into it, and then examine the transfer log. (See Chapter 5 for information about creating devices and databases.)

EXERCISE 10.1

Using the SQL Transfer Management Interface

1. Start SQL Enterprise Manager.

2. Create a new database named **pubs_copy** on a data device of 3MB named **pubs_copy_data**. Use a 1MB device named **pubs_copy_log** for the log. Your New Database dialog box should look like the one shown below.

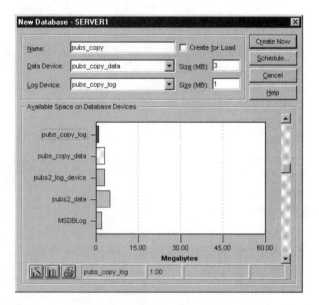

3. Start the transfer management interface by choosing Tools ➤ Database/Object Transfer.

4. In the Database/Object Transfer dialog box, select your server as both the source and destination server (in the Source Server and Destination Server boxes). Select the pubs database in the Source Database box. Choose the pubs_copy database in the Destination Database (see Figure 10.1).

5. In the Advanced Options section at the bottom of the dialog box, deselect Transfer All Objects and click on the Choose Objects button.

6. In the Choose Objects to be Transferred dialog box, select the All Stored Procedures option. All four stored procedures move to the box on the right side of the dialog box, as shown below.

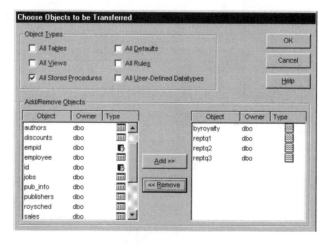

7. Click on Cancel (we want to transfer all the objects). Back in the Database/Object Transfer dialog box, reselect Transfer All Objects.

8. Deselect Use Default Scripting Options, and then click on the Scripting Options button. This displays the Transfer Scripting Options dialog box. Here, you can control exactly which type of objects and security are transferred (see Figure 10.3).

9. Click on Cancel (we want to use the default options), and then reselect the Use Default Scripting Options option.

10. Click on the Start Transfer button to begin the transfer operation. You should see progress bars showing the progress of the transfer operation. The transfer could take a minute or two.

11. When the operation is finished, you will see a message notifying you that the transfer was completed, and whether there were any warnings (in our example, there will probably be warnings). Click on OK to close the screen.

12. To examine the log of the session, click on the View Logs button in the Database/Object Transfer dialog box. The log will look something like the one shown below.

13. Click on Close in Transfer Logs window, and then click on Close in the Database/Object Transfer dialog box to exit the transfer management interface.

14. Open the Pubs_copy database, open the Objects folder, and open the Tables folder. You should see all of the tables that were in the original Pubs database, as shown below.

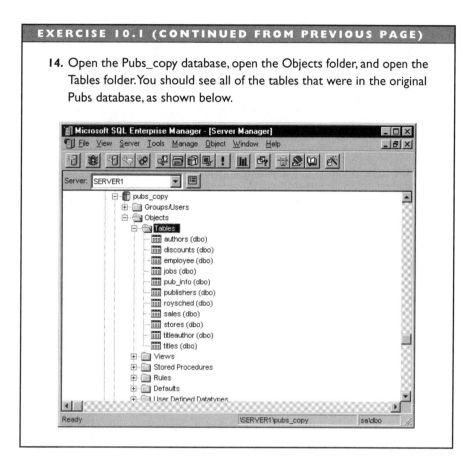

Transfer Log and Script Files

The transfer process creates two major log files. Additionally, all of the scripts that were created for the process are kept. The log and script files are stored in the \MSSQL\Log directory (by default), and they can be examined after the transfer to analyze any errors or warnings. Table 10.1 lists the log and script files created by the transfer process. Although you can examine the destination server transfer log file from within SQL Enterprise Manager, you need to use Notepad or a similar program to examine the scripting files.

	File Name*	Purpose
TABLE 10.1 Log and Script Files Created by the Transfer Process	SSQL.SDATA.LOG	Log of errors and warnings about the source database
	DSQL.DDATA.LOG	Log of errors and warnings about the destination database
	SSQL.SDATA.BND	Tables bindings
	SSQL.SDATA.DEF	Script used to create defaults
	SSQL.SDATA.DP1	Script used to drop table constraints
	SSQL.SDATA.DP2	Script used to drop database objects
	SSQL.SDATA.DR1	Script used to add primary keys to tables
	SSQL.SDATA.DR2	Script used to add defaults, rules, and other integrity constraints
	SSQL.SDATA.FKY	Script used to add foreign keys to tables
	SSQL.SDATA.GRP	Script used to add groups to the database
	SSQL.SDATA.ID1	Script used to create clustered indexes
	SSQL.SDATA.ID2	Script used to create nonclustered indexes
	SSQL.SDATA.LGN	Script used to create SQL Server logins
	SSQL.SDATA.PRC	Script used to create stored procedures
	SSQL.SDATA.PRV	Script used to create permissions
	SSQL.SDATA.RUL	Script used to create rules
	SSQL.SDATA.TAB	Script used to create tables
	SSQL.SDATA.TRG	Script used to create triggers
	SSQL.SDATA.UDT	Script used to create user-defined datatypes
	SSQL.SDATA.USR	Script used to create usernames and statement permissions
	SSQL.SDATA.VIW	Script used to create views

*SSQL stands for Source_SQL_Server, SDATA stands for Source Database, DSQL stands for Destination_SQL_Server, and DDATA stands for Destination Database.

Bulk Copying

The BCP.EXE command-line program, which comes with SQL Server, is designed for bringing ASCII and native (binary) data into or out of SQL Server.

Microsoft Exam Objective

Identify the best uses for bcp when managing data.

NOTE Exam objectives are subject to change at any time without prior notice and at Microsoft's sole discretion. Please visit Microsoft's Training & Certification Web site (www.microsoft.com/Train_Cert) for the most current exam objectives listing.

To use BCP, you must have the following permissions:

- Select on any tables or views that you wish to bulk-copy out of SQL Server.

- Insert on any tables or views that you wish to bring data into.

Although any user with appropriate rights can use the BCP utility, usually it is the DBO's responsibility.

Fast versus Slow BCP Sessions

There are two ways to conduct an import session with BCP:

- *Fast BCP* happens when there are no indexes on the table being imported to, and when the Select Into/Bulk Copy database option is set.

- *Slow BCP* happens when there are either indexes on the table being imported into, or when the Select Into/Bulk Copy is not set.

Fast BCP has the advantage of being considerably faster for importing data, because there are no indexes to be updated for each row. Another advantage is that because the import is not logged, there is little chance of the transaction log filling up during the import process.

In some cases, using fast BCP may be the only option. This will depend on the size of the database and the amount of data that needs to be imported. For example, suppose that you have a 50MB database that has a 20MB transaction log, and you want to import 30MB of data. If the import is logged, it will fill the transaction log before it can be completed. Even though the data will all fit into the database, the size of the transaction log limits the amount of data that can be imported before the transaction log needs to be truncated. (For details on clearing the transaction log, see Chapter 8.)

The steps involved in fast BCP can be summarized as follows:

- Back up the database. It is always a good idea to run a backup procedure before performing major maintenance on a database; that way, the database can be quickly restored to its previous state if something goes wrong. You might want to back up the database before doing regular maintenance, especially as a precaution the first few times that you use BCP. If the BCP import works flawlessly every time, this step can be eliminated.

- Set the Select Into/Bulk Copy switch to on (select it). This switch allows the import to bypass the transaction log and go directly into the database. You can set this switch by using the sp_dboption stored procedure or from SQL Enterprise Manager (from the Options tab of the Edit Database dialog box).

- Drop all indexes on the affected tables. If you're importing a large number of records, it is actually faster to drop the indexes and re-create them after the data is imported than to have the indexes active during the import process.

- Use BCP to import the records into the database.

- Set the Select Into/Bulk Copy switch back to off (deselect it). At this point, you want the transaction log to become fully active again.

- Back up the database (optional). If the import takes a long time (hours), you may want to back up the database before proceeding. If you don't run a backup, and you need to restore from earlier backups, you will need to redo the import. (The transaction log isn't active during the import process.)

- Check and fix any rule, trigger, and constraint violations. Because SQL Server doesn't check to see if you have imported invalid data, you may want to import your data into a temporary table, validate it, and then move it to its final destination table.

- Re-create indexes on affected tables. You should re-create your indexes after all the data has been imported and cleaned up.

■ Back up the database. Cleaning the data and re-creating indexes could involve a lot of time and effort. If you've done a lot of work and don't want to redo it, back up the database before proceeding.

The BCP Command

BCP supports command-line keywords and switches to control the way it works. The command has the following syntax:

```
bcp <database..table> in/out <file_path_and_name> <type_of_file
field_and_row_delimiters> /S<sql_server> /U<user> /P<password>
```

Table 10.2 lists the BCP keywords and switches. Note that the switches are case-sensitive.

TABLE 10.2 BCP Switches	Keyword or Switch	Function
	in/ out	Specifies whether the data is going into the specified database and table, or out of it.
	/a	Sets the packet size. Valid packet sizes are from 512 to 65,535 bytes. This setting may have little effect, or it may help to speed up BCP. It depends on your network topology and equipment.
	/b	The number of rows included as a batch. Each batch is sent as a single transaction (if logging is enabled).
	/c	Specifies the data is to be read from/stored in ASCII format. The /c switch also implies the /t and /r switches will be used to set the delimiters.
	/E	Specifies how Identity datatypes in fields will be handled.
	/e <error file>	Creates an error file.
	/F	Specifies the first row to start with. If omitted, BCP will start with the first row encountered.
	/f <format file>	Specifies a format file to be used.
	/i <input file>	Specifies an input file.
	/L	Specifies the last row to end with. If omitted, BCP will end with the last row encountered.

T A B L E 10.2 (cont.) BCP Switches	**Keyword or Switch**	**Function**
	/m	The maximum number of errors allowed before the BCP operation will cancel. The default (if not specified) is 10.
	/n	Specifies the data is to be read from/stored in native or binary format. This format works only when you are transferring data between compatible SQL Server machines.
	/o <output file>	Specifies an output file.
	/r	Specifies the row delimiter. One of the most common delimiters is the end-of-row or carriage return, which is specified by \n.
	/t <"delimiter">	Specifies the field delimiter. For example, /t " , " specifies a comma-delimited file.

Because you may not want every column to be imported or exported, BCP allows the creation and use of format files. Format files can not only be used to specify which columns to ignore, but can also be used to set up an unattended BCP session. In order to create a format file, do an initial bulk copy without using the /c or the /n switch. You will be prompted through the BCP session, and a format file will be created. To reuse the format file, specify the file after the /f switch.

Using BCP

There are a few factors to consider when you use BCP:

- When you use BCP to bring data into a table, it is dynamic; that is, other users can be using the table.

- When you export data using BCP, it is best if you are the only user in that table. This becomes an even more important factor if you are using BCP to export multiple tables, because any changes that take effect on any of the tables may not be included, so your referential integrity may suffer.

- When performing an import BCP, datatypes and defaults are obeyed, but rules, triggers, keys, and constraints are ignored.

- It's a good idea to use the /o switch, so a log file of the errors will be saved for the BCP session. The /e switch saves the actual row(s) that caused the errors.

In Exercise 10.2, we will bulk-copy some data out of the Pubs_copy database. Then we will edit the data we exported and use BCP to bring the data back into the Pubs_copy database.

EXERCISE 10.2

Exporting and Importing Data Using BCP

1. Open a Windows NT Command Prompt window.

2. Go to the C:\Temp folder (make one if you don't already have one).

3. Open a file called DOBCP.BAT for editing by issuing the following command:

   edit dobcp.bat

4. In the editor window, enter the following command. Type it in as a single, long line, as shown below. A BCP command should not have any returns.

   bcp pubs_copy out c:\temp\employee.txt /m100 / ec:\temp\bcp_errors.txt /c /t "," /r\n /b500 /S<*your server name*> /Usa /P<*password of SA account*>

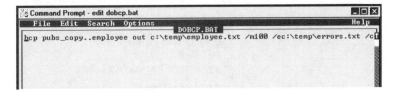

5. Save the batch file, exit the editor, and run the batch file by issuing the following command:

   dobcp.bat

6. If the command ran successfully, you should see that 43 rows were copied.

You may have added rows or changed the Pubs database during earlier exercises. If your count is off, don't worry. The most important thing is that we are going to import two new rows in, so you should have two more rows at the end of the exercise than you did at the beginning of the exercise.

7. Open the output from the BCP command by issuing the following command:

```
edit employee.txt
```

You should see a comma-delimited file, as shown below.

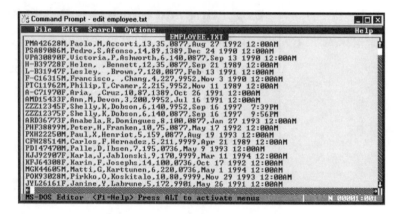

8. In the editor window, delete all but the last two employees. Edit the existing employee ID numbers and names (the first four columns) so that you will have two unique rows to add.

9. Copy the original batch file and then open it for editing by issuing the following two commands:

```
copy dobcp.bat dobcp2.bat
edit dobcp2.bat
```

10. In the editor window, change the keyword out to **in**, and verify that the batch file contains the following command:

```
bcp pubs_copy in c:\temp\employee.txt /m100 /
ec:\temp\bcp_errors.txt /c /t "," /r\n /b500 /S<your server
name> /Usa /P<password of SA account>
```

EXERCISE 10.2 (CONTINUED FROM PREVIOUS PAGE)

11. Save the file.

12. Run the batch file by issuing the following command:

    dobcp2.bat

You should see that two rows were copied.

13. Start ISQL/W, go to the Pubs_copy database, and run the following query:

    Select * from employee

There should now be 45 employees. (The two you added should be sorted alphabetically because of a clustered index.)

14. Close ISQL/W, and then close the Command Prompt window.

Importing Data from a Backup

Backing up a database and then restoring it to another database is a quick way to get a copy of the data, to move it to another device, or to move it to another SQL Server machine.

Microsoft ✓ *Exam Objective*

Identify the best uses for the dumping command and the loading command in managing data.

You will need the appropriate rights to back up and restore databases. Only the SA and DBO have default rights to back up a database, although that right can be given to others. The right that cannot be given to ordinary users is the ability to restore a database, which applies only to the SA and DBO.

Keep in mind that when you load a database from a backup, there is no merging of the data—all old objects, data, and security are deleted and replaced with whatever is contained in the backup.

Also remember that backups can be loaded only onto like systems with like sort order and character sets. For example, if you had a server with an Intel CPU, you could not load a backup made on the Intel machine into a database on a server with a Digital Alpha CPU.

See Chapter 8 for details about the procedures for backing up and restoring databases.

There are no log files created during the database backup or restore procedures.

Replication Scenarios

Replication is when one or more tables of one database are linked to tables in another database so that any changes in the first database are reflected in the second database. We will cover the replication process in detail in Chapter 11. We bring it up now so that you can compare it to the other methods for transferring data.

There are several different replication models:

- Single publisher (the server that has the original data) to single subscriber (the server that gets the data)

- Single publisher to multiple subscribers

- Multiple publishers to single subscriber

- Multiple publishers to multiple subscribers

As you might guess, the major advantage of replication is that two (or more) databases can be kept in constant synchronization. However, replication is relatively complicated to set up, troubleshoot, and maintain when compared with the other methods described in this chapter.

Removable Media Databases

As you learned in Chapter 5, SQL Server 6.5 has the ability to create databases on removable media, such as CD-ROMs or floppy disks. Removable media databases can be sent to another location for later use. When a removable media database is installed at the target site, the transaction log and system tables are copied to the hard drive. This makes it possible to add users, groups, security, views, and stored procedures to the database, while the data continues to reside on read-only media.

The details about the procedures for creating and installing removable media databases are in Chapter 5. Here, we are focusing on how using removable media databases compares with the other methods for transferring data.

In some cases, removable databases provide a good solution to a business problem. For example, you might use a removable media database when your branch offices need a copy of a master parts list or customer list, and this list is updated relatively infrequently. Another use would be to send a new database to all of your clients periodically, such as to send an up-to-date inventory list once a quarter.

There are a few factors to consider when you are using removable media databases:

- You must use Transact-SQL commands and stored system procedures to create removable media databases. You cannot do this from a SQL Enterprise Manager dialog box.

As far as we know, the MCSE test will not contain syntax questions about removable media databases (thank goodness). However, you may be asked about when and how to use them, and how they work.

- The database must be created on devices that are used for only this database. The devices used for removable media databases must not contain any other databases.

- After the receiving site installs the database, the data remains read-only, even if the devices are copied to a hard drive before being installed.

Steps for the Originating Site

At the site where the removable media database is being created, a few steps must be followed:

- Create the database using the `sp_create_removable` stored procedure. At least three devices need to be specified: one for the transaction log, one for the system tables, and one or more for the data.

- Certify it as removable by using the `sp_certify_removable` stored procedure. This procedure calls the `sp_check_removable` procedure, which makes sure that the SA or DBO owns all the objects and that there are no users or groups in the database; and then truncates the transaction log, moves it to the system device, and drops the transaction log device. The `sp_certify_removable` procedure then checks that device fragments are contiguous and in sequence. It also verifies that row-level locking is not enabled for any tables in the database and sets the database to offline status.

- Put the database on removable media, and send the media to the receiving site with the corresponding parameters used to install the database. Parameters are saved in a file called \MSSQL\Log\CertifyR_*databasename*.txt in case you need to find them later.

- Delete references to the database and devices with the `sp_dbremove` procedure after you no longer need the database. You will need to delete the physical files (the device files) by hand.

Steps for the Receiving Site

At the site where the removable media database is to be used, the following steps are followed to install the database:

- Install the devices and database by using the `sp_dbinstall` stored procedure with the parameters supplied.

- Bring the database online by using the `sp_dboption` procedure.

- Use the database normally. Users and groups can be added, security set, and views and stored procedures created.

- Take the database offline (eventually) by using the `sp_dboption` stored procedure. There cannot be any users in the database in order to take the database offline. Taking a database offline not only prevents anyone from using it, but it is also required before it can be removed.

- If you need to remove the database and devices, use the `sp_dbremove` stored procedure. This procedure will not remove any files; it just deletes their entry in SQL Server. You will need to delete the files by hand, or simply replace them once you receive a newer version.

In Exercise 10.3, we will create a removable database on a floppy disk.

This exercise requires precise typing. You will be entering some long command lines, and a mistake at the beginning could come back to haunt you later.

EXERCISE 10.3

Creating a Removable Database

1. Format two high-density floppy disks. Label them **Data** and **System**.

2. Start ISQL/W, make sure you are in the Master database, and issue the following command:

```
sp_create_removable payroll, pay_sys, 'c:\temp\pay_sys.dat',
1, pay_log, 'c:\temp\pay_log.dat', 1, pay_data,
'c:\temp\pay_data.dat', 1
```

This will create three devices named pay_sys, pay_log, and pay_data, which will hold the system tables, log, and data for a database named Payroll. You should see the following results:

```
CREATE DATABASE: allocating 512 pages and then Extending
Database by 512 pages twice.
```

If the command didn't work properly, double-check your entry for syntax errors.

3. Certify that the database is removable by issuing the following command:

```
sp_certify_removable payroll
```

The results should say that the following devices are ready for removal, and list the devices, as shown below. This information is what the receiving site will need to install the devices and databases.

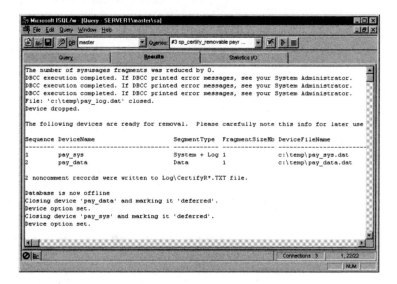

4. Insert the floppy labeled Data and copy the C:\Temp\Pay_data.dat file to it.

5. Insert the floppy labeled System and copy the C:\Temp\Pay_sys.dat file to it.

6. In ISQL/W, clean up the originating server by issuing the following command:

   sp_dbremove payroll, dropdev

7. Go to the C:\Temp folder and delete the three .DAT files.

8. Make sure that the floppy labeled System is in the floppy disk drive.

9. In ISQL/W, install the system tables and the transaction log by issuing the following command:

   sp_dbinstall payroll, pay_sys, 'a:\pay_sys.dat', 1, 'System', 'c:\temp\pay_sys.dat'

10. Insert the floppy labeled Data.

EXERCISE 10.3 (CONTINUED FROM PREVIOUS PAGE)

11. In ISQL/W, install the data device by issuing the following command:

    ```
    sp_dbinstall payroll, pay_data, 'a:\pay_data.dat', 1, 'data'
    ```

    The results should say that the Payroll database has been marked offline.

12. Change the status of the database to online by issuing the following command:

    ```
    sp_dboption 'payroll', 'offline', false
    ```

    The results should say that the database is now online. The database is ready for use. Users, groups, views, and stored procedures can all be added normally.

13. In ISQL/W, take the database offline by issuing the following command:

    ```
    sp_dboption 'payroll', 'offline', true
    ```

    If you get a message saying that it can't be placed offline because it is in use, try closing SQL Enterprise Manager and any other SQL Server utilities. Make sure that the ISQL/W session is not using the database (use the Master database to be safe).

14. Remove the database and devices by issuing the following command:

    ```
    sp_dbremove payroll, dropdev
    ```

Upgrading from SQL Server 4.2x to 6.5

If you have an earlier version of SQL Server, you can easily upgrade to SQL Server 6.5.

Microsoft ✓ ***Exam Objective***   **Upgrade SQL Server 4.2x to SQL Server 6.5.**

There are two major ways to upgrade SQL Server 4.2x (or SQL Server 6.0) to version 6.5.

- Perform a live upgrade of the SQL Server 4.2x engine to 6.5. If SQL Setup detects an earlier installation of 4.2x installed in the server, it will default to an upgrade of the old server to the latest version.

- Leave a SQL Server 4.2x engine intact, install SQL Server 6.5 into a separate folder (or even separate computer), and copy the databases into SQL Server 6.5.

Since the first method is automatic, here we will focus on the second one. If you specify a new folder for SQL Server 6.5, then the 4.2x version will remain intact. The services under SQL Server 4.2x are named differently and can thus coexist with SQL Server 6.5 services. When you load a backup from a previous version of SQL Server into version 6.5, SQL Server will convert it to the latest version. If you're restoring from an earlier version, you should run the CHKUPG65 program to make sure that the earlier database will work with the current version of SQL Server.

In order to load a SQL Server 4.2x backup into a SQL Server 6.5 database, you will need the same permissions you would need to work with any version 6.5 database: SA or DBO rights in the receiving database.

Checking for Problems before Upgrading

When you are upgrading databases to SQL Server 6.5, you may encounter one of the following types of problems:

- Reserved keywords are used in the original database. SQL Server 4.2x followed the ANSI 88 specifications. These were changed in the ANSI 92 specifications, which are what SQL Server 6.5 follows. Because of this, database objects from 4.2x may contain keywords that are reserved under 6.5.

- Some syscomments table code is missing. When a stored procedure is created, the source code that it was created from is stored in the syscomments table. When a database is upgraded to SQL Server 6.5, the stored procedure is re-created using the code stored in the syscomments table. If the code is missing, the stored procedure cannot be re-created during the upgrade process.

■ The database status is set to read-only. If the database is set to read-only, it cannot be upgraded, because the upgrade process changes the database.

In order to determine if the backup from a SQL Server 4.2x database is compatible with SQL Server 6.5, you can run the CHKUPG65.EXE program before proceeding with the upgrade.

Running the CHKUPG65 Utility

The CHKUPG65 program connects to a SQL Server machine and checks all the databases for keyword validity and to see if stored procedures and other objects can be reconstructed through the use of the syscomments table. It also checks to see if any databases have been marked as read-only.

The syntax for the command is as follows:

```
chkupg65 /S<sqlserver> /U<login_id> /P<password> /o<output_file>
```

If there are keyword violations or missing rows in the syscomments table, you may still be able to import the database into SQL Server 6.5, but you may not have full functionality until the problems have been resolved.

CHKUPG65 doesn't change anything; it merely checks to see if all the databases follow the SQL Server 6.5 specifications.

In Exercise 10.4, we will run the CHKUPG65 program on SQL Server and look at the results.

EXERCISE 10.4

Running CHKUPG65

1. Open a Windows NT Command Prompt window.

2. Go to the C:\Temp folder.

3. Enter the following command:

   **chkupg65 /S<sqlserver> /Usa /P<password of sa> /
   oc:\temp\chkupg65.out**

4. To examine the output, issue the following command:

   notepad chkupg65.out

Look for the results from the Master database. There shouldn't be any errors, as in the Notepad window shown below.

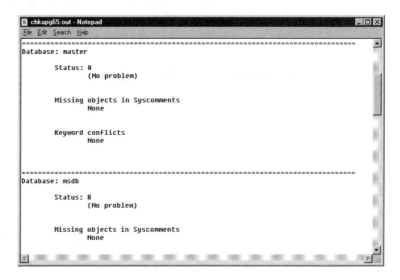

5. Examine the rest of the output file, looking for errors. For example, you might see keyword conflicts, as in the example below.

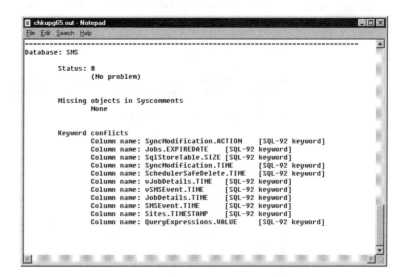

6. Close Notepad and the Command Prompt window.

Summary

There are various tools and utilities that are available to the SQL Server administrator for the administration and manipulation of data, database objects, and entire databases. As you learned in this chapter, there may be more than one tool that will work for any given situation, although one tool may be easier to use than others.

First, we talked about SQL Enterprise Manager's ability to transfer database objects, security, and data. Using the transfer management interface, you can create live connections between two SQL Server machines and copy information from one server to another. Transferring data is a one-step process using this method.

Next, we covered bulk copying. BCP is a command-line program that allows data to be imported and/or exported from dissimilar systems to or from SQL Server. BCP is especially useful when ASCII data is involved. BCP operates on a table-by-table basis.

We then discussed backups as a method for copying information. Backing up a database and then restoring to another database is a quick and easy way to make a copy of the original database. Its major disadvantages are that it is an "all or nothing" solution and that it works only on similar installations of SQL Server (except when you're loading a backup from a previous version of SQL Server, because SQL Server will convert it during the restore process).

We briefly mentioned replication, which is when tables from one SQL Server machine are linked to tables in another SQL Server machine. Use this method if you need for two (or more) databases to be kept in constant synchronization. In the next chapter, we'll go into details about the replication process.

We also talked a bit about creating removable media databases. This type of database can be duplicated, sent to another location, and installed there (for example, in branch or client offices).

Finally, we covered upgrading from SQL Server 4.2*x* to version 6.5. You learned that you should first run the CHKUPG65 utility to check the 4.2*x* databases for compliance with ANSI 92 specifications, and thus for compliance with SQL Server 6.5. Databases from earlier versions of SQL Server may be missing rows from the syscomments table, have reserved words in use, or be set to read-only, all of which present problems when you're upgrading to SQL Server 6.5.

Exercise Questions

1. Which tool would you use to import a mainframe data tape to SQL Server?

   A. Replication

   B. Backup and restore the database

   C. SQL Enterprise Manager's transfer management interface

   D. BCP

2. Which tool would you use to copy the stored procedures from one database to another?

   A. Replication

   B. Backup and restore the database

   C. SQL Enterprise Manager's transfer management interface

   D. BCP

3. Which tool would you use to keep branch offices databases in near-real-time synchronization with a central office database?

   A. Replication

   B. Backup and restore the database

   C. SQL Enterprise Manager's transfer management interface

   D. BCP

4. Which tool would you use to keep a hot standby server up to date?

   A. Replication

   B. Backup and restore the database

   C. SQL Enterprise Manager's transfer management interface

   D. BCP

5. What rights do you need on the originating database using SQL Enterprise Manager's transfer management interface?

    A. SA rights

    B. DBO rights

    C. Insert rights

    D. Select/Execute rights

6. What minimum rights do you need on the receiving database using SQL Enterprise Manager's transfer management interface?

    A. SA rights

    B. DBO rights

    C. Insert rights

    D. Select/Execute rights

7. What rights do you need on a table when using BCP to export records?

    A. SA rights

    B. DBO rights

    C. Insert rights

    D. Select/Execute rights

8. What rights do you need on a table when using BCP to import records?

    A. SA rights

    B. DBO rights

    C. Insert rights

    D. Select/Execute rights

9. BCP ignores which of the following when doing an import? (Choose all that apply.)

A. Rules

B. Triggers

C. Datatypes

D. Defaults

10. A fast BCP goes through the transaction log.

A. True

B. False

11. A slow BCP requires you to rebuild your indexes.

A. True

B. False

12. The data on removable media databases can be edited by the receiving site.

A. True

B. False

13. Users, groups, views, stored procedures, and security can be added to a removable media database that has been sent on CD-ROM.

A. True

B. False

14. The CHKUPG65 utility will fix problems with older databases.

A. True

B. False

15. SQL Server 4.2x and 6.5 can coexist on the same computer.

A. True

B. False

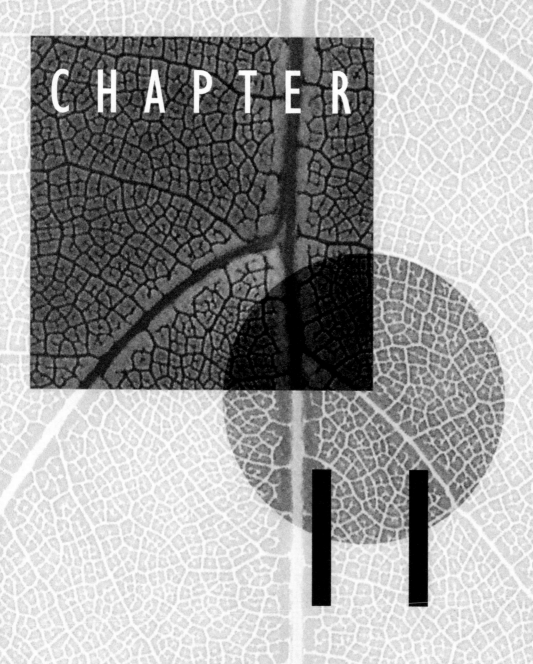

CHAPTER

11

Replication of Data

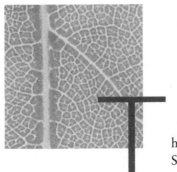

This chapter will focus on one of the more interesting abilities of SQL Server—the ability to replicate or copy data to other servers. SQL Server, starting with version 6.0, can replicate its data to databases on other servers or to databases on the same server.

Not only can SQL Server replicate its data to other SQL Server machines, but it can also replicate its data to database servers from other companies, as long as they follow the ODBC (Open Database Connectivity) replication specifications. Examples of other servers that SQL Server can replicate to are Oracle from Oracle Corporation, Microsoft's Access, and IBM's DB2.

The real advantage of replication is that you can start to design SQL Server and your databases around the way your company works, instead of changing the company to fit within the limitations of the software.

In this chapter, we will first look at generic models for replication, which should spark your interest and give you some ideas for your own setup. We will then look at the requirements for replication and how to set it up.

Another type of data replication is called *two-phase commit*. This is when two or more SQL Server computers either complete a transaction simultaneously or not at all. Two-phase commit guarantees consistency between servers better than standard replication, but it incurs a higher cost in terms of programming and network bandwidth. The Distributed Transaction Coordinator (MSDTC service) is designed to help manage these types of transactions. For more information about two-phase commit, refer to a book devoted to advanced Transact-SQL programming.

Replication Terminology

Replication is the ability to automatically copy data and changes made to data from one server to another server. The data may not be copied immediately, so replication is used when "real-enough" data replication is needed. In replication, the change is made to one server and then sent out to one or more servers.

Replication borrows heavily from the world of publishing for its terminology. The following are the terms you should know:

Term	Definition
Publishing server	The SQL Server server that has the original data and is making it available to other servers.
Subscribing server	The server that gets data that originated on the publishing server and updates one or more tables with new data and changes.
Distribution server	The SQL Server server that keeps track of replication. It copies the data from the publishing server, stores it, and then forwards it to all subscribing servers. The distribution server uses a database (named Distribution, by default) to keep track of these changes.
Article	The basic unit of replication. An article is one or more columns and rows of a table.
Publication	A collection of articles. Subscribing servers can subscribe to an entire publication or to individual articles within a publication.

WARNING   The data on the subscribing servers that has been sent from the publishing server should be designated as read-only, because any changes made to this data will be lost. By default, the data is not replicated back to the publishing database.

A single SQL Server machine can be a publishing, subscribing, and distribution server at the same time. This means that the server can publish certain databases and tables, as well as subscribe using different databases and tables.

Requirements for Replication

To make replication work, the various servers must meet certain requirements and your system must be configured properly.

Microsoft Exam Objective

Identify prerequisites for replication.

Exam objectives are subject to change at any time without prior notice and at Microsoft's sole discretion. Please visit Microsoft's Training & Certification Web site (www.microsoft.com/Train_Cert) for the most current exam objectives listing.

The requirements for the servers are as follows:

- The publishing server should be running at least SQL Server version 6.0, although version 6.5 is highly recommended. SQL Executive must be configured and running on the publishing server.

- The subscribing server must be ODBC-compliant. Compatible servers include Microsoft SQL Server, Access, Oracle, and DB2.

- The distribution server must have at least 16MB of RAM dedicated to SQL Server. SQL Executive must be configured and running on this server. Also, the distribution server must have a new database created for the sole purpose of tracking replication. The default name of the database is Distribution, although any name can be chosen.

- The publishing server and the distribution server should be running the same version of SQL Server (6.0 or 6.5).

- The publishing server and the distribution server should have the same Service Pack version (Service Pack 1, Service Pack 2, or Service Pack 3) installed.

- Each server must be registered in SQL Enterprise Manager on the computer where replication will be set up. Registration of servers can be done during the installation and configuration of publishing.

- The SQL Executive service must be configured and running on all servers involved in replication, and must be configured to run under a user account rather than the LocalSystem account.

In addition, the following system setup and rights are required:

- Because the SQL Executive service will be making secured connections between SQL Server computers, either named pipes or multi-protocol support must be installed (to enable a trusted connection).

- Tables to be published must have a primary key in place.

- SA rights are required to set up replication.

 System databases (Master, Model, Tempdb, Msdb) cannot be replicated; only user databases can be replicated.

Replication Models

There are several generic models for data replication: single publisher to single publisher, single publisher to multiple subscribers, multiple publishers to single subscriber, and multiple publishers to multiple subscribers. Let's take a look at how each of these models works and when you might use them.

Microsoft Exam Objective   **Identify the appropriate replication scenario to use.**

Single Publisher to Single Subscriber

In the single publisher to single subscriber model, one server functions as both publisher and distributor, while another single server is set up as a subscriber. This design, which is by far the simplest of any of the replication models, is illustrated in Figure 11.1.

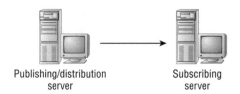

FIGURE 11.1

The single publisher to
single subscriber model

Publishing/distribution
server

Subscribing
server

You might use this model for the following purposes:

- Replicating the data to a backup system (although this is probably not the best way to set up a backup system)

- Replicating the data for a Web server database

- Replicating just part of the database for security purposes

- Replicating the data from an OLTP (online transaction processing) system into a report-optimized system

- Replicating the data across a WAN for better performance than a single server could otherwise give

Single Publisher to Multiple Subscribers

The single publisher to multiple subscribers design is not a lot more complex than the single publisher to single subscriber model. In this setup, the data is changed in one place, and the changes are sent out to multiple SQL Server computers, as illustrated in Figure 11.2.

FIGURE 11.2

The single publisher to
multiple subscribers
model

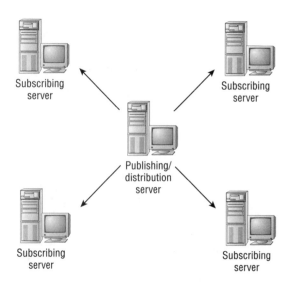

Subscribing
server

Subscribing
server

Publishing/
distribution
server

Subscribing
server

Subscribing
server

You might use the single publisher to multiple subscribers design to replicate the data from a central office to multiple branches, or for any replication that involved more than one branch or secondary offices.

Multiple Publishers to Single Subscriber

In the multiple publishers to single subscriber design, many SQL Server computers are sending their changes into a central subscriber. Although this is a little tricky to set up, this model works well for databases that need to be updated from more than one source, as illustrated in Figure 11.3. Each publisher also serves as its own distribution server.

FIGURE 11.3

The multiple publishers to single subscriber model

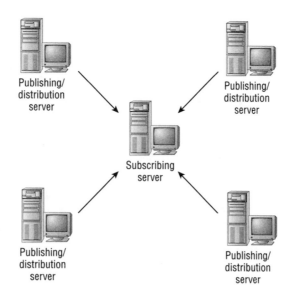

Publishing/
distribution
server

Publishing/
distribution
server

Subscribing
server

Publishing/
distribution
server

Publishing/
distribution
server

To make this design work, you must ensure that each publishing SQL Server machine has a unique location identifier as part of the primary key for the replicated data. Figure 11.4 illustrates this concept.

This model is appropriate for the following situations:

- Branch offices updating a central database

- Warehouses updating a master inventory database

- Remote offices reporting data to a central site

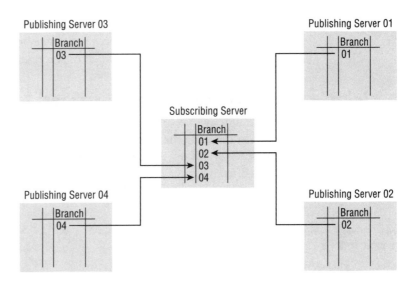

FIGURE 11.4

Unique location identifiers are required for each publisher in a multiple publishers to single subscriber model.

Multiple Publishers to Multiple Subscribers (Round Robin)

The multiple publishers to multiple subscribers design is by far the most difficult to set up, and unfortunately, it is also one of the most popular. In this design, SQL Server computers update each other so that data can be changed on any of the servers and the change will appear (eventually) on all of the servers. Figure 11.5 illustrates how the multiple publishers to multiple subscribers design works. Each server is a publisher and distributor of its own data, as well as a subscriber to every other server's data.

FIGURE 11.5

The multiple publishers to multiple subscribers model

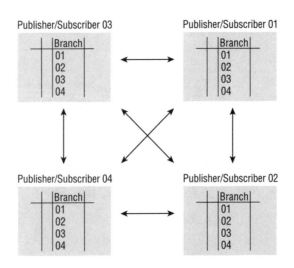

As with the multiple publishers to single subscriber model, it is imperative that each publishing SQL Server machine has a unique location identifier as part of the primary key of the replicated data (see Figure 11.4).

To make this model work properly, you will probably need to use custom scripts. The BackOffice Resource Kit and TechNet are good resources for more information about implementing a multiple publishers to multiple subscribers design.

Publishing Data

There are several steps that must be taken to install SQL Server as a publishing server. You need to install support for publishing data, and then define the actual publications and articles.

Microsoft Exam Objective	**Implement replication.**

The steps required for publishing data include the following:

- Decide which replication model to use.
- Choose a distribution server (local or remote).
- Set up all SQL Server machines in SQL Enterprise Manager or create ODBC definitions (for non-SQL Server subscription partners).
- Install and configure publishing support (one-time installation).
- Create publications and articles (ongoing).

These steps are described in more detail in the following sections.

Deciding Which Model to Use

Microsoft Exam Objective	**Set up various replication scenarios.**

First, you must decide which replication design best suits your purposes:

- Single publisher to single publisher (Figure 11.1)

- Single publisher to multiple subscribers (Figure 11.2)

- Multiple publishers to single subscriber (Figure 11.3)

- Multiple publishers to multiple subscribers (Figure 11.5)

These models were discussed in the previous section.

You will need to decide which server will be the publishing server, which will be the distribution server, and which one(s) will be the subscribing server(s). You will also need to decide which database, tables, and columns you want to replicate.

Choosing a Distribution Server

Replication works by initially synchronizing the tables and then applying the changes that are made to the original table to all subscribing tables. It does this by copying the transaction log into the Distribution database until it can apply those changes to all of the subscribing servers. Figure 11.6 illustrates the role of the distribution server.

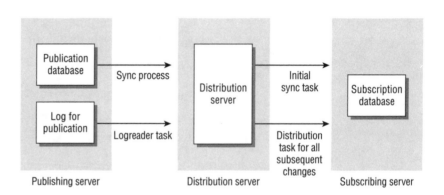

FIGURE 11.6

The role of a distribution server

The Distribution database contains a copy of the transaction log for databases that are being published. It acts as a warehouse, storing changes until all subscription databases have the transactions applied to them or until the configured storage interval expires.

WARNING

Remember, the publishing server and the distribution server should not only be the same version of SQL Server, but they should also have the same Service Pack (1, 2, or 3) installed.

As explained earlier, the server where the Distribution database resides is referred to as the distribution server. The distribution server makes connections to each of the subscribing servers in order to keep the servers synchronized.

You can place the Distribution database on the local publishing server or on a remote server. Your choice will depend on how your network is set up, as explained in the next sections.

Using a Local Distribution Server

If you designate the SQL Server machine where you are installing publishing to hold the Distribution database, you are installing a local distribution server. Although this is simpler than designating a remote SQL Server as the distribution server, there may be performance ramifications to consider. For instance, if you have five subscribing servers that are all in Asia, your distribution server will make five connections across your WAN. Another consideration may be the extra performance hit that your publishing SQL Server machine will take by being a distribution server. Figure 11.7 illustrates a local distribution server setup.

FIGURE 11.7

A local distribution server

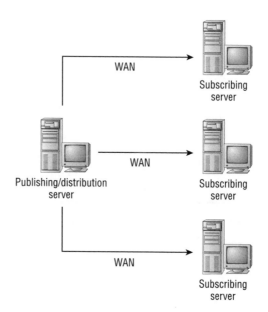

Using a Remote Distribution Server

Designating a remote server rather than a local one as your distribution server may make better use of your WAN. In this setup, the publishing server makes a single connection to your distribution server, and it then makes individual connections to the subscribing servers, as illustrated in Figure 11.8. For example, you could place the distribution server in your office in Asia, where it would make local LAN connections to the subscribing servers, instead of slower WAN connections. You might also choose this model if you need to reduce the work required of your publishing server.

FIGURE 11.8

A remote distribution server

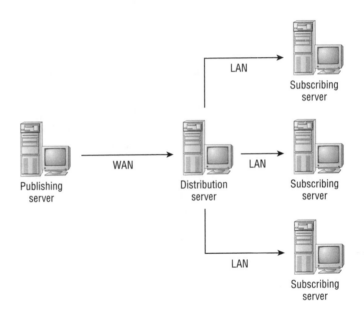

Setting Up All Servers in SQL Enterprise Manager

After you've decided on which model to use and which server to use as the distribution server, you need to register all of the servers involved in replication in SQL Enterprise Manager.

Microsoft ✓ ***Exam Objective***

Configure the servers used for setting up replication.

If your SQL Server computers are situated across domains, you will need to set up the appropriate trusts and security, because the SQL Executive service will need to make integrated security connections between servers. As explained in Chapter 6, integrated security requires Windows NT authentication before SQL Server will allow access.

Installing Publishing Support

The actual installation of publishing takes only a couple of minutes. You do this through the Server menu in SQL Enterprise Manager:

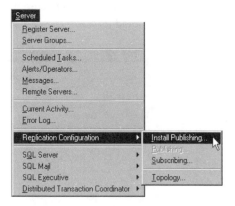

For this installation procedure, you set up the distribution server and database, and you specify how often you want the data refreshed. Follow the steps in Exercise 11.1 to install support for publishing. For this exercise, we will create new devices for the database and log. See Chapter 5 if you need a refresher on creating devices and databases.

EXERCISE 11.1

Installing Replication Publishing

1. Start SQL Enterprise Manager.

2. Double-click on your server to make a connection to it. A red squiggly line should appear next to your server.

EXERCISE 11.1 (CONTINUED FROM PREVIOUS PAGE)

3. Highlight your server and select Server ≻ Replication Configuration ≻ Install Publishing. You will see the Install Replication Publishing dialog box, with the default database name (distribution), and the default distribution server location (local).

4. In the Data Device drop-down list, select New. Then create a new device for the database. Give it the name **dist_data** and a size of 10MB.

5. In the Log Device drop-down list, select new. Then create a new log device. Give it the name **dist_log** and a size of 5MB. Your dialog box should look like the one shown below.

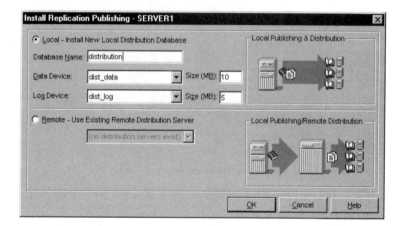

6. Click on OK to save your changes and create the database. (This may take a minute or two.) When the installation is complete, you will see the message box shown below.

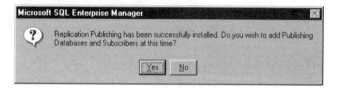

7. As you can see, you could continue and set up publishing databases and subscribers now. Since we're going to do that a bit later, click on No.

Configuring Publishing Support

After you've installed publishing support, you need to configure it. The following are the main items that can be configured:

- Which servers will be published to. For security reasons, all servers that can receive publications must be enabled.

- Whether any subscribing servers will be non-SQL Server machines. You can configure non-SQL Server servers, such as Access, Oracle, and DB2 servers. Note that SQL Server 6.0 is considered a "foreign" server, just like Oracle or DB2.

- Which databases will be published. All of the databases that will allow publishing must be enabled.

- When the data will be published. By default, the data is published continuously, in batches of no more than 100 transactions. You can change this to publish data at certain intervals rather than continuously.

- Whether other publishing servers will be allowed to use this server as their distribution server. By allowing other publishing servers to use this one as their distribution server, you are setting up remote distribution.

Microsoft Exam Objective

Schedule a replication event.

In Exercise 11.2, we will look at some of the publishing options and configure publishing for SQL Server.

EXERCISE 11.2

Configuring Publishing Support

1. In SQL Enterprise Manager, highlight your server and select Server ➤ Replication Configuration ➤ Publishing. You will see the Replication—Publishing dialog box. Before we make any selections, let's take a look at some of the options that are available.

2. Click on the Distribution Publishers button in the lower-left corner of the dialog box. You will see a list of those publishing servers that can use this server as their distribution server, as follows. Note that Server1 (the local server) is not checked, because it is already installed as a local distribution server, and doesn't need rights to use itself as a remote distribution server. Select Cancel to close this dialog box.

3. Click on the New Subscriber button to open the New Subscriber dialog box, as shown below. If you click on the New Server button, you are taken to the server registration window, where you can register a new SQL Server machine in SQL Enterprise Manager. If you click on the ODBC Subscriber button, you can enter information about third-party SQL engines compatible with SQL Server. Click on Cancel to close this dialog box.

4. Click on the Distribution Options button. The Distribution Options dialog box, shown on the next page, lets you change the way that transactions are sent to subscription servers. The default is continuous. The Scheduled button lets you select when updates are sent to the subscribing servers. Click on Cancel to close this dialog box.

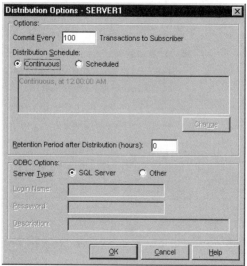

5. Enable publishing to Server1 by checking it in the Subscribing Server list of the Replication—Publishing dialog box.

6. In the Database list, check the Pubs database to enable publishing for that database. Your dialog box should look like the one shown below.

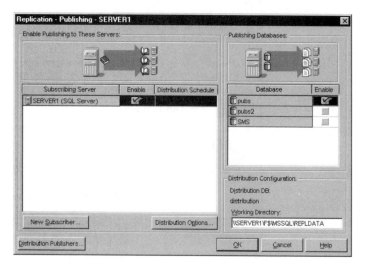

7. Click on OK to save your changes and close the dialog box.

Creating Publications and Articles

After you've installed and configured publishing support, you're ready to build publications and articles. Articles are based on tables, but you don't need to publish the entire table. There are two major ways to filter your data:

- Through *horizontal partitioning,* you can publish only certain rows of a table. To horizontally partition a table, enter the standard Transact-SQL command `column = value` in the restriction box. (The `Where` portion of the Transact-SQL syntax that would normally be used to restrict output is not required.)

- Through *vertical partitioning*, you can publish only certain columns of a table. To vertically partition a table, simply select the columns you want published.

Horizontal and vertical partitioning can be combined in a single article.

You create publications and articles through the Replication option on SQL Enterprise Manager's Manage menu.

In Exercise 11.3, we will create a publication and an article based on the employees table of the Pubs database. We will also explore some of the options available for publications and articles.

EXERCISE 11.3

Creating a Publication and an Article

1. In SQL Enterprise Manager, select Manage ➤ Replication ➤ Publications. The Manage Publications window appears. Notice the Pubs database is listed. This is because it is the database we tagged earlier (in Exercise 11.2) as one that would be publishing data.

2. Click on the New button (upper right) to create a new publication.

3. In the Publication Title text box, enter the name **Publish_Employees**.

---

4. In the Database Tables list box, highlight the dbo.employee table and click on the Add button, as shown below. Notice that only tables with a primary key show up in the Database Tables list. This creates an article based on that table.

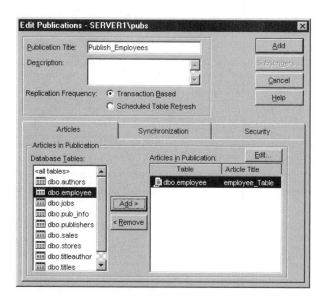

5. Click on the Edit button (on the right side of the dialog box, above the Article Title column) to display the Manage Article dialog box.

6. Create a vertically partitioned article by selecting only the first four columns and the next to last column (pub_id).

7. Create a horizontally partitioned article by adding the following command in the Restriction Clause box:

pub_id='8077'

8. Select the Use Column Names in SQL Statements checkbox. This tells replication to use column names, which is useful if the receiving table has columns out of order. Your dialog box should look like the one shown below.

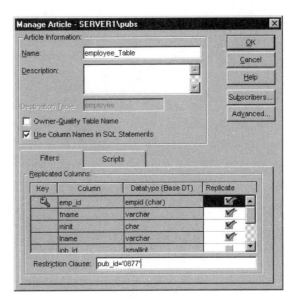

9. Click on OK to save the changes and return to the Edit Publications dialog box.

10. Click on the Synchronization tab. This tab includes options for the initial synchronization method and schedule. If this were a non-SQL Server machine (or SQL Server on another platform), you would need to change the Bulk Data Copy type to Character Format (Compatibility) option.

As you can see on this tab, by default, the initial synchronization checks for new subscribers every five minutes and then synchronizes the tables. You can also adjust the start synchronization time and how often the synchronization process happens to lessen the impact on your network. Let's change it to every one minute (to make it happen faster on your server).

11. Click on the Change button, and change the Occurs Every 5 Minute(s) setting to Occurs Every 1 Minute(s). Then click on OK to save the change. Your dialog box should look like the one shown below.

12. Click on the Security tab. By default, all marked subscription servers have access to this publication. You can enable publication security by checking only the server you will be replicating to, as shown below.

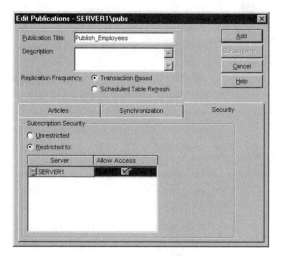

13. Click on the Add button to create the publication.

Subscribing to Data

After you created your publication and defined one or more articles, you need to set up a subscription to actually start the replication process.

If the publishing server has enough rights on the subscribing server (SA rights), then the publishing server can do a "push" installation and force the subscription to happen. The subscription process can also be initiated from the subscribing server, which is called a "pull" installation.

Microsoft ✓ *Exam* **Objective**

Recognize the situations in which you must perform manual synchronization.

There are three basic synchronization methods from which you can choose when you establish the subscription:

Automatic This is the default. SQL Server makes a snapshot of the table and loads the snapshot on the subscribing server.

SQL Server synchronizes the tables exactly. The table is actually dropped and re-created as part of the process, and the data then bulk copied in. Any existing data will be lost unless custom synchronization and replication are used.

Manual SQL Server relies on you, the operator, to make sure that the synchronization happens. Custom stored procedures are usually written and used for manual synchronization. In this method, the administrator manually synchronizes the tables, and then tells SQL Server to start sending the changes.

No Synchronization SQL Server will assume that the data is in sync if this option is chosen, and only changes will be replicated, not the original synchronization. The changes are sent by the distribution server immediately without any sort of synchronization. You should use this option only if you are going to do something like a backup/restore of the database, and can guarantee that *nothing* has changed between the time the backup was made and the time you set up the subscription.

You can choose to subscribe to publications through SQL Enterprise Manager's Manage Subscriptions dialog box. In Exercise 11.4, we will subscribe to the publication we created in Exercise 11.3. This is an example of a single publisher to single subscriber design.

EXERCISE 11.4

Subscribing to a Publication

1. In SQL Enterprise Manager, select Manage ➢ Replication ➢ Subscriptions to display the Manage Subscriptions dialog box.

2. Expand your server's folder, and then the Pubs database folder. The publication we created in Exercise 11.3 should be listed.

3. Highlight the publication and click on Subscribe, as shown below.

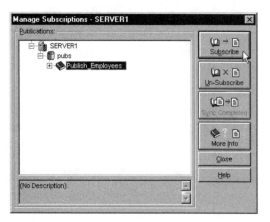

4. The Pubs2 database should be listed by default. Leave the synchronization on the default setting of Automatically Applied, as shown below. Then click on OK.

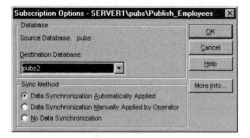

5. Click on Close in the Manage Subscriptions dialog box to save your subscription changes and close the dialog box.

Testing Replication

After you've set up all the replication elements, you should test the system to make sure it is working as you intended. In Exercise 11.5, we will test the replication we've established in the previous exercises by adding, editing, and deleting information in a database.

EXERCISE 11.5

Testing Replication

1. Start the ISQL/W utility.

2. Select the Pubs database.

3. Run the following query:

   `Select * from employee`

The Results window should show 8 columns and 43 rows.

4. Select the Pubs2 database.

5. Run the same query you did in step 3. The Results window should show only 5 columns (because of vertical partitioning) and only 10 rows (because of horizontal partitioning), as shown below.

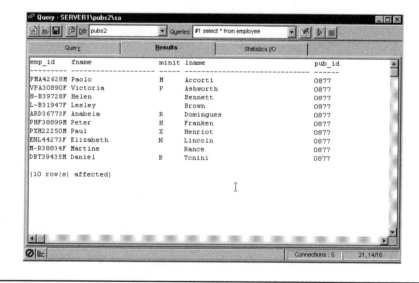

6. Go back to the Pubs database and add a row with the following commands:

```
INSERT employee VALUES ('XXX12345F', 'Katie', 'R', 'Mortensen',
6, 140, '0877',(getdate()))
```

This will add a new employee with the publisher ID of 8077. This addition should be replicated.

7. Add another employee with the following command:

```
INSERT employee VALUES ('ZZZ12345F', 'Shelly', 'K', 'Dobson',
6, 140, '9952',(getdate()))
```

This will add an employee with the publisher ID 9952.

8. Select the Pubs2 database. Run the same query you did in step 3. You should have 11 rows—only Katie has been added, but not all the columns, as shown below. Note that Shelly was not replicated because the pub_id column did not have the value of 0877.

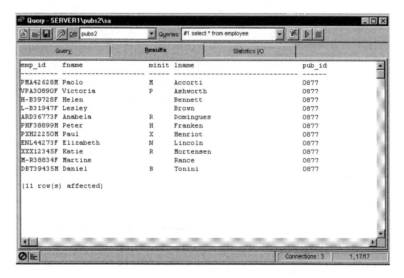

9. Now we will edit a row and watch the change replicate. Run this query in the Pubs database:

```
Update employee set fname='KatieRose' where emp_id='XXX12345F'
```

EXERCISE 11.5 (CONTINUED FROM PREVIOUS PAGE)

The results should say "1 Row affected."

10. Go to the Pubs2 database. Run the same query you did in step 3.
    Katie's first name should now be KatieRose.

11. We will now delete Katie's record, and watch the replication also
    delete the row from the Pubs2 database. Run the following query:

    ```
    Delete employee where emp_id='XXX12345F'
    ```

Katie's record should be deleted.

12. Go to the Pubs2 database. Run the same query you did in step 3. You
    should now have only 10 rows.

Troubleshooting Replication

Although replication is relatively easy to set up, there will probably be times where you will need to troubleshoot some aspect of it. There are various tools and tables that you can use to help troubleshoot replication. Here, we will talk about viewing the Replication Topology window, monitoring replication tasks, and checking replication system tables. Microsoft's Resource Kit for BackOffice (Part 2), the Replication chapters in SQL Server Books Online, and TechNet are also invaluable sources of information regarding replication, problems you may encounter, and fixes for various problems.

Microsoft ✓ *Exam* *Objective*   **Resolve setup problems.**

If replication doesn't work initially, check the requirements to make sure that they have all been satisfied. If replication was once working, but now isn't, check the history of the replication tasks and make sure that the databases involved have not filled up their transaction log files.

Replication Topology

One nice feature of SQL Enterprise Manager is its Replication Topology window. From this window, you can not only see the layout of your replication servers, but you can configure and manage publications and subscriptions as well. To open the Replication Topology window, select Server ➤ Replication Configuration ➤ Topology.

You can use the Zoom button (the one with a + in a magnifying glass) to zoom in on your topology. In Figure 11.9, notice how our server is the publication, distribution, and subscription server.

FIGURE 11.9

Topology view of a replication server

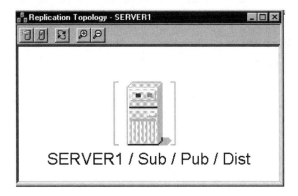

To access the replication options, right-click on the server and select from the context menu.

Monitoring Replication Tasks

There are four different replication tasks that are created when replication is set up:

- A separate logreader task will exist for each published database on each publication server. The task is created when the database is marked as published. This is the task that reads the log of the published database.

- A separate sync task will exist for each publication created. This task makes sure that the tables have a baseline synchronization.

- There will be one distribution task for every published database/subscribed database combination. This is the task that copies the changes to the subscription server.

■ The cleanup task is a Transact-SQL task that will exist for each publication/subscription server combination. This task triggers the `sp_replcleanup` stored procedure, which removes transactions from the Distribution database after they have been replicated successfully.

NOTE All scheduled tasks related to replication will run on the distribution server.

Microsoft* ✓ *Exam* *Objective **Resolve fault-tolerance problems and recovery problems.**

By default, the cleanup task will remove all applied and completed transactions. It can be set to wait a certain number of hours after data has been applied by setting the Retention Period after Distribution (in hours) option. This option is in the Distribution Options dialog box, accessed from the Replication—Publishing dialog box (see Exercise 11.2, step 4).

All of the replication tasks can be monitored in the same way that you monitor other SQL Server tasks. See Chapter 9 for more information about monitoring tasks and viewing task history.

Checking Replication System Tables

When you set up replication, SQL Server creates several system tables in the publishing, distribution, and subscribing databases.

Microsoft* ✓ *Exam* *Objective **Identify the system tables that are used in replication.**

The system tables used in replication are listed in Table 11.1.

	System Table	Database	Contents
T A B L E 11.1 System Tables Used for the Replication Process	msjob_commands	Distribution	Commands that will be sent to the subscription server for each job. By executing a `Select * from msjob_commands` statement in the Distribution database, you can see all of the Transact-SQL code that will be reapplied at the subscribing server.
	msjobs	Distribution	Information about the jobs, including the date of the job.
	mssubscriber_jobs	Distribution	Information for each subscriber about the commands it needs to receive.
	mslast_job_info	Subscribing	Information about the last command that was run on the subscribing database. The job IDs match those found in the msjob_commands table of the Distribution database.
	sysarticles	Publishing	A list of the articles for this database.
	syspublications	Publishing	A list of the publications for this database.
	syssubscriptions	Publishing	A list of the subscribers to the publications for this database.

Summary

This chapter covered the replication process. The ability to replicate data in real-time is a feature of SQL Server that first appeared in version 6.0.

You learned that replication requires there to be a publishing server, which holds the original data; a distribution server, which records, tracks, and sends out updates; and a subscribing server, which receives the replicated data. One SQL Server machine can function as all three types of replication servers.

Next, we talked about the various models for replication. The single publisher to single subscriber is the easiest to set up, and is the model we used in the exercises in this chapter. In this model, there is just one publisher and just one subscriber. Another relatively simple model is the single publisher to multiple subscribers design. This is a good model for a central database that needs to update multiple branch databases. The multiple publishers to a single subscriber model is useful for setups in which many branch offices need to update a central database. The main consideration is that each branch has an identifying code so that the central database knows where the records came from. The most difficult model to set up is the multiple publishers to multiple subscribers model, or the round robin model. In this model, each database both publishes its changes to other databases and subscribes to changes from those other databases.

Then we moved on to a discussion of implementing replication. The replication process works by initially synchronizing the tables, and from there the distribution server copies the transaction log of the replicated database and applies those changes to the subscribing server. Replication can be set for real-time or can be set to happen at scheduled times.

You learned how to install and configure publishing support, and create publications and articles. You also learned how to set up subscribing, and then to test the replication process.

The final section of this chapter covered troubleshooting replication. You can view the Replication Topology window from SQL Enterprise Manager, examine the replication tasks, and query the replication system tables (from the publishing, distribution, and subscribing databases).

Exercise Questions

1. Which database has the original data?

   A. Publishing

   B. Subscribing

   C. Distribution

   D. Replication

2. Which database controls replication?

   A. Publishing

   B. Subscribing

C. Distribution

D. Replication

3. Which database receives the replicated data?

   A. Publishing

   B. Subscribing

   C. Distribution

   D. Replication

4. Which network library can be used with replication? (Choose all that apply.)

   A. Named pipes

   B. IPX/SPX

   C. AppleTalk

   D. Multi-protocol

5. The subscribing database should be treated as read-only.

   A. True

   B. False

6. Which type of server should have at least 16MB of RAM devoted to SQL Server?

   A. Publishing

   B. Subscribing

   C. Distribution

   D. Replication

7. The publishing server is running SQL Server 6.0 and the distribution server is running SQL Server 6.5. This system meets the recommended specifications.

  A. True

  B. False

8. A branch updating a central database is an example of which model?

  A. Single publisher to single subscriber

  B. Single publisher to multiple subscribers

  C. Multiple publishers to single subscriber

  D. Multiple publishers to multiple subscribers

9. Regional databases maintaining synchronization with each other are an example of which model?

  A. Single publisher to single subscriber

  B. Single publisher to multiple subscribers

  C. Multiple publishers to single subscriber

  D. Multiple publishers to multiple subscribers

10. A vice president's weekly report that gets updated from all 15 of his managers' budgets is an example of which model?

  A. Single publisher to single subscriber

  B. Single publisher to multiple subscribers

  C. Multiple publishers to single subscriber

  D. Multiple publishers to multiple subscribers

11. Which task is in charge of reading data from the publishing database?

    A. Logreader

    B. Sync

    C. Distribution

    D. Cleanup

12. Which task is in charge of applying updates as they happen?

    A. Logreader

    B. Sync

    C. Distribution

    D. Cleanup

13. Which task can be set to not affect data until 24 hours after it has been applied?

    A. Logreader

    B. Sync

    C. Distribution

    D. Cleanup

14. Which table contains information about the last change applied to the subscribing database?

    A. syssubscriptions

    B. msjob_commands

    C. mssubscriber_jobs

    D. mslast_job_info

15. You can perform all publication and subscription tasks from the Replication Topology window.

   A. True

   B. False

CHAPTER

12

Performance and Tuning of SQL Server

A lthough it can be frustrating at times, getting every last ounce of performance that you can out of SQL Server is the most exciting and dynamic part of a database administrator's job. Tuning is as much an art as it is a science. There are no right or wrong answers, although there are some rules of thumb to follow and some outstanding tools that you can use to identify where the problems may exist.

In this chapter, we will introduce you to some of these tools and tricks that can make your tuning job a much easier one. Be ready for an adventure, because this task can turn up the most unexpected monsters and hidden treasures that you will ever encounter.

What Is Performance Tuning?

E veryone is interested in getting the best performance possible out of SQL Server, yet very few really know how. This is because tuning SQL Server requires more cross-discipline knowledge than any other SQL Server task:

- You must know your hardware well enough to understand its advantages and limitations.

- You must know your operating system platform (Windows NT) and how it interacts with the hardware and the SQL Server system that you are tuning.

- You must be a network engineer, capable of identifying all of the possible network problems that may exist.

- You must be a proficient database administrator, who is completely comfortable with all of the configuration options that SQL Server has to offer.

- You must be a developer, who understands how the server-side applications are written and the effects that this might have on your indexing strategy.

These are a lot of hats to wear—all things considered, a pretty good day's work.

There are three primary roles in performance tuning with SQL Server: tuning the platform, tuning the server, and tuning the application.

Tuning the platform involves ensuring that the Windows NT operating system is functioning as efficiently as possible. This is critical to a well-tuned application server. Network troubleshooting also falls in this category.

Tuning the server is the focus of this chapter. SQL Server is designed to be essentially self-tuning. However, there are many server and database configuration options that you can and probably should evaluate.

Finally, tuning the application is also important to performance. Some approaches to application development inherently provide better performance than others. A poorly written application will destroy all of the work done at the platform and network levels.

This book is written as a resource to help you prepare for the SQL Server 6.5 System Administration exam. For that reason, it makes no sense to clutter these pages with an extensive discussion of programming or Windows NT architecture. Our focus will be on tuning the server. But in order to do a good job as a database administrator, you should also familiarize yourself with the other aspects of SQL Server performance tuning—if not now, then at some point in the future.

In this chapter, we will focus on the primary issues surrounding server tuning: Tempdb database configuration, memory management, thread management, locking, I/O, and the query optimizer. These factors alone, when properly managed, can have a substantial impact on the performance of your server.

Configuring the Tempdb Database

During installation of SQL Server 6.5, the Tempdb database is created on the Master device, with a size of 2MB. There is only one Tempdb database on a server, and it is shared by all the other databases on the server. Without Tempdb, many of the most basic functions of SQL Server would not be possible. Tempdb has three major functions:

- Storing interim results from system functions

- Storing user-created temporary data sets

- Maintaining pointers and overhead for server-side cursors

Tempdb can sometimes be one of the biggest mysteries of SQL Server tuning. The initial size of 2MB is rarely enough Tempdb space to accommodate your users' needs, especially if you have a large number of users or an application that is written to be Tempdb-intensive. How large your Tempdb database should be and its location will depend on a number of factors:

- The developer's use of explicitly created temporary tables

- If there is improper indexing on tables, which forces the system to create work tables in Tempdb

- The number of server-side cursors used

- The number of users accessing the server

The number of concurrent users that the server supports is a much more important factor than the number of users accessing any individual database. For example, if a particular database makes extensive use of server-side cursors, this will use a significant amount of Tempdb space. Since Tempdb space is shared among all databases on the server, a user attempting to use a stored procedure in a different database may get an error if there is not enough Tempdb space to handle the request.

A *cursor,* in database terminology, is a set of pointers that relate back to rows in the database. Normally, when you extract data from a SQL Server database, you retrieve a set of records. You do not have the ability to move through the set; you must use the set as a whole. A cursor gives you the ability to isolate an individual row in the result set and scroll to other rows as needed.

If you need to increase the size of the Tempdb database, you have three primary options:

- You can expand the Master device and increase the size of Tempdb in that location.

- You can create a new device for Tempdb and move Tempdb to the new device.

- You can use RAM to store Tempdb.

While this last option looks very attractive at first, placing Tempdb in RAM has some disadvantages. We will discuss all three options in the following sections.

Making More Room on the Master Device

If you choose to expand Tempdb in its current location, you do not have much room to work with unless you expand the Master device as well. By default, the Master device is 25MB, and 23MB is currently being used by the system databases stored on the Master device. Figure 12.1 shows the default population of the Master device.

FIGURE 12.1

The default members of the Master device

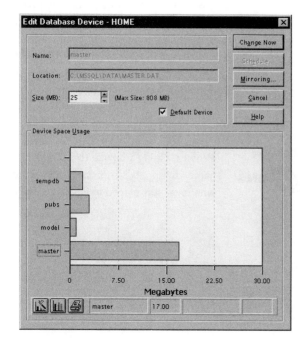

Notice that the Pubs database is stored in the Master device. The Pubs database is 3MB in size, and since it is merely an example provided with SQL Server, you can feel free to drop it (if you do not need the sample data that it provides for testing and training purposes). This will give you an additional 3MB in the Master device, for a total of 5MB for the Tempdb to grow before the Master device must be expanded. Unfortunately, this is still usually not enough for a production installation of SQL Server.

Moving Tempdb to Another Device

If you need more space than the Master device has to offer and you are not very excited about the prospect of expanding that device, you might consider moving your Tempdb database to a device other than Master. By moving Tempdb to a different device, you leave more room for the Master database to expand. More important, assuming that you are not using RAID 5 striping, you can place this device on your fastest physical disk. This will help make access to Tempdb to be as fast as possible.

The process of moving Tempdb takes a few steps, but it is well worth the effort. You need to move Tempdb into RAM and then back out again, changing the default attribute of the Master device and the new device in the interim. When Tempdb is pulled out of RAM, it will automatically choose the first available default device, in alphabetical order, to rebuild. Exercise 12.1 takes you through the process of moving Tempdb from the Master device.

 When creating a device to build your relocated Tempdb, do not use the name "temp_db." This name is given to the virtual device that holds Tempdb whenever it is placed in RAM. Use of this name could cause a naming conflict.

After you've moved Tempdb to a new device, you can expand that device (with the Alter Database command) to whatever size you need for Tempdb.

EXERCISE 12.1

Moving Tempdb from the Master Device

1. Start SQL Enterprise Manager and create a new device (select Manage ➤ Database Devices and click on the New Device button). Name the device **devTempdb** and make it 5MB in size, as shown below. Make sure that the Default Device checkbox is selected.

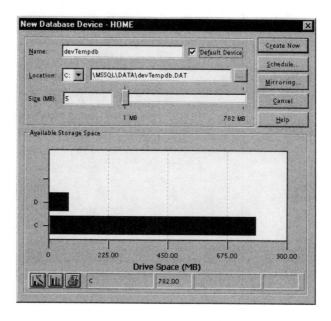

2. In the Manage Database Devices window, double-click on the bar representing the Master device.

3. If it is selected, clear the Default Device checkbox in the Master device window. Then click on the Change Now button and close the Manage Database Devices window.

4. Select Server ➤ SQL Server ➤ Configure. Choose the Configuration tab.

EXERCISE 12.1 (CONTINUED FROM PREVIOUS PAGE)

5. Scroll down the list of configuration options until you find Tempdb in RAM (MB). Change the value from 0 to 2, as shown below, and then click on OK.

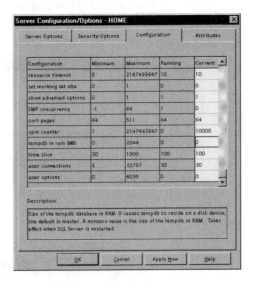

6. Stop the SQL Server service (click on the traffic light button on the toolbar and double-click on the red light on the large traffic light).

7. After SQL Server stops, restart the service (double-click on the green light).

8. Expand the Database Devices folder in the Server Manager window. Notice the device named TEMP_DB. This is the RAM device currently holding Tempdb.

9. Reset the Tempdb in RAM (MB) configuration option back to 0. Stop and restart the SQL Server service.

10. Expand the Database Devices folder in the Server Manager window. You should no longer see the TEMP_DB device.

11. Double-click on the devTempdb device and verify that Tempdb has been moved to the new device.

Storing Tempdb in RAM

Many application developers use a temporary table to store result sets, lookup tables, intermediate results, and other critical data. It should be obvious that the speed of access to this data is critical to the performance of the application. One way that you can speed up this access is to place your Tempdb device on the fastest physical disk. Another way is to place the Tempdb database in RAM.

Microsoft ✓ ***Exam Objective***

Identify the benefits of installing the tempdb database in RAM.

NOTE Exam objectives are subject to change at any time without prior notice and at Microsoft's sole discretion. Please visit Microsoft's Training & Certification Web site (www.microsoft.com/Train_Cert) for the most current exam objectives listing.

The benefits of placing the Tempdb database in RAM can be significant. Tempdb in RAM speeds up access to temporary resources since memory access is so much faster than disk access. If the temporary tables are global objects serving multiple connections, memory-resident objects can also provide less multiuser conflict due to the faster access.

If the performance benefit can be so astounding, then why not make this a standard when configuring a server? Because, as with most performance tuning actions, there is an equally negative reaction. In this case, the downside is memory starvation.

Memory Considerations

In order to understand the ramifications of placing Tempdb in RAM, you need to be aware of how SQL Server allocates memory. When you allocate memory for SQL Server by setting the Memory configuration option, SQL Server divides this memory among all of the objects that need memory in order to function. These include locks, user connections, open databases, and open objects. One of the most important areas of reserved memory is data cache.

Microsoft
Exam
Objective

Tune and monitor memory use.

No data modifications in SQL Server are ever made directly to disk. Data is changed by pulling a data page into cache and then making the modifications. The change is made to disk when a system process such as checkpoint writes a page back down to disk and frees the buffer that held that page. The idea is that the data can be read and/or modified many times while in cache, thus avoiding the need to hit the disk every time that a page is needed.

When Tempdb is placed in RAM, it indirectly affects the size of data cache. If you want to place Tempdb in RAM without adding more memory to the computer, you need to reduce the amount of memory allocated to SQL Server so that your operating system is not starved for memory resources. This action of reducing allocated memory will directly affect both procedure and data caching, with data caching taking the majority of the hit. This could bring your server down to a crawl if there is not enough memory to cache the data so that it can be effectively accessed in RAM rather than from disk.

When placing Tempdb in RAM, the memory that you are requesting is not allocated from the preallocated memory reserved for SQL Server that was set from the Memory configuration option. If you are not careful when placing Tempdb in RAM, you can starve the operating system, and perhaps even prevent the SQL Server service from starting, due to insufficient memory.

Microsoft generally recommends that your system have at least 64MB to 128MB of RAM before placing Tempdb in RAM. However, what is most important here is how that memory is being used. Since Tempdb cannot be split between RAM and disk, your RAM device must be large enough to satisfy your entire Tempdb needs. As stated earlier, these needs depend on the number of users, how the application is written, and other usage factors.

If you have enough memory in your computer to place a fully functioning Tempdb in RAM and also have enough data cache to provide buffers for all of your most frequently accessed databases, then it may be a good idea to place Tempdb in RAM. On the other hand, given a choice between a RAM-resident Tempdb and more data cache, you may find that the cache will usually give better performance. Test it for yourself and then take the appropriate action based on the results of your testing.

Configuring Tempdb in RAM

You can configure Tempdb to be stored in RAM either through SQL Enterprise Manager or with a Transact-SQL statement.

In SQL Enterprise Manager, select Server ➤ SQL Server ➤ Configure to display the Configuration tab. The Tempdb in RAM (MB) configuration option is set to 0 by default. Change it to the size you want for Tempdb (see step 5 in Exercise 12.1), and then click on OK.

The stored procedure for configuring Tempdb in RAM is `sp_configure`. Here is its syntax:

```
sp_configure [config_name [, config_value]]
```

For example, to configure the Tempdb database in RAM with a size of 2MB, use the following statement:

```
EXEC sp_configure 'tempdb in ram (MB)', 2
RECONFIGURE
```

Configuring Worker Threads

One of the best models of organization that occurs in the natural world is the beehive. A single queen sits in control, carefully monitoring the needs of the hive. Some of the bees in the hive are worker bees. These females are responsible for all of the various duties of the hive, from gathering food, to building comb, to caring for eggs and newly hatched bees. When more workers are needed, the queen can lay more eggs destined to become worker bees; however, a single hive can become only so large before the size becomes a drain on the resources of the hive.

Microsoft ✓ **Exam** **Objective**　　**Configure the number of worker threads.**

Before you wonder where we're going with this diversion into the wild kingdom, have you ever thought that SQL Server is very much like a beehive? Just as a beehive has a single queen with many worker bees, SQL Server is a single process with many threads. The beehive is most efficient when a single bee is responsible for a single task. The same can be said about threads in SQL Server. When the task list becomes larger than the number of threads, efficiency decreases. If more threads are needed, the process can create them, but there is only a finite pool of resources available for those threads, and the total number can grow only to a certain point.

Every user connection gets a thread from this pool. When a connection makes a request to the server, it is the assigned worker thread that performs that function on the server. If there are not enough threads to go around, thread pooling will occur. When thread pooling begins, the connection waits until a thread is available to run the request. This may diminish the responsiveness of the system.

Worker threads are responsible for almost all of the activity on a SQL Server. The system uses a few of them for system processes such as checkpoint and lazywriter, but most of them are reserved for satisfying user requests.

To avoid thread pooling, you can configure SQL Server to use a higher value for its maximum worker threads configuration. As you might expect, this also has its drawbacks. When a thread is created for a user connection, additional memory, about 20KB, is allocated for threading resources. If the maximum worker threads value is configured too high, this may consume unnecessary resources, since a new thread is automatically created for every user connection.

When determining the number of worker threads that should be configured, you once again must walk that thin line between resource consumption and system responsiveness. Too few threads will make the system unresponsive; too many threads will waste precious resources.

Monitoring Server Activity

Fortunately, thread pooling is not always a bad thing. Every connection is not always active. Sometimes, connections made by a client application lie dormant while a user inputs data, prints a report, or engages in other activities. If this is the case, that thread can be used by another connection without causing any delay. The secret is to configure the maximum worker threads to represent the value of average active connections. You can check the Current Activity window in SQL Enterprise Manager (select Server ➤ Current Activity) to evaluate the current connection activity. Figure 12.2 shows an example of this display.

FIGURE 12.2

Monitoring activity on the
server

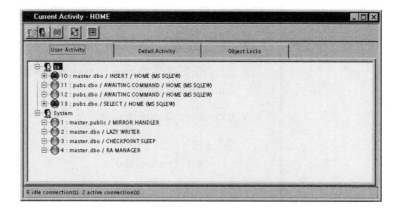

In the Current Activity window, you will see the connections currently accessing this SQL Server machine. Every connection has a number to identify it. This number is called a server process ID, or SPID. In Figure 12.2, notice that the icons next to SPIDs 10 and 13 are darkened, while all the others are dimmed. SPIDs 10 and 13 are the only active processes on this server. In the status bar of the window, you can see exactly how many connections are active and how many are idle. Monitoring this information can tell you how many active connections you have over time. Pad this value by a few connections, and you have a good starting place for configuring worker threads. The steps in Exercise 12.2 show you how to monitor connections to a server.

The Current Activity window is static. It will only update when it is closed and reopened or when you refresh the display. Click on the Refresh button on the Current Activity window's toolbar (the fourth button from the left) to refresh the results.

EXERCISE 12.2

Monitoring Current Activity

1. In SQL Enterprise Manager, select Server ➤ Current Activity to open the Current Activity window.

2. Note the number of SPIDs in the list. You will see at least five: one for the SA communication with the Master database and four for system connections.

3. Close the Current Activity window.

4. Start the ISQL/W utility (by selecting Tools ➤ SQL Query Tool in SQL Enterprise Manager).

5. Enter and execute the following query:

```
USE pubs
Select * from authors
GO
```

6. Add a new query (by selecting File ➤ New) and repeat step 5.

7. Reopen the Current Activity window. You should now see two new connections, both idle. Close the Current Activity window.

8. Add a new query. Enter and execute the following code:

```
USE pubs
DECLARE @X int
SELECT @X=1
WHILE @X=1
SELECT * FROM authors
LOOP
GO
```

9. Open the Current Activity window again. You should now see a new SPID. This one will be an active connection.

10. Close the Current Activity window and ISQL/W.

Setting the Maximum Worker Threads

After you have monitored your server activity and determined how many active connections you need, you can set the maximum worker threads value. You can change the maximum worker thread configuration through SQL Enterprise Manager or a Transact-SQL statement. In SQL Enterprise Manager, select Server ➤ SQL Server ➤ Configure and choose the Configuration tab of the Server Configuration/Options dialog box. The Max Worker Threads configuration option is set to 255 by default; you can change it to a value between 10 and 1024.

The stored procedure for configuring the maximum worker threads is `sp_configure`. For example, to set the Max Worker Thread value to 20, use the following statement:

```
EXEC sp_configure 'max worker threads', 20
RECONFIGURE
```

Working with Read-Ahead

When data is accessed from a SQL Server, the query optimizer will usually select an index that will make this process more efficient. Sometimes, however, the optimizer might determine that rather than using an index, it will result in less I/O to read every page of the table sequentially. When the optimizer makes this choice, it is called a *table scan*.

A table scan is sometimes referred to as a *horizontal operation*. This is because performing a table scan is a bit like reading a book from cover to cover to find a certain group of facts. The action intuitively progresses from page to page in a horizontal fashion from beginning to end.

Table scans are not the only types of horizontal operations. Some of the DBCC commands, such as `DBCC CheckTable`, also read every page of the table to get the required information. Although horizontal operations tend to be quite resource-consuming, there are ways to make them more efficient. One of these is *read-ahead*.

What Is Read-Ahead?

Read-ahead is a process by which SQL Server pulls pages from disk to cache before a query will actually need them, thus reducing the number of pages that the query will need to retrieve from disk itself. For example, imagine yourself on a toy truck assembly line where your job is to fasten a wingnut to a widget. You have two large boxes next to you, one full of wingnuts and the other full of widgets. In order to assemble the part, you must bend over to each box, place the pieces on a table in front of you, and tighten the wingnut to the widget. This could be fairly time-consuming with all of that bending and stooping, wouldn't you agree? Your trucks-per-hour ratio would probably be very low.

Now imagine that you have two other workers also on the assembly line whose responsibility it is to place the pieces on the table for you. In fact, they are so efficient that they can place pieces in front of many assembly workers at the same time. Your entire team should be much more productive as a result of their efforts.

Just like the two workers in our example, read-ahead threads can place the necessary pieces of data in front of the query-worker thread so that the query can be processed much faster. This only works with horizontal operations, because that is the only time that the read-ahead threads can predict exactly which page will be needed next.

Read-ahead is designed to reduce physical I/O, not logical I/O. A physical I/O is a page read from disk. A logical I/O is a page read from either cache or disk.

Configuring Read-Ahead

Read-ahead behavior is one of the more configurable features that SQL Server has to offer. Figure 12.3 shows the Server Configuration/Options dialog box in SQL Enterprise Manager. The read-ahead attributes all begin with *RA* and are in the center of the list.

FIGURE 12.3

Read-ahead configuration options

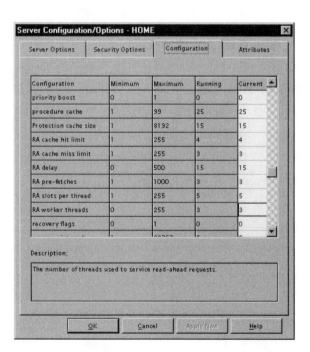

Configuration	Minimum	Maximum	Running	Current
priority boost	0	1	0	0
procedure cache	1	99	25	25
Protection cache size	1	8192	15	15
RA cache hit limit	1	255	4	4
RA cache miss limit	1	255	3	3
RA delay	0	500	15	15
RA pre-fetches	1	1000	3	3
RA slots per thread	1	255	5	5
RA worker threads	0	255	3	3
recovery flags	0	1	0	0

Description:

The number of threads used to service read-ahead requests.

Microsoft
✓ *Exam*
Objective

Select the appropriate settings for read ahead.

There are six different configuration options, each supporting different attributes of read-ahead behavior:

- RA Cache Hit Limit

- RA Cache Miss Limit

- RA Delay

- RA Pre-fetches

- RA Slots Per Thread

- RA Worker Threads

All of the read-ahead configuration options, with the exception of RA Worker Threads, are advanced options. To see them in the Server Configuration/Options dialog box, you must set the Show Advanced Options option to 1, and then close and reopen this dialog box.

You can also set read-ahead configuration options through the `sp_configure` stored procedure. For example, to set the RA Cache Miss Limit value to 5, use the following statement:

```
EXEC sp_configure 'RA cache miss limit', 5

RECONFIGURE
```

The following sections describe each of the read-ahead configuration options and possible settings.

RA Cache Hit Limit

If read-ahead has been activated for a particular query, the RA Cache Hit Limit setting will be used to specify when read-ahead threads should stop working on that query. If a read-ahead worker thread sees that a page it is supposed to retrieve is already in cache, that is marked as a cache hit. If the configured cache hit limit is reached before a cache miss occurs, all read-ahead activity will stop. If the pages are already found in cache, then there is no need for the read-ahead worker threads to attempt to retrieve them. A single cache miss after the read-ahead stops will cause the read-ahead threads to continue reading once again. The default value is 4. This should be adequate in most implementations.

RA Cache Miss Limit

The RA Cache Miss Limit setting is the number of pages that the query must retrieve from disk before read-ahead will begin. This value should be set low enough that read-ahead will properly engage when needed, but not so low that it starts unnecessarily. The default value is 3. This is a good place to start.

You might consider using the SET STATISTICS IO ON statement periodically in some of your queries that are satisfied with a table scan to identify how productive read-ahead is for your system. You can then play with some of these settings to identify if more physical reads can be transformed to read-ahead reads by changing these settings.

Immediately after a query runs, all pages for that query are in cache. Subsequent tests of read-ahead I/O without clearing cache would produce results that are not relevant.

RA Delay

The RA Delay setting configures the amount of time that a query thread will wait for read-ahead to start after read-ahead has been activated. It does take a little time for the operating system and disks to respond to the thread-creation request and the initial retrieval of data from disk. Although this delay is not significant, if the query thread does not wait for the read-ahead thread to begin, the query will always access the next needed page before the read-ahead thread. Think of this configuration as the "head start" provided for the read-ahead thread to allow it to get in front. The default is 15 milliseconds. This is usually adequate.

RA Pre-Fetches

Read-ahead is so efficient that it does not take long for the read-ahead threads to get way ahead of the query. The RA Pre-fetches value indicates how far ahead the read-ahead threads can get of the executing query. This value is measured in *extents*. An extent is a set of eight 2KB pages that is allocated to a specific table or index. Since every page of the table will be read anyway, the data is retrieved from disk in extent blocks. The default value is 3. This means that the read-ahead threads will always stay three extents ahead of the query.

Sometimes, a table can get very fragmented and pages that are in contiguous order in the page chain can end up on different extents. When a horizontal operation must go from one extent to another to get the next page in the chain, this is called an *extent switch*. This is very damaging to read-ahead performance. The optimal number of extent switches would be the minimum number of extents on which the data could reside minus one. To check the level of extent switching in your tables, use DBCC Showcontig(). Excessive extent switching can be repaired by rebuilding your clustered index with the SORTED_DATA_REORG option.

RA Slots Per Thread

Every read-ahead worker thread can handle multiple requests for assistance. An individual read-ahead activity will use one or more slots on one or more threads to handle the request. The default value for the RA Slots Per Thread setting is 5, meaning that each thread has five context areas that can handle read-ahead traffic. The value of this setting depends on the efficiency of your I/O subsystem. If you have extremely efficient I/O, then each thread may be able to get its work done more quickly, leaving idle time to be utilized. Setting this value higher could allow you to decrease the number of actual threads needed, thus saving on threading overhead.

Setting this value too high could cause very unresponsive and inefficient read-ahead behavior because the read-ahead threads would have a difficult time keeping up with the requests. On the other hand, setting it too low puts an unnecessary resource drain on the system, because more threads must be created. The default value of 5 is appropriate for most server hardware.

RA Worker Threads

The RA Worker Threads configuration option represents the total number of threads that can be created to support read-ahead activity. It is very important that this value be adequate for the number of users on your system.

The total number of read-ahead worker threads multiplied by the read-ahead slots per thread indicates the total number of concurrent connections performing horizontal operations that can be supported. If a connection requests read-ahead assistance and there is no free slot to satisfy the request, this will log a warning in the error log. Consult the error log periodically and look for this warning to see if you need to increase the RA Worker Threads value. You can also consult the Windows NT Performance Monitor utility's counter RA – Slots Used. This counter is part of the SQL Server object.

You can disable read-ahead by setting the RA Worker Threads value to 0. Disabling read-ahead can be very handy during some testing activities, but it is usually not recommended in production systems.

SQL Server Locking

One of the primary responsibilities of the server in a client/server scenario is managing concurrency. Since multiple clients could be accessing the same data at the same time, ensuring data integrity and managing concurrency are critical tasks of the server. SQL Server manages concurrency by placing locks on data when it is being accessed by a client application.

> *Concurrency* is defined as the ability of SQL Server to support multiple users at the same time, even if these users want the same data.

Appropriate locks can prevent two users from changing data at the same time. Locking can also be used to prevent a user from reading data that another transaction has changed but not yet committed. Without locking, SQL Server would be of no use at all—there would be no way to determine what data was changed, when it was changed, where it was changed, and by whom. We will look at the specific types of locks first and then discuss the different configuration options for managing locks.

Lock Types

SQL Server locks are primarily page locks. This means that when a client accesses a single record on a 2KB page, SQL Server will lock the entire page until it is appropriate to release the lock. SQL Server also supports table locks for times when it would make more sense to lock the entire table rather than locking individual pages.

SQL Server 6.5 does not support row-level locking, except during some data inserts. To turn on insert row locking, use `sp_tableoption`. This locking is controlled on a table-by-table basis.

> As of this writing, SQL Server row locks are limited to insert operations. SQL Server 7.0 will support dynamic row-level locking.

Page locks and table locks can be broken down into three different types. These types indicate the duration of the lock and its compatibility with locks of other types. The different lock types are as follows:

- *Shared locks* are read locks. They are placed at the page or table level when a connection is reading data from a page. Shared locks are held on a page until the page is no longer being read, and then they are released.

Shared locks are compatible with other shared locks. This allows two connections to read the same page at the same time. Since the data is not being altered, this will not cause a data-integrity problem.

■ *Exclusive locks* are write locks. When data is being altered with an insert or delete statement, the page is held with an exclusive lock. Exclusive locks are held for the duration of the transaction that requested the lock. When the transaction commits or rolls back, the lock is released. Exclusive locks are not compatible with shared locks or other exclusive locks.

■ *Update locks* are designed to promote concurrency. Many update operations actually take multiple passes through the data. Initially, updates are simply reading the data to identify which records need to be changed. Another pass is then made as the update process actually makes the changes to the data. When in the initial read stages, other users could also be reading, but it is important that no other data modifications be made on these pages after the read has begun. For this reason, update locks are compatible with shared locks but not other update locks or exclusive locks. After the initial read phase, the update lock is escalated to an exclusive lock as the modifications are actually being made.

There are also other types of locks that SQL Server supports, including extent locks, spin locks, resource locks, intent locks, and others. These are used in special cases, and we will not concern ourselves with them here.

Configuring Locks

One of your server-level configuration options is locks. The number of locks that you can configure ranges from a minimum of five thousand to more than two billion. This value reflects the total number of simultaneous locks that can be held. Note that is does not specify which types of locks. To SQL Server, all locks are the same.

Microsoft
✓ *Exam*
Objective

Select the appropriate settings for locks.

Like the other server-level configuration options, the Locks setting can be changed through SQL Enterprise Manager's Server Configuration/Options dialog box or with the `sp_configure` stored procedure. When choosing a value for locks, you must be liberal enough to allow for all users to have the locks that they need without allocating unnecessary resources to locking. Each lock allocated will require about 32 bytes of memory from SQL Server allocated memory. Like user connections (worker threads), this memory is used whether the lock is being used or not. If a user connection attempts to place a lock and there are no locks available, this will cause an error. The client will be informed that SQL Server is out of locks.

You will want to configure locks so that you have enough to satisfy the spikes that occur in daily business and no more. You can monitor the number of locks over time by using the Windows NT Performance Monitor utility. If you log this information from Performance Monitor over time, you will be able to find where those spikes occur. The steps in Exercise 12.3 demonstrate how locks are monitored.

EXERCISE 12.3

Monitoring Locks

1. From Windows NT, select Start ➢ Programs ➢ Administrative Tools ➢ Performance Monitor.

2. Add a new counter by selecting Edit ➢ Add to Chart from the menu.

3. In the Object drop-down list, select SQL Server - Locks

4. Look at the various options available in the Counter list box. Select Total Locks and click on the Add button. Click on Done to close the dialog box.

If no other activity is on this server, you should see that only one lock is being held.

5. Start ISQL/W by selecting Start ➢ Programs ➢ Microsoft SQL Server 6.5 ➢ ISQL_w. Log in as the SA user.

6. Enter and execute the following query:

```
USE pubs
Begin Transaction
SELECT * FROM titles (HOLDLOCK)
GO
```

7. Return to Performance Monitor. You should see that another lock is being held.

8. Return to ISQL/W and close it. This will roll back the transaction.

9. Return to Performance Monitor. The lock has been released.

Setting Lock Escalation

Along with the maximum number of locks, you can also set lock escalation thresholds so that page locks can be escalated to table locks when needed. SQL Server uses exactly the same resources for any lock, no matter what type. This means that if you can use fewer table locks instead of many page locks, you can reduce total locking overhead. There is a cost to this, however. Using table locks for efficiency does reduce total concurrency on the system, and you will need to consider this when you set lock escalation.

Determining the proper settings for lock escalation requires you to know your data very well. You must know your user base and the level of concurrency required by these users. Setting liberal lock escalation thresholds reduces resource consumption by allowing you to reduce the configured number of locks. This comes at the expense of concurrency, as more connections need locks on larger objects.

There are three settings for lock escalation:

- LE Threshold Maximum

- LE Threshold Percent

- LE Threshold Minimum

Figure 12.4 shows three tables of different sizes: large, medium, and small. The different lock escalation threshold values can be used to support all three sizes of tables. The following sections describe how each of the lock escalation threshold settings works.

Lock escalation threshold values are server level. You cannot have alternate escalation values on different databases on the same server.

F I G U R E   12.4

Lock-escalation scenarios

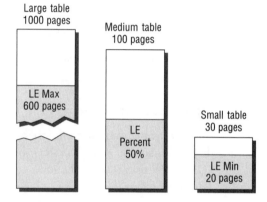

LE Threshold Maximum   This value sets the total number of pages of a table that an individual transaction can hold before the page locks are escalated to a single table lock. This setting can support very large tables. The default value is 200. In the example in Figure 12.4, a very large table (1000 pages) would escalate to a table lock as soon as 600 page locks are requested. This would reduce the locking overhead from 600 locks or more to 1 lock.

LE Threshold Percent   This value indicates the percentage of a table that can be locked at the page level before escalation to a table lock occurs. This is helpful for moderate-sized tables. In the example in Figure 12.4, the LE Threshold Maximum value would never occur because there are only 100 pages in the table. Sometimes, the configured percentage will trigger the escalation before the maximum, and in this case, the maximum would never start the escalation at all. The escalation occurs when 50 percent of the table is locked with page locks.

The default value for the LE Threshold Percent setting is 0, which disables the percentage escalation. Escalation will occur only when the LE Threshold Maximum value is reached.

LE Threshold Minimum   This setting will allow an override of the lock escalation percent for smaller tables. For example, in Figure 12.4 there is a very small table consisting of only 30 pages. If the LE Threshold Percent value is set to 50, this would escalate the locks on that table as soon as 15 page locks were held by a single transaction. But this table may be too small and the overhead too negligible to make it worth escalating at 15 page locks. In the example, the LE Threshold Minimum value, which is set to 20, specifies the minimum number of page locks to hold before the locks are escalated. Even though we may have passed the level of 15 page locks dictated by the LE Threshold Percent value, the escalation will not occur until 20 page locks are held. The default for this value is 20. This option is not used if the LE Threshold Percent value is at 0.

LE Threshold Minimum is an advanced option. To see this option in the Server Configuration/Options dialog box, set Show Advanced Options to 1, and then close and reopen the dialog box.

Monitoring the Transaction Log

One of the most important components of any SQL Server database is the transaction log. As explained in earlier chapters, every data modification that is issued against the server is written to the transaction log. The transaction log provides fault tolerance, a mechanism for reliable backups, automatic recovery functionality, replication functionality, and much more.

Microsoft ✓ ***Exam Objective***   **Monitoring log size.**

For all of the advantages that the transaction log provides, it can also be the SQL Server administrator's most frustrating monster. If the transaction log fills up, no more data modifications can be issued to the database. If the transaction log is too large, it can eat up too much disk space and become difficult to manage.

A database administrator does not have many options available to "tune" the transaction log. You cannot decide what is logged and what is not logged. Since you did not write the code for the application, you cannot ensure that the coding techniques that were used will result in minimal logging. There are only three things that you can do with the transaction log:

- Determine where it goes.

- Determine how large it should be.

- Monitor how full it currently is.

We talked about transaction log placement in Chapter 5. The following sections discuss transaction log size and monitoring.

Determining Transaction Log Size

Because of its importance to the integrity of your data, transaction logging cannot be turned off. If your database application is responsible for significant OLTP (online transaction processing) activity, the transaction log can be quite large. Your goal as a database administrator is to ensure that the transaction log always has space free to accept new transactions into the database. How large should a transaction log be? Like all of the other configuration options that we have discussed in this chapter, the right setting depends on your particular situation. You should consider the following factors in determining the appropriate log size:

Transaction activity in the database Is your application a data warehouse? In this case, you will be reading from the database as your primary function. This does not require a large transaction log, since read activities are not logged. If your application is an OLTP application, then you are making frequent additions, deletions, and changes to the data. This requires a larger transaction log. If you are using replication, your log may also need to be larger. The transaction log in SQL Server is a write-ahead log. This means that all data modifications are written to the transaction log before they are actually written to the database. Unless there is adequate space in the transaction log to store these modifications, the transactions will fail.

Number or users that your database supports Supporting more users usually translates into more transactions. The type of transactions also has an effect on the transaction log. Update operations tend to be more logging intensive than either insert or delete operations.

Your backup strategy   How often you intend to back up your transaction log will also help determine the size of the log. The more often that you intend to back up your transaction log, the smaller that log can be. To put it simply, you can empty a small bucket more often or a large bucket less often. The choice is yours.

Tracking Transaction Log Space

You must continually monitor the transaction log to ensure that there is enough space remaining for the users of the database to perform their tasks. The easiest way to watch this is through the Windows NT Performance Monitor utility. By selecting the SQL Server – Log object, you can select counters to watch log sizes and percentages for all of your databases. Tracking these over time will allow you to find the right balance between log size, transaction activity, and backup strategy. The percentage counters specify how full the transaction log actually is. If this value is allowed to reach 100%, no more transactions can be issued against the database until the log is backed up or truncated. As you watch these counters, you will want to take the appropriate actions if the percentage counters get high enough for concern.

The percent of log counters can be monitored only when a database has been created with a transaction log device. If one device is used to hold both the database and transaction log, the log is never explicitly sized. No percentage can be calculated.

Exercise 12.4 will show you how to monitor the contents of a transaction log.

EXERCISE 12.4

Monitoring the Transaction Log

1. Start the Windows NT Performance Monitor utility. If necessary, start a new chart by selecting File ➢ New Chart from the menu.

2. Add a new counter by selecting Edit ➢ Add to Chart. Select SQL Server - Log from the Object drop-down list. Select Log Space Used(%) from the Counter list box. Select msdb from the Instance list box. Click on Add, and then click on Done to close the dialog box.

EXERCISE 12.4 (CONTINUED FROM PREVIOUS PAGE)

The line you see will most likely be flat at 1. However, watching this over time will give you the status of the transaction log.

3. Save the chart. This will eliminate the need to re-create the counters every time you wish to monitor the transaction log.

4. Exit the Performance Monitor utility.

Monitoring and Managing I/O

The performance bottleneck in almost every SQL Server database application is the I/O subsystem. This operating system component always seems to be working overtime to accommodate all of the users' requests for data. Fortunately, there are things that you can do to reduce the I/O on your server before it becomes a serious bottleneck.

Microsoft ✓ ***Exam Objective*** | **Tune and monitor physical and logical I/O.**

I/O is the process of reading or writing from a database. The smallest unit of I/O in SQL Server is the 2KB page. All data is read in pages, and all data is written in pages. All I/O in SQL Server is logical I/O, but some I/O is physical I/O. Logical I/O is defined as a data read or write operation that is made to cache or disk. Physical I/O is subclassified as a data read or write that is made to disk only.

When configuring I/O, your ultimate goal is to reduce logical I/O as much as possible. However, there are additional steps that you can take to reduce physical I/O specifically.

Managing Physical I/O

Most of the effects of a reduction in physical I/O are cumulative; that is, they will reduce logical I/O at the same time. In the following sections, we will look at how data read and write operations use the I/O subsystem and how you can reduce this drain on resources.

Increasing Memory for Data Cache

As stated earlier, physical I/O is caused by data reads and writes to and from disk. The best way to reduce the amount of data accessed from disk is to increase data cache so that the data can be in cache when it is needed instead of sitting on disk. Therefore, the best way to reduce the volume of physical I/O is to add more memory and increase the configured allocation of memory to SQL Server through the Memory configuration option.

Microsoft ✓ *Exam* *Objective*

Tune and monitor memory use.

There is a point of diminishing returns for memory applied to data cache. If you have enough cache for your most commonly accessed data, this is usually sufficient. If you add any more than that, the less-used data will just be bumped out for more less-used data.

For example, imagine that you have a restaurant storehouse where you keep containers that hold all of the ingredients for your menu. Some of these things you use every day, so you keep these containers on the bottom shelves. Other things you use less frequently, and these are kept on the upper shelves. You have devised a system that you believe will keep the most important ingredients in lower positions. When an ingredient is used, it stays on the lower shelves until it is bumped out by another ingredient. When space is needed on the lower shelf, the ingredient that has been used last is moved up and the new ingredient is moved down.

You have enough lower shelf space to hold all of your most common ingredients, and your system seems to be working. You do a little bit of shuffling every once in while because you have quite a few ingredients that are rarely used. You now have the opportunity to spend some of your profits to expand the warehouse and create more bottom shelves. Will this reduce the amount of shuffling that you do? No, it will probably not help you much.

If you have many seldom used ingredients, then these will always work their way to the end of the line before any of the common ingredients anyway. You will probably spend the same amount of time shuffling ingredients; you will just have more of them on the bottom shelves. It is possible that the longer they stay on the bottom shelves, the more likely they are to be used again, thus extending their life for another trip through; however, the effect that this would have on your back would be negligible.

If you increase the memory configuration to allocate more memory to SQL Server, this will split this memory between data cache and procedure cache. If you want to allocate all of this new memory to data cache, you must reduce the procedure cache configuration, because this setting specifies the percentage of remaining memory allocated to procedure caching.

Using Read-Ahead

Earlier in this chapter, we discussed the advantages that read-ahead could have for reducing physical I/O. Actually, it does not reduce physical I/O—it simply shifts responsibility for physical I/O from the query thread to read-ahead threads. This shift allows the query to view these reads as logical reads rather than physical reads.

Remember that read-ahead is a factor for only those operations that are horizontal in execution.

Configuring System I/O Processes

When a transaction modifies a record in the database, that change is made to the page sitting in cache. If the page is not in cache already, then the query reads the page into cache from disk, resulting in a physical read. After the modification is made to the page in cache, it is not immediately written out to disk. The page stays in cache until it is flushed out by the system. There are two system processes that have primary responsibility to flush a page from cache: the checkpoint and the lazywriter.

Configuring the Checkpoint   The checkpoint is a sleeping system process that wakes up about every minute and evaluates how much work has been done on each database since it went to sleep. When evaluating a database, it may choose to perform a checkpoint operation on that database if enough work has built up since the last time it actually performed a checkpoint. The amount of accumulated work that can build up before the database check-points is called the *recovery interval*. The Recovery Interval configuration option can be set in the Server Configuration/Options dialog box in SQL Enterprise Manager. The default value is 5 minutes.

Although recovery interval is a server-level configuration, the value is used at the database level. The default of 5 minutes specifies that the dirty cached pages of an individual database will be flushed to disk as soon as 5 minutes of recovery work accumulates for that database.

If the checkpoint process finds that the recovery interval has been reached, the database will be checkpointed. A checkpoint is the process of copying all dirty pages (pages that have been changed since they were last brought into cache) in cache to disk. This includes data pages and transaction log pages, and may include pages that contain uncommitted transactions. If the recovery interval has not been reached, the checkpoint process will skip that database and move on to the next database. When it has finished evaluating all of the databases on the server, it will go back to sleep.

In order to maintain data integrity, transaction log pages are always flushed to disk as soon as the transaction commits. This allows any committed transactions that may be waiting to be checkpointed to be rolled forward during SQL Server automatic recovery.

The reason that this approach is used rather than simply writing data modifications directly to disk is that the longer the page can remain in cache, the greater the likelihood that page may be modified more than once. Since the smallest unit of I/O is the page, the more of these that can be logical rather than physical, the better off you are. A change to a page in cache is logical I/O; a write of a page to disk is physical I/O.

If you increase the recovery interval value, a page might be allowed to stay in cache longer. This is because if more work is required to accumulate before the database is flushed, then the physical act of flushing will occur less often. The page may not be forced out as it works up the LRU chain. This will reduce physical I/O.

Of course, increasing the recovery interval value also has its downside. Increasing the recovery interval increases the amount of accumulated transaction work that would need to be rolled forward during automatic recovery in the event of a system failure that did not corrupt physical media. Since this value is database-specific, every database that needs to recover could take as long as the recovery interval value to complete its work. For example, if you increase the recovery interval on your server to 10 minutes and you have six databases on your server, a normal recovery in the event of a system failure could take up to an hour.

Configuring the Lazywriter   The lazywriter is another system process responsible for physical I/O. The role of the lazywriter is to flush pages from cache to disk as free buffers are needed by the system. The lazywriter differs from the checkpoint in how it performs its work. The checkpoint process executes its work in spikes and then goes back to sleep. The lazywriter may be continually active, writing out pages from cache to disk as needed.

To determine an appropriate time to "wake up," the lazywriter uses a configuration value called Free Buffers, which can be set in the Server Configuration/Options dialog box in SQL Enterprise Manager or through the sp_configure stored procedure. The free buffers value specifies how many free 2KB buffers are to remain in cache at any time to be used by query or read-ahead threads. The default value for this configuration is five percent of the allocated memory for SQL Server. For example, if you have set the memory configuration to 8192, then the free buffers configuration would be set to 409.

The free buffers configuration resets to five percent of memory every time you change the memory configuration value. If you set free buffers to a desired value and then reset the memory configuration, you will need to reset the free buffers configuration to its desired value.

The number of free buffers determines lazywriter activity. As soon as the actual number of free buffers falls below this configured value, the lazywriter will begin freeing pages by writing them from cache out to disk. It is good practice for the lazywriter to be continually active. This offloads some of the pressure from the checkpoint process, since some pages may have been flushed earlier by the lazywriter. Set the free buffers to a value that has the lazywriter remain active but not so active that it falls behind in its task.

Configuring Maximum Asynchronous I/O

Unlike the other approaches that we have discussed, setting the Max Async IO configuration option (in the Server Configuration/Options dialog box in SQL Enterprise Manager) does not reduce physical I/O; rather it makes all physical I/O more efficient. The checkpoint and lazywriter processes perform asynchronous I/O. This means that the order in which the I/O requests are issued is actually unimportant, and multiple requests can be handled at the same time provided that the hardware can handle these asynchronous I/O requests.

The default value for the maximum asynchronous I/O setting is 8, meaning that eight individual I/O requests can be run against the I/O subsystem at any given time. If you have a very efficient I/O subsystem, you may be able to increase this value. If your hardware can handle more work than you are throwing at it, you are simply wasting capacity. You will want to increase this value until you no longer see any performance benefit from the increase.

After your server goes into production, you may want to check some Performance Monitor counters to see if an increase in maximum asynchronous I/O would be beneficial. You should watch two counters that are associated with the SQL Server object: Batch writes/sec and Transactions/sec. Monitor the value of these two counters over time. Let them run a little while at production levels to get an idea of actual values.

After you get these values, go to the Server Configuration/Options dialog box in SQL Enterprise Manager. Increase the value of Max Async IO by one. This is a dynamic option, so you do not need to stop and restart the server after changing this value.

Monitor these same two counters (through Performance Monitor) over a representative amount of time. If the new numbers for these counters are notably higher, you can increase the value of Max Async IO by one again. If you see no change in values or the performance is worse than before, reduce the value by one.

Here, you are concerned with how fast the requests for data can be processed and how many requests are being processed at any single point in time, rather than how much physical I/O is actually being requested. Through a combination of reducing physical I/O and increasing the efficiency of that I/O, you can create an environment that will be self-tuning from the physical perspective. You can then turn to logical I/O tuning to take care of the rest.

Managing Logical I/O

In our discussion of physical I/O, our focus was on turning physical I/O into logical I/O. In other words, when users read and write from a database, you want it to happen in cache rather than on disk. When tuning logical I/O, you concentrate on ways to eliminate page access, whether those pages lie in cache or on disk.

Of course, it is impossible to eliminate page I/O completely. After all, that is the very work that the server is designed to perform. You can reduce page I/O significantly, however. This is done mainly through proper index usage and efficient application development techniques.

The reality is that much of the task involved in tuning logical I/O is beyond your control as an administrator. The database developer has much of the control over logical I/O. Some ways of developing an application are more efficient than others. If the developer uses efficient coding techniques, this can significantly reduce I/O. The way that you ask for data does matter.

Using Indexes

One specific technique that a database administrator can use to reduce logical I/O is the proper use of indexes.

An index is a data structure that provides a mechanism for resolving queries more efficiently by working through a subset of the data rather than all of the data. When an index is used, a full table scan can be avoided. This allows a query to be resolved with less logical I/O. Less logical I/O usually translates into less physical I/O somewhere along the line.

As explained in Chapter 5, indexes in SQL Server are called *B-Tree* indexes. B-Tree is short for balanced tree. It is called a balanced tree because every page of the index is exactly the same distance from the root as every other page at the same level. Figure 12.5 shows a generic B-Tree index.

FIGURE 12.5

A B-Tree index structure

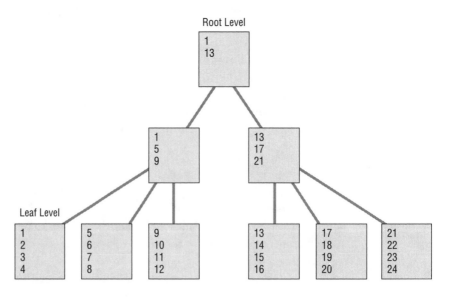

At the leaf level of the index, every record in the database is referenced in indexed order. The layers above the leaf level provide a path from the root to every record in the table by starting at the root level and traversing the index downward until the record searched is found. For example, if the query is looking for record 18 in the example in Figure 12.5, it would start at the root page and find the starting path through the index. Since 18 is greater than 13, it would move to the level below on the right path. Since 18 is greater than 17 and less than 21, the query moves to the fifth page from the left on the leaf level. Total I/O for this process is three pages—one for each index level. If a table scan were performed, it would result in more I/O than the index provides.

As a database administrator, you will be required to evaluate the effect that indexing has on performance, with the goal of reducing logical I/O as much as possible. One way to do this is to use run a query with a statement that will show you I/O statistics as well as the results of the query. The statement Set Statistics IO allows you to identify how much I/O resulted for a query.

When you run a query with Statistics IO enabled, you will see the following information below each query output.

Scan Count   The number of times the system needed to iterate through the table to satisfy the query. Unless you are joining tables together, this value will always be 1.

Logical Reads   The number of logical page I/Os that were needed to resolve the query.

Physical Reads   The number of the above logical reads that actually came from disk rather than cache.

Read Ahead Reads   The number of needed pages that were brought into cache from disk by read-ahead threads. If this value is 0, then read-ahead was not used.

Follow the steps in Exercise 12.5 to evaluate I/O for a query.

WARNING   When using Set Statistics IO, or any other Set statement, the statement will not take effect unless the batch that contains the statement executes. GO is the batch-execution statement, and it should be placed in the script immediately following any group of Set statements.

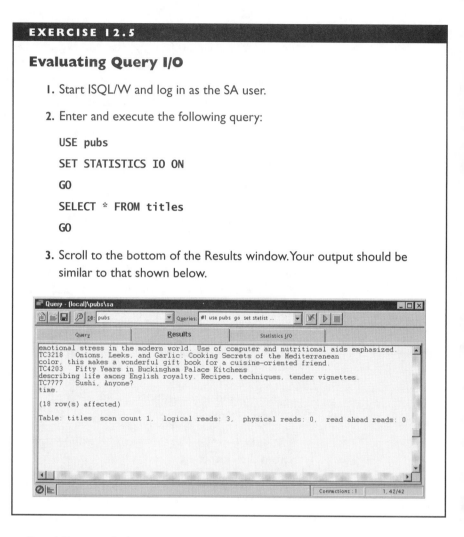

By adding new indexes or restructuring existing ones, you may be able to reduce logical I/O. But be careful here. Indexes, although beneficial to extracting data, are very costly to maintain if you have too many of them. Every time that you add, delete, or modify a record, some or all of the indexes on that table may need updating. The more indexes you have, the longer that this process will take.

In Chapter 1, we mentioned that data warehousing applications and OLTP applications are often on different ends of the optimization strategy. The primary reason that this is the case is that data warehousing applications love indexes. They thrive on them. OLTP applications are ambivalent toward indexes. Although they are useful for finding the value to modify, over-indexing can lead to unnecessary index maintenance and slow down the data modifications in the application. You must consider this when devising the "perfect" indexing strategy.

Updating Distribution Statistics

The ultimate test of performance is whether the users are satisfied with the speed of their queries. Ironically, one of the factors that impacts performance the most is completely beyond the scope of all server or database configurations. This factor is the specific execution path that is chosen for the resolution of a query. When a query is evaluated prior to execution, there are many potential strategies that can be used to resolve it. Sometimes, there is a choice of indexes that can be used. There is always the option of reading every page of the table in a table scan. The best option will be the one that results in the lowest amount of logical I/O. With all of these different options, how do you make the best choice?

Microsoft
✓ ***Exam***
Objective

Update statistics.

It is the role of the query optimizer to determine which index (or no index) will result in the lowest amount of logical I/O. This is done by evaluating the data and the restrictions that the query is requesting. With this information, the query optimizer estimates how many pages will be read for each possible scenario and chooses the scenario with the lowest estimated page I/O. This estimation is made possible through the use of distribution statistics.

An index is based on keys that define the order of the index. Along with the pages that hold the index levels, every index also stores a page of distribution statistics that holds information about how the index keys are distributed throughout the index. This distribution statistics page is used by the query optimizer in its estimation of page I/O. Without good distribution statistics, the query optimizer could not pick which index to use to satisfy a query.

These distribution statistics pages are completely static. They are never updated unless you ask for the update. There are two ways to perform an update on the distribution statistics of an index: through SQL Enterprise Manager or with the Transact-SQL statement Update Statistics.

Here is the syntax of the Transact-SQL statement:

UPDATE STATISTICS *tablename*

When used with just a table name, the Update Statistics statement updates the statistics of all of the indexes on that table. If you want to update the statistics for only a single index, follow the table name with a space and the index name.

Follow the steps in Exercise 12.6 to update statistics using both SQL Enterprise Manager and the Transact-SQL statement.

EXERCISE 12.6

Updating Distribution Statistics

1. Start ISQL/W and log in as the SA user.

2. Enter and execute the following query. This will update the statistics for all of the indexes on the Authors table.

   USE pubs

   UPDATE STATISTICS authors

   GO

The Results window should read:

> This command did not return data, and it did not return any rows

3. Close ISQL/W.

4. Open SQL Enterprise Manager. Expand the Databases folder in the Server Manager window and select the Pubs database.

5. Select Manage ➢ Indexes. You should now be viewing information regarding the clustered index on the Authors table.

6. Click on the Distribution button on the right side of the window to display the Index Distribution Statistics dialog box, as shown below. Notice that the list box contains the actual distribution statistics. Immediately above the list box is the date of last update. This should be about a minute ago.

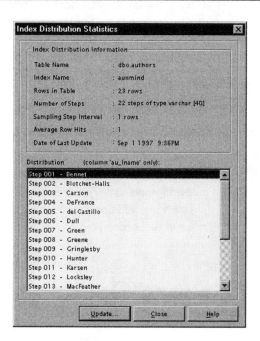

7. Click on Close in the Index Distribution Statistics dialog box.

8. Select the Titles table from the Table drop-down list in the upper left of the dialog box, and click on the Distribution button again. The date of update should read April 3, 1996 at 3:46 AM.

9. Click on the Update button at the bottom of the dialog box.

10. You have the option to apply the update to all of the indexes on the Titles table. If you do not select this checkbox, the update will affect only the current index. Select this checkbox and click on Execute Now. You should now see that the date of last update has changed to the current date.

11. Close the Index Distribution Statistics dialog box and the Manage Indexes window.

You should update distribution statistics whenever data distribution for an index key changes significantly. When you add or delete a substantial amount of data from one end of the table, this changes data skew and should be followed with an update to the statistics as soon as possible.

Updating statistics is a horizontal operation. This implies that it will require a significant amount of I/O in order to execute. This task might be best scheduled for the evening or sometime when the users will not be trying to access the same data.

A full discussion of indexing strategy is beyond the scope of both this book and the exam. A basic understanding of the purpose of indexing and the tools used for evaluating indexes should suffice. However, you will want to investigate some additional resources for more information on this topic when you begin supporting your production servers.

Setting Database Options

The configuration options that we have been discussing up to this point have been server-level. SQL Server also has some settings that are specific to each database. Even though they are not server-level options, database options may play a significant role in the performance of your application.

Microsoft ✓ **Exam Objective** | **Set database options.**

You can set database options through SQL Enterprise Manager or by using the stored procedure sp_dboption.

Using SQL Enterprise Manager to Set Database Options

In SQL Enterprise Manager, the database options are on the Options tab of the Edit Database dialog box. To access this dialog box, select Manage ➤ Databases, double-click on the database for which you want to set options, and select the Options tab. Figure 12.6 shows the database options for the Pubs database. These options are dynamic, so you do not need to shut down and restart the server in order for these options to take effect.

FIGURE 12.6

Default database options
for the Pubs database

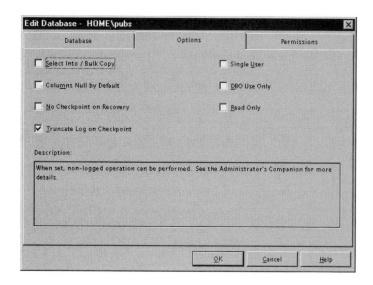

These options work as follows:

Select Into/Bulk Copy   You cannot turn off transaction logging in SQL Server, however there are some operations that are not logged by design. Two of these are fast BCP and Select Into, which were discussed in Chapter 10. Turning on this switch will allow a BCP (bulk copy operation) into a table to proceed without being logged. Select Into is a Transact-SQL command that creates a new table and populates that table with data in a single statement. Select Into is also not logged. This switch must be enabled for this statement to be allowed.

Immediately after any nonlogged operation, you should perform a full database backup. Since the data was not placed into the transaction log, your database is not recoverable until you perform a database backup.

Columns Null by Default   When you create a table in SQL Server, you specify for each column whether it will allow null values. If you do not specify this explicitly, the default is used. The default status of this checkbox is cleared. If you want your application to be compatible with ANSI standard behavior, you must select this checkbox.

No Checkpoint on Recovery   Whenever the SQL Server service is restarted, the server goes into a state of recovery, where transactions are committed or rolled back depending on the status of the transaction and the data that has been flushed to disk. As explained in our earlier discussion of recovery interval configuration, this can be a lengthy process. In order to prevent the same recovery from being needed again, a checkpoint is normally performed on each database after the recovery of that database. If you have another system failure before the completion of the entire recovery, the checkpoint will enable the server to simply continue where it left off. Selecting this option allows the recovery to happen a little faster, but eliminates the benefits provided by this checkpoint. If you are maintaining a standby server, you should select this option to ensure that the transaction log on the production server and the one on the standby server will always be in sync.

Truncate Log on Checkpoint   When a checkpoint occurs, the portion of the transaction log to the next previous checkpoint is considered inactive. The inactive portion of the transaction log is that portion which lists all completed transactions up to the point of the first open transaction. When this option is selected, the transaction log is automatically cleared of this inactive portion without making a backup. This switch makes all transactions since the last full database backup completely unrecoverable. While very helpful during your development stages to keep the transaction log from filling up during testing, this option should be used with great caution on a production server. The default state of this checkbox is cleared.

The SA has the authority to call a checkpoint on any database by using the SQL command CHECKPOINT. If the Truncate Log on Checkpoint option is set, this action by the SA will *not* cause the transaction log to truncate. This will occur only during a system-initiated checkpoint.

Single User   This switch prevents more than one user from having an open connection to the database at any point in time. This switch does not specify what position on the user hierarchy this user must be. When the database is placed into single-user mode, no other users can have open connections to the database other than the user performing the change to the setting. If this is not the case, the request to change this setting will fail. Some operations, such as DBCC ShrinkDB, require a database to be in single-user mode.

Do not confuse the Single User database option with the ability to start the server in single-user mode. The database setting affects only that database; starting the server in single-user mode means that only one user will be able to access the entire server.

DBO Use Only   When this checkbox is selected, only the database owner or other logins aliased as DBO can access the database. When a database is created using the For Load option, the DBO Use Only option is automatically set and must be cleared before your users will have access to the database.

Read Only   When this option is selected, the database is explicitly marked as read-only. No data modifications to the database may be made. If your database application is truly a data warehouse with no data modifications being made, you may want to consider setting the Read Only option on. This will significantly improve performance. When a database is marked as read-only, SQL Server completely disengages all locking on that database.

If you will be replicating to a database using SQL Server replication, the subscriber cannot be marked as read-only, even if your users will be making no changes to the data. This prevents the distribution server from issuing replicated transactions on the subscribing database.

Using Transact-SQL to Set Database Options

All of the database options listed in the previous section also can be changed by using the `sp_dboption` stored procedure. Here is its syntax:

```
sp_dboption [dbname, optname, {true | false}]
```

For example, to mark the Pubs database as read-only, use the following statement:

```
EXEC sp_dboption pubs,'read only', true
```

Summary

In this chapter, we discussed numerous approaches to tuning a SQL Server server, as well as configuring a database stored on a SQL Server machine.

We have looked at expanding and/or moving the Tempdb database, threading, locking, I/O configuration, and database-specific options. We have also discussed how many of these features interact with each other.

If nothing else, you should now have a grasp on the tightrope walk that is performance tuning. As you have seen, every action that you perform seems to always have two consequences, one positive and one negative. That is the standard approach to performance tuning. You must choose which actions to take to give you the greatest possible benefits at the lowest cost.

The job of tuning a database and a server is never done. The best that you can ever do is buy yourself some time occasionally. The systems will require retuning as the needs of the users change, the data changes, your hardware changes, and so on. A SQL Server server is much like a piano—constant tuning is required if it is to make beautiful music.

Exercise Questions

1. Which of the following commands is used to turn on insert row locking?

A. `sp_dboption`

B. `sp_tableoption`

C. `sp_configure`

D. `Alter Table`

2. Which of the following is not a read-ahead configuration option?

A. RA Worker Threads

B. RA Delay

C. RA Pre-fetches

D. RA Extent Switches

3. Which kind of lock is placed on a page when it is being read by a transaction?

A. Intent

B. Shared

C. Exclusive

D. Extent

4. What is the default value of LE Threshold Maximum?

A. 20 pages

B. 20 percent

C. 200 pages

D. 0

5. Which of the following operations would most benefit from an index on the Authors table?

A. `SELECT * FROM authors where au_lname = 'Smith'`

B. `SELECT * FROM authors`

C. `UPDATE STATISTICS authors`

D. `DBCC NewAlloc`

6. The benefits of placing Tempdb in RAM will always outweigh the cost.

A. True

B. False

7. Which of the following Performance Monitor counters are helpful for monitoring physical I/O? (Choose two.)

   A. Log Space Used (%)

   B. IO – Batch Writes / Sec

   C. RA – Slots Used

   D. IO – Transactions / Sec

8. A checkpoint does which of the following? (Choose all that apply.)

   A. Writes dirty pages to disk ever minute

   B. Evaluates the option of writing dirty pages to disk every minute

   C. Writes dirty pages to disk whenever the recovery interval has been reached

   D. Reads pages from disk before a query will need them

9. Which of the following configuration options will *not* affect the size of data cache?

   A. Max Async IO

   B. Procedure Cache

   C. Locks

   D. User Connections

10. Tempdb can be split between RAM and disk.

   A. True

   B. False

11. A shared lock and an update lock can be placed on the same page at the same time.

   A. True

   B. False

12. Read-ahead can substantially reduce logical I/O.

    A. True

    B. False

13. SQL Server uses which of the following approaches for managing pages in data cache?

    A. Last in first out

    B. Last in last out

    C. Last used first out

    D. Last used last out

14. What is the name that SQL Server gives the logical device that holds Tempdb in RAM?

    A. devTempdb

    B. temp_db_dev

    C. tempdb

    D. temp_db

15. Which of the following is a benefit of setting the database option Truncate Log on Checkpoint on?

    A. Your database will always be recoverable

    B. Your transaction log will most likely never fill up

    C. Long running transactions will be automatically committed at checkpoint

    D. SQL Executive can read the transaction log at checkpoint

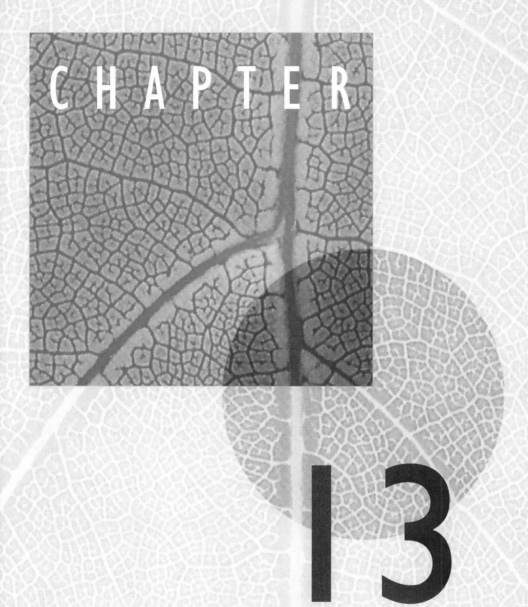

CHAPTER

13

Troubleshooting SQL Server

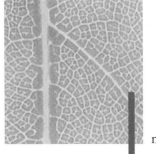

n this chapter, you will learn how to troubleshoot and resolve some of the most common problems with SQL Server. First, we'll explain how to gather information about SQL Server errors and how to break error messages down into their components and discover what they mean.

Then we will discuss some common network problems and how to resolve them. Next, we will review the DBCC commands used to check database object integrity. We will then explain how to check on SQL Server processes and when you might need to kill (cancel) a process. We will finish the chapter with a look at fault-tolerance and recovery problems encountered in replication.

Troubleshooting is one of the largest sections on the Prometric Exam for System Administration for Microsoft SQL Server 6.5 (10 to 12 percent), so study this chapter carefully and get as much hands-on experience as you can before you take the exam. Be sure to study the other chapters as well and keep an eye out for troubleshooting issues.

Checking Error Logs

If you start SQL Server as a Windows NT service through the auto-start setting, from Control Panel ➤ Services, or from a command line with the command NET START MSSQLSERVER, messages will be sent to both the SQL Server error log and the Windows NT event (Application) log. Both logs may contain informational messages as well as error messages.

Microsoft ✓ *Exam* *Objective* | **Locate information relevant to diagnosing a problem.**

Exam objectives are subject to change at any time without prior notice and at Microsoft's sole discretion. Please visit Microsoft's Training & Certification Web site (www.microsoft.com/Train_Cert) for the most current exam objectives listing.

Viewing the SQL Server Error Log

The SQL Server error log is a group of ASCII text files located in the \MSSQL\Log folder. The most recent log file is called ERRORLOG (with no extension). As each new log is created, the old log file is renamed to ERRORLOG.1, the existing ERRORLOG.1 file is renamed to ERRORLOG.2, and so on, for up to six history logs. The oldest log file, ERRORLOG.6, is not renamed but is overwritten by the old ERRORLOG.5.

Since the error logs are in ASCII format, you can use any text editor, such as Notepad or MS-DOS Edit, to view them. Word processing programs that are capable of reading ASCII files (sometimes referred to as MS-DOS text), such as Microsoft Word and Corel's WordPerfect, can also be used to view the information.

To view a log from SQL Enterprise Manager, select Server ➢ Error Log. This opens the Server Error Log window, with the current log file displayed, as shown in Figure 13.1. You can change to a different log file by selecting one from the drop-down list box on the Server Error Log window's toolbar. To refresh your view of the log, click on the Refresh button on the toolbar (to the right of the drop-down list).

The location of event and error logging depends on how you start SQL Server. For example, if you start SQL Server from the command line using the command SQLSERVR.EXE, events and errors will be sent to the SQL Server error log. Error messages may also be sent to the screen, or even redirected to another location. See SQL Server Books Online for more information about redirecting logging.

Using the NT Event Viewer

As you've learned in previous chapters, Windows NT also logs SQL Server events and errors, and you can view these with the NT Event Viewer (see Exercise 2.3 in Chapter 2).

FIGURE 13.1

The Server Error Log window in SQL Enterprise Manager

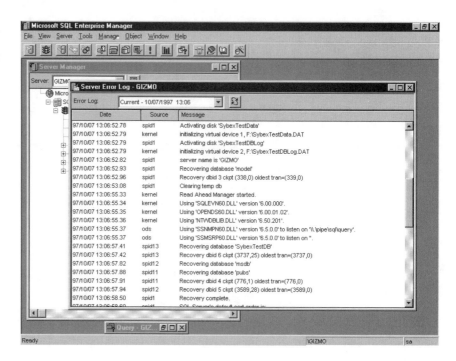

For SQL Server administrators, the disadvantage of using the NT Event Viewer is that it not only logs SQL Server events, but also events from other applications running under Windows NT.

Exercise 13.1 demonstrates the differences between the SQL Server error log and the NT Event Viewer. We will view the same two error messages in each of these log files.

EXERCISE 13.1

Searching for Errors

1. Start ISQL/W and run the \scripts\script13.sql script (which is on the CD that comes with this book). This script generates the same error with three different states, or levels of severity. You will see several error messages appear in your ISQL/W window. Ignore these and close the utility.

2. In SQL Enterprise Manager, select Server ➢ Error Log to display the Server Error Log window.

---

3. Click on the Refresh button, and then scroll down to the bottom of the log. You should see something similar to the entries shown below. You can see that the log lists the date, the SPID (system process ID), and the error message.

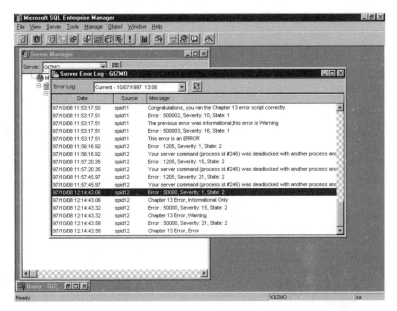

4. Let's take a look at the same error messages in the NT Event Viewer. From Windows NT, select Start ➤ Programs ➤ Administrative Tools ➤ NT Event Viewer.

5. Select Log ➤ Application to switch to the Application log.

6. To refresh the data, select View ➤ Refresh (or simply press the F5 key). You should now see something similar to the window shown below.

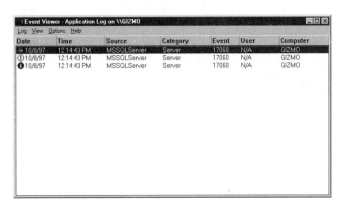

EXERCISE 13.1 (CONTINUED FROM PREVIOUS PAGE)

7. Double-click on the first error (the error with the stop sign). Note that the error is number 50,000, with a severity of 21 and a state of 2. The error message is on the following line.

8. Close the NT Event Viewer.

Error Message Components

An error message has the following components:

- The error number uniquely identifies the error message.

- The severity level tells you what type of problem has occurred in SQL Server. Severity levels range from 0 to 25. In a nutshell, errors from 0–10 are informational, 11–16 are user errors, 17 and 18 are resource problems (a user's session is not normally interrupted when one of these errors occurs), and 19–25 are fatal errors in the program code. Table 13.1 lists the security levels, with some details about levels 17 through 25.

Fatal errors are very rare and should be investigated as quickly as possible. Errors with a severity of 20 and higher will terminate a user's connection to SQL Server.

- The error state identifies the source of the error. This can be especially useful if the same error could occur in several locations.

- The error message text tells you what the error is. Sometimes, this text also includes a possible solution. For example, you might get an error message that includes the text "incorrect syntax near FOO." This could indicate that you forgot a comma or quotation marks, or you made another syntactical error.

Although you won't be tested on the components of an error message in the System Administration for Microsoft SQL Server 6.5 exam, this knowledge will be very helpful in your work as a database administrator. It is particularly useful to know what the different severity levels imply.

	Security Level	Definition
TABLE 13.1 Error Message Severity Levels	Severity 0–10	Informational messages, which do not usually prevent a user from working with SQL Server. User-defined errors (error numbers 50,000 and higher) will have a severity of 0–10.
	Severity 11–16	Errors generated by users, which need to be fixed by the user. These are generally errors in the syntax of SQL statements.
	Severity 17	Insufficient Resources. The resources referred to could be configurable resources like locks or open databases allowed. The SA should handle this error by using the sp_configure stored procedure to reconfigure the system.
	Severity 18	Non-Fatal Internal Error Detected. There has been some type of internal error detected. The SA should handle this error. Stopping and restarting the SQL Server service will generally fix the problem. A user's session is not normally interrupted when this error occurs.
	Severity 19	SQL Server Error in Resource. This error occurs when a nonconfigurable limit has been exceeded. The SA should investigate the error and may need to call for some type of technical support.
	Severity 20	SQL Server Fatal Error in Current Process. This error occurs when SQL Server code runs into a problem. Because this error affects only one process, there is a good chance that the database is still intact. The SA should kill the process.
	Severity 21	SQL Server Fatal Error in Database Process. This error occurs when SQL Server finds an error in code that affects all current connections or processes running on a database. Although this error sounds disastrous, the database itself is generally still intact.
	Severity 22	SQL Server Fatal Error Table Integrity Suspect. This error occurs when an application damages an index or a table. See the "Database Object Integrity" section for actions to take.
	Severity 23	SQL Server Fatal Error Database Integrity Suspect. See the "Database Object Integrity" section for actions to take.

T A B L E 13.1 (cont.)	**Security Level**	**Definition**
Error Message Severity Levels	Severity 24	Hardware Error. This error occurs when there is a hardware problem. The SA and possibly the network administrator should investigate the problem. In the event of media failure, you should start your recovery procedures (see Chapter 8).
	Severity 25	Internal System Error. The SA should be contacted and may need to call Microsoft's product support team.

Troubleshooting Network Problems

The first step in handling network problems is to isolate where the problem is occurring. The errors could be coming from SQL Server, the network, the front-end application, or any combination of these three components.

Microsoft ✓ *Exam* *Objective*

Resolve network error messages.

To troubleshoot a network problem, check your connections as follows:

- Check your local connection to SQL Server first. From the server machine, go to a command prompt and run the ISQL utility without the /S parameter. This will verify that you do have access to SQL Server and that the named pipes protocol is working on the local machine.

- Verify that you have network connectivity by running a NET VIEW statement from a command prompt. Alternatively, double-click on the Entire Network icon in Network Neighborhood. If something shows up in Network Neighborhood other than your own computer, then you know that you can see the rest of the network.

- Check your remote connection to SQL Server over named pipes. You can do this by using the MAKEPIPE and READPIPE utilities (see Exercise 2.4 in Chapter 2).

- If named pipes comes up successfully, but you still cannot connect, you probably have a DB-Library problem. Verify that you have the same network library and DB-Libraries on both the server and the client computer. This can be done with the Setup program or with the Client Configuration utility (see Chapter 4).

Checking Database Object Integrity

You can check the integrity of database objects by using the DBCC commands. There are several that you should know for the exam, and several more that you may need to use in your work as a SQL Server administrator.

Microsoft ✓ *Exam* *Objective*	**Check object integrity.**

If the DBCC commands generate errors, you can try to recover data or drop and rebuild the individual database objects in question. For example, if your system has a severity 22 (SQL Server Fatal Error Table Integrity Suspect) or severity 23 (SQL Server Fatal Error Database Integrity Suspect) error, DBCC commands may help you track down the problem. You can use the DBCC CheckTable, DBCC CheckDB, and DBCC NewAlloc commands to investigate the consistency of your database. If you find that only one object is corrupted, you might try dropping and re-creating that object. If multiple objects are corrupted, there is still a chance that the error is in cache and not on the hard disk. Try stopping and restarting the SQL Server service or rebooting Window NT, and then run the DBCC commands again. (If this did not fix the problem, then the errors have migrated to your hard disk, and you should start your recovery procedures, as outlined in Chapter 8.)

Table 13.2 provides a quick overview of some of the most common DBCC commands.

TABLE 13.2	DBCC Command	Function
Overview of Common DBCC Commands	DBCC CheckTable	Verifies that index and data pages are correctly linked and that your indexes are sorted properly. It will also verify that the data stored on each page is reasonable and that the page offsets are reasonable.
	DBCC CheckDB	Same as DBCC CheckTable, but it does the verification for every table in a database.
	DBCC CheckCatalog	Checks for consistency in and between system tables. For example, if there is an entry in the sysobjects table for a table, there should be a matching entry (or entries) in the syscolumns table.
	DBCC NewAlloc	Verifies that extents are being used properly and that there is no overlap between objects that reside in their own separate extents.
	DBCC MemUsage	Provides a detailed report of the server memory allocated at startup, and how much memory is being used by the 20 largest in objects in both the procedure and data caches.
	DBCC TextAlloc/TextAll	Checks the allocation of text and image columns in a table or a database. The command has two options: FULL generates a report, and FAST does not generate a report.

Investigating a Suspect Database

A database can be marked as suspect for a number of reasons. You need to discover why a particular database was marked suspect before you can troubleshoot the problem.

Microsoft ✓ *Exam* *Objective*

Investigate a database that is marked suspect.

If a database device is offline, then all of the databases that have allocations on that device will be marked suspect. To resolve this problem, find out why the device is offline and bring it back online. Stop and restart the SQL Server service. The automatic recovery should unmark the suspect databases.

If a database device has been moved or renamed, or if it doesn't exist, you can bet that the error log will contain Error 822 (severity 21—Could Not Start I/O for Request). If the database device has been renamed, you should name it back to its original name and stop and restart the SQL Server service. If the database device is missing, you should start your recovery procedures.

The sp_movedevice stored procedure can also be useful for moved or renamed database devices. See SQL Server Books Online for more information about this stored procedure.

Another possible reason for a database to be suspect is a lack of permissions. This can happen only if you are using NTFS and the device is on the NTFS partition. You can fix this problem by making the administrator the owner of the device file and making sure that the SQL Server service has read/write permissions on the file as well.

If the database appears to be fine, but you cannot remove the suspect status, you could run the following Transact-SQL script to manually reset the status of the database:

```
sp_configure 'allow updates', 1
GO
RECONFIGURE WITH OVERRIDE
GO
USE master
GO
BEGIN TRAN
GO
UPDATE sysdatabases
set status=0 where name='your database name'
GO
```

If more than one row is affected by the UPDATE statement, issue a ROLLBACK statement and do some further investigation; otherwise, continue with the rest of these statements:

```
COMMIT TRAN

GO

sp_configure 'allow updates', 0

GO

RECONFIGURE WITH OVERRIDE

GO

CHECKPOINT

GO

SHUTDOWN

GO
```

Resolving Process Problems

Every process in SQL Server is assigned an SPID (system process ID) when the process is started. The SPID is stored in the sysprocesses table in the Master database, along with the following:

- Information on the process status (running, runnable, sleeping, and so on)

- A login ID

- A hostname, which is usually a computer name but can be an application name

- A block, which will contain the SPID of the blocking process

- The database name to which the process is attached

- A command that is running or waiting

Microsoft ✓ *Exam Objective*

Cancel a sleeping process.

You can view process information and cancel processes in two ways. As you might have guessed, those two ways are through SQL Enterprise Manager and by using Transact-SQL statements.

Using SQL Enterprise Manager to Kill a Process

To view process information from SQL Enterprise Manager, click on the toolbar button that looks like a bar graph, or select Server ➤ Current Activity. You will see the Current Activity window, as shown in Figure 13.2.

FIGURE 13.2

The Current Activity window

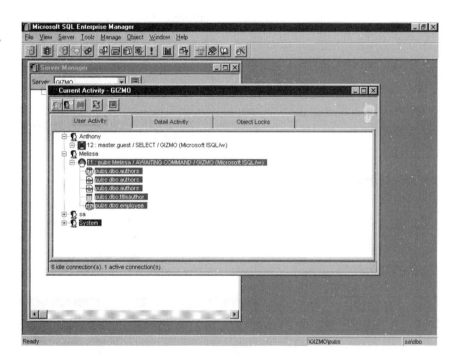

In the figure, Melissa is currently blocking and Anthony is being blocked. You know this by the icons that are shown. Click on the rightmost button on the Current Activity window toolbar to see a legend. To see what line of code a user is currently running, double-click on the activity line for that user. In the example, we would double-click on Melissa's activity line:

```
11:pubs.Melissa / AWAITING COMMAND / GIZMO (Microsoft ISQL/w)
```

This displays the Process Details dialog box, with the line of code Melissa is currently running, as shown in Figure 13.3.

F I G U R E   13.3

The Process Details dialog box shows the code that a user is currently running.

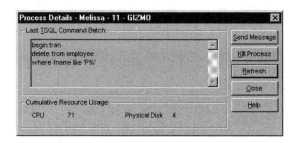

Then we would double-click on Anthony's activity line:

```
12: master.guest / SELECT / GIZMO (Microsoft ISQL/w)
```

We see that Anthony is attempting to run a SELECT query from the Employees table, which is where Melissa's transaction is currently running.

From the Process Details dialog box, you can send a message to the user (click on the Send Message button) or kill the process (click on the Kill Process button), which will cancel it.

Using Transact-SQL to Kill a Process

Although the Current Activity window in SQL Enterprise Manager is useful, you may find the sp_who stored procedure to be much more valuable as a resource for finding blocking problems and killing them. Figure 13.4 shows an example of the results of executing an sp_who statement.

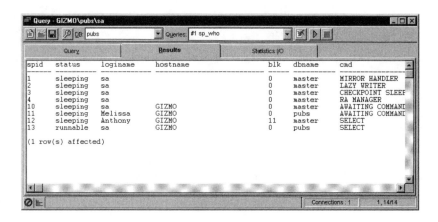

As you can see in the example, the processes for both Anthony and Melissa are sleeping. You will further note that Anthony is blocked by SPID 11 (shown by the 11 in Anthony's blk column), which is Melissa. You can kill Melissa's process, which will roll back her transaction, by issuing the KILL statement, as follows:

```
KILL 11
```

Anthony's blocked process, which was a simple SELECT statement, would then finish processing. You can check this by executing the sp_who statement again. Figure 13.5 shows the results. Note that Anthony is no longer blocked and Melissa's process (SPID 11) is no longer running.

FIGURE 13.5

Output from the sp_who stored procedure after the KILL statement

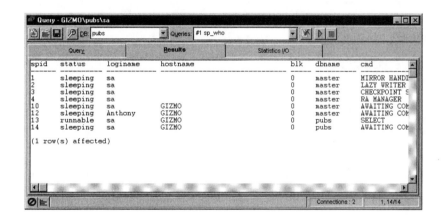

There are a few rules to keep in mind when you are using the KILL statement:

- Only the SA can kill a process.

- System processes (such as Mirror Handler, Lazy Writer, Checkpoint Sleep, and RA Manager) cannot be killed.

- Processes running extended stored procedures (ones that begin with xp) cannot be killed.

Replication Fault-Tolerance and Recovery Problems

In Chapter 11, you learned that SQL Server replication is log-based. This means that the logreader process looks through the transaction logs of a published database and extracts appropriate transactions. These transactions are then placed in the distribution database. At scheduled intervals, subscribers are passed these transactions through the distribution process. The transactions are then applied at the subscribing database.

Microsoft ✓ Exam Objective | **Resolve fault-tolerance and recovery problems.**

Troubleshooting Logreader and Distribution Process Problems

Several different things can go wrong with replication. The sources for potential problems are in the logreader process and in the distribution process. Let's look at a couple of scenarios, and then see how to troubleshoot them.

No Subscribers Are Receiving Transactions

If no subscribers are receiving transactions, it is unlikely that the distribution process is corrupted, since none of the subscribers is receiving changes. It is much more likely that the logreader process is not working properly.

First, you need to determine whether the logreader or the distribution process is failing. The easiest way to check this is to look at the command column in the msjob_commands table, which is stored in the Distribution database. As SA, you can run the following Transact-SQL commands using the Distribution database:

```
SELECT command
FROM msjob_commands
```

If there are no transactions stored here, then you know that the problem exists with the logreader process. If there are transactions stored here, then you know that the distribution task has errors. If a logreader or distribution task does not appear to be running, you should edit the scheduling information for that particular task (see Exercise 13.2).

One Subscriber of Many Is Not Receiving Changes

If only one subscriber is not getting the changes and others are, you know that the logreader process is working properly. Check for the following problems:

- The distribution process for that particular subscriber is not working properly (see Exercise 13.2).

- The subscribing database is unavailable (because it is in DBO Use Only mode or single-user mode, marked suspect, or for some other reason).

- The subscribing server is unavailable (because it is shut down, in single-user mode, or for some other reason).

- The replication login ID has been removed from the subscribing server.

- The distribution task is waiting for a manual synchronization event.

Initial Synchronization Jobs Not Applied to the Subscriber

If initial synchronization jobs are not being applied to the subscribing database, it is likely that either the synchronization task or the distribution task is failing. Check the command column of the msjob_commands table to determine whether or not Sync commands have been stored there. If there are no Sync commands stored there, then you know that the synchronization process is failing; otherwise, it is the distribution process that is failing.

If the logreader or distribution tasks do not appear to be running, you should edit the scheduling information for that particular task. Exercise 13.2 will walk you through that procedure.

EXERCISE 13.2

Troubleshooting Replication

1. Start SQL Enterprise Manager and verify that the SQL Executive service is running.

2. Select the distribution server and click on the Manage Scheduled Tasks icon (it looks like a calendar with a checkmark on it) or select Server ➤ Scheduled Tasks. This will open the Manage Scheduled Tasks window, as shown below.

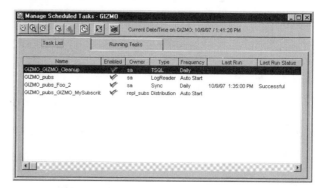

3. In the Type column, look for a Logreader, Sync, or Distribution task that has failed and double-click on it. This will open the Edit Task dialog box, as shown below.

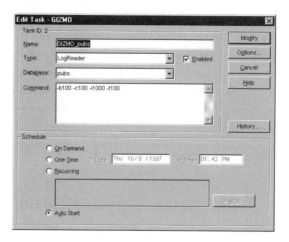

4. Click on the History button to view the history of the process. If you see an error here, click on it to gather more information about the problem.

5. To resolve a logreader or distribution problem, try scheduling it as a recurring task. Click on the Change button to display the Task Schedule dialog box, as shown below.

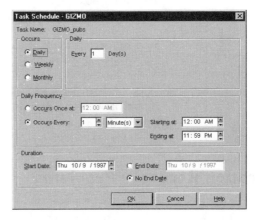

6. Change the process to daily, occurring every 1 minute. Click on OK in the Task Schedule dialog box, and then click on Modify in the Edit Task dialog box.

7. Stop and restart the SQL Executive service (right-click on SQL Executive and choose Stop/Start).

8. If your tasks are still not being distributed, try changing the commit parameter. Return to the Edit Task dialog box for the distribution process (steps 2 and 3 above), find the -c option in the Command box, and change its default from 100 (-c100) to 1 (-c1). This will force the process to distribute (commit) transactions for every 1 transaction received rather than for every 100 transactions.

EXERCISE 13.2 (CONTINUED FROM PREVIOUS PAGE)

9. For synchronization problems (the tasks are not synchronized), click on the Sync process in the Manage Scheduled Tasks window and then click on the Run Task button in the toolbar (the fourth button from the left with an icon of a clock with a green arrow). This will force the synchronization process.

10. If everything appears to be working properly again, return to the Edit Task dialog box for any processes you changed and change their schedules back to the times that you want them to run.

11. Stop and restart the SQL Executive service again to make sure that your problems are resolved.

12. Since you have made significant changes to the Msdb database, you should back up that database now. You may also want to back up the Distribution database.

Replication Recovery Problems

Due to the design of replication in SQL Server, it can normally recover itself automatically after a disaster. However, there are a few considerations to keep in mind regarding the publishing server, distribution server, and the sub-scribing servers.

Publishing Server Recovery

The distribution server keeps a pointer to track where it left off reading in a published database. This makes recovery simple if the publishing server is offline for some reason. When the publishing database is online again, the logreader will continue where it left off.

If the publishing database is rebuilt and reloaded from backups, you should resynchronize with the subscribers.

It's also important to monitor the publishing server's transaction log to make sure that it does not fill up. See Chapters 8 and 12 for details on clearing and monitoring transaction logs.

Distribution Server Recovery

Distribution servers keep track of where they left off replicating to the subscribers. When a distribution server is offline and then comes back online, it will continue processing where it left off. You should have a coordinated backup scheme to guarantee that distribution server backups match up with publishing server backups. In this way, information from the logreader process will be synchronized and automatic recovery can take place.

If the synchronization fails for some reason (you restore an old backup of the distribution database and the logreader pointers are off), the logreader process will log errors. The easiest way to fix this problem is to unsubscribe the subscribers and then resubscribe and resynchronize.

Subscribing Server Recovery

Subscribing servers are the easiest of the three to recover. Since transactions are stored in the Distribution database, when the subscribing server comes back online, the stored transactions will be processed.

If the subscribing server is down for an extended period of time, you don't want the transactions stored for it in the Distribution database to age out and therefore not be applied. To help ensure that aging does not take place, you can disable the scheduled cleanup task associated with the subscriber in the Distribution database.

In the event you must restore a subscribing database and the transactions have aged out from the distributor, it is easiest to just resynchronize the databases.

Summary

In this chapter, you learned how to gather information about events and errors from both the SQL Server error log and the Windows NT Application log (through the NT Event Viewer). You then learned how to break an error message down into its component parts. You learned that errors with a severity of 0–10 are informational, errors from 11–16 are user-generated, and errors of severity 19 or higher are fatal.

We then looked at networking problems. To resolve these types of errors, you should first verify that you have network connectivity through named pipes, and then check other connectivity-related issues. The most common communication problem is a mismatched DB-Library and Net-Library in the client and server. This problem can be fixed by using the SQL Setup utility or the SQL Client Configuration utility, which we discussed in Chapter 4.

You then learned how to check for object integrity by using some DBCC commands. (Make sure you know these for the exam!)

Next, we looked at how two processes might block each other and how to read the Current Activity window and the output of the sp_who stored procedure. You learned how to stop a blocking process by using the KILL statement.

We finished this chapter by learning a little bit about replication fault tolerance and recovery. For the most part, the servers involved in replication will take care of themselves, but you should know where to look for common problems as they occur. The Manage Scheduled Tasks window is the first place to begin your troubleshooting.

Exercise Questions

I. Which of the following can be used to gather information on SQL Server errors? (Choose all that apply.)

A. SQL Server error log

B. SQL Server transaction log

C. Windows NT event log

D. Windows NT Server Manager

2. What type of error message has a severity level of 0–10?

A. Informational

B. Warning

C. User

D. Fatal

3. What type of error message has a severity level of 11–16?

A. Informational

B. Warning

C. User

D. Fatal

4. What type of error message has a severity level of 19–25?

   A. Informational

   B. Warning

   C. User

   D. Fatal

5. Which command can you run to verify that index and data pages are correctly linked and that your indexes are sorted properly, and to verify that the data stored on each page is reasonable and that the page offsets are reasonable for an entire database?

   A. DBCC CheckTable

   B. DBCC CheckDB

   C. DBCC CheckCatalog

   D. DBCC NewAlloc

6. Which command can you run to verify that index and data pages are correctly linked and that your indexes are sorted properly, and to verify that the data stored on each page is reasonable and that the page offsets are reasonable for a single table in a database?

   A. DBCC CheckTable

   B. DBCC CheckDB

   C. DBCC CheckCatalog

   D. DBCC NewAlloc

7. Which command can you use to verify that extents are being used properly and that there is no overlap between objects that reside in their own separate extents?

   A. DBCC CheckTable

   B. DBCC CheckDB

   C. DBCC CheckCatalog

   D. DBCC NewAlloc

8. Which command could you use to check for consistency in and between system tables?

A. DBCC CheckTable

B. DBCC CheckDB

C. DBCC CheckCatalog

D. DBCC NewAlloc

9. Which of the following can cause a database to be marked suspect? (Choose all that apply.)

A. The database device is offline

B. The database device is in DBO Use Only mode

C. The database device is on an NTFS partition that SQL Server does not have rights on

D. The database device has been renamed

10. Who can kill a process?

A. SA

B. The object owner

C. The process owner

D. Anyone can kill a process

11. Suppose that you looked at the output of an sp_who statement and noticed that Gary was being blocked by SPID 16. SPID 16 is Lisa's process, which is sleeping and awaiting a command. How could you allow Gary's process to finish processing?

A. By issuing a KILL 15 statement, which would end Gary's runaway process and then automatically restart it

B. By issuing a KILL 16 statement, which would end Lisa's sleeping process

C. By clicking on Gary in the output window of ISQL/W and then selecting End Task from the Task menu

D. By clicking on Lisa in the output window of ISQL/W and then selecting End Task from the Task menu

12. The SA can kill which of the following?

   A. Mirror Handler

   B. Lazy Writer

   C. A Waiting Command

   D. RA Manager

13. If no subscribers are receiving replicated transactions, what is most likely the problem?

   A. The logreader process is dead

   B. The distribution process is dead

   C. The subscription process is dead

   D. The problem is internal to SQL Server and has nothing to do with replication

14. If only one subscriber of many isn't receiving replicated transactions, what is the most likely problem?

   A. The logreader process

   B. The distribution process

   C. The subscription process

   D. The problem is internal to SQL Server and has nothing to do with replication

15. If you are having problems with replication, where is the easiest location to begin gathering information to troubleshoot the problem?

    A. The Manage Alerts window

    B. The Current Activity window

    C. The Publication window

    D. The Manage Tasks window

16. Replication can usually fix itself in the event of problems with the publishing, distribution, or subscribing databases.

    A. True

    B. False

APPENDIX

A

Exercise Answers

Chapter 1

1. SQL Server is part of Microsoft's Office Suite.

A. True

B. False

Answer: B

2. SQL Server is part of Microsoft's BackOffice Suite.

A. True

B. False

Answer: A

3. Which of the following is a database object? (Choose all that apply.)

A. Table

B. Index

C. Rule

D. Default

Answer: A, B, C, D

4. Which role is responsible for backing up databases?

A. The database administrator

B. The database developer

C. Database users

D. The Windows NT administrator

Answer: A

5. Who is responsible for ongoing database security?

A. The database administrator

B. The database developer

C. Database users

D. The Windows NT administrator

Answer: A

6. Who is responsible for ongoing SQL Server optimization?

   A. The database administrator

   B. The database developer

   C. Database users

   D. The Windows NT administrator

   Answer: A

7. What is the process of breaking related information into tables called?

   A. Fragmentation

   B. Database design

   C. Normalization

   D. Tablizing the data

   Answer: C

8. Data warehousing emphasizes fast reads.

   A. True

   B. False

   Answer: A

9. Online transaction processing (OLTP) emphasizes fast reads.

   A. True

   B. False

   Answer: B

10. When a query is run in client/server computing, who actually runs the query?

   A. The client

   B. The server

   C. Both the client and the server

   D. Neither; a middleware piece runs the query

   Answer: B

11. SQL Server is an example of which kind of a database system?

   A. Flat-file

   B. 3-D

   C. RDBMS

   D. DB2

   Answer: C

12. Data in relational databases is organized into what format?

   A. Fields

   B. Files

   C. Reports

   D. Tables

   Answer: D

Chapter 2

1. Where should you install SQL Server?

   A. Onto a PDC or BDC—the server will have direct access to domain accounts and will therefore run much more quickly

   B. Onto any machine in the enterprise with access to the domain accounts directly or through a trust relationship (preferably not a PDC or BDC)

   C. Onto any machine in the enterprise that is running TCP/IP, because this is the default protocol for most machines

   D. Onto any machine that is not a member of a domain—because the machine is not involved in any domain-related activities, it will run much more efficiently

   Answer: B

2. Which of the following if changed would force you to rebuild your databases and reload all of your data? (Choose all that apply.)

   A. The character set

   B. The Net-Library

   C. The SQL Executive logon account

   D. The sort order

   Answer: A, D

3. Which of the following can be used to start and stop SQL Server? (Choose all that apply.)

   A. The Services Control Panel

   B. The command prompt

   C. SQL Service Manager

   D. SQL Enterprise Manager

   Answer: A, B, C, D

4. When installing the client software, the client's operating system is of no concern and all of the components get loaded onto every client.

   A. True

   B. False

   Answer: B

5. What platforms can SQL Server be installed on? (Choose all that apply.)

   A. Intel 486 and later

   B. MIPS

   C. DEC Alpha

   D. PowerPC

   Answer: A, B, C, D

6. When installing SQL Server onto an Intel x86 machine, which subdirectory is used?

   A. \Intel

   B. \Macintosh

   C. \X86

   D. \i386

   Answer: D

7. What is the minimum amount of RAM needed to install and run SQL Server?

   A. 12MB; 24MB for replication

   B. 16MB; 32MB for replication

   C. 24MB; 32MB for replication

   D. 32MB; 48MB for replication

   Answer: B

8. What is the SQL Executive logon account used for?

   A. By the MSDTC to distribute transactions for the SQL Executive service

   B. By the SQL Executive managers to log on to SQL Server and perform automation tasks, alerts processing, event firing, and replication

   C. By the MSSQLServer service to log on to SQL Server and perform automation tasks, alerts processing, event firing, and replication

   D. By Windows NT to log on to SQL Server and place all error messages in the NT Event Viewer

   Answer: B

9. You have one SQL Server in your enterprise and you are planning on adding two more in the next month. Which licensing option would best suit this environment?

   A. Per Server—by using the Per Server licensing option, you can add as many servers as you want in the enterprise and you do not need to purchase any more client licenses

   B. Per Seat—by using the Per Seat licensing option, you have a one-time one way upgrade to a Per Server client license

   C. Per Seat—by using the Per Seat licensing option, you can add as many servers as you want in the enterprise, and you do not need to purchase any more client licenses

   D. Per Server—by using the Per Server licensing option, you have a one-time one way upgrade to a Per Seat client license

   Answer: C

10. What is the minimum and default size of the Master database device?

   A. 20MB

   B. 30MB

   C. 25MB

   D. 35MB

   Answer: C

11. In an MS-DOS environment, you may install only a single network client in the AUTOEXEC.BAT file.

A. True

B. False

Answer: A

12. In a Windows 3.*x* (16-bit) environment, you may install only a single network client. The network client options will be found only in the *.INI files.

A. True

B. False

Answer: B

13. In a Windows 95 or Windows NT environment, you may install multiple network clients. The network client options will be found in the Windows Registry.

A. True

B. False

Answer: A

14. What happens when you pause SQL Server?

A. The entire SQL Server is paused, and everyone who was using SQL Server is disconnected until the SQL Server is started again

B. The entire SQL Server is paused, and everyone who was using SQL Server continues to process normally but new connection requests are denied

C. Only the users currently connected to SQL Server are paused; their work is halted and they are disconnected

D. Only the users currently connected to SQL Server are paused; their work is halted, but they are not disconnected, and once the SQL Server is restarted, they will resume their processing

Answer: B

15. Which of the following will start the SQL Server service from a command prompt?

A. SQLSERVR.EXE

B. MSSQLServer

C. NET START SQLSERVR.EXE

D. NET START MSSQLServer

Answer: D

16. Which of the following will start the SQL Executive service from a command prompt?

A. SQLEXEC.EXE

B. MSSQLExecutive

C. NET START SQLEXEC.EXE

D. NET START SQLExecutive

Answer: D

17. Where could you look for troubleshooting information if your installation did not proceed properly? (Choose all that apply.)

A. SQL Server error log

B. NT application log

C. *.OUT in the \MSSQL\Install directory

D. \MSSQL\SQLInstError directory

Answer: A, B, C

18. You wish to install support for the Banyan Vines client on an MS-DOS-based machine. Which of the following will you load in the AUTOEXEC.BAT file?

A. DBMSPIPE.EXE

B. DBMSVINE.EXE

C. DBMSSPX.EXE

D. DBMSTCP.EXE

Answer: B

Chapter 3

1. What is the default folder for a SQL Server installation?

A. \MSSQLServer

B. \SQL65

C. \MSSQL

D. \SQLServer

Answer: C

2. In which folder are database devices saved by default?

A. \MSSQLServer\Data

B. \MSSQL\Data

C. \MSSQLServer\Devices

D. \SQLServer\Devices

Answer: B

3. A device can store what type of information? (Choose all that apply.)

   A. Transaction logs

   B. Databases

   C. Database dumps (backups)

   D. Transaction log dumps (backups)

   Answer: A, B, C, D

4. The Master database device has which of the following databases on it? (Choose all that apply.)

   A. Master

   B. Model

   C. Msdb

   D. Tempdb

   Answer: A, B, D

5. The SQL Executive utilities use which database?

   A. Master

   B. Model

   C. Msdb

   D. Pubs

   Answer: C

6. The task manager, alerts manager, events manager, and replication manager make up which component of SQL Server?

   A. The MSSQLServer service

   B. The SQLExecutive service

   C. The server engine

   D. The MSSQL utilities

   Answer: B

7. In which Registry key(s) will you find configuration information for SQL Server? (Choose all that apply.)

A. \HKEY_LOCAL_MACHINE\Software\Microsoft\MSSQLServer

B. \HKEY_LOCAL_MACHINE\Software\Microsoft\SQLExecutive

C. \HKEY_LOCAL_MACHINE\SYSTEM\CurrentControlSet\Services\MSSQLServer

D. \HKEY_LOCAL_MACHINE\SYSTEM\CurrentControlSet\Services\SQLExecutive

Answer: A, C, D

8. SQL Server error messages can be viewed in the SQL Server error log and which Windows NT application?

A. Windows NT Performance Monitor

B. Windows NT Network Control Panel

C. Windows NT Network Monitor

D. Windows NT Event Viewer

Answer: D

9. SQL Server is a multithreaded application. Which Windows NT kernel process gives the SQL threads CPU time?

A. Windows NT Threader

B. Windows NT Scheduler

C. Windows NT Network Service

D. Windows NT Local Application Service

Answer: B

10. SQL Server can be integrated with Windows NT logon security. What needs to be in place before this can happen? (Choose all that apply)

A. SQL Server must be running in integrated security mode, and the Windows NT user accounts must be mapped into SQL Server

B. SQL Server must be running in integrated security mode and the SQL Server login IDs must be mapped out to the Windows NT SAM database

C. You must be running any protocol other than named pipes because named pipes is used for SQL installation only

D. You must be running named pipes or multi-protocol

Answer: A, D

11. SQL Enterprise Manager uses which component of the SQL Distributed Management Framework (DMF) to communicate with SQL Server?

    A. The SQL-DMO (Database Management Objects) or its OLE interface

    B. It doesn't need any components; it works directly with the database engine and the SQL Executive utilities

    C. The SQL Executive

    D. SQL Enterprise Manager doesn't communicate with SQL Server at all

    Answer: A

12. What is the default login ID to SQL Server?

    A. Guest

    B. SA

    C. Probe

    D. Administrator

    Answer: B

13. You should be careful when you create passwords for your user IDs because they may be case-sensitive.

    A. True

    B. False

    Answer: A

14. SQL Server Books Online is a fairly useless feature and just an excuse for Microsoft to quit printing books.

    A. True

    B. False

    Answer: B

15. SQL Server can send e-mail messages to which of the following mail providers?

    A. MS Exchange

    B. CC:Mail

    C. Profs

    D. All the above and any MAPI-compliant mail provider

    Answer: D

16. There are no restrictions on the SA account in SQL Server.

A. True

B. False

Answer: A

Chapter 4

1. Which of the following is true regarding server groups? (Choose all that apply.)

A. You can use drag-and-drop to move registered servers from group to group

B. You can use drag-and-drop to move a server group to a subgroup

C. You can use drag-and-drop to move server groups in SQL Enterprise Manager on machine A to SQL Enterprise Manager on machine B

D. You can use the stored procedure sp_movesvrgrp to move server groups from machine A to machine B

Answer: A, B

2. Before you can administer a SQL Server machine in SQL Enterprise Manager, you must first register it and supply the proper login credentials, or use a trusted connection.

A. True

B. False

Answer: A

3. You can force a user who is working with the xp_cmdshell extended stored procedure into the security context of the client rather than the server by setting an option in the SQL Enterprise Manager's Server Configuration/Options dialog box.

A. True

B. False

Answer: A

4. The SQL Setup utility can be used to do which of the following? (Choose all that apply.)

A. Add network libraries

B. Add database libraries

C. Install languages

D. Rebuild the Master database

Answer: A, C, D

5. The SQL Client Configuration utility can be used to do which of the following? (Choose all that apply.)

   A. Add network libraries

   B. Add database libraries

   C. Configure languages

   D. Rebuild the Master database

   Answer: A, B

6. The SQL Client Configuration utility needs to be run on only the server running SQL Server because all SQL Server clients get their configuration information from SQL Server itself.

   A. True

   B. False

   Answer: B

7. Which of the following will start the ISQL command-line utility and log you in?

   A. `isql /Login sa /Pwd *****`

   B. `isql /Lsa /S`

   C. `isql /Usa /P`

   D. `sqlservr /Usa /P`

   Answer: C

8. You can run any Transact-SQL command from the ISQL/W window, but you cannot run any DBCC commands from the ISQL/W window.

   A. True

   B. False

   Answer: B

9. You can run any Transact-SQL command from the ISQL command line, but you cannot run any DBCC commands from the ISQL command line.

   A. True

   B. False

   Answer: B

10. You can run multiple Transact-SQL commands, each in their own window, in the ISQL/W utility.

A. True

B. False

Answer: A

11. You can specify the database you wish to work with in the ISQL/W utility in which of the following ways? (Choose all that apply.)

A. Use the :USE <databasename> command in your SQL script

B. Click on the Databases list box and select your database

C. Just run the command—it will know which database you want to use

D. Drag-and-drop the database you wish to work with onto the ISQL/W window

Answer: A, B

12. What does the following Transact-SQL script do?

```
SELECT Employee.FirstName, Employee.LastName, WorkInfo.YearsExp
FROM Employees, WorkInfo WHERE Employee.EmpID = WorkInfo.EmpID.
```

A. Displays all information in an employee record and all associated work information

B. Displays the first name and last name in an employee record, and if the employee has work experience, it will display that too

C. Displays all employees' first names and last names and their work experience where there are records that have a matching employee ID in the WorkInfo table

D. Displays all employees' first names and last names and their work experience whether or not they have a matching employee ID in the WorkInfo table

Answer: C

13. The ORDER BY clause in a Transact-SQL SELECT statement is used to change the default sort order from descending to ascending.

A. True

B. False

Answer: B

14. The MSQuery utility can be used to create complex Transact-SQL statements using a graphical interface.

A. True

B. False

Answer: A

15. The MSQuery utility allows you to cut and paste Transact-SQL statements into other applications.

A. True

B. False

Answer: A

16. The MSQuery tool is useful only for creating Transact-SQL queries to run in SQL Server.

A. True

B. False

Answer: B

17. What are the benefits of stored procedures? (Choose all that apply.)

A. They are precompiled and therefore run more efficiently than normal queries

B. They can be used in Transact-SQL batches

C. They are not precompiled and therefore run more efficiently than normal queries, because the optimizer can look at the current conditions and make the necessary optimizations in real-time

D. They are not used in Transact-SQL batches

Answer: A, B

18. The SELECT statement can be used to both horizontally and vertically partition a table.

A. True

B. False

Answer: A

19. Anyone can register an extended stored procedure.

    A. True

    B. False

    Answer: B

20. DBCC commands generally fix problems in your databases, whereas stored procedures are used to report on the integrity of your database.

    A. True

    B. False

    Answer: B

21. The SQL Trace utility can be used to view logins to SQL Server and to filter out Transact-SQL statements run by those logins.

    A. True

    B. False

    Answer: A

Chapter 5

1. Which of the following system tables is used to store information about the relationship between databases and devices?

    A. sysdatabases

    B. sysdevices

    C. sysusages

    D. sysfragments

    Answer: C

2. How large can a device in SQL Server be?

    A. 32MB

    B. 32GB

    C. 32TB

    D. There is no limit to device size

    Answer: B

3. How many fragments can a SQL Server database contain?

A. 2

B. 3

C. 32

D. There is no limit to the number of fragments that a SQL Server database can contain

Answer: C

4. All of the databases created on a SQL Server share a common transaction log.

A. True

B. False

Answer: B

5. What is the basic unit of I/O in SQL Server?

A. Record

B. Page

C. Extent

D. Allocation unit

Answer: B

6. What is the basic unit of database allocation?

A. Page

B. Extent

C. Allocation unit

D. Database space can be allocated with any unit of granularity

Answer: C

7. What is the basic unit of table or index allocation?

A. Page

B. Extent

C. Allocation unit

D. Table and index space can be allocated with any unit of granularity

Answer: B

8. What is the unit of measure for the `Size` parameter when using the `Disk Resize` statement?

    A. Incremental change in 2KB pages

    B. Final size in 2KB pages

    C. Incremental change in megabytes

    D. Final size in megabytes

    Answer: B

9. What is the unit of measure for the `Size` parameter when using the `Alter Database` statement?

    A. Incremental change in 2KB pages

    B. Final size in 2KB pages

    C. Incremental change in megabytes

    D. Final size in megabytes

    Answer: C

10. Which stored procedure is used to find out what virtual device numbers are available?

    A. `sp_vdevno`

    B. `sp_virtual_device`

    C. `sp_helpdb`

    D. `sp_helpdevice`

    Answer: D

11. How much space is available for data in a data page?

    A. 1962 bytes

    B. 2016 bytes

    C. 2048 bytes

    D. 2KB

    Answer: B

12. Which command is used to shrink a device?

    A. `sp_shrinkdevice`

    B. `sp_changedevice`

C. DBCC ShrinkDevice

D. You cannot shrink a device

Answer: D

13. You have used the statement sp_dbremove mydb, dropdev on the database Mydb, a removable media database. What will be the result?

   A. Only the database will be removed from the system

   B. The database and the devices will be removed from the system

   C. The database and devices will be removed and any physical files will be deleted

   D. The database will be brought offline; all references to the database and devices will remain in the system tables

   Answer: B

14. You are estimating the storage requirements for a table defined with the following fields: Char(15), Int, Float, Char(10). How many bytes will be used to store each row assuming no fields allow nulls?

   A. 35

   B. 37

   C. 39

   D. 41

   Answer: D

15. If a row requires 34 bytes of space to store, how many rows can be placed on a page with a fill factor of 80?

   A. 60

   B. 59

   C. 48

   D. 47

   Answer: D

Chapter 6

1. Which system table holds information about login IDs?

   A. sysusers

   B. syslogins

   C. sysprotects

   D. sysalternates

   Answer: B

2. Which system table holds information about user aliases?

   A. sysusers

   B. syslogins

   C. sysprotects

   D. sysalternates

   Answer: D

3. There can only be one user acting as the database owner in a database.

   A. True

   B. False

   Answer: B

4. Which of the following security modes support standard connections? (Choose all that apply.)

   A. Standard

   B. Integrated

   C. Mixed

   D. None of the above

   Answer: A, C

5. Which of the following security modes support trusted connections? (Choose all that apply.)

   A. Standard

   B. Integrated

   C. Mixed

   D. None of the above

   Answer: A, B, C

6. Which Transact-SQL stored procedure is used to change ownership of a database to another user?

   A. sp_defaultdb

   B. sp_helpdb

   C. sp_changedbowner

   D. sp_addalias

   Answer: C

7. Which of the following login IDs is not created during SQL Server installation?

   A. guest

   B. repl_publisher

   C. sa

   D. probe

   Answer: A

8. An SA user attempts to transfer ownership of a database to another login and this action returns an error. What might be the problem?

   A. The login is accessing the database under a standard connection

   B. The login has an entry in the sysalternates system table in that database

   C. The SA does not have the authority to do the transfer of ownership; only the DBO has this authority

   D. The database is corrupt and must be repaired before the transfer of ownership can take place

   Answer: B

9. When using the Transact-SQL stored procedure sp_addlogin, if a password is not provided when the login is created, what will be the password for the new login?

   A. null

   B. "password"

   C. The same as the login name

   D. The value provided in the Default Password text box of the Security Options dialog box

   Answer: A

10. The SA is attempting to drop a group from a database using `sp_dropgroup`. This statement fails on execution. What might be the problem?

A. One of the users in the group owns an object in the database; the group and its users can't be deleted with `sp_dropgroup` if any user owns any objects

B. The SA does not have authority to drop groups from a database; only the DBO has that authority

C. The group is empty and deleting it would have no effect

D. The group is not empty and you cannot drop a group with members

Answer: D

11. The DBO is attempting to drop a login from the server using `sp_droplogin` and the attempt fails. What might be the problem?

A. The DBO does not have authority to drop logins; only the SA has that authority

B. The login owns an object in a database and cannot be dropped until the object is dropped

C. The login is part of a group and must be removed from the group before the login can be dropped

D. Logins can only be dropped through SQL Enterprise Manager

Answer: A

12. A user can be a member of how many groups including Public?

A. 1

B. 2

C. 3

D. 4

Answer: B

13. After ownership of a database was transferred from SA to another user, all users who used to be able to access the database under DBO aliases report that they can no longer access the database at all. What went wrong?

A. The database ownership was transferred with SQL Enterprise Manager; this is a known bug in SQL Enterprise Manager

B. When the `sp_changedbowner` stored procedure was called, the `true` flag was not included, indicating that existing aliases were to be maintained

C. Nothing went wrong—it is not possible to retain aliases to DBO during ownership transfer

D. The users who were formerly aliased as DBO already had usernames in the database, and aliases cannot be maintained unless these usernames are dropped

Answer: B

14. Which of the following Transact-SQL statements will drop the Grover user from the Monsters group?

   A. `sp_dropgroup Monsters, Grover`

   B. `sp_helpgroup Grover, Monsters`

   C. `sp_transfergroup null, Grover`

   D. `sp_changegroup public, Grover`

   Answer: D

15. When are trusted connections established under mixed security?

   A. Always

   B. Never

   C. Whenever possible

   D. Only when requested

   Answer: C

Chapter 7

1. Which of the following users can perform these tasks: `Disk {Init, Mirror, Refit, Reinit, Remirror, Unmirror}`? (Choose all that apply.)

   A. SA

   B. DBO

   C. DBOO

   D. Database user with permissions

   Answer: A

2. Which of the following users can perform these tasks: `Shutdown, Reconfigure, Kill,` add and drop extended stored procedures? (Choose all that apply.)

   A. SA

   B. DBO

   C. DBOO

   D. Database user with permissions

   Answer: A

3. Anyone can issue the `Kill` statement.

   A. True

   B. False

Answer: B

4. Only the SA can `Kill` a system process.

   A. True

   B. False

Answer: B

5. A DBO can use the `Alter Database` statement when which of the following is true? (Choose one.)

   A. The DBO is the SA

   B. The DBO has the Create Database permission in addition to the Alter Database permission

   C. Neither A nor B

   D. Both A and B

Answer: D

6. If a user in a database has created an object, and has not given permissions on that object to the DBO, the DBO can still access the object by using the `SetUser` statement.

   A. True

   B. False

Answer: A

7. Statement permissions can be granted to others.

   A. True

   B. False

Answer: B

8. You should grant permissions on individual columns in a table because this is much more efficient than granting permissions on a view.

   A. True

   B. False

Answer: B

9. Database users are always a member of which group?

A. Users

B. Everyone

C. Public

D. The World

Answer: C

10. If you grant Tanisha permissions and then later revoke permissions from the Sales group of which Tanisha is a member, Tanisha will *not* have access.

A. True

B. False

Answer: B

11. If James creates a table, and then James creates a view on his table and gives Laura permission on his view, Laura can select data from the view.

A. True

B. False

Answer: A

12. James creates a table, and then James creates a view on his table and gives Laura permission on his view, and Laura creates a view based on James's view and then gives Amanda permissions on her view. Where will permissions be checked? (Choose all that apply.)

A. On Laura's view

B. On James's view

C. On James's table

D. Permissions will not be checked

Answer: A, B

13. James can create a view on a table that he does not have access to because permissions on views are not checked until the view is run.

A. True

B. False

Answer: A

14. If you grant a permission with the WITH GRANT OPTION option, the grantee will be able to grant that permission to other users.

A. True

B. False

Answer: A

15. If you want to revoke permissions from grantees and anyone that they might have granted permissions to on your object, you can use the REVOKE statement with the CASCADE option.

A. True

B. False

Answer: A

Chapter 8

1. What is the Transact-SQL command to back up databases?

A. Backup Database

B. Dump Database

C. Backup Device

D. Dump Device

Answer: B

2. How do you edit a recurring (scheduled) backup? (Choose all that apply.)

A. You can't—you need to delete and re-create them

B. From the Database/Tasks dialog box

C. From SQL Executive/Tasks dialog box

D. From the SQL Server/ Manage Scheduled Tasks dialog box

Answer: C, D

3. What is the Transact-SQL command to back up a transaction log?

A. Dump Database /Log

B. Dump Log

C. `Dump Transaction`

D. `Backup Log`

Answer: C

4. What does the `no_log` switch do on a transaction log backup?

   A. There is no such switch

   B. It removes committed transactions from the log without making a backup

   C. It makes a backup of the log without removing committed transactions

   D. It is a "last resort" switch for when the log has become full

   Answer: D

5. What does the `no_truncate` switch do on a transaction log backup?

   A. There is no such switch

   B. It removes committed transactions from the log without making a backup

   C. It makes a backup of the log without removing committed transactions

   D. It is a "last resort" switch for when the log has become full

   Answer: C

6. What does the `truncate_only` switch do on a transaction log backup?

   A. There is no such switch

   B. It removes committed transactions from the log without making a backup

   C. It makes a backup of the log without removing committed transactions

   D. It is a "last resort" switch for when the log has become full

   Answer: B

7. What is the most efficient form of disk fault tolerance with six drives?

   A. Stripe set

   B. Mirror set

   C. Duplex set

   D. Stripe set with parity

   Answer: D

8. Windows NT supports which of the following? (Choose all that apply.)

   A. Mirroring

   B. Duplexing

   C. Striping

   D. Striping with parity

   Answer: A, B. C, D

9. What program allows you to do backups through a graphical user interface?

   A. Transfer Manager

   B. Backup Manager

   C. SQL Security Manager

   D. SQL Enterprise Manager

   Answer: D

10. What is the Transact-SQL command to restore a database?

   A. Restore Database

   B. Run Database

   C. Load Database

   D. Undo Database

   Answer: C

11. What is the Transact-SQL command to restore a log?

   A. Restore Log

   B. Load Log

   C. Restore Transaction

   D. Load Transaction

   Answer: D

12. What is the switch that initializes a backup device?

   A. with init

   B. with format

   C. overwrite

   D. without protect

   Answer: A

13. Which feature of SQL Server allows backups to run faster?

   A. SCSI support

   B. Stripe backups

   C. Mirror backups

   D. Parallel striped backups

   Answer: D

14. You can restore log files out of order.

   A. True

   B. False

   Answer: B

Chapter 9

1. What rights does the SQL Executive service account user need? (Choose all that apply.)

   A. Log on as a Service right

   B. Administrator group membership

   C. Backup Operators membership

   D. Server Operators membership

   Answer: A, B

2. What is the API set that allows SQL Server to send and receive e-mail?

   A. TAPI

   B. EAPI

   C. OLE

   D. MAPI

   Answer: D

3. Which database holds alert and task information?

   A. The Master database

   B. The Model database

   C. The Msdb database

   D. None—it is held in the Registry

   Answer: C

4. How can you rebuild the Msdb database?

A. You can't; you must reinstall SQL Server

B. Run SQL Setup and choose Rebuild Master Database

C. Run SQL Setup and choose Rebuild Msdb Database

D. Stop and restart SQL Server; the Msdb database will be rebuilt automatically

Answer: B

5. Where do alerts look for errors?

A. The Windows NT event Application log

B. The SQL Server event log

C. The Master database error log

D. SQL Server sends errors directly to the alert engine

Answer: A

6. What kinds of tasks can be created? (Choose all that apply.)

A. TSQL (Transact-SQL)

B. CmdExec (Command Prompt)

C. Replication

D. Windows NT Kernel

Answer: A, B, C

7. You can create new error messages in SQL Server.

A. True

B. False

Answer: A

8. Alerts can be defined but not activated.

A. True

B. False

Answer: A

9. What is the operator of last resort called?

   A. Weekend operator

   B. Last-chance operator

   C. Notification operator

   D. Fail-safe operator

   Answer: D

10. What is the central server that receives alerts from other SQL Server servers called?

   A. Central alerter

   B. Standardized alerter

   C. Central control

   D. Unhandled events server

   Answer: D

11. Which of these four services is in charge of the others?

   A. Alert Manager

   B. Task Manager

   C. SQL Executive

   D. Event Manager

   Answer: C

Chapter 10

1. Which tool would you use to import a mainframe data tape to SQL Server?

   A. Replication

   B. Backup and restore the database

   C. SQL Enterprise Manager's transfer management interface

   D. BCP

   Answer: D

2. Which tool would you use to copy the stored procedures from one database to another?

A. Replication

B. Backup and restore the database

C. SQL Enterprise Manager's transfer management interface

D. BCP

Answer: C

3. Which tool would you use to keep branch offices databases in near-real-time synchronization with a central office database?

A. Replication

B. Backup and restore the database

C. SQL Enterprise Manager's transfer management interface

D. BCP

Answer: A

4. Which tool would you use to keep a hot standby server up to date?

A. Replication

B. Backup and restore the database

C. SQL Enterprise Manager's transfer management interface

D. BCP

Answer: B

5. What rights do you need on the originating database using SQL Enterprise Manager's transfer management interface?

A. SA rights

B. DBO rights

C. Insert rights

D. Select/Execute rights

Answer: D

6. What minimum rights do you need on the receiving database using SQL Enterprise Manager's transfer management interface?

A. SA rights

B. DBO rights

C. Insert rights

D. Select/Execute rights

Answer: B

7. What rights do you need on a table when using BCP to export records?

    A. SA rights

    B. DBO rights

    C. Insert rights

    D. Select/Execute rights

    Answer: D

8. What rights do you need on a table when using BCP to import records?

    A. SA rights

    B. DBO rights

    C. Insert rights

    D. Select/Execute rights

    Answer: C

9. BCP ignores which of the following when doing an import? (Choose all that apply.)

    A. Rules

    B. Triggers

    C. Datatypes

    D. Defaults

    Answer: A, B

10. A fast BCP goes through the transaction log.

    A. True

    B. False

    Answer: B

11. A slow BCP requires you to rebuild your indexes.

    A. True

    B. False

    Answer: B

12. The data on removable media databases can be edited by the receiving site.

    A. True

    B. False

    Answer: B

13. Users, groups, views, stored procedures, and security can be added to a removable media database that has been sent on CD-ROM.

    A. True

    B. False

    Answer: A

14. The CHKUPG65 utility will fix problems with older databases.

    A. True

    B. False

    Answer: B

15. SQL Server 4.2x and 6.5 can coexist on the same computer.

    A. True

    B. False

    Answer: A

Chapter 11

1. Which database has the original data?

    A. Publishing

    B. Subscribing

    C. Distribution

    D. Replication

    Answer: A

2. Which database controls replication?

    A. Publishing

    B. Subscribing

    C. Distribution

D. Replication

Answer: C

3. Which database receives the replicated data?

   A. Publishing

   B. Subscribing

   C. Distribution

   D. Replication

   Answer: B

4. Which network library can be used with replication? (Choose all that apply.)

   A. Named pipes

   B. IPX/SPX

   C. AppleTalk

   D. Multi-protocol

   Answer: A, D

5. The subscribing database should be treated as read-only.

   A. True

   B. False

   Answer: A

6. Which type of server should have at least 16MB of RAM devoted to SQL Server?

   A. Publishing

   B. Subscribing

   C. Distribution

   D. Replication

   Answer: C

7. The publishing server is SQL Server 6.0 and the distribution server is SQL Server 6.5. This system meets the recommended specifications.

   A. True

   B. False

   Answer: B

8. A branch updating a central database is an example of which model?

   A. Single publisher to single subscriber

   B. Single publisher to multiple subscribers

   C. Multiple publishers to single subscribers

   D. Multiple publishers to multiple subscribers

   Answer: A

9. Regional databases maintaining synchronization with each other are an example of which model?

   A. Single publisher to single subscriber

   B. Single publisher to multiple subscribers

   C. Multiple publishers to single subscribers

   D. Multiple publishers to multiple subscribers

   Answer: D

10. A vice president's weekly report that gets updated from all 15 of his managers' budgets is an example of which model?

   A. Single publisher to single subscriber

   B. Single publisher to multiple subscribers

   C. Multiple publishers to single subscriber

   D. Multiple publishers to multiple subscribers

   Answer: C

11. Which task is in charge of reading data from the publishing database?

   A. Logreader

   B. Sync

   C. Distribution

   D. Cleanup

   Answer: A

12. Which task is in charge of applying updates as they happen?

   A. Logreader

   B. Sync

C. Distribution

D. Cleanup

Answer: C

13. Which task can be set to not affect data until 24 hours after it has been applied?

   A. Logreader

   B. Sync

   C. Distribution

   D. Cleanup

   Answer: D

14. Which table contains information about the last change applied to the subscription database?

   A. syssubscriptions

   B. msjob_commands

   C. mssubscriber_jobs

   D. mslast_job_info

   Answer: D

15. You can perform all publication and subscription tasks from the Replication Topology window.

   A. True

   B. False

   Answer: A

Chapter 12

1. Which of the following commands is used to turn on insert row locking?

   A. sp_dboption

   B. sp_tableoption

   C. sp_configure

   D. Alter Table

   Answer: B

2. Which of the following is not a read-ahead configuration option?

A. RA Worker Threads

B. RA Delay

C. RA Pre-fetches

D. RA Extent Switches

Answer: D

3. Which kind of lock is placed on a page when it is being read by a transaction?

A. Intent

B. Shared

C. Exclusive

D. Extent

Answer: B

4. What is the default value of LE Threshold Maximum?

A. 20 pages

B. 20 percent

C. 200 pages

D. 0

Answer: C

5. Which of the following operations would most benefit from an index on the Authors table?

A. `SELECT * FROM authors where au_lname = 'Smith'`

B. `SELECT * FROM authors`

C. `UPDATE STATISTICS authors`

D. `DBCC NewAlloc`

Answer: A

6. The benefits of placing Tempdb in RAM will always outweigh the cost.

A. True

B. False

Answer: B

7. Which of the following Performance Monitor counters are helpful for monitoring physical I/O? (Choose two.)

   A. Log Space Used (%)

   B. IO – Batch Writes / Sec

   C. RA – Slots Used

   D. IO – Transactions / Sec

   Answer: B, D

8. A checkpoint does which of the following? (Choose all that apply.)

   A. Writes dirty pages to disk every minute

   B. Evaluates the option of writing dirty pages to disk every minute

   C. Writes dirty pages to disk whenever the recovery interval has been reached

   D. Reads pages from disk before a query will need them

   Answer: B, C

9. Which of the following configuration options will *not* affect the size of data cache?

   A. Max Async IO

   B. Procedure Cache

   C. Locks

   D. User Connections

   Answer: A

10. Tempdb can be split between RAM and disk.

    A. True

    B. False

    Answer: B

11. A shared lock and an update lock can be placed on the same page at the same time.

    A. True

    B. False

    Answer: A

12. Read-ahead can substantially reduce logical I/O.

A. True

B. False

Answer: B

13. SQL Server uses which of the following approaches for managing pages in data cache?

A. Last in first out

B. Last in last out

C. Last used first out

D. Last used last out

Answer: D

14. What is the name that SQL Server gives to the logical device that holds Tempdb in RAM?

A. devTempdb

B. temp_db_dev

C. tempdb

D. temp_db

Answer: D

15. Which of the following is a benefit of setting the database option Truncate Log on Checkpoint on?

A. Your database will always be recoverable

B. Your transaction log will most likely never fill up

C. Long running transactions will be automatically committed at checkpoint

D. SQL Executive can read the transaction log at checkpoint

Answer: B

Chapter 13

1. Which of the following can be used to gather information on SQL Server errors? (Choose all that apply.)

A. SQL Server error log

B. SQL Server transaction log

C. Windows NT event log

D. Windows NT Server Manager

Answer: A, C

2. What type of error message has a severity level of 0–10?

A. Informational

B. Warning

C. User

D. Fatal

Answer: A

3. What type of error message has a severity level of 11–16?

A. Informational

B. Warning

C. User

D. Fatal

Answer: C

4. What type of error message has a severity level of 19–25?

A. Informational

B. Warning

C. User

D. Fatal

Answer: D

5. Which command can you run to verify that index and data pages are correctly linked and that your indexes are sorted properly, and to verify that the data stored on each page is reasonable and that the page offsets are reasonable for an entire database?

A. DBCC CheckTable

B. DBCC CheckDB

C. DBCC CheckCatalog

D. DBCC NewAlloc

Answer: B

6. Which command can you run to verify that index and data pages are correctly linked and that your indexes are sorted properly, and to verify that the data stored on each page is reasonable and that the page offsets are reasonable for a single table in a database?

   A. DBCC CheckTable

   B. DBCC CheckDB

   C. DBCC CheckCatalog

   D. DBCC NewAlloc

   Answer: A

7. Which command can you use to verify that extents are being used properly and that there is no overlap between objects that reside in their own separate extents?

   A. DBCC CheckTable

   B. DBCC CheckDB

   C. DBCC CheckCatalog

   D. DBCC NewAlloc

   Answer: D

8. Which command could you use to check for consistency in and between system tables?

   A. DBCC CheckTable

   B. DBCC CheckDB

   C. DBCC CheckCatalog

   D. DBCC NewAlloc

   Answer: C

9. Which of the following can cause a database to be marked suspect? (Choose all that apply.)

   A. The database device is offline

   B. The database device is in DBO Use Only mode

   C. The database device is on an NTFS partition that SQL Server does not have rights on

   D. The database device has been renamed

   Answer: A, C, D

10. Who can kill a process?

   A. SA

   B. The object owner

   C. The process owner

   D. Anyone can kill a process

Answer: A

11. Suppose that you looked at the output of an sp_who statement and noticed that Gary was being blocked by SPID 16. SPID 16 is Lisa's process, which is sleeping and awaiting a command. How could you allow Gary's process to finish processing?

   A. By issuing a KILL 15 statement, which would end Gary's runaway process and then automatically restart it

   B. By issuing a KILL 16 statement, which would end Lisa's sleeping process

   C. By clicking on Gary in the output window of ISQL/W and then selecting End Task from the Task menu

   D. By clicking on Lisa in the output window of ISQL/W and then selecting End Task from the Task menu

Answer: B

12. The SA can kill which of the following?

   A. Mirror Handler

   B. Lazy Writer

   C. Awaiting Command

   D. RA Manager

Answer: C

13. If no subscribers are receiving replicated transactions, what is most likely the problem?

   A. The logreader process is dead

   B. The distribution process is dead

   C. The subscription process is dead

   D. The problem is internal to SQL Server and has nothing to do with replication

Answer: A

14. If only one subscriber of many isn't receiving replicated transactions, what is the most likely problem?

A. The logreader process

B. The distribution process

C. The subscription process

D. The problem is internal to SQL Server and has nothing to do with replication

Answer: B

15. If you are having problems with replication, where is the easiest location to begin gathering information to troubleshoot the problem?

A. The Manage Alerts window

B. The Current Activity window

C. The Publication window

D. The Manage Tasks window

Answer: D

16. Replication can usually fix itself in the event of problems with the publishing, distribution, or subscribing databases.

A. True

B. False

Answer: A

APPENDIX

B

Using ODBC with SQL Server

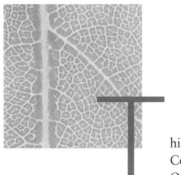

This appendix provides an overview of ODBC (Open Database Connectivity) and its effect on client programming.

ODBC is not a subject that you will see on the System Administration for Microsoft SQL Server 6.5 exam. However, a knowledge of ODBC and its various implementations is extremely helpful when rounding out your understanding of SQL Server. It also gives you the tools necessary to access your data from a variety of applications. This can be critical during the testing of a new installation of SQL Server, as well as when you are working with the developers who will be writing applications for your SQL Server system.

What Is ODBC?

Data access is at the heart of any database application. While SQL Server provides the functionality to store, retrieve, and summarize the data, this information must be available from other applications in order for it to be useful. For example, data held in a SQL Server database may be the source for a report that is generated in Microsoft Excel. The data must somehow get from SQL Server to Excel. The application that is requesting the data from SQL Server is often called a *client*. There are many different approaches to data access; some are more complex than others. ODBC is designed to simplify the data-access process as much as possible.

Every database has a unique method for accessing data from a client application. The methods of data access that are specific to a certain database management system are called *proprietary interfaces* or the *native API (Application Programming Interface)*. Although the native API is usually an extremely efficient method of accessing data, it is specific to a particular database system. This means that if you use the native API of a server to access your data, the client application is not portable to other database systems.

An API is usually implemented as a DLL (dynamic link library) or set of DLLs that provides access to the functionality provided by an operating system, service, or application. Client applications can call the functions in these DLLs to use the services.

The native API of SQL Server comes with two interfaces: one that is designed for data access from client applications written in C/C++, called DB-Library, and another designed for use from Visual Basic and Visual Basic for Applications (VBA) applications, called VBSQL. Although these libraries provide the fastest possible data access to SQL Server from a client application, they are not valid for accessing data in any other format, such as Microsoft Access, Microsoft FoxPro, or other database servers like Sybase or Oracle.

Because of their limited use and complexity, the native APIs are very frustrating for database developers who wish to build truly interoperable clients. These developers want a method of data access that is common to all database systems, thus removing the need to learn the native API of every database system that the client might access. In response to this need, Microsoft spearheaded the development of an open standard for database access called *Open Database Connectivity,* or ODBC. The intent of ODBC is to provide a common API that can be used to access any ODBC-compliant database.

ODBC Architecture

So how does ODBC really work? Well, imagine yourself sitting in a conference at the United Nations General Assembly in New York City. The speaker today is a representative of a small North African nation who speaks a language that you do not know. You are confident that this intelligent dissertation would be extremely valuable to you if you could just understand what was being said. Fortunately for you, there is a translator present who speaks your language as well as the native language of the speaker. This translator will interpret as closely as possible the messages that are being conveyed by the speaker. You leave that day with a well-spring of knowledge thanks to the translator. Since translators cannot be provided for every possible combination of languages, the issue is simplified by requiring every attendee to learn a common language such as English or French. This makes the translation process much more reasonable.

ODBC works in a similar way. Figure B.1 illustrates how this happens. The database that you wish to access does not speak your application's language. Therefore, your application learns a common language and enlists the services of a translator to translate your requests in the common language into the native language of the database. This common language is called the ODBC API.

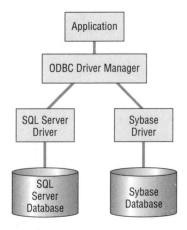

Calls made to the ODBC API are initially processed by a common component of ODBC called the *driver manager*. The driver manager is responsible for setting up the initial communication between the client and the database and then forwarding all specific requests directly to the translator. The translator is called an *ODBC driver*.

Installing and Configuring ODBC

ODBC must be installed and configured correctly for your client application to see your database. You need to have the ODBC components installed on the machine where the client application is running, and the client application must also have a Data Source Name (DSN) properly registered.

Installing ODBC

Before ODBC can be used in your applications, it must first be installed. Unlike MAPI (Messaging Application Programming Interface) or the Windows API, ODBC is not part of the operating system itself.

Components installed on Windows 95 or Windows NT include the driver manager (ODBC32.DLL) and any drivers that you wish to use. These components must be installed on the machine where the client application is running, not on the server where the data is located. The driver manager is usually installed with any data source that supports ODBC. If you install Microsoft SQL Server or Microsoft Office, you will have the option of installing ODBC. This discussion will focus on ODBC 3.0, the current version that ships with Visual Studio 97.

To verify that ODBC is installed on your system, open the Control Panel and look for the 32-bit ODBC icon. This icon is added as part of the ODBC installation, and it launches the ODBC Data Source Administrator.

Next, you must install the ODBC drivers for the data sources that you will be using. If you have Microsoft SQL Server installed, the SQL Server ODBC driver should also be installed. This is one of the last things that happens during the SQL Server installation process. If you are accessing a data source other than SQL Server, you must get the ODBC driver from the vendor of that data source. Some vendors ship these drivers with their database management systems; other vendors require these drivers to be purchased separately.

To verify which ODBC drivers you have installed, open the ODBC Data Source Administrator by clicking on the 32-bit ODBC icon in the Control Panel. Then click on the Add button in the upper-right corner of the window. You should now see a dialog box with a list of ODBC drivers installed on your system, as shown in Figure B.2. If the driver you wish to use is not listed, you must first acquire that driver from the vendor and install it on your system.

FIGURE B.2

Installed ODBC drivers

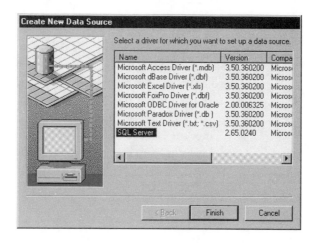

Setting Up a Data Source Name

Before client applications can access the data in your SQL Server database, you must create a *Data Source Name* (DSN). A DSN is a set of instructions to ODBC indicating where your data source is and how it should be accessed. The DSN must be created on every machine on which the client application will run.

A DSN is created with the ODBC Data Source Administrator. The DSNs that you create are usually entries in the Windows NT or Windows 95 Registry, however, ODBC 3.0 may use other types of DSNs, including file DSNs. The DSN contains all of the information required to locate the remote data source:

- The name of the server that hosts the data source

- The name of the driver that will be used to access the data

- Optionally, the name of the database that you wish to access (if the database name is included in the DSN, you won't need to provide this information when the connection is made from the client application)

WARNING   When adding a DSN, you have the option of a user DSN or a system DSN. User DSNs are available only to the user that created them. System DSNs are available to the entire system. If you create a user DSN, your application will not run properly when another user is logged on to the system or when a system process needs to access the DSN.

To install a DSN for SQL Server, open the ODBC Data Source Administrator from the Control Panel. From the list of data sources, choose a user DSN or a system DSN by clicking on the appropriate tab in the window. Click on the Add button to display the Create New Data Source dialog box (see Figure B.2). Select the SQL Server driver from the list and click on the Finish button. You will see the ODBC SQL Server Setup dialog box.

Enter the DSN in the top text box. In the example shown in Figure B.3, the DSN is Pubs. You can enter a description of this DSN in the Description text box. In the Server text box, indicate the name of the server that is hosting the SQL Server database.

FIGURE B.3

The ODBC SQL Server
Driver Setup dialog box

FIGURE B.3

The ODBC SQL Server
Driver Setup dialog box

At this point, if you click on the Options button on the right side of the window, the dialog box will expand to reveal other optional settings. Unless you must use the same DSN to access multiple databases on your server, it's a good idea to enter the name of the database in the Database text box. This will eliminate the need to refer to a database every time you make an ODBC connection.

After you've finished filling in the dialog box, click on OK. You will now see your new DSN listed in the ODBC Administrator window. Click on the OK button in the ODBC Administrator window to complete the process.

After a DSN has been created on a client system, it can be used to access data in your SQL Server database from any application that can use ODBC. These applications range from popular desktop applications, such as Microsoft Office, to report writers, administrative utilities, and custom applications created in development systems such as Microsoft Access, Visual Basic, or Visual C++.

Programming with ODBC

You may never need to write any programming code to access data from an ODBC data source. Nevertheless, if you are responsible for the system administration of a SQL Server system, you will undoubtedly be required to work with programmers who are writing custom applications for your SQL Server data store. Programmers have a language of their own. Here, we will provide a primer of programming concepts and terminology, or a survival guide for dealing with programmers.

Programming Roles in Client/Server Development

Programming client/server applications requires developers to be fluent in more than one development environment. Client/server programming can be defined as the intelligent distribution of a task across tiers in an application architecture in such a way that the efficiency of all aspects of the physical architecture is maximized.

What this means is that in a client/server application, all of the processing does not take place on just one computer. Multiple computers are involved. Some of these computers are dedicated to providing data storage and data processing, such as the computer running Microsoft SQL Server. Other computers are responsible for interacting with the users of the application directly by providing a friendly interface for data input, data formatting, and reporting. Still other computers may be involved in running ActiveX components designed to run between the application and the server to provide encapsulation of data-access methods, business rules, and security. The goal is to ensure that every piece of software in the system takes full advantage of the computer on which it is running and contributes to the efficiency of the system as a whole.

There are two main types of client/server architectures in production today: two-tier architecture and multitier architecture.

Two-Tier Architecture

The two-tier, or traditional, model divides the entire application in two pieces: the client and the server.

Server-side development is usually done in a database management system such as Microsoft SQL Server. The developer responsible for the server would define the data store and create the tables; provide server-side data integrity;

and program the server with views, triggers, and stored procedures. Essentially, the server is responsible for accepting data input from the client, protecting data integrity, and providing result sets back to the client when requested.

Client-side development could take place in a product as simple as Excel or as robust as Visual C++. The client-side developer is responsible for providing a user interface for the application, accepting user input and passing it to the server, making requests of information from the server, and formatting these requests into screens or printed reports.

The most popular client-side development tools are those that support Rapid Application Development (RAD). These include Microsoft Visual Basic, Borland Delphi, and PowerSoft PowerBuilder.

A single developer or group of developers might work on both the client and server portions of an application, or different individuals or groups might focus on their respective tier.

Multitier Architecture

Multitier, or *n*-tier, development adds another tier into the architecture by shifting many of the client activities to collections of ActiveX components or DLLs that hide the complexities of specific data and other models from the developer.

For example, a client-side developer might want to use a login routine in every application developed for a specific project. Rather than putting this login routine, including its forms and program code, in every client application, a single component can be built that encapsulates the login logic and forms, and then this component can be called from each of the client applications. If the routine and forms must be changed at some point, the changes can be made in only one place—in the component—and the applications can simply continue to call the updated component.

Data-Access Models

It has been said that the only constant in the universe is change, and client/server development is no exception. If you have read the trade magazines, you have undoubtedly heard about some of the many data-access models, each of which is the self-proclaimed "best" way to access data. Microsoft itself is responsible for a large number of the choices that you have today to access your data from a client application. Here, we will discuss some of the current choices for accessing server-side data. These are terms that you will undoubtedly hear your developers mention.

Native API

Every data source has a set of interfaces that can be used directly from a client application to avoid the need for ODBC. In fact, it is these native interfaces that the ODBC drivers interact with in order to translate generic ODBC calls into something that the back-end data source can understand.

Native interfaces have one distinct advantage: speed. This is execution speed, however, not development speed. In fact, this can be the greatest problem with native interfaces. They are usually quite cumbersome to learn and use. This investment might be worthwhile if the same methods could be used to access other data sources, but this is not the case. Native interfaces are applicable only to the database management system for which they were built. If a developer wishes to access data from more than one database system, that developer must learn the native interface of each system.

ODBC API

Another option is to write your client applications directly to the ODBC API. This has the advantage of giving you a generic interface that can be applicable to many different data sources. A developer needs to learn only one interface and can apply that knowledge to numerous database systems.

Of course, this approach does require the developer to learn a traditional function-based API interface, which can be a bit of a learning curve. There are hundreds of ODBC API calls, each of which has its own syntax. Although this approach will provide the fastest execution speed that ODBC can offer, it does not lend itself to RAD, which is the client/server buzzword of the decade.

Another problem to note with ODBC in general is that the speed of execution against Indexed Sequential Access Method (ISAM) data files is very slow. ISAM data access is nothing more than file I/O routines with indexing and a few enhanced features. This is why you can't create a client/server application with Microsoft Access unless you are using a database server like SQL Server as the data store. The Access portion is nothing more than a file. Jet is responsible for all processing and data access.

Jet and the DAO

For many Access and Visual Basic developers, the DAO was the first data-access model that they learned. DAO is an object interface to the Jet database engine. Since Jet is designed primarily for ISAM databases, the DAO is also designed for access to ISAM data structures.

DAO is a set of programmable objects that Access developers use to manip-ulate data through Jet, the data-access engine for Microsoft Access and other Microsoft desktop products. Microsoft Access ships with Jet and the DAO. Microsoft Visual Basic also utilizes Jet as its native data-access method. Jet can also be accessed by Excel, Word, Project, and PowerPoint through VBA.

Although DAO prefers ISAM structures, ODBC data sources are available by providing specific connection information through Jet. This is often a very easy approach for most developers who already have experience with Access or Visual Basic because they are already familiar with the object model.

Because of this familiarity and ease of implementation, the DAO is a superb choice for RAD. However, against ODBC data sources, the speed of execution can often be disappointing. With one engine (Jet) talking to another engine (SQL Server), this scenario can be dubbed a poster model for inefficiency.

If you choose to use DAO with an ODBC data source and are using DAO 3.5, you may wish to consider the use of ODBC Direct. ODBC Direct allows you to create a DAO workspace that does not use Jet, but actually uses a subset of RDO (discussed in the next section) to get access to the data. ODBC Direct allows you to continue to work in the general DAO object model, and it does not require special licensing (as does RDO).

Remote Data Objects (RDO)

Unlike DAO, the RDO model does not call a data engine directly. RDO repre-sents a Component Object Model (COM) encapsulation of the ODBC API. In other words, RDO is a very thin layer of software that provides an object model for calling the ODBC API. This gives you the performance benefit of using the ODBC API and avoiding Jet, while providing an object interface that is very similar to DAO in structure.

COM is the specification that defines all interaction between objects and is the original specification upon which OLE was based. As OLE progressed toward the true implementation of COM, the name was changed to reflect the progress that had been made since the early implementations of OLE.

This would seem to solve the weaknesses of both the ODBC API and DAO while capitalizing on their respective strengths. However, this approach cannot solve the one inherent weakness of ODBC: poor performance when accessing ISAM data structures. If an application needs to access data from both an ODBC data source and an ISAM data structure, the developer must use a combination of DAO and RDO to provide maximum performance.

OLE DB

OLE DB is Microsoft's latest solution to the problem of ODBC execution against ISAM data sources. In the ODBC environment, a common interface is provided in the driver manager. The driver manager then loads a driver. In the case of SQL data sources, this driver translates ODBC calls to native calls. In the case of ISAM data sources, this driver provides the entire I/O component for accessing data from the ISAM file.

OLE DB changes this by defining a standard COM interface for data access. Data-access models can be written for client applications, and OLE DB service providers, analogous to ODBC drivers, can be provided for the back-end database. These service providers are actually COM wrappers written directly around the data sources themselves, thus eliminating the need for a driver manager layer. Since this layer has no bias toward the data-storage method, SQL or ISAM, maximum efficiency is provided for all data sources regardless of type.

At the time of this writing, OLE DB is in the early stages of implementation. Service providers are not readily available for many databases. Currently, the Microsoft OLE DB Service Provider for ODBC is being provided as a bridge between ODBC and OLE DB.

ActiveX Data Objects (ADO)

Unlike ODBC, OLE DB is a very low-level COM specification. So low-level, in fact, that a developer is unable to access OLE DB directly from a development tool like Visual Basic. To make OLE DB data sources available to the widest range of clients, Microsoft created a COM object set called the ActiveX Data Objects (ADO). It is Microsoft's intention to replace all other object models with ADO in future releases of Microsoft products.

ADO is potentially a very robust object model in that it defines a core set of functions and allows extensions to be built into the model to support the individual features of certain types of databases. Since it is designed to access OLE DB data sources, the performance problems of ODBC against ISAM data structures are avoided.

At this writing, ADO is in its 1.0 implementation, primarily being used in Web development as a means of accessing data storage through Active Server Pages. A Web project development tool called Microsoft Visual InterDev simplifies this approach significantly.

There are two weaknesses of note with ADO as of this writing:

- Currently, there are few (if any) native OLE DB service providers available. The Microsoft OLE DB Service Provider for ODBC, code named Kangera, is the only way to access data sources through ADO. It must be noted, however, that this relationship between ADO and ODBC is one only of convenience. There is no architectural relationship between ADO and ODBC. ADO promises future implementations that do not depend on ODBC and may replace ODBC entirely at some future point.

- Not all desired database functionality may be available. For example, while ADO will handle the return of multiple result sets from a single request, asynchronous queries are not possible. This is a basic feature of ODBC and of all the other models that we have discussed in this appendix.

APPENDIX

C

SQL Server and the Internet

his appendix will introduce you to different ways of accessing data in SQL Server from Internet applications. SQL Server 6.5 includes a Web Assistant designed to make accessing static Web pages easier than ever before. There are also ways that you can access SQL Server data dynamically through interactive Web pages. We'll begin with an explanation of the differences between static and interactive Web pages.

Static versus Interactive Web Pages

In the early days of the World Wide Web, most pages were not designed to give the user an interface for extensive interaction. Sure, there were stunning graphics and even some animations, but the pages were essentially static in nature.

When a user accesses a static Web page, the presentation consists primarily of links and text. The text and/or links might be updated periodically by the Web master, but the page does not accept any input from the user other than to follow a link to another static page.

Static pages have their place. If the user has no need to "drill down" to specific data and can use the contents of the page as a whole, the static approach is valid. Properly planned links, good organization, and maintenance of current information can give a static site the appearance of being fairly dynamic in response to user requests.

Interactive pages have an entirely different concept and purpose than static pages. The key participant in an interactive Web page is the user. The user can provide input about the information to be retrieved, enter data into a data store by filling out a Web-based form, and even cause events to happen halfway around the world. (I even found a Web site that let me remote-control a model train in Germany—not bad considering I never left the basement of my house in Utah.)

One of the most recent applications for interactive Web pages is to provide merchant services. A Web site can be built to handle merchandising activities ranging from taking orders in an online bookstore to transferring funds between two financial institutions. This is accomplished through tools such a Microsoft Internet Information Server (to handle the Web traffic), Merchant Server (to maintain the security of the transactions), and SQL Server (to provide the data storage and transactional integrity). Adding Microsoft Transaction Server to the mix contributes the extra element of distributed transaction processing, allowing you to coordinate the activities of multiple SQL Server machines, or even other database management systems such as Oracle or Sybase.

As you can see, with interactive Web pages, the only limit is the imagination of the site architect and the developer. Whether you are building your Web site for internal use, as with an intranet or an extranet, or planning on luring Internet customers to your site, the entire reason for building your site is to provide services for a user. The more richly interactive the experience, the more likely that the users will return to purchase the product or service that you have to offer.

Using the SQL Server Web Assistant

Although there are advantages to providing the user with an interactive experience, sometimes there is no need to dynamically extract information from a SQL Server database. If your goal is to create static Web pages that will be periodically updated, either by the administrator or by an automated service, the SQL Server Web Assistant might be exactly the tool that you need. It doesn't make sense to pound a pin into the wall with a sledgehammer, and sometimes a static Web page is completely adequate.

The Web pages created by the Web Assistant can be based on a stored procedure or a free-form query that you type as you initially run the Web Assistant, or you can select the fields you want to include graphically. These pages are sometimes called *push* pages because the data is pushed out of SQL Server by the queries or stored procedures that access the data. These queries or stored procedures are completely static, however. They cannot be changed by the user interacting through a Web browser, nor can parameters be passed to the stored procedure through the browser.

Running the SQL Server Web Assistant

To run the SQL Server Web Assistant, first make sure that the SQL Server service is running. If the SQL Server service is not running, the Web Assistant will not be able to forward the query or stored procedure call to SQL Server for processing.

Logging On

The SQL Server Web Assistant is not available from within SQL Enterprise Manager. To access the Web Assistant, go to the Microsoft SQL Server 6.5 program group. This should start the introductory screen shown in Figure C.1. From here, you will need to provide login information for SQL Server in order to continue.

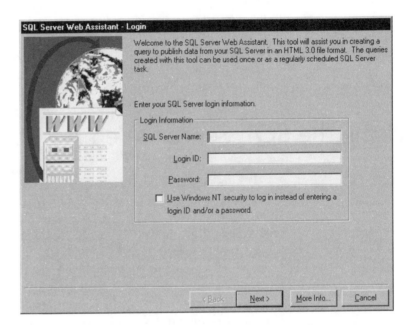

To successfully log in to SQL Server, you must provide a login ID and a password. If the server to which you wish to connect is located on a computer other than the one from which you are running the SQL Server Web Assistant, you must also include the name of the server in the SQL Server Name text box. If you need more information about this window, click on the More Info button at the bottom of the window.

If you are using SQL Server integrated security, you have the option of selecting the checkbox to use Windows NT security. In order to use this option, you must have previously mapped your Windows NT login ID to a specific level of SQL Server security using the SQL Security Manager utility (see Chapter 6 for more information about using integrated security and other security modes).

By default, any member of the Windows NT Administrators group is allowed to access SQL Server as an SA through a trusted connection. If you are logged in to Windows NT under an administrative account, you should be able to select this option and continue without entering a login ID and password.

After you've entered your login information, click on the Next button to move to the Query window.

Creating Your Query

In the SQL Server Web Assistant Query window, you have three choices of how to create the query:

Build a Query from a Database Hierarchy   Using this option, you can simply expand your databases to the field level and select which columns you want in your Web page results. Figure C.2 shows an example of this "drill-down" option. Although this approach looks very intuitive at first, it really won't save you much coding. If you wish to provide any aggregation or summarization of your data, you must write the appropriate clauses in the blank text box below the database tree. By the time you do this, you might as well have just typed in the query yourself.

Enter a Query as Free-Form Text   Selecting this option gives you a blank text box where you can write a Transact-SQL query. The contents of this text box will be submitted to the server exactly as you type them, so make sure that the query is syntactically correct. If it isn't, a parsing error will occur as you attempt to leave this page of the Web Assistant.

Use a Query in a Stored Procedure   This option lets you select a stored procedure to run as the Web page is created. If the Web page update task also must modify or copy data elsewhere in your database, you might consider using a stored procedure; however, this stored procedure must return a result set (a Select statement) in order for the page to display information.

FIGURE C.2

Creating a query with the
SQL Web Assistant

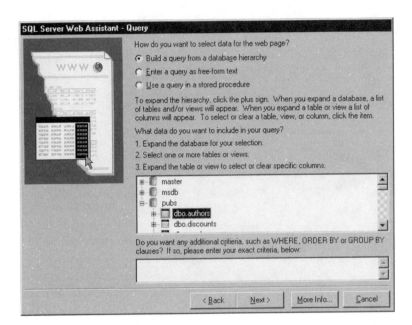

Stored procedures can do much more than return result sets to a requesting client. You can use stored procedures wherever any group of tasks, including administrative tasks, can be organized in a batch and called initially with a single statement.

When you're finished composing your query using one of these three methods, click on the Next button to continue.

Scheduling Web Page Generation

The Web Assistant next presents the Scheduling window, as shown in Figure C.3. Here, you specify when your Web page will be created, and if you like, re-created.

You have five choices for the generation of this page, as listed below. The option that you select will determine what additional information you need to supply here.

Now   The page is generated immediately. No future regenerations are scheduled.

FIGURE C.3

Scheduling a Web page
generation task

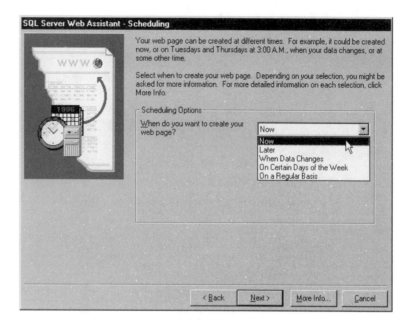

Later   You are presented with scheduling options to schedule a generation at a single point in the future. No additional regenerations are scheduled.

When Data Changes   You are presented with a "drill-down" list so that you can select which underlying data changes will trigger the regeneration task.

When you choose the When Data Changes option, the data modifications must be initiated by a process other than the browser. A browser cannot ask for a static Web page to be dynamically updated from SQL Server (this would require an interactive page). You can mix and match, however. A browser working in an interactive page could cause an update of a static page.

On Certain Days of the Week   You are presented with a list of days so that you can select from one to seven days for scheduled regeneration. A single time of regeneration for all scheduled days is given.

On a Regular Basis   You are offered a choice for regeneration at intervals, such as every 2 hours, every 4 days, and so on.

After making your scheduling selections, click on the Next button to continue.

Setting File Options

The next Web Assistant window contains file options, as shown in Figure C.4. This window requires you to make some choices about how the Web page will be organized and which files will be used in the process.

FIGURE C.4

Setting file options

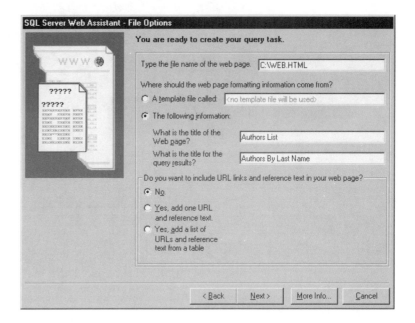

The first choice is the filename for the Web page. Any valid filename can be used. Here are some tips for specifying the Web page's filename:

- Use an .htm or .html extension to your filename.

- Use a full path or UNC name. Don't leave any room for ambiguity.

- Make sure that the directory location is a directory managed by your Web server. The browser must be able to make a request for the page from the Web server in order to retrieve the data.

Your next decision is whether to use an HTML template file or to enter basic title information into the Web Assistant for your Web page. If you choose to enter information directly into the Web Assistant, you do not have a great deal of flexibility concerning the type of formats you can work with. You can enter a page title and a table title and include links at the bottom of your Web page in this window. If you want to enter a link (or links) at the bottom of your Web page, you can select the appropriate option button at the bottom of the File Options window. This will change the appearance of the area on the bottom right of the window, allowing you to provide additional information about the links. Note that Microsoft conveniently provides an example of how to link to its Web site.

If you want links placed anywhere other than the bottom of the page, you must use an HTML template file. The SQL Server Web Assistant does not offer an option for the placement of these links.

If you want the greatest amount of flexibility with your Web page, you should use an HTML template file. If you choose to use an HTML template, the other options on this form will no longer be available. This means that if you wish to specify a page title, table title, or links in your Web page, you must include them in your template file.

The template file is created in the same way that any other HTML page is created. You can create the HTML template yourself by using Notepad or a GUI editor such as Microsoft Front Page. Create the page exactly as you want your finished page to appear, with the exception of the data that will be coming from SQL Server. In the location that will hold the SQL Server data, put the HTML marker <%insert_data_here%>. This marker will be used by the Web Assistant as a key for inserting the results of the query.

Put the full path of the template file into the appropriate text box in the File Options window. This template will be used by the Web Assistant every time the page is regenerated. If you wish to make modifications to the formatting and display of your Web page, you will not need to run the SQL Server Web Assistant again. Just open the template in your favorite editor, make the changes, and save the file. You are ready for your next regeneration—SQL Server with take care of the rest of the updating work.

Click on the Next button in the File Options window after you've entered the appropriate information.

Formatting Your Web Page

The Formatting window, shown in Figure C.5, contains all of the formatting options that the Web Assistant will let you control. These include font type and characteristic, timestamps, and column options.

FIGURE C.5

Choosing formatting options for your Web page

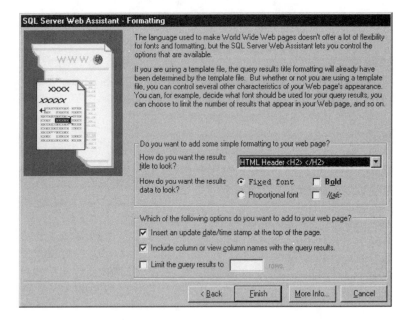

Unlike when you create a document with a word processor, when you create a page with HTML, you cannot be sure how your Web page will appear when it is run inside a browser. This is because different browsers have different capabilities. In order to allow a page to be viewed from the various types of browsers, HTML provides soft codes called *tags* rather than hard codes for formatting a Web page. For example, a Web page may use a header tag that is displayed differently in different browsers, perhaps as underlined text in one browser and as bold text in another. Ultimately, it is up to the browser to determine how each of the tags will be interpreted.

There are six levels of header tags defined in HTML. <H1> is the heaviest, and <H6> is the lightest. <H1> should be reserved only for substantial emphasis, such as the main concept or idea of a Web page.

The first drop-down list in the Formatting window allows you to choose a header for the title of the query result table. The default is <H2>. Usually, this will be sufficient for most pages. If you have elected to use an HTML template file in the previous window, this option will be dimmed; you must define any result title attributes in the template file.

The next options let you choose some simple formatting for the actual data that will be written as part of the Web page. You can choose between fixed or proportional fonts, although you cannot choose exactly which typeface will be used (the typefaces available depend on the browser). You can also choose to make the results appear as bold or italic by selecting the appropriate checkboxes. Note that bold and italic print tend to be fuzzy at small font sizes in most browsers. If you choose to use these, do so sparingly in small fonts and test your page in a number of browsers for readability.

The three checkboxes at the bottom of the Formatting window deal with other miscellaneous features that you may wish to include in your Web page. By selecting the appropriate boxes, you can include a timestamp at the top of the page or include column names at the top of each column. If your query results have the potential of being very large, you can also restrict the number of rows that will be generated into the Web page.

To support a large number of rows in your data result, consider breaking the results into pieces by including a Where clause in the original query. For example, you can create a page based on a query that selects authors whose last name begins with the letters A through F. Access the page through a link labeled "Authors A - F." Continue this process for logical breaks in your data set.

Finishing Your Web Page

Congratulations! You are now ready to create your Web page. If you wish to make any changes at this point, you can click on the Back button. Otherwise, click on the Finish button. When you choose Finish, you will be presented with a message box informing you that the task you've created has been started. If you've entered a complicated query, generating the Web page could take a few minutes.

Viewing Your Web Page

If you selected the Now option in the SQL Server Web Assistant's Scheduling window (Figure C.3), your page has been created and is ready to be viewed. If you selected any of the other scheduling options, the page will be generated when the scheduled task occurs.

Viewing the Page in a Browser

To examine your page in a browser, you can either go through your Web server or load the file directly into your browser.

To view the page using Microsoft Internet Explorer 3.*x*, simply type the path of the file into the address bar at the top of the browser's window. This should load the page into the browser, as shown in the example in Figure C.6. The result in Figure C.6 is based on a query selecting the author id, first name, and last name columns from the Authors table in the Pubs database, and sorting by last name.

The Pubs database is a sample database that is installed when you install SQL Server. See Chapter 3 for more information about this and the other databases that are installed by default.

FIGURE C.6

The results of an Authors table query in the Internet Explorer window

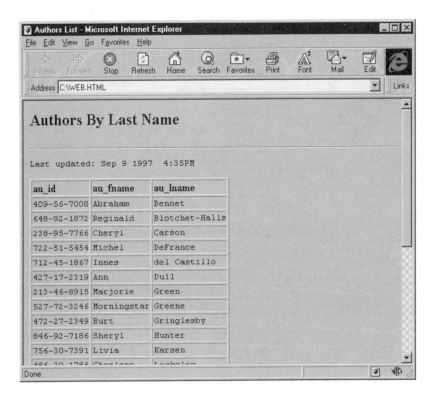

Viewing the HTML Code

To view the actual HTML code that was generated by the Web Assistant, select View ➤ Source from the Internet Explorer menu. This will open Notepad and place the HTML source code there for viewing and editing. If you wish to make changes to the HTML source code directly, you can do this in Notepad or in an HTML editor, such as Microsoft Front Page. Figure C.7 shows the source code for the Web page shown in Figure C.6. If you are familiar with HTML code, you will note that everything that you asked for in the Web Assistant windows is here in the code. A standard HTML table was used to hold your results, and the formatting is exactly as requested.

FIGURE C.7

The source code for the page generated by the Authors table query

```
Web.html - Notepad                                                   _ □ ×
File  Edit  Search  Help
<HTML>

<HEAD>

<TITLE>Authors List</TITLE>

</HEAD>

<BODY>

<H2>Authors By Last Name</H2>
<HR>

<PRE><TT>Last updated: Sep 9 1997  4:35PM</TT></PRE>

<P>
<P><TABLE BORDER=1>
<TR><TH ALIGN=LEFT>au_id</TH><TH ALIGN=LEFT>au_fname</TH><TH ALIGN=LEFT>au_lname</TH></TR>
<TR><TD NOWRAP><TT>409-56-7008</TT></TD><TD NOWRAP><TT>Abraham</TT></TD><TD NOWRAP><TT>Bennet<,
<TR><TD NOWRAP><TT>648-92-1872</TT></TD><TD NOWRAP><TT>Reginald</TT></TD><TD NOWRAP><TT>Blotchr
<TR><TD NOWRAP><TT>238-95-7766</TT></TD><TD NOWRAP><TT>Cheryl</TT></TD><TD NOWRAP><TT>Carson</
<TR><TD NOWRAP><TT>722-51-5454</TT></TD><TD NOWRAP><TT>Michel</TT></TD><TD NOWRAP><TT>DeFrance·
<TR><TD NOWRAP><TT>712-45-1867</TT></TD><TD NOWRAP><TT>Innes</TT></TD><TD NOWRAP><TT>del Casti:
<TR><TD NOWRAP><TT>427-17-2319</TT></TD><TD NOWRAP><TT>Ann</TT></TD><TD NOWRAP><TT>Dull</TT></
<TR><TD NOWRAP><TT>213-46-8915</TT></TD><TD NOWRAP><TT>Marjorie</TT></TD><TD NOWRAP><TT>Green<,
<TR><TD NOWRAP><TT>527-72-3246</TT></TD><TD NOWRAP><TT>Morningstar</TT></TD><TD NOWRAP><TT>Grer
<TR><TD NOWRAP><TT>472-27-2349</TT></TD><TD NOWRAP><TT>Burt</TT></TD><TD NOWRAP><TT>Gringlesby·
```

WARNING Although you can edit the Web page directly after it has been generated, any changes that you make will be lost the next time the page is generated. If you wish to make permanent changes to the formatting of the page, you must either change the settings inside the Web Assistant or, for a more robust approach, use an HTML template file.

What is really happening when you run the SQL Server Web Assistant? The truth might be a little disappointing. There is absolutely no magic involved. Its just another one of those pesky system stored procedures creating a scheduled task.

If you look at the list of system stored procedures in the Master database, you will see one in the list called sp_makewebtask. This system stored procedure takes all of the information that was gathered from the Web Assistant windows and generates a Web page creation task based on those parameters.

What this means is that if you want to create your own custom application that calls the stored procedure and passes the necessary parameters, you could accomplish this quite easily. You could then create custom interfaces and defaults, enabling you to set standards for the creation of Web pages in your enterprise.

Creating Interactive Web Pages

Although static Web pages are simple to produce with the SQL Server Web Assistant, you may have more sophisticated requirements for your Web site. For example, if your users need to enter information into a database or retrieve information based on custom parameters, you may need to look at interactive Web pages as a solution. Interactive Web pages are sometimes called *pull* pages because the user's input will pull data out of your SQL Server database.

Pull pages tend to place more of a strain on your server because, rather than simply generating a Web page at certain intervals, the browser is actually calling information directly out of the database. Significant hits to your Web site can negatively impact the performance of SQL Server.

When you are creating interactive Web pages, there are three basic ways to get at your SQL Server data:

- Internet Database Connector (IDC)

- Remote Data Services (RDS), formerly known as the Advanced Data Connector (ADC)

- ActiveX Data Objects (ADO)

Although these approaches are not necessarily difficult to implement, they do require programming that is beyond the scope of this book. There are numerous resources available for additional exploration of these topics. Also, these are other approaches to creating interactive Web pages to data sources, such as CGI scripts and ISAPI applications.

APPENDIX

D

Common Transact-SQL Commands

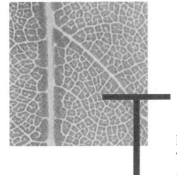

he tables in this appendix list the most commonly used Transact-SQL commands, organized by the items that they affect, as follows:

- Devices (see Chapter 5)

- Databases (see Chapters 5, 12, and 13)

- SQL Server logins (see Chapter 6)

- Database users and groups (see Chapter 6)

- Database permissions (see Chapter 7)

- Backup and restore procedures (see Chapter 8)

- Miscellaneous (see Chapters 10, 12, and 13)

T A B L E D.1	Command	Description	Syntax

Commands Related to Devices	DISK INIT	Create a new database device.	DISK INIT
			   NAME = 'logical_name',
			   PHYSNAME = 'physical_name',
			   VDEVNO = virtual_device_number,
			   SIZE = number_of_2K_blocks
			   [,VSTART = virtual_address]

	DISK RESIZE	Increase the size of a database device.	DISK RESIZE
			   NAME = logical_device_name,
			   SIZE = final_size

T A B L E D.I (cont.) Commands Related to Devices	**Command**	**Description**	**Syntax**
	sp_dropdevice	Remove a database device. Use DELFILE to delete an operating system file.	sp_dropdevice logical_name [, DELFILE]
	sp_helpdevice	Retrieve information about a database device.	sp_helpdevice [logical_name]

T A B L E D.2 Commands Related to Databases	**Command**	**Description**	**Syntax**
	ALTER DATABASE	Increase the size of a user database.	ALTER DATABASE database_name [ON {DEFAULT | database_device} [= size] [, database_device [= size]]...] [FOR LOAD]
	CREATE DATABASE	Create a user database.	CREATE DATABASE database_name [ON {DEFAULT | database_device} [= size] [, database_device [= size]]...] [LOG ON database_device [= size] [, database_device [= size]]...] [FOR LOAD]
	DBCC DBREPAIR	Drop a user database marked as suspect.	DBCC DBREPAIR (database_name, DROPDB [, NOINIT])
	DBCC SHRINKDB	Reduce the size of a user database.	DBCC SHRINKDB (database_name [, new_size [, 'MASTEROVERRIDE']])
	DROP DATABASE	Drop a user database.	DROP DATABASE database_name [,database_name...]

T A B L E D.2 (cont.) Commands Related to Databases	**Command**	**Description**	**Syntax**
	sp_change- dbowner	Change the login mapped to the DBO user in a database.	sp_changedbowner login_id [, true]
	sp_dboption	Change the value of a database option.	sp_dboption [dbname, optname, {true | false}]
	sp_dbremove	Drop a user database (including one that is marked as suspect).	sp_dbremove database[, dropdev]
	sp_helpdb	Retrieve information about a user database.	sp_helpdb [dbname]

T A B L E D.3 Commands Related to SQL Server Logins	**Command**	**Description**	**Syntax**
	sp_addlogin	Create a login on the server.	sp_addlogin login_id [, passwd [, defdb [, deflanguage]]]
	sp_defaultdb	Change the default database for a login.	sp_defaultdb login_id, defdb
	sp_droplogin	Drop a login from the server.	sp_droplogin login_id
	sp_helplogins	Gather information about logins.	sp_helplogins [login_id]
	sp_password	Change your password.	sp_password old, new [, login_id]

	Command	Description	Syntax
TABLE D.4 Commands Related to Database Users and Groups	sp_addalias	Create a user alias in a database for a login.	sp_addalias login_id, username
	sp_addgroup	Create a group in a database.	sp_addgroup grpname
	sp_adduser	Create a user in a database.	sp_adduser login_id [, username [,grpname]]
	sp_change-group	Change group membership for a database user.	sp_changegroup grpname, username
	sp_dropalias	Drop a user alias from a database for a login.	sp_dropalias login_id
	sp_dropgroup	Delete a group from a database.	sp_dropgroup grpname
	sp_dropuser	Drop a user from a database.	sp_dropuser username
	sp_helpgroup	Retrieve information about database groups.	sp_helpgroup [grpname]
	sp_helpuser	Retrieve information about database users.	sp_helpuser [username]

T A B L E D.5	Command	Description	Syntax
Commands Related to Database Permissions	GRANT	Grant database object and statement permissions for a user.	**Statement permissions:** GRANT {ALL | statement_list} TO {PUBLIC | name_list} **Object permissions:** GRANT {ALL | permission_list} ON {table_name [(column_list)] | view_name [(column_list)] | stored_procedure_name | extended_stored_procedure_name} TO {PUBLIC | name_list} [WITH GRANT OPTION]
	REVOKE	Remove database object and statement permissions from a user.	**Statement permissions:** REVOKE {ALL | statement_list} FROM {PUBLIC | name_list} **Object permissions:** REVOKE {ALL | permission_list} ON {table_name [(column_list)] | view_name [(column_list)] | stored_procedure_name | extended_stored_procedure_name} FROM {PUBLIC | name_list} [WITH GRANT OPTION] [CASCADE]
	sp_helpprotect	Retrieve permission information about an object or a user.	sp_helprotect name [, username]

T A B L E D.6	Command	Description	Syntax
Commands Related to Backup and Restore Procedures	DBCC CHECK-CATALOG	Check consistency in and between system tables.	DBCC CHECKCATALOG [(database name)]
.	DBCC CHECKTABLE	Check the consistency of a table.	DBCC CHECKTABLE (table_name [, NOINDEX | index_id])

	Command	Description	Syntax
T A B L E D.6 *(cont.)* Commands Related to Backup and Restore Procedures	DBCC NEWALLOC	Check and correct resource allocation information in a database.	DBCC NEWALLOC [(database_name [, NOINDEX])]
	DBCC TEXTALL	Check the consistency of text and image columns.	DBCC TEXTALL [({database_name | database_id} [, FULL | FAST])]
	DUMP DATABASE	Perform a database backup.	DUMP DATABASE {dbname | @dbname_var} TO dump_device [, dump_device2 [..., dump_device32]] [WITH options [[,] STATS [= percentage]]]
	DUMP TRANS-ACTION	Perform a transaction log backup.	DUMP TRANSACTION {dbname | @dbname_var} [TO dump_device [, dump_device2 [..., dump_device32]]] [WITH {TRUNCATE_ONLY | NO_LOG | NO_TRUNCATE}{options}]
	LOAD DATABASE	Perform a database restoration.	LOAD DATABASE {dbname | @dbname_var} FROM dump_device [, dump_device2 [..., dump_device32]] [WITH options [[,] STATS [= percentage]]]
	LOAD HEADERONLY	Perform a header information only restoration.	LOAD HEADERONLY FROM dump_device
	LOAD TRANS-ACTION	Perform a transaction log restoration.	LOAD TRANSACTION {dbname | @dbname_var} FROM dump_device [, dump_device2 [..., dump_device32]] [WITH options]
	sp_addump-device	Create a backup device.	sp_addumpdevice {'disk' | 'diskette' | 'tape'}, 'logical_name', 'physical_name' [, {{cntrltype [, noskip | skip [, media_capacity]]} | {@devstatus = {noskip | skip}}}]

TABLE D.7	Command	Description	Syntax
Miscellaneous Commands	CHECKPOINT	Issue an explicit checkpoint.	CHECKPOINT
	DBCC UPDATEUSAGE	Report and correct inaccuracies in the sysindexes table that may be reported by sp_spaceused.	DBCC UPDATEUSAGE ({0 | database_name} [, table_name [, index_id]])
	KILL	Kill a current user process.	KILL spid
	RECONFIGURE	Install server configurations.	RECONFIGURE [WITH OVERRIDE]
	SHUTDOWN	Shut down the MSSQLServer service.	SHUTDOWN [WITH NOWAIT]
	sp_certify_removable	Certify the consistency of a database created for removable media distribution.	sp_certify_removable dbname[, AUTO]
	sp_configure	Set server configurations. Must be followed by RECONFIGURE.	sp_configure [config_name [, config_value]]
	sp_create_removable	Create a database for removable media distribution.	sp_create_removable dbname, syslogical, 'sysphysical', syssize, loglogical, 'logphysical', logsize, datalogical1, 'dataphysical1', datasize1 [..., datalogical16, 'dataphysical16', datasize16]

T A B L E D.7 _(cont.)_ Miscellaneous Commands	**Command**	**Description**	**Syntax**
	sp_dbinstall	Install a database from removable media.	sp_dbinstall database, logical_dev_name, 'physical_dev_name', size, 'devtype' [,'location']
	sp_helpsql	Return the syntax of a Transact-SQL statement or system stored procedure.	sp_helpsql ['topic']
	sp_helptext	Return the SQL code used to create a stored procedure.	sp_helptext objname
	sp_lock	Report current server locks.	sp_lock [spid1 [, spid2]]
	sp_logdevice	Move a transaction log to another device.	sp_logdevice dbname, database_device
	sp_rename	Rename a database object.	sp_rename objname, newname [, COLUMN | INDEX]
	sp_who	Report current server activity.	sp_who [login_id | 'spid']
	UPDATE STATISTICS	Update the distribution page for an index.	UPDATE STATISTICS [[database.]owner.]table_name [index_name]
	USE	Reset a user's current database.	USE database_name

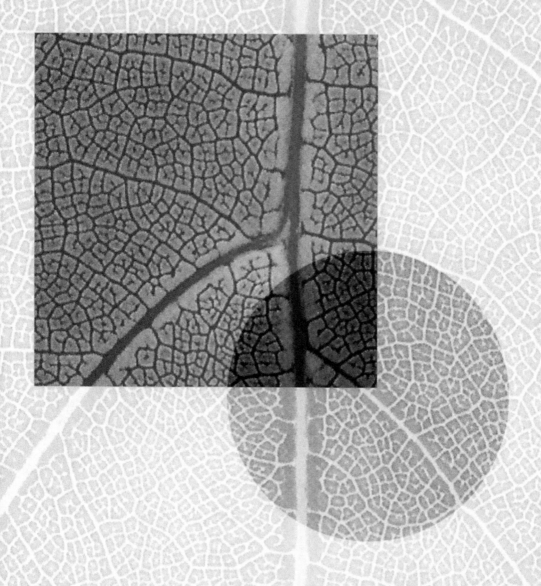

Glossary

ActiveX Data Objects (ADO) A COM (Component Object Model) object set created by Microsoft intended to replace all other object models in future releases of Microsoft products. ADO is potentially a very robust object model in that it defines a core set of functions and allows extensions to be built into the model to support the individual features of certain types of databases. It is designed to access OLE DB data sources. See also *OLE DB*.

ADO See *ActiveX Data Objects*.

alert A mechanism that tells SQL Server which error codes to look for in the Windows NT event log, and what action to take if an event is found. Alerts can be based on a severity level, an error code, and the database in which the error occurred. An alert can notify an operator and/or perform a task. Alerts are stored in the Msdb database.

alias A mechanism that allows a login to access a database under the username assigned to another login. The alias is stored in the sysalternates system table of the database. Each login can have either a username in a database or an alias, but not both. An alias can be used to consolidate permissions under special user accounts, such as DBO.

allocation unit In SQL Server, a structure designed to provide a method of keeping track of which pages are allocated to which objects. When a database is created, it is divided into allocation units. When an allocation unit is created, it is built from 32 pieces called *extents*. The very first page of the first extent of the allocation unit is called the *allocation page*. The allocation page is responsible for keeping track of every extent in the allocation unit. Allocation units

affect the size of the database. Databases must be created and maintained in full allocation unit intervals, which are 512KB in size.

article The basic unit of SQL Server replication. An article is one or more columns and rows of a table.

automatic recovery A feature built into SQL Server that ensures that a database is brought up-to-date, only completed transactions are put into the database, and partially done transactions are removed. Every time that SQL Server is restarted, SQL Server runs its automatic recovery feature.

B-Tree format The format used for indexes in SQL Server. B-Tree is short for balanced tree. It is called a balanced tree because every page of the index is exactly the same distance from the root as every other page at the same level.

BackOffice Microsoft's line of client/server support applications that run on Windows NT Server. Some components of BackOffice include Microsoft SQL Server, Systems Management Server (SMS), Internet Information Server (IIS), Exchange Server, SNA Server, and Proxy Server.

backup device A file or tape to which SQL Server backs up a database. Also called a *dump device*. SQL has no built-in backup devices that point to files or tapes. You will need to create all of your backup devices that point to files or tapes.

backup domain controller (BDC) A server that keeps a copy of the authentication database from the primary domain controller (PDC). Users can log in to either the PDC or to any of the BDCs. See also *primary domain controller*.

BCP (Bulk Copy Program) A command-line utility used for transferring information into and out of SQL Server. See also *fast BCP, slow BCP.*

broken ownership chain See *ownership chain.*

browser See *Web browser.*

caching A speed optimization technique that keeps a copy of the most recently used data in a fast, high-cost, low-capacity storage device rather than in the device upon which the actual data resides. Caching assumes that recently used data is likely to be used again. Fetching data from cache is faster than fetching data from the slower, larger storage device. Most caching algorithms also copy the next most likely to be used data and perform write caching to further increase speed gains.

character set The set of characters that SQL Server will recognize and therefore store. Of the 256 characters contained in each character set, the first 128 characters are the same throughout the various code pages. The last 128 characters, also known as extended characters, are different.

checkpoint The mechanism by which SQL Server periodically writes modified data to a database. The DBO of a database may also issue a checkpoint at any time by running the command Checkpoint in the appropriate database.

CHKUPG65 A utility used to check the compatibility between a current version of SQL Server and older user-defined databases that are being upgraded.

client A computer on a network that subscribes to the services provided by a server.

client/server A network architecture that dedicates certain computers called *servers* to act as service providers to computers called *clients,* which users operate to perform work. Servers can be dedicated to providing one or more network services, such as file storage, shared printing, communications, e-mail service, and Web response.

client/server application An application that is split into two components: computer-intensive processes that run on application servers and user interfaces that run on clients. Client/server applications communicate over the network through interprocess communication mechanisms.

column The component of a table that holds individual pieces of the data.

COM See *Component Object Model.*

commit The process whereby completed transactions are put into the database. SQL Server will automatically commit the data at regular intervals, or a manual commit can be initialized by the DBO or SA.

Component Object Model (COM) The specification that defines all interaction between objects. COM is the original specification upon which OLE was based.

computer name A 1- to 15-character NetBIOS name used to uniquely identify a computer on the network.

concurrency The ability of SQL Server to support multiple users at the same time, even if these users want the same data.

Control Panel A Windows utility that controls the function of specific operating system services by allowing users to change default settings for the service to match their preferences. The Windows Registry contains the Control Panel settings on a system and/or per user basis.

DAO See *Data Access Objects*.

Data Access Objects (DAO) A set of programmable objects that Microsoft Access developers use to manipulate data through Jet, the data-access engine for Access and other Microsoft desktop products.

data cache SQL Server's own cache of data to speed up access to databases. The size of the data cache can be indirectly manipulated by allocating more or less RAM to SQL Server. After SQL Server fulfills its requirements for RAM from the RAM that has been assigned to it, the rest is assigned to cache. The cache is divided into a data cache and procedure cache. The percentage of procedure cache versus data cache can be set by the SA. See also *caching, procedure cache*.

Data Source Name (DSN) A user-created identifier used by ODBC to negotiate connections to any ODBC-compliant data source. A DSN consists of a server location and a driver name and can optionally contain a database name and authentication information. See also *ODBC*.

data warehousing Storage and querying of historical data, also referred to as *decision-support systems*. The main focus of data warehousing is the ability to quickly query existing data and perform complex analysis, usually looking for patterns or other relationships that are difficult to locate during day-to-day operations of a company.

Database Consistency Checker See *DBCC*.

database device A file that stores one or more SQL Server databases. When databases are created, they can be assigned space on one or more devices.

Database Maintenance Plan Wizard A wizard provided with SQL Server 6.5 that helps you schedule backups and perform optimizations and consistency checking.

database management system (DBMS) An environment specifically created for the purpose of working with databases. The term database management system usually refers to an electronic system or a computer program designed to work with databases. Microsoft Access and FoxPro are both examples of database management systems.

database object owner See *DBOO*.

database owner See *DBO*.

database user See *user*.

datatype A component of a SQL Server database that determines what kinds of data can be stored in a column, such as character data, numeric data, or date/time data. A column can hold data of only a single datatype.

DB-Library A set of functions and connectivity programs that allow clients to communicate with database engines.

DBCC (Database Consistency Checker) SQL Server commands used to check the consistency of databases. These commands are generally used to gather information about the status of a database rather than to make changes to a database.

DBMS   See *database management system.*

DBO (database owner)   In SQL Server, a user who has full permissions in a particular database. This includes the ability to back up and restore the database and transaction log. The SA is also considered the DBO of every database. The DBO is specified through the sp_changedbowner stored procedure.

DBOO (database object owner)   In SQL Server, a user who creates a particular database object. The DBOO has all rights on that object, including the right to allow others to use the object.

DDE   See *Dynamic Data Exchange.*

default   A SQL Server object assigned to a column or user-defined datatype in a table. If no data is entered, the default value will be used.

Desktop   A directory that the background of the Windows Explorer shell represents. By default, the Desktop holds objects that contain the local storage devices and available network shares. Also a key operating part of the Windows GUI.

Distributed Transaction Coordinator (DTC)   A service (the MSDTC service) that helps coordinate transactions between two or more SQL Server machines so that the transaction is done simultaneously on both servers.

distribution server   For replication in SQL Server, the server that keeps track of replication. It copies the data from the publishing server, stores it, and then forwards it to all subscribing servers. If you designate the SQL Server machine where you are installing publishing as the one that holds the Distribution database,

you are installing a *local distribution server.* Designating a remote server rather than a local one as your distribution server may make better use of a WAN.

DLL   See *dynamic link library.*

domain   In Microsoft networks, an arrangement of client and server computers referenced by a specific name that share a single security permissions database. On the Internet, a domain is a named collection of hosts and subdomains, registered with a unique name by the InterNIC.

domain controller   A server that authenticates workstation network logon requests by comparing a username and password against account information stored in the user accounts database. A user cannot access a domain without authentication from a domain controller. See also *primary domain controller, backup domain controller.*

DSN   See *Data Source Name.*

DTC   See *Distributed Transaction Coordinator.*

dump device   See *backup device.*

dynamic backup   A type of backup that allows you to back up your SQL Server databases while they are in use. Users can stay connected to the server while a dynamic backup is in progress.

Dynamic Data Exchange (DDE)   A method of interprocess communication within the Microsoft Windows operating systems.

dynamic link library (DLL)   A set of modular functions that can be used by many programs simultaneously. There are hundreds of functions stored within DLLs.

electronic mail (e-mail) A type of client/server application that provides a routed, stored-message service between any two user e-mail accounts. E-mail accounts are not the same as user accounts, but a one-to-one relationship usually exists between them. Because all modern computers can attach to the Internet, users can send e-mail over the Internet to any location that has telephone or wireless digital service.

Enterprise Manager See *SQL Enterprise Manager*.

enterprise network A complex network consisting of multiple servers and multiple domains over a large geographic area.

Exchange See *Microsoft Exchange*.

Explorer The default shell for Windows 95 and Windows NT 4.0. Explorer implements the more flexible Desktop object paradigm rather than the Program Manager paradigm used in earlier versions of Windows. See also *Desktop*.

extended stored procedure See *stored procedure*.

extent In SQL Server, the unit of allocation for tables and indexes. All SQL Server objects and data are stored in tables. Tables and indexes are organized into extents. Each extent consists of eight 2KB pages. When a table or an index requires additional storage space, a new extent is allocated.

extranet A World Wide Web network between two or more closely related companies. For example, suppliers and wholesalers could be connected through an extranet.

fast BCP A form of importing data into SQL Server with the BCP utility that takes place when there are no indexes on the table being imported

to, and when the Select Into/Bulk Copy database option is set. See also *slow BCP*.

file allocation table (FAT) The file system used by MS-DOS and available to other operating systems such as Windows (all variations), OS/2, and Windows NT. FAT has become something of a mass-storage compatibility standard because of its simplicity and wide availability. FAT has few fault-tolerance features and can become corrupted through normal use over time.

flat-file database A database whose information is stored in a single file and is accessed sequentially. Examples of flat-file database programs include dBASE, Access, FoxPro, and other personal computer databases.

group A security entity to which users can be assigned membership for the purpose of applying a broad set of group permissions to the user. By managing permissions for groups and assigning users to groups, rather than assigning permissions to users, security administrators can more easily manage large security environments. SQL Server differs from most network applications in that it allows a user to be a member of only one other group besides the Public group (per database).

guest user A user account in SQL Server. If a specific user doesn't exist in the database permissions list, but a user called guest does, then that user will have the rights of the guest user in that particular database.

horizontal partitioning In SQL Server replication, a method by which you can publish only certain rows of a table. See also *vertical partitioning*.

HTML See *Hypertext Markup Language*.

HTTP See *Hypertext Transfer Protocol.*

hyperlink A link in text or graphics files that has a Web address embedded within it. By clicking on the link, you jump to another Web address. You can identify a hyperlink because it is a different color from the rest of the Web page.

Hypertext Markup Language (HTML) A textual data format that identifies sections of a document as headers, lists, hyper links, and so on. HTML is the data format used on the World Wide Web for the publication of Web pages.

Hypertext Transfer Protocol (HTTP) An Internet protocol that transfers HTML documents over the Internet and responds to context changes that happen when a user clicks on a hyperlink.

IDE See *Integrated Drive Electronics.*

IIS See *Internet Information Server.*

index A data structure that provides a mechanism for resolving queries more efficiently by working through a subset of the data rather than all of the data. When an index is used, a full table scan can be avoided. In SQL Server, each table is allowed one *clustered* index. This index is the actual sort order for the data in the table. *Nonclustered* indexes consist of a list of ordered keys that contain pointers to the data in the data pages. Numerous nonclustered indexes can be created, but these occupy more space than clustered indexes.

Indexed Sequential Access Method (ISAM) A method of data access that utilizes file I/O routines with indexing and a few enhanced features.

Industry Standard Architecture (ISA) The design standard for 16-bit Intel compatible motherboards and peripheral buses. The 32/64-bit PCI bus standard is replacing the ISA standard. Adapters and interface cards must conform to the bus standard(s) used by the motherboard in order to be used with a computer.

Integrated Drive Electronics (IDE) A simple mass-storage device interconnection bus that operates at 5Mbps and can handle no more than two attached devices. IDE devices are similar to but less expensive than SCSI devices.

integrated security A SQL Server security mode in which SQL Server accepts, or trusts, the Windows NT validation of a user. The Windows NT account information is used to validate the user to SQL Server. These connections are referred to as *trusted connections.*

Internet A voluntarily interconnected global network of computers based on the TCP/IP protocol suite. TCP/IP was originally developed by the U.S. Department of Defense's Advanced Research Projects Agency to facilitate the interconnection of military networks and was provided free to universities. The obvious utility of worldwide digital network connectivity and the availability of free complex networking software developed at universities doing military research attracted other universities, research institutions, private organizations, businesses, and finally the individual home user. The Internet is now available to all current commercial computing platforms.

Internet Explorer A World Wide Web browser produced by Microsoft and included free with Windows 95 and Windows NT 4.0.

Internet Information Server (IIS)   A server produced by Microsoft that serves Internet higher-level protocols like HTTP and FTP to clients using Web browsers.

Internet Protocol (IP)   The network layer protocol upon which the Internet is based. IP provides a simple connectionless packet exchange. Other protocols such as UDP or TCP use IP to perform their connection-oriented or guaranteed delivery services.

Internet service provider (ISP)   A company that provides dial-up or direct connections to the Internet.

Internetwork Packet eXchange (IPX)   The network protocol developed by Novell for its NetWare product. IPX is a routable protocol similar to IP but much easier to manage and with lower communication overhead. The term IPX can also refer to the family of protocols that includes the Synchronous Packet eXchange (SPX) transport layer protocol, a connection-oriented protocol that guarantees delivery in order, similar to the service provided by TCP.

interprocess communications (IPC)   A generic term describing any manner of client/server communication protocols, specifically those operating in the session, presentation, and application layers. Interprocess communications mechanisms provide a method for the client and server to trade information.

intranet   A privately owned network based on the TCP/IP protocol suite.

I/O (input/output)   The process of reading and writing data back and forth from cache to disk. The smallest unit of I/O in SQL Server is the 2KB page. All I/O happens in page increments.

Logical I/O is defined as a data read or write operation that is made to cache or disk. *Physical I/O* is subclassified as a data read or write that is made to disk only.

IP   See *Internet Protocol.*

IP address   A four-byte number that uniquely identifies a computer on an IP internetwork. InterNIC assigns the first bytes of Internet IP addresses and administers them in hierarchies. Huge organizations like the government or top-level ISPs have class A addresses, large organizations and most ISPs have class B addresses, and small companies have class C addresses. In a class A address, InterNIC assigns the first byte, and the owning organization assigns the remaining three bytes. In a class B address, InterNIC or the higher-level ISP assigns the first two bytes, and the organization assigns the remaining two bytes. In a class C address, InterNIC or the higher-level ISP assigns the first three bytes, and the organization assigns the remaining byte. Organizations not attached to the Internet are free to assign IP addresses as they please.

IPC   See *interprocess communications.*

IPX   See *Internetwork Packet eXchange.*

ISA   See *Industry Standard Architecture.*

ISAM   See *Indexed Sequential Access Method.*

ISP   See *Internet service provider.*

ISQL   A command-line utility that provides a query interface to the SQL Server. You can run Transact-SQL statements as well as stored procedures and DBCC commands from ISQL.

ISQL_w   An interactive SQL interface for Windows, also called ISQL/W. This utility allows you to run all of the same commands that the ISQL command-line utility does. It has an added advantage of being a Windows interface. This allows you to run multiple queries and view the results of multiple queries in their own separate windows.

Jet   The data-access engine for Microsoft Access and other Microsoft desktop products. Microsoft Access ships with Jet. Microsoft Visual Basic also utilizes Jet as its native data-access method. Jet can also be accessed by Excel, Word, Project, and PowerPoint through VBA (Visual Basic for Applications).

kernel   The core process of a preemptive operating system, consisting of a multitasking scheduler and the basic services that provide security. Depending on the operating system, other services such as virtual memory drivers may be built into the kernel. The kernel is responsible for managing the scheduling of threads and processes.

LAN Manager   The Microsoft brand of a network product jointly developed by IBM and Microsoft that provided an early client/server environment. LAN Manager/Server was eclipsed by NetWare, but was the genesis of many important protocols and IPC mechanisms used today, such as NetBIOS, named pipes, and NetBEUI. Portions of this product exist today in OS/2 Warp Server and Windows NT.

LAN Server   The IBM brand of a network product jointly developed by IBM and Microsoft. See also *LAN Manager*.

lazywriter   A system process responsible for physical I/O. The role of the lazywriter is to flush pages from cache to disk as free buffers are needed by the system. The lazywriter differs from the checkpoint in how it performs its work. The checkpoint process executes its work in spikes and then goes back to sleep. The lazywriter may be continually active, writing out pages from cache to disk as needed.

LFN   See *long filename*.

local group   A group that exists in a Windows NT computer's local security database. Local groups can reside on NT Workstation or NT Server computers and can contain users or global groups.

lock   A mechanism by which SQL Server manages concurrency. SQL Server places locks on data when it is being accessed by a client application. SQL Server locks are primarily *page locks*. This means that when a client accesses a single record on a 2KB page, SQL Server will lock the entire page until it is appropriate to release the lock. SQL Server also supports table locks for times when it would make more sense to lock the entire table rather than locking individual pages. Row-level locking can also be enabled with SQL Server 6.5.

lock escalation   The SQL Server process of increasing a lock from the page to the table level. When a transaction acquires a configured number of page locks, a table lock is set and the page locks are released. This behavior is configured through lock-escalation thresholds.

logging   The process of recording information about activities and errors in the operating system.

logical I/O   See *I/O*.

login   A name that, when combined with a password, allows access to SQL Server resources. Logins are stored in the syslogins system table. This table is located in the Master database only, and there is only one per server.

long filename (LFN)   A filename longer than the eight characters plus three-character extension allowed by MS-DOS. In Windows NT and Windows 95, filenames can contain up to 255 characters.

MAKEPIPE   A command-line utility that can be used in conjunction with the READPIPE utility to verify that the named pipes protocol is working properly.

MAPI   See *Messaging Application Programming Interface*.

Master device   The device that stores SQL Server's Master database, Model database, Tempdb database, and Pubs database. The Master device has a default size of 25MB.

Messaging Application Programming Interface (MAPI)   The messaging application standard developed by Microsoft to allow for interaction between an application and various message service providers.

Microsoft Exchange   Microsoft's messaging application. Exchange implements Microsoft's MAPI as well as other messaging protocols, such as POP, SMTP, and faxing to provide a flexible message composition and reception service.

Microsoft Query   A utility used to graphically create SQL statements for any ODBC-compliant data source. Microsoft Query (also called MS Query) can link to Microsoft Office applications (such as Word and Excel), and other ODBC-compliant applications and databases.

mixed security   A SQL Server security mode that combines the functionality of both standard and integrated security. In the mixed mode, preference is given to trusted connections, but standard security can be implemented if a trusted connection is not possible.

Model database   The template database for SQL Server that is used when new databases are created. Any users, groups, and security existing in this database are automatically part of any new databases, but changes made to the Model database will not affect existing databases.

MS Query   See *Microsoft Query*.

Msdb database   A SQL Server database that stores information about the alerts, tasks, events, and replication tasks created on that server. The Msdb database also includes information about system operators.

multiprocessing   Using two or more processors simultaneously to perform a computing task. Depending on the operating system, processing may be done asymmetrically, wherein certain processors are assigned certain threads independent of the load they create, or symmetrically, wherein threads are dynamically assigned to processors according to an equitable scheduling scheme. The term usually describes a multiprocessing capacity built into the computer at a hardware level in that the computer itself supports more than one processor. However, multiprocessing can also be applied to network computing applications achieved through interprocess communication mechanisms. Client/server applications are, in fact, examples of multiprocessing.

multi-protocol　A network library available with SQL Server 6.5. Multi-protocol allows SQL Server to communicate over any interprocess communications (IPC) mechanism. It also provides support for integrated security. Multi-protocol takes advantage of remote procedure calls (RPCs) to pass information between the client and server.

multitasking　The capacity of an operating system to rapidly switch among threads of execution. Multitasking allows processor time to be divided among threads as if each thread ran on its own slower processor. Multitasking operating systems allow two or more applications to run at the same time and can provide a greater degree of service to applications than single-tasking operating systems like MS-DOS.

multithreaded　Refers to programs that have more than one chain of execution, thus relying on the services of a multitasking or multiprocessing operating system to operate. Multiple chains of execution allow programs to simultaneously perform more than one task. In multitasking computers, multithreading is merely a convenience used to make programs run smoother and free the program from the burden of switching between tasks itself. On multiprocessing computers, multithreading allows the compute burden of the program to be spread across many processors. Programs that are not multithreaded cannot take advantage of multiple processors in a computer.

named pipes　An interprocess communications (IPC) mechanism that is implemented as a file system service, allowing programs to be modified to run on it without using a proprietary API. Named pipes was developed to support more robust client/server communications than those allowed by the simpler NetBIOS. Named pipes is

the default SQL Server protocol and is required for integrated security mode.

native API　The methods of data access that are specific to a certain database management system. Also called the *proprietary interface.*

network operating system　A computer operating system specifically designed to optimize a computer's ability to respond to service requests. Servers run network operating systems. Windows NT Server is a network operating system.

New Technology File System (NTFS)　A secure, transaction-oriented file system developed for Windows NT that incorporates the Windows NT security model for assigning permissions and shares. NTFS is optimized for hard drives larger than 500MB and requires too much overhead to be used on partitions smaller than 50MB.

normalization of data　The process of organizing data into tables, in a consistent and complete format, in order to create a relational database.

NT Event Viewer　A Windows NT utility used to view Windows NT events and errors. The Application log records SQL Server events and errors, as well as events from other applications running under Windows NT.

NTFS　See *New Technology File System.*

object permissions　SQL Server permissions that generally allow users to manipulate data that a database object controls. For example, to view the information in a table, you must first have the Select permission on that table. If you want to run a stored procedure, you must first have the Execute permission on that stored procedure. Object permissions can be granted by the SA, DBO, or DBOO.

ODBC (Open Database Connectivity) An API set that defines a method of common database access. Client applications can be written to the ODBC API. ODBC uses a Data Source Name (DSN) to make a connection to a database and to load an appropriate ODBC driver. This driver will translate client calls made to the ODBC API into calls to the native interface of the database. The goal of ODBC is to provide interoperability between client applications and data resources.

OLE DB A method of common database access which defines an interface based on the COM (Component Object Model) rather than a traditional API interface like ODBC. The goal is similar to ODBC, which is to provide interoperability between client applications and data resources.

OLTP See *online transaction processing*.

online transaction processing (OLTP) A type of database activity that involves live, continually changing data.

Open Database Connectivity See *ODBC*.

operator A user who is notified about certain network events. In SQL Server, operators can be defined by name, along with their e-mail and pager addresses, and can be notified about the success and/or failure of scheduled or triggered tasks and alerts. Operator information is stored in the Msdb database.

optimization Any effort to reduce the workload on a hardware or software component by eliminating, obviating, or reducing the amount of work required of the component through any means. For instance, file caching is an optimization that reduces the workload of a hard disk drive.

ownership chain In SQL Server, the result of a user who owns an object creating another object based on the original one, such as when a user creates a view based on a table. This ownership chain has only one object owner. If another user creates an object based on the original owner's object, this now becomes a *broken ownership chain*, because different users own objects within the permission chain. If a person who owns objects that are dependent on each other grants another person rights to the final object, then the ownership chain is unbroken. However, if the second person then grants rights to a third person, the ownership chain becomes broken, as the third person needs rights from the first person, not the second person.

page The smallest unit of data storage in SQL Server. Every page is 2KB in size with a 32-byte header. Data rows are written to data pages, index rows to index pages, and so on.

parallel striped backup A SQL Server backup created across two or more devices.

PCI See *Peripheral Connection Interface*.

PDC See *primary domain controller*.

Per Seat License A type of SQL Server license that allows you to pay once for each seat (person) in your company, and then use any number of connections to any number of servers.

Per Server License A type of SQL Server license that allows you to pay for only a single server. You are then limited to the number of connections you have paid for.

Performance Monitor A Windows NT utility that tracks statistics on individual data items, called *counters*. You can view information about the performance of SQL Server through Performance Monitor. For example, you can monitor log space used, number of current connections, and memory usage.

Peripheral Connection Interface (PCI)   A high-speed 32/64-bit bus interface developed by Intel and widely accepted as the successor to the 16-bit ISA interface. PCI devices support I/O throughput about 40 times faster than the ISA bus.

permissions   SQL Server security constructs that regulate access to resources by username or group affiliation. Administrators can assign permissions to allow any level of access, such as read-only, read/write, or delete, by controlling the ability of users to initiate object services. Security is implemented by checking the user's security identifier against each object's access control list.

physical I/O   See *I/O*.

preemptive multitasking   A multitasking implementation in which an interrupt routine in the kernel manages the scheduling of processor time among running threads. The threads themselves do not need to support multitasking in any way because the microprocessor will preempt the thread with an interrupt, save its state, update all thread priorities according to its scheduling algorithm, and pass control to the highest priority thread awaiting execution. Because of the preemptive nature, a thread that crashes will not affect the operation of other executing threads.

primary domain controller (PDC)   In a Microsoft network, the domain server that contains the master copy of the security, computer, and user accounts databases and that can authenticate workstations or users. The PDC can replicate its databases to one or more backup domain controllers (BDCs).

procedure cache   A SQL Server cache that contains stored procedures that have been run by users or the system. After SQL Server fulfills its requirements for RAM from the RAM that has been assigned to it, the rest is assign to cache. The cache is divided into data cache and procedure cache. The percentage of procedure cache versus data cache can be set by the SA. See also *caching*, *data cache*.

process   A running program containing one or more threads. A process encapsulates the protected memory and environment for its threads.

Program Developers Kit (PDK)   Extra SQL Server documentation and programming examples useful to developers who wish to know which DLL (dynamic link library) functions are available and what they do concerning SQL Server.

Public group   A group that exists in every SQL Server database. Any rights granted to the Public group automatically apply to all users in the database, including the guest user (if present).

publication   In SQL Server replication, a collection of *articles*. Subscribing servers can subscribe to an entire publication or to individual articles within a publication.

publishing server   In SQL Server replication, the server that has the original data and is making that data available to other replication servers.

pull page A model of Web page creation in which a server-side process requests data dynamically from the database when the Web browser makes the request. No static page is created. The HTML response to the request is created dynamically by the server-side process.

push page A model of Web page creation in which static Web pages are created by executing queries on a SQL Server and formatting the output in HTML. This HTML page is placed on a Web server and can be accessed by a Web browser. Although the pages can be updated frequently, they are still static pages.

query A request sent to SQL Server to manipulate or retrieve data.

query optimizer In SQL Server, a mechanism that determines which index (or no index) will result in the lowest amount of logical I/O. This is done by evaluating the data and the restrictions that the query is requesting. With this information, the query optimizer estimates how many pages will be read for each possible scenario and chooses the scenario with the lowest estimated page I/O.

RAID 5 A hard drive subsystem that writes files across multiple hard disks and multiple partitions in what are called *stripes*. It also keeps track of the information contained in each piece of the stripe with a parity checksum. A RAID 5 system provides faster disk access and fault tolerance.

RDBMS See *relational database management system*.

RDO See *Remote Data Objects*.

read-ahead A SQL Server mechanism for retrieving data from disk into cache before the data is actually needed. Separate read-ahead

threads pull data into cache, thus freeing the query thread to process the data that it finds in cache.

READPIPE A command-line utility that can be used in conjunction with the MAKEPIPE utility to verify that the named pipes protocol is working properly.

Registry A database of settings required and maintained by Windows NT and its components. The Registry contains all the configuration information used by the computer. It is stored as a hierarchical structure and is made up of keys, hives, and value entries. You can use the Registry Editor (REGEDT32 or REGEDIT) to change these settings.

relational database A database composed of tables, which contain related data, and other objects such as views, stored procedures, rules, and defaults.

relational database management system (RDBMS) A database management system that supports true data and transactional integrity, and a server-side relational database engine. SQL Server is an RDBMS.

Remote Data Objects (RDO) A COM (Component Object Model) encapsulation of the ODBC API. RDO is a very thin layer of software that provides an object model for calling the ODBC API.

Remote Procedure Calls (RPC) A network interprocess communications (IPC) mechanism that allows an application to be distributed among many computers on the same network.

removable media database A SQL Server 6.5 database created on a removable medium, such as a CD-ROM or floppy disk. Removable media databases can be sent to another location and used from that location.

replication For SQL Server systems, the ability to automatically copy data and changes made to data from one server to another server. The data may not be copied immediately, so replication is used when "real-enough" data replication is needed. In replication, the change is made to one server and then sent out to one or more servers.

roll back To cancel an entire transaction if any part of the transaction fails.

row In a SQL Server database, a complete set of columns within a single table which represents a single item of data.

RPC See *Remote Procedure Calls*.

rule In a SQL Server database, an object that is assigned to a column so that data being entered must conform to standards you set.

SA (System Administrator) The default login ID for SQL Server; the global administrator of the SQL Server system. This ID has no restrictions on what it can do within the SQL Server environment.

SAM See *Security Accounts Manager*.

scheduling The automation of tasks in SQL Server. Tasks that can be automated include backups, transfers, index creation and reorganization, and other maintenance procedures.

script A saved query that has an .sql extension by default. Scripts can be loaded, edited, and run from the ISQL/W utility. Scripts can also be created for existing databases and objects by SQL Enterprise Manager. Scripts are saved as ASCII text.

SCSI (Small Computer Systems Interface) A high-speed, parallel-bus interface that connects hard disk drives, CD-ROM drives, tape drives, and many other peripherals to a computer.

security Measures taken to secure a system against accidental or intentional loss of data, usually in the form of accountability procedures and use restrictions. SQL Server security is based on the server, database, and database objects.

Security Accounts Manager (SAM) The module of the Windows NT Executive that authenticates a username and password against a database of accounts, generating an access token that includes the user's permissions. Also known as the *directory database*.

security identifier (SID) A unique code that identifies a specific user or group to the Windows NT security system. Security identifiers contain a complete set of permissions for that user or group.

server A computer dedicated to servicing requests for resources from other computers on a network. Servers typically run network operating systems such as Windows NT Server. The basic functionality of a server can be added to by installed programs such as SQL Server.

server process ID See *SPID*.

service A process dedicated to implementing a specific function for other processes. Most Windows NT components are services. SQL Server is composed of two main services: MSSQLServer, which is the database engine, and SQLExecutive, which is the helper service.

Service Pack A group of bug fixes and enhancements offered by Microsoft on a (semi) regular basis. There are various Service Packs for different applications. As of this writing, some of the current Service Packs are Windows NT 3.51 Service Pack 5, NT 4.0 Service Pack 3, and SQL Server 6.5 Service Pack 3.

severity level For a system error, a component of the error message that provides information about the error. Levels from 0 to 10 are informational, 11 to 16 are user errors, 17 and 18 are resource problems, and 19 to 25 are fatal errors.

SID See *security identifier*.

slow BCP A form of importing data with the BCP utility that takes place when there are either indexes on the table being imported into or when the Select Into/Bulk Copy database option is not set. See also *fast BCP*.

Small Computer Systems Interface See *SCSI*.

sort order In SQL Server, an option that determines how the system will collate, store, and present data. The sort order options available depend on the chosen character set. The most important sort order descriptions include dictionary order, binary order, case-sensitive, and case-insensitive.

SPID (server process ID) In SQL Server, the number that identifies a connection currently accessing the SQL Server machine.

SQL (Structured Query Language) A database language originally designed by IBM that can not only be used for queries, but can also be used to build databases and manage security of the database engine.

SQL Client Configuration Utility A utility used to configure SQL Server clients' network libraries. It also reports on the DB-Libraries that are in use for a particular client.

SQL-DMO (SQL Server Distributed Management Objects) An interface that exposes OLE automation objects that other programs can take advantage of to manipulate the SQL Server Engine and the SQL Executive utilities.

SQL Enterprise Manager The main SQL Server administration program provided with SQL Server 6.5. Multiple servers can be monitored and maintained by SQL Enterprise Manager.

SQL Executive A SQL Server service that can take care of automating tasks on your server. The service includes managers that can handle alerts processing, tasking, event processing, and replication. It works for local automation with the local system account, but for many activities that occur over the network, the SQL Executive service needs to be assigned a separate logon account that has administrative rights to the computer, as well as the Log On as a Service right.

SQL login See *login*.

SQL Security Manager A utility used to "map" Windows NT user accounts into SQL Server.

SQL Server administrator The individual usually responsible for the day-to-day administration of SQL Server databases. The administrator takes over where the programmer left off.

SQL Server Books Online All of the books that normally ship with Microsoft SQL Server in an electronic format. SQL Server Books Online takes advantage of the original TechNet style interface, complete with a search engine for key words and phrases, bookmarks, and the ability to copy and paste from within it.

SQL Server developer   The individual responsible for designing, programming, and populating SQL Server databases.

SQL Server Distributed Management Objects   See *SQL-DMO*.

SQL Server Engine   The core service (MSSQLServer) that performs all query-related activities of SQL Server.

SQL Server Web Assistant   A SQL Server 6.5 utility that facilitates the creation of push Web pages. It can use the SQL Executive service to schedule the creation of the static Web pages in order to keep them more current.

SQL Trace   A SQL Server utility used to monitor who is running what on a SQL Server machine. It also allows you to enable auditing of SQL Server.

SQLMaint   A SQL Server utility that can be used to create tasks that will take care of day-to-day administration of SQL Server. This includes automating backups, updating statistics, and rebuilding indexes. SQLMaint is configured by the Database Maintenance Plan Wizard.

standard security   A SQL Server security mode in which SQL Server validates all connections to SQL Server regardless of that user's authentication to Windows NT. These connections are referred to as *standard* or *nontrusted* connections. Note that even in standard security mode, you can explicitly request a trusted connection to SQL Server.

statement permissions   SQL Server permissions that allow database users and groups to perform tasks that are not specific to objects. These permissions are generally related to the creation of certain database objects.

Structured Query Language   See *SQL*.

stored procedure   In SQL Server, a set of Transact-SQL statements combined together to perform a single task or set of tasks. This object is like a macro, in that SQL code can be written and stored under a name. By invoking the name, you actually run the code. Because stored procedures are precompiled, they run much more quickly and efficiently than regular queries do. There are three types of stored procedures: system, user-defined, and extended. *System stored procedures* are shipped with SQL Server and are denoted with an sp_ prefix. These are typically found in the Master database. *User-defined stored procedures* can be registered with the system by the SA. *Extended stored procedures* work outside the context of SQL Server and generally have an xp_ prefix. These are actually calls to DLLs.

subscribing server   In SQL Server replication, the server that gets data that originated on the publishing server and updates one or more tables with new data and changes to that data.

suspect database   A database which SQL Server believes to be corrupt or otherwise unavailable. A database can be marked suspect for a number of reasons, such as when a database device is offline or because a database device has been removed or renamed.

system stored procedure   See *stored procedure*.

system table   A table in a relational database that is used for administrative purposes by SQL Server. For example, the syslogins system table in the Master database holds SQL Server logins and passwords.

table In a SQL Server database, the object that contains rows and columns of data.

task A job performed by a system, such as a backup procedure. In SQL Server 6.5, you can schedule tasks to run at regular intervals or when an alert is triggered. A task can run a Transact-SQL command, a command prompt utility, or replication procedures.

Task Manager An application that manually views and can close running processes. Task Manager can also be used to view CPU and memory statistics. Press Ctrl+Alt+Del or Ctrl+Shift+Escape to launch the Task Manager.

Taskbar In Windows NT, the gray bar at the bottom of the screen which replaces the Task Manager in previous versions of Windows. The Taskbar holds buttons which represent running programs as well as the Start menu button. Used to switch between running programs and choose the Start menu.

TCP See *Transmission Control Protocol*.

TCP/IP See *Transmission Control Protocol/ Internet Protocol*.

TechNet Microsoft's monthly CD-ROM set that contains patches to existing programs, technical notes about issues (bugs), and white papers describing technologies in more detail. Most all of the information in TechNet can also be found on Microsoft's Web site.

Tempdb database A SQL Server database reserved for storing temporary objects. These may be tables or stored procedures and can be created implicitly by SQL Server or explicitly by the user. The Tempdb database is also used to store server-side cursors.

thread A list of instructions running in a computer to perform a certain task. Each thread runs in the context of a process, which embodies the protected memory space and the environment of the threads. Multithreaded processes can perform more than one task at the same time. SQL Server is a single process with many threads. Every user's connection is given a dedicated thread until the level of maximum worker threads is reached.

T-SQL See *Transact-SQL*.

Transact-SQL An enhanced version of the SQL language used by SQL Server as its native database language.

transaction A logical set of one or more commands that need to be processed as a whole in order to make a complete unit of work.

transaction log In SQL Server, a reserved area in the database that stores all changes made to the database. All modifications are written to the transaction log before writing to the database. The transaction log provides a durable record of database activity and can be used for recovery purposes.

Transaction SQL See *Transact-SQL*.

Transmission Control Protocol (TCP) A transport layer protocol that implements guaranteed packet delivery using the Internet Protocol (IP). See also *TCP/IP, Internet Protocol*.

Transmission Control Protocol/Internet Protocol (TCP/IP) A suite of network protocols upon which the global Internet is based. TCP/IP is a general term that can refer either to the TCP and IP protocols used together or to the complete set of Internet protocols. TCP/IP is the default protocol for Windows NT.

trigger   A SQL Server object that is a stored procedure. A trigger activates when data is added, updated, or deleted from a table. Triggers are used to ensure that tables linked by keys stay internally consistent with each other.

trusted connection   See *integrated security*.

two-phase commit   A type of data replication for SQL Server. With two-phase commit, two or more SQL Server computers either complete a transaction simultaneously or not at all. The Distributed Transaction Coordinator (MSDTC service) is designed to help manage these types of transactions.

UNC   See *Universal Naming Convention*.

Uniform Resource Locator (URL)   An Internet standard naming convention for identifying resources available via various TCP/IP application protocols. For example, http://www. microsoft.com is the URL for Microsoft's World Wide Web server site, and ftp://gateway.dec.com is a popular FTP site. A URL allows easy hypertext references to a particular resource from within a document or mail message.

Universal Naming Convention (UNC)   A multivendor, multiplatform convention for identifying shared resources on a network.

URL   See *Uniform Resource Locator*.

user   In SQL Server, a database-specific identifier that maps to a login and allows access to database resources. If a user is mapped to a login entry in the syslogins system table of the server, that login is allowed access to the database and can be permitted to access database objects. Users are stored in the sysusers system table of each database.

username   A user's account name in a logon-authenticated system (like Windows NT and SQL Server).

VBSQL   One of the interfaces provided with the native API of SQL Server. VBSQL is designed for use from Visual Basic and Visual Basic for Applications (VBA) applications.

vertical partitioning   In SQL Server replication, a method by which you can publish only certain columns of a table. See also *horizontal partitioning*.

view   In SQL Server, an object that is usually created to exclude certain columns from a table or to link two or more tables together. A view appears very much like a table to most users.

Web browser   An application that makes HTTP requests and formats the resultant HTML documents for the users. The preeminent Internet client, most Web browsers understand all standard Internet protocols.

Web page   Any HTML document on an HTTP server.

Win16   The set of application services provided by the 16-bit versions of Microsoft Windows: Windows 3.1 and Windows for Workgroups 3.11.

Win32   The set of application services provided by the 32-bit versions of Microsoft Windows: Windows 95 and Windows NT.

Windows 3.11 for Workgroups   The current 16-bit version of Windows for less-powerful, Intel-based personal computers; this system includes peer-networking services.

Windows 95 The current 32-bit version of Microsoft Windows for medium-range, Intel-based personal computers; this system includes peer-networking services, Internet support, and strong support for older DOS applications and peripherals.

Windows NT The current 32-bit version of Microsoft Windows for powerful Intel, Alpha, PowerPC, or MIPS-based computers; the system includes peer-networking services, server-networking services, Internet client and server services, and a broad range of utilities. Windows NT Workstation is a version of Windows NT that is primarily used on desktop and laptop computers, but can act as a server for up to ten simultaneous connections at a time. Windows NT Server is a version of Windows NT that is primarily used as a file/application server that can theoretically have thousands of simultaneous users connected to it. SQL Server 6.5 runs on either version of Windows NT.

workgroup In Microsoft networks, a collection of related computers, such as a department, that don't require the uniform security and coordination of a domain. Workgroups are characterized by decentralized management as opposed to the centralized management that domains use. See also *domain*.

World Wide Web (WWW) A collection of Internet servers providing hypertext formatted documents for Internet clients running Web browsers. The World Wide Web provided the first easy-to-use graphical interface for the Internet and is largely responsible for the Internet's explosive growth.

WWW See *World Wide Web*.

Index

Note to the Reader: First level entries are in **bold**. Page numbers in **bold** indicate the principal discussion of a topic or the definition of a term. Page numbers in *italic* indicate illustrations.

W

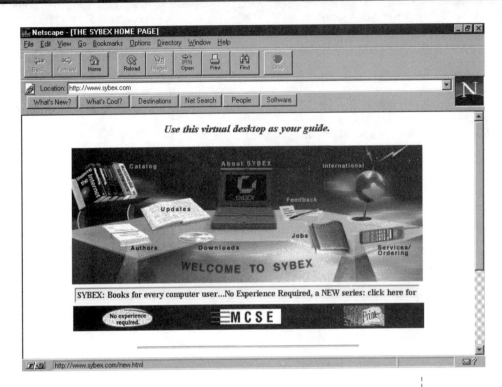

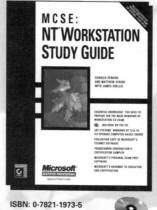

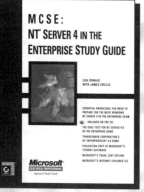
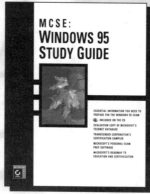

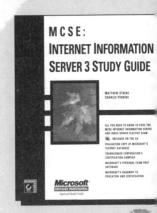
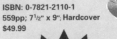

Official Microsoft Objectives for Exam 70-026: System Administration for Microsoft SQL Server 6.5

 NOTE Exam objectives are subject to change at any time without prior notice and at Microsoft's sole discretion. Please visit Microsoft's Training & Certification Web site (www.microsoft.com/Train_Cert) for the most current exam objectives listing.